Free Books for All

THE PUBLIC LIBRARY
MOVEMENT IN ONTARIO, 1850–1930

Have a happy retirement Dave !

LORNE BRUCE

November 2001

Lorne

ONTARIO
Heritage
BOOK
AWARD

This publication has been assisted by an Ontario Heritage Book Award
from the Ontario Heritage Foundation, an agency of the
Ministry of Culture, Tourism and Recreation

Toronto & Oxford
Dundurn Press

Edited by Michael Power
Printed and bound in Canada by Best Book Manufacturers

The author and publisher are particularly grateful to the **Ontario Heritage Foundation,** an agency of
the **Ontario Ministry of Culture, Tourism and Recreation,** for a research grant and a grant in aid of
publication.

The publisher wishes to acknowledge the generous assistance and ongoing support of the **Canada Council,**
the **Book Publishing Industry Development Program** of the **Department of Canadian Heritage,** the
Ontario Arts Council, and the **Ontario Publishing Centre.**
　　Care has been taken to trace the ownership of copyright material used in the text (including the illustrations). The author and publisher welcome any information enabling them to rectify any reference or
credit in subsequent editions.

J. Kirk Howard, Publisher

Canadian Cataloguing in Publication Data

Bruce, Lorne, 1948–
　　Free books for all : the public library movement in Ontario

Includes bibliographical references and index.
ISBN 1-55002-205-9

1. Public libraries – Ontario – History. I. Title.

Z735.05B7 1994　　027.4713　　C94-932135-4

Dundurn Press Limited	Dundurn Distribution	Dundurn Press Limited
2181 Queen Street East	73 Lime Walk	1823 Maryland Avenue
Suite 301	Headington, Oxford	P.O. Box 1000
Toronto, Canada	England	Niagara Falls, N.Y.
M4E 1E5	0X3 7AD	U.S.A. 14302-1000

CONTENTS

PREFACE

This book deals with the genesis and expansion of public library service in Ontario, Canada's most populous province. It does not claim to be a complete history of all the province's libraries; this would necessitate many volumes. Instead, I have chosen to describe and discuss the "public library movement," a term that fell into disuse after 1930 as the character of library leadership changed from lay persons to a professional cadre and as a modern service ethic for libraries replaced a grand Victorian vision of beneficial societal change. It is a broad examination of the ideas of people who participated in the movement in the late nineteenth and early twentieth centuries and gave it strength. My object is threefold: to render a factual account of what the movement achieved; to use the actual writings and words of the men and women who participated; and to illustrate its phases as much as possible.

I have long felt a need for a history of the people and ideas that shaped the modern conception and work of public libraries in Ontario. In tracing the history of the movement between 1850 and 1930, I have not attempted to present a complete chronological or event-by-event account; rather, I have sought to examine interconnections with other contemporary societal developments in a national and international setting. This book, in part, is a study of evolving Canadian nationalism and international influences in local government in the contexts of Anglo-American culture. Since no account of the growth of public libraries should omit a consideration of the influence of the interests and ideas of those involved in the movement, I have drawn a general outline of its main periods and tried to present the evidence that participants left first-hand. Many types of documents – reports, letters, speeches, newspaper columns, photographs, memorandums, statutes – have been incorporated into my narrative and analysis. I recognize that my interpretation for parts of the evidence, much of which has never been presented before, may be questioned. Of course, this fate must befall most writers. I assume full responsibility for any errors and dissatisfaction with the analysis.

For help during the writing of this book many persons and institutions deserve my thanks. The University of Guelph provided time for research and writing. The Ontario Heritage Foundation granted money for editing and publication. The McLaughlin Library's interlibrary loan section, particularly Marlene Robertson, gave very valuable assistance. Marie Puddister, from the Geography Department, drew the maps for this volume. Many public librarians and public library staffs offered assistance with local sources at various stages of my research and writing: Thomas Rooney in Ottawa; Deborah Defoe in Kingston; David Kotin, head of the Baldwin Room in Toronto; Brian Henley and Margaret Houghton in Hamilton; Glen Curnoe in London; Ryan Taylor in Kitchener; and Linda Kearns in Guelph. Michael Power's editorial assistance was invaluable. My chief debt is to my wife, Karen, whose constructive criticism of my drafts and help compiling tables and indexes made the whole work more readable and enlightening.

The development of library service in Ontario is a subject in Canadian history too long neglected to remain untold. The movement to use the power of local governments to deliver rate-supported services for all citizens typified the efforts of Victorians and Edwardians to improve Canadian society and enrich its culture. Some of the difficulties in assembling the story are related to the diversity of participants and places associated with the public library movement. To the men and women who joined the movement, libraries were only one of a number of reform and working concerns in which they were engaged; the majority did not write extensively about their library activities. Although the work of gathering source materials scattered across the province is laborious, the results can be rewarding. It is my hope that this book will stimulate readers to turn to the history of Ontario's libraries for themselves, thus deepening our understanding of the processes that have shaped modern public libraries in Canada.

Introduction

A DREAM FOR ONTARIO

There are numerous references to the concept of a public library movement in Ontario throughout the late Victorian and Edwardian eras. Three will suffice to introduce the subject. John Hallam, Ontario's "Father of Free Libraries," in his inaugural address to Toronto's library board of management in February 1883, spoke glowingly of a "far reaching movement [that] is likely to extend to every city and considerable town in this Province."[1] Eugène Rouillard, a Quebec journalist and civil servant, who published the first extensive examination of public libraries in Canada, took note of Ontario's enthusiasm in 1890: "Dans l'organization de ce mouvement, la province d'Ontario a déjà pris le pas sur nous depuis assez longtemps."[2] More than a decade later, in April 1901, James Bain's presidential address at the first Ontario Library Association conference was appropriately entitled "The Library Movement in Ontario." He outlined an ambitious agenda for mobilizing public opinion and action:

> The time is propitious. With the beginning of a new century we venture to look forward to new lines of work, to vast increase in the number and sizes of our libraries, and to extension in every direction which aims at the development to their true end – the mental advancement and culture of the people of this province.[3]

Clearly, these three men believed that public libraries had important roles to fulfill, and that it was proper for government to support them at public expense. The increase in the number of public libraries before the First World War indicates that many Ontario communities were in agreement.

In Canada there have been few attempts to study the public library movement on a national or regional basis or to examine its historical development in an international context.[4] Indeed, definitions for the central terms, "movement" and "public library," are usually lacking in Canadian library histories. I am using the first term, "movement," broadly in the sense that people and groups organize formally or informally to support and produce change in society. At its core a successful social movement should have a set of values and beliefs which inspire a sense of common purpose among citizens as well as a sound program to effect societal change. It may be organized by means of voluntary linkages or display a unified arrangement of interdependent parts under various types of leadership. If it is successful in challenging the established social order by gaining public recognition for its program, a social movement may become institutionalized and solidify into formal, bureaucratic structures and organizations.[5]

The Victorian era spawned many social and political movements, some transient, some lasting. The labour, temperance, Grange, and nine-hour movements are accepted historical examples. The public library movement, a progressive, collective effort, was a successful and resilient phenomenon. It benefited from the presence of favourable political and societal conditions that valued public service in municipalities, a factor critical to its longevity. I have proposed previously that between 1880 and 1920 public library development in Ontario unfolded within a conducive decentralized political structure at a time when society was evolving from a small town rural base to an industrialized urban base.[6] This political culture reflected a consensus about the need for provincial direction and local administration; the demographic trend also accommodated the formation of free libraries in municipalities, especially larger urban ones where public library leadership resided. Thus, structural conditions in provincial political life helped shape the development of the public library movement to a significant degree as a component of evolving Canadian nationalism.

The second term, "public library," is largely a matter of perception. Its meaning is reflected in political arrangements and legal regulations that define and maintain the concept within the encompassing social organization of the state. It is difficult, therefore, to analyze public library service diachronically because it has remained essentially a local, optional service rather than a provincial or national public concern. Local conditions not only vary from place to place, but also change over time. The *American Library Association Glossary* defined the early Anglo-American public library, circa 1850, as "a library accessible to all residents of a given community, but not generally free, as distinguished from a private library."[7] Its main features countenanced fees, strictly voluntary endeavours, and limited public access. However, legislation, intergovernmental processes, and standards advanced by public library protagonists in Great Britain and the United States, during the last quarter of the nineteenth century, either eliminated or substantially altered these initial ideas and practices.

In their place emerged a broader vision of public library service in Anglo-American countries. Over time, twentieth century state bureaucracy has codified that vision, and another more modern definition of "public library" has come into force, namely:

> Any library which provides general library services without charge to all residents of a given community, district, or region. Supported by public or private funds, the public library makes its basic collections and basic services available to the population of its legal service area without charges to individual users, but may impose charges on users outside its legal service area. Products and services beyond the library's basic services may or may not be provided to the public at large and may or may not be provided without individual charges.[8]

This concept of public library service has supplanted the earlier version.

In the mid-nineteenth century a public library could assume many forms; it was not synonymous with the second definition recognized in the twentieth century. William Rhees' 1859 *Manual of Public Libraries*, which carefully included a survey of British North America, adopted the earlier interpretation of public library service.[9] His handbook enumerated libraries open to the public in a variety of public institutions: academies, public schools, colleges, and historical, scientific or other associations or societies. Libraries were either institutional – they were attached to Mechanics' Institutes, literary, scientific or philosophical bodies – or they were subscription libraries managed by private or commercial concerns. In these circumstances, public libraries might be reference collections or lending libraries or both; reading rooms might share other quarters; fees might be charged; private organizations might retain the right of ownership or provide most of the revenue; the public might be restricted to certain classes of people; and access might be limited by physical conditions or hours of service. In short, the concept of a public library was broadly conceived.

Yet, by about 1850, more precise terminology was emerging. It would eventually capture the imagination of advocates on both sides of the Atlantic. In 1849 the British Select Committee on Public Libraries recommended legislation that would differentiate between permanent municipal public libraries and other libraries accessible to the public.

> They [the Committee members] have recognised in the establishment of Libraries, the general principles that they

should be based on a firm and durable foundation; that they should be freely accessible to all the public; that they should be open during the evening; and that they should, as far as possible, be Lending Libraries. The last consideration is one of great importance. Many men, in order to derive the fullest advantage from books, must have them not only in their hands, but in their homes.[10]

Shortly afterwards, the Public Libraries Act of 1850 was steered through the British parliament by the reformer William Ewart. On the other side of the Atlantic, American state legislatures previously had introduced tax-supported libraries for public use in school districts, following the prompting of eastern educators such as Horace Mann in Massachusetts and Henry Barnard in Rhode Island. As well, state municipal public library laws began appearing in New England after 1849. For many American citizens the new public library concept complemented the growth of democracy and derived strength from its egalitarian values.[11]

Although this particular manifestation of the municipal tax-supported public library was still in its infancy, its popularity grew steadily after 1850. It subsequently attracted a younger generation of progressive-minded men and women, librarians such as the American Joseph Harrison, who articulated a dynamic version of library progress in the 1890s.

The modern library movement is a movement to increase by every possible means the accessibility of books, to stimulate their reading, and to create a demand for the best. Its motive is helpfulness; its scope, instruction and recreation; its purpose, the enlightenment of all; its aspiration, still greater usefulness. It is a distinctive movement, because it recognizes, as never before, the infinite possibilities of the public library, and because it has done everything within its power to develop those possibilities.[12]

It was this spirited, expanded public library activity that became pre-eminent by the early years of the twentieth century.

For the most part, after Confederation Canadian efforts were patterned on British and American precedents. In Ontario a fundamental impetus to promote public libraries stemmed from the late nineteenth-century liberal creed that encouraged governments to undertake a positive role in the improvement of society as a whole and in the lives of individual citizens regardless of class. Also, Ontario public library promoters were willing to carry on their activities within organized societal channels and laws. The expectation that their cause would triumph seemed unshakeable. The governing party of the late Victorian era helped foster this attitude by enacting various legislative measures which permitted collective action on behalf of free public libraries. Oliver Mowat's Liberal administration introduced the first free library legislation in Canada. His government's motivation for reform was summed up by the education minister, who proclaimed the need for "progressive changes in government as from time to time may be developed."[13]

In the field of social reform, Victorians emphasized the self-improvement of the individual. They seldom attempted to identify causes within the broader social structure or to propose far-ranging government measures to change society. They supposed that individual changes (especially the cultivation of good character) would aggregate and result in beneficial societal change. Support for libraries existed because people felt that they contributed to the creation of a literate, prosperous, devout, moral, and knowledgeable society. At a public library individuals could seek information for educational self-development, vocational training, recreation, and societal roles, such as citizenship. Furthermore, public libraries were politically nonpartisan and nonsectarian; they were impartial instruments of government capable of effecting or impeding change. These orthodoxies were to remain part of the library gospel long after the death of Queen Victoria in 1901.

A concerted effort by many individuals on behalf of the municipal public library was required for it to achieve accepted status within the evolving confines of Ontario's system of local government. Many library enthusiasts were from the middle- and upper-classes. Edwin A. Hardy eloquently captured their missionary zeal in 1904.

> On the boards of our libraries throughout the province there are scores of college men and it has been so for years. They have been the backbone of the movement, and I am satisfied that the greatest work before us [the Ontario Library Association] is the placing before these trustees the needs and the methods of the public library as conceived by the leaders of the movement. Once they grasp the possibilities as to the results and methods, the burden of the work is done. Funds will be found and methods perfected to bring the library into its proper place as one of the greatest educational factors in the community.[14]

There was a broad base of support and loyalty for a program that encompassed all classes and political persuasions. Ontarians could accept publicly funded libraries because they offered individuals an equal opportunity to improve their social well-being, and because they claimed to cure social ills: poverty, ignorance, irreligion, alcoholism, and crime. Many people also were swayed by the utilitarian social doctrine of "the greatest happiness of the greatest number" as it applied to libraries.

Some of the movement's conservative or well-to-do, upper-class members were convinced that public libraries could help preserve social stability. They shared a concern about the possibility of widening social divisions, industrial upheaval, and class antagonism. Education was one solution to these problems. An educated public would not desire radical political change if the provision of socially accepted book collections and library programs encouraged conformity among readers. But the desire for social control (the regulation of society by acceptable behaviour to attain certain social values) by itself does not explain adequately the growth of public libraries in Ontario. Educational attainment has many complex purposes and consequences.

There were many limitations on the concept of social control via public libraries: the heterogeneous nature of library resources available to the public; the permissive feature of enabling legislation which regulated the establishment of libraries; the different levels of public use of libraries; and the general acceptance of library promoted ideology.[15] I follow the interpretation that "a widespread faith in factual knowledge as the alkahest for utopia was behind the founding of free libraries and that their purpose was to provide for all men the knowledge necessary for the improvement of their own lot and of all mankind."[16] The public library movement's goals, its plan of action to meet its goals, and its "ideology" – the values, beliefs, and attitudes which informed its members and governed its actions – will be dealt with in subsequent chapters. For the moment, though, only a brief summary will be given.

A prolonged dialectical interchange took place between 1850 and 1930. During that time, public libraries underwent successive conceptual transformations. These changes were defined by the limits of public opinion, the evolving goals of the movement, and the exchange of ideas between the movement's leaders, its rank and file, and its opponents.[17] Change is inextricably linked with motion, and, at the risk of generalizing, it appears that the Ontario branch of the movement passed through three distinguishable phases: an initial period when the modern concept of free public libraries coexisted alongside an older version that predated the Victorian era; a mobilization stage when lay leaders came forward and created the decentralized structure of municipal service during the last two decades of the nineteenth century; and, shortly after 1900, an institutional phase during which the ideology of the movement began to achieve widespread public acceptance, to the point where library service became part of the accepted fabric of local government and was complimented by a professionally educated leadership and stronger organizations embodying the movement's goals.

This historical pattern of development must not be regarded as a rigid typology, but as a useful outline for study. The people constituting the movement in Ontario believed in its eventual success. They were not passive captives of preordained events or societal structures; rather a confluence of conditions and factors affected their decisions to participate. Often, they were activated by the charisma of ideas, friends, and voluntary organizations. Since public library development occurred on a transatlantic scale, Canadian promoters benefited greatly from progress in Great Britain and the United States, and, consequently, they formed part of an international movement that was able to exert a positive influence on public library growth, thereby laying the foundation for public library service today.

The public library movement grew at varying rates during its three phases. Before 1850 it hardly existed. The social library and Mechanics' Institute, which catered to popular or particular local tastes depending on their membership, predominated. As part of his general educational reforms, Egerton Ryerson supported different categories of free public libraries operated primarily by school boards and municipalities. The results over a quarter century were decidedly equivocal. His tax-supported libraries provided a rationale for carefully supervised free circulating collections, in which the number of novels and range of political literature was restricted on the basis of immoral, controversial, subversive, risqué, or sectarian grounds. Common school libraries in Upper Canada supplied by the book depository at Toronto served a potentially diverse reading public, yet the attempt to exclude many popular novels from the Education Office's official catalogue, because they were deemed to be undesirable, precluded mass use.[18]

The confinement of circulating public school libraries to officially sponsored proper books – too often, a steady diet of religion, biography, history, and innocuous fiction – led to a conflict between two objectives, one centring on democratic reading rights, the other on purposeful moral uplift. During this initial stage of coalescence, the free libraries in common schools championed by Ryerson languished after a promising beginning because reading matter for adults could not be restricted to conventional social values. The colonial government encouraged another alternative, town libraries, which were governed by private boards of management in either Mechanics' Institutes or literary societies, under the aegis of its agriculture department. Despite subscription fees, these organizations were popular because their directors usually were more attuned to the demand for "best-selling" fiction and non-fiction published in Britain and the United States.

The birth of an informed library public, even if a small one, was crucial, as was the creation of a small, dedicated, altruistic public library collectivity backed by government aid.[19] First, educators, booksellers, politicians, and the reading public among the general populace began to realize that the concept of municipally controlled public library service differed from other types of public libraries, as Thomas D'Arcy McGee's remarks to a Montreal audience shortly after Confederation show.

> Of public libraries, I grieve to say that we have not so far as I know, a single one, in the whole Dominion. There is a Society Library, containing some good books, at Quebec; there are, of course, college libraries, more or less incomplete; there are law libraries at Osgoode Hall, and elsewhere, there is our own excellent Parliamentary Library (some 60,000 chosen volumes) at Ottawa; but no public library in any of our chief towns.[20]

This was an important step in consciousness raising, for a general shift in public opinion could lead to advantageous structural changes that would formalize library service at the community level.

At the same time, a growing public need for improved library service became evident, partly in response to the advancement of literacy in Ontario and partly in response to the international success of library legislation in the British Isles and American states after 1850. Because Canadian culture was essentially colonial, library progress in Britain and the United States provided obvious models that could be adapted by a young Dominion striving to achieve nationhood and maturity in the arts, sciences, and letters. The most significant Canadian library modification concerned provincial financial support in the form of generous conditional grants for library books, an inducement that heartened many Ontario library boosters both in Ryerson's system and among the urban-based institutes. Without this financial stimulus, local progress would have been confined to a few major urban centres.

There were signs of a new stage of development, one of mobilization toward better defined goals, following the retirement of Ryerson in 1876. This second phase coincided with the reformulation of Ontario's educational policies and the birth of national library associations in the United Kingdom and United States between 1876-77. Free library legislation appeared in 1882, in conjunction with the work of two library leaders in Toronto, John Hallam and John Taylor. The 1882 act formulated by the Liberal administration of Oliver Mowat rationalized government policies and gave an aura of legitimacy to local supporters of municipal public libraries, a quality missing in Ryerson's hierarchical system. People discontented with library service provided by Mechanics' Institutes or other organizations began to organize and share their plans with friends and associates. Library advocates openly challenged opponents who treasured the canon of civic economy and who cautioned against the temptations of immoral fiction. Informal, decentralized leadership based in communities, combined with provincial financial support and legislative encouragement, were features of this period.

Improved adult services organized by municipal public libraries in larger communities – reference departments, larger circulating collections, branch libraries, better trained staff – demonstrated the advantages inherent in this structure. Some enthusiasts observing Ontario's progress believed that the formation of municipal libraries could be used as a popular call to action, a cause that would arouse genuine, sympathetic support in every part of the country among citizens who took it upon themselves to improve local service.[21] Chief librarians, like James Bain in Toronto, helped raise the profile of the library by the strength of their personalities and plans for better service. Most importantly, a cogent public library ideology began to achieve grudging public acceptance. Explanations for the necessity of free libraries were formulated to satisfy members, to entice prospective recruits, and to justify the passage of library bylaws in community referendums.

Candidates for the movement were enticed by the benefits proclaimed to emanate from free public library service. Many Victorians agreed that the library was a lifelong educator, a logical "missing link" in an expansionist educational system, a role which the slogan "a people's university" aptly described. The concerns of technical education for workingmen also were addressed partly in the library's *raison d'être*. As a result, the differentiation of the free category of service from the generalized version of public libraries proceeded apace. The trend developed later in Ontario than in Britain or the United States. As late as 1886, the education department continued to categorize libraries in Mechanics' Institutes, the Ontario Legislative Assembly, the University of Toronto, and various colleges as "public" in one of its key handbooks.[22]

At the turn of the century the commencement of another phase can be discerned, institutionalization, a process whereby the movement's objectives gradually were incorporated into distinct, recognizable societal structures. Andrew Carnegie's liberality dramatically altered the public's perception of libraries. It swamped the counter argument of civic economy and erected more than one hundred state-of-the-art neoclassical library buildings (many inadequately planned) on the downtown streets of Ontario's cities, towns, and villages before 1914.[23] It was at the start of this period that an enthusiastic spokesman, Lawrence Burpee, believed that "the library spirit, the true library spirit, has come to Canada, and has come to stay."[24] The idea of the public library as an active force in the service of all the people had arrived. Ingrained resistance to free books for all citizens steadily crumbled as attractive new ideas came to the fore: open access to collections; the removal of age restrictions on children; standardized classification; catalogues with author/title/subject access; specialized staff training; improved architecture and internal organization; and programs for different groups. Thus, the scope of service, as well as its administration, was better tailored to public use.

The formation of the Ontario Library Association in 1900 was a vital step in the creation of a viable organization able to influence public opinion, mobilize resources, and develop strategies for successful change. Also, the OLA became a forum for authorized spokesmen and representatives to sanction and disseminate ideas. This centralization of decision making by a dominant group eliminated the potential for conflict within the public library movement. The government, through the education department, immediately recognized the OLA's role. Indeed, it helped fund its activities on a modest scale: it hosted annual conferences; published OLA's conference proceedings; and financed regional library institutes, which were designed to impart library techniques and concepts to trustees and librarians. The OLA was fortunate in that public opinion sympathetic toward the fiction issue also was evolving. The bias towards larger circulating collections of popular "light" fiction attenuated as the reading stepladder theory expounded by librarians gained more credence.

Shortly before the Great War, a prominent English librarian, Louis Stanley Jast, pronounced favourably on Ontario's progress: "In Ontario the right men seem to have taken hold of the movement in its infancy, to their influence and knowledge of library methods, and to their foresight of the possibilities of the movement much of the success is due."[25] At this stage, as the concept of a modern public library began to crystallize, the "right men" were mostly male trustees, a distinctive characteristic of the OLA before 1914. The male leadership in the OLA successfully promoted libraries and avoided conflict within the movement by a variety of constructive means. On the one hand, they allied themselves with other groups, in particular the library branch of the education department, local library boards, and American library associations. On the other hand, they skillfully resisted their opponents: they spread a library ideology; they promoted Carnegie philanthropy; and they introduced modern methods in library work.

The ideas propounded by the OLA were set out concisely in its original constitution drafted by Edwin Hardy. While the association was interested in all libraries, the public library's advancement was foremost on its agenda. This was not surprising given the municipal origin of most OLA members. Hardy's publication of his Ph.D. thesis on the public library was the most complete and eloquent explanation of Ontario's public library movement prior to 1914. Hardy stood for an energetic, expanded educational role, but he was prepared to admit the reality of circulating recreational reading. He outlined four major purposes for the modern library: 1) to provide general, scientific, and reference literature; 2) to provide fiction for recreation; 3) to provide children's literature and programs; and 4) to supply newspapers and periodicals.[26] His vision was forthright: an active library board, a trained librarian, suitable premises, and adequate services based on public demand could fulfill the promise of better library service in local communities across Ontario.

Throughout this period the government continued its long-standing support for libraries. It established a travelling library service for rural southern communities and the new northern districts beyond Muskoka. This was a service which acknowledged its supportive role in providing free books to the entire populace. The government modified legislation at frequent intervals to improve conditions, 1909 and 1920 being notable instances. Between these legal landmarks the department of education sponsored regional library institutes and began publication of the quarterly *Ontario Library Review and Book-Selection Guide* as evidence of its "interest in the public library movement" and its desire to keep libraries abreast of "modern library ideas."[27] As well, in response to urgings from the Ontario Library Association, the department of education established short summer training programs after 1911 to standardize and mechanize library work on the apprenticeship model.

Women joined these training classes in large numbers, as male dominance in the movement started to ebb. Library work was now viewed as a suitable female occupation, a fact the National Council of Women of Canada publicized in 1900.

> A large percentage of those employed in Library work are women, but not many women are heads of Libraries, excepting in the small institutions. Salaries vary from nothing to a maximum of $600. The Public Library of Toronto, the largest circulating Library in the Dominion, gives employment to 25 persons, of whom 22 are women.[28]

Within a decade these brief introductory courses had created the nucleus for meaningful steps toward professional status. By 1922 George Locke was stressing the need to recruit people for librarianship on the basis of sound professional objectives, enhanced recognition, and improved pecuniary rewards.[29] Later, in 1928, a formal program leading to a library diploma appeared in the University of Toronto's calendar of studies; subsequently, a one-year Bachelor

of Library Science requiring an undergraduate degree for entrance was introduced in 1936.[30] As university library education thus became a professional
standard, the significance and attraction of vocational training programs and
library institutes gradually declined.

Although the background of public library history is sketched in the
chapters that follow, much has been omitted by necessity; in fact, many source
materials for that history only recently have come to light for examination
using contemporary historical methods. I have traced the broad spectrum of
the public library movement from 1850 to 1930, but the scope of this work
did not allow me to deal with the stories of individual libraries or biographies
of librarians and trustees. For example, there is no detailed discussion of the
Toronto Public Library's impact on the movement in the rest of the province,
nor is there a search for other historical explanations to account for the development of public libraries in Ontario. The constructive causal role the movement played in relation to total library advancement must necessarily be the
focal point. Turn-of-the-century librarians acknowledged this centripetal
influence, especially the role of the OLA. The University of Toronto's chief
librarian, Hugh H. Langton, wrote in 1903:

> A further indication of the progress of the library movement
> in Ontario is perhaps afforded by the fact that a Library
> Association for the province was formed in 1900, which has
> met with gratifying success. Although not expecting to
> become a rival to the American Library Association in num-
> bers or strength, it will endeavor to emulate the activity and
> usefulness of that body in its own limited sphere.[31]

The OLA succeeded far beyond Langton's unassuming prose. Twice in the
next three decades, in 1912 and 1927, the ALA would convene at Ottawa and
Toronto, thereby solidifying Ontario's international library standing and holding forth the promise of universal service across Ontario's disparate municipal
structure.

By the time of the Diamond Jubilee celebration of Confederation, in
1927, the modern public library concept and its supporting structure had
taken firm root in Ontario. The municipal system of public library service,
not the spirited enterprise of men and women, had become the locus for
future growth. Toward the close of this period, in 1926, Edwin Hardy made a
prediction that embodied the confidence of the public library movement and
the successes it had achieved in promoting the "service ethic." Hardy felt that

his forecast was warranted because the movement, truly progressive in spirit, had always aspired to better service. He wrote:

> My dream for the Ontario of 1976, then, in a word, is a free library service for every man, woman and child in all parts of the province, central or remote, utilizing every contrivance of organization and transportation, staffed by educated men and women specially trained, adequately paid and ranking with the other learned professions.[32]

He could make his prediction with relative assurance. The movement had undergone lively and varied transmutations, resulting in an "establishment" status and integration with government structures by the beginning of the 1930s.[33] Its resilience and successful tactics in establishing hundreds of libraries had created the foundation for continued growth under government aegis. Hardy realized that time alone would be the major obstacle in bringing free books to people in every corner of the province.

PART ONE
Origins

Chapter 1

COMMON SCHOOL AND MECHANICS' INSTITUTE LIBRARIES

The first library for public use in Upper Canada was a small subscription library at Newark (Niagara-on-the-Lake) founded in 1800. One of its organizers, the Anglican minister Robert Addison, possessed an exceptional personal library, but he seldom used it; nevertheless, he recognized the need for a public circulating library and generously assisted in its foundation.[1] The Niagara library, like other proprietary or subscription libraries that flourished in the early part of the nineteenth century, was a voluntary undertaking, by necessity charging fees and limiting its range of activity to comparatively few members. In a fledgling colony, with a low rate of public literacy and few avid readers, the need for libraries was not pressing. It was not until the Reverend Egerton Ryerson became chief superintendent of education in 1844 that strong administrative support for a tax-supported system of public libraries throughout the colony came into prominence.

Ryerson (Illus. 1) was of Loyalist stock. A former editor of the *Christian Guardian* and manager of the Methodist Book Room, he left publishing and bookselling in 1840 to become Principal of Victoria College in Cobourg. He was well acquainted with the book trade, with European and American educational systems, and with the role libraries could play in the education of the people.[2] According to Ryerson, a universal system of education held the promise of creating a society based on Christian virtues, self-discipline, and allegiance to duly constituted authority. At the heart of his concept of education stood the common school: it ought to provide the most complete schooling possible for Upper Canadians, excepting the few elite students who would continue their studies beyond this general level. At this time, the common school in the rural townships was a familiar centre of community activities. Included in Ryerson's expansive vision of public education was his own view of public library service.

The colony Ryerson embarked on reaching through his comprehensive system of education (officially known as Canada West between 1841 to 1867 although the name used prior to 1841, Upper Canada, continued in use) numbered about one million people. According to the census of the Canadas in 1851, Canada West's demographic pattern was relatively homogeneous: more than half the population, fifty-eight percent, were native born and mainly of British stock; another thirty-five percent had been born in the British Isles. The number of Methodists, Presbyterians, and Anglicans was overwhelming – just over sixty percent of the population worshipped in these congregations. The vast majority of people lived in rural conditions; there were few major cities or towns.[3] Learning was centred in small log-clad schoolhouses where the headmaster's word, backed by his rod, ruled.

The flavour of Ryerson's ideas concerning free libraries in common schools may be judged from his 1847 publication on general public elementary instruction in which he referred to circulating libraries in the final passages. Ryerson wrote of the need for efforts to improve public education by extending book collections to the entire community, thereby satisfying the taste for reading which the school had created.

> I mean the establishment of *Circulating Libraries* in the various Districts, and as far as possible in the School Sections. To the attainment of this object, local and voluntary co-operation is indispensable. Government may perhaps contribute; it may assist by suggesting regulations, and recommending lists of books from which suitable selections can be made; but the rest remains for individual and local efforts to accomplish. And the advantages of the School can be but very partially enjoyed, unless they are continued and extended by means of books.[4]

In his scheme the provision of circulating libraries was obviously an important supplement to teaching.

Even though Ryerson had the power "to promote the establishment of school libraries for general reading," according to the Common School Act of 1846 (9 Vic., c. 20, s. 2), no government funding was specified, and, as a result, the growth of school libraries remained sporadic. In his 1847 annual report, the superintendent lamented that the New York legislature appropriated $55,000 for libraries "while not a farthing has yet been appropriated by our legislature for the same object in Upper Canada."[5] Ryerson encouraged local officials to support the formation of libraries, and he also featured libraries in his newly founded *Journal of Education for Upper Canada*. Robert Bell, the member for Lanark and Renfrew in the Legislative Assembly, wrote to the *Journal* with a proposal to finance libraries by using money from the sale of "spirituous liquors" and from the revenues generated by a tavern license fund.[6] Another correspondent, Dexter D'Everardo, a school inspector in the Niagara District, wrote Ryerson in 1849 to say that small, private libraries could not satisfy the public thirst for reading. He agreed with Ryerson that the creation of common school libraries would be a popular measure.[7] When a special committee of the British House of Commons studied public libraries in 1849, the *Journal* outlined its deliberations and gave some prominence to selected European public libraries.[8]

Commencing in 1847, Ryerson began to include library statistics in his annual reports. For this purpose he devised a classification of public libraries that remained standard in the government's education report for the next three decades. Libraries reported under three categories: common school libraries, Sunday school libraries, and other public libraries. By school libraries Ryerson meant those libraries whose collections were housed in school buildings but were intended for the entire population. Public libraries, on the other hand, were usually in a building other than a school and might be managed by a municipal council or other group that charged a small fee for using the collection. Sunday school collections were an important element of instilling Christian faith and ideas. Ryerson, in common with other authorities, interpreted a public library in a broad sense. The terminology used in 1850 by the American Charles Jewett was typical: public libraries were those which were not strictly private ones.[9] Thus, when the University of Toronto's library and public reading room opened in 1859, the public was permitted to use the collection and study hall without charge.[10]

By 1850 Ryerson was identifying a significant number of public libraries across the province in his annual report: 70 common school libraries, 528 Sunday school libraries, and 77 public libraries. Together these libraries held 96,165 volumes, a significant resource in a growing colony. The geographic distribution of common school and public libraries was reasonably even across the southern counties (Table 1: Public Libraries in 1850 by County). The number of public libraries is perhaps surprising on first consideration. Library historians have identified 24 Mechanics' Institutes in operation before 1850,[11] leaving more than 50 subscription, institute, college, government, and other social libraries in existence according to Ryerson's tally. A later, more comprehensive list of North American public libraries compiled by William Rhees in 1859 revealed that small cities such as Kingston, Hamilton, and London were served by eight, six, and seven libraries respectively; this information, with the inclusion of Toronto's 41 libraries in Rhees' count, makes Ryerson's earlier tabulations reasonably accurate.[12] With the advent of established points of library service, Ryerson could begin to implement his designs for a public school library system.

Public School Libraries and the Book Depository

The revised School Act of 1850 (13 & 14 Vic., c. 48) gave Ryerson the latitude he desired to institute ideas nurtured by his travels in Europe and the United States. The new legislation was sweeping. County and township councils were allowed to levy taxes for township, city, and town libraries. The Council of Public Instruction, the agency Ryerson reported to but often controlled, received £3,000 annually (a handsome sum at this time) for library purposes. This fund served as a central reservoir for matching grants set at fifty percent of local contributions. The Council had the authority to examine and accept or reject books, maps, globes, and other apparatus for use in schools or school libraries. An education depository was established on a non-profit basis to supply the needs of schools and libraries from Toronto.

There is no doubt that the superintendent believed that libraries were an integral part of public education. In a July 1849 letter to the Governor General, James Bruce, Earl of Elgin and Kincardine, with whom he was on good terms, Ryerson wrote:

> There can be but one opinion as to the great importance of introducing into each township of Upper Canada, as soon as possible, a Township Library, with branches for the several school sections, consisting of a suitable selection of entertaining and instructive books, in the various departments of biography, travels, history (ancient and modern), natural philosophy and history, practical arts, agriculture, literature, political economy, &c., &c., &c., It is not easy to conceive the vast and salutary influence that would be exerted upon the entire population, the young portion especially, in furnishing useful occupation for leisure hours, in improving the tastes and feelings, in elevating and enlarging the views, in prompting to varied and useful enterprize, that would flow from the introduction of such a fountain of knowledge and enjoyment in each township in Upper Canada.[13]

This was an expansive, purposeful design, requiring careful implementation and ongoing attention.

To accomplish his plans, Ryerson believed that the Education Office he had inherited needed to establish a firm set of regulations to govern the administration of public school libraries. He also decided it was necessary to publish a catalogue of acceptable literature from which councils and school trustees could purchase books at prices about one-third less than those Canadian booksellers usually charged. From his vantage point, booksellers were not adequately prepared to provide the type of educational service he thought could be managed from the central book depository. He travelled to England in 1850-51 to establish arrangements with English publishers and agencies such as the Society for the Diffusion of Useful Knowledge and the Religious Tract Society. In London, the Committee of the Council on Education gave him permission to deal directly with British publishers, thereby dispensing with the fee their own national agent, Longman's, normally enjoyed for arranging this type of service. Ryerson also visited the Irish National Board of Education in Dublin. His deputy, John George Hodgins, remained in Toronto to correspond with American publishing houses in Boston and New York that were acquainted with the general operation of district school libraries in American states on the eastern seaboard and in the midwest.

Familiar with the workings of the publishing industry and the library book trade, Ryerson was confident his system would be successful. In his lengthy letter to Lord Elgin, in July 1849, he wrote:

> According to these arrangements, I propose to secure, at the cheapest rate possible, to the reading youth and people of Canada, the best popular works which emanate from the British and American press. There will thus be a *British* and an *American* series, with the price affixed to each, and directions where and how they may be procured, leaving to local councils or committees the option of selecting from either series, or from both, at their discretion.
>
> In the catalogue of these library books, I think a characteristic notice of each book should be inserted (including two or three sentences, but of course, requiring considerable thought, judgment and labor in the preparation). A catalogue should be furnished to each local council, and the books generally be also brought to the notice of the public, in the columns of the *Journal of Education*, and personally by the Chief Superintendent, during his visits to the various districts ...[14]

Fortunately for Ryerson, Lord Elgin was an enthusiastic supporter of public school libraries.

To ensure good reading or, more correctly, the "diffusion of useful knowledge," the Council of Public Instruction published guidelines that governed the selection of books for the general catalogue that Ryerson was developing. Works considered licentious, vicious, immoral, hostile to Christianity, theologically controversial, or sectarian in viewpoint were expressly forbidden.

This official censorship effectively ensured a great deal of opposition and apathy towards the colony's recently formed public libraries.[15] The Education Office worked diligently to sort through thousands of books, and, by the beginning of 1853, the library catalogue was nearing completion. At this time, Ryerson organized county conventions of clergymen, magistrates, municipal councillors, school trustees and superintendents, and other interested persons to promote the establishment of schools and school libraries throughout Canada West. Ryerson wholeheartedly favoured the development of township libraries with circulating collections in school sections because he expected school trustees, not municipal councillors, to promote libraries. Only in Stormont and Glengarry did the local assembly favour the creation of a county system to provide "large and expensive works, such as Encyclopedias for reference etcetera."[16] Virtually all conventions concurred with Ryerson's administrative preference for townships.

In the summer of 1853, the general catalogue, along with the detailed regulations adopted by the Council of Public Instruction in August, was published in the *Journal of Education*. The regulations, which remained virtually unchanged for the next two decades, elaborated upon the responsibilities of municipalities and school sections to hire librarians and to acquire books from the depository as well as the duties of librarians to account for circulation and finances relating to books, cataloguing of collections, acquisition of book cases, filing of annual reports, and so on. Every book was to be accessioned with the number recorded on a printed label pasted on the inside cover or printed on the first blank leaf. Each monograph had to be covered by strong wrapping paper with the title and number on the back. For circulation purposes there was a prescribed minute book with five columns, one for each of the following categories: book title and number, borrower, date charged out, date returned, and condition on return.

To make his scheme more attractive, Ryerson introduced amendments. He arranged for school boards to levy a general rate on property or to raise other (voluntary) sums for libraries in the Supplementary School Act of 1853 (16 Vic., c. 185, s. 1). In 1854, the matching portion of the grant increased to one hundred percent, and, in 1855, the Grammar and Common School Improvement Act (18 Vic., c. 132, s. 4) raised the total amount of the central fund to £3,500. However, the superintendent was rebuffed in his efforts to extend the depository's services to Mechanics' Institutes or other public organizations on the same terms as schools boards and township municipalities.[17] These bodies, which received financial aid voted by the Legislative Assembly, could continue purchasing books from the depository, but they were not eligible for a grant.

Ryerson's designs for an administrative structure and his development of legislation for a system of public libraries are to be admired. There were four types of public library that could be established:

1. A common school library in a schoolhouse available to children and ratepayers;
2. A general public library under municipal control available to all ratepayers in a community;
3. A professional library of books on teaching, school organization, etc., for teachers;
4. A library in an institution for public use or specific use of inmates, etc., which operated under a public statute.

In practice, Sunday school and common school libraries were in abundance, other types were less numerous and under utilized. When one considers the pedagogical content of the depository stock, it comes as no surprise that its usefulness to the general community was limited and bound to be contentious. Under such circumstances, consistent growth in the system was virtually impossible.

From 1853 to 1857, Ryerson's system was in full operation. Orders for library books threatened to submerge the small staff working at the Education Office. During this period more than 160,000 books were dispatched to various libraries throughout the province. Enthusiasm for the chief superintendent's plan was reflected in public praise. When Lord Elgin remarked at the Provincial Exhibition of 1854 that the "Township and County Libraries are becoming the Crown and Glory of the Institutions of the Province,"[18] he was expressing the government's favourable verdict. Although the education office was hard pressed to organize its regular shipments, Ryerson successfully persuaded some municipalities to use money from the sale of the Clergy Reserve lands for school and library purposes, thus spurring the sale of books and increasing the depository's business.

To cope with the flood of orders, Ryerson hired more clerks and officers for the central office. One new recruit, Samuel Passmore May, a recent arrival from England, was destined to play an important role in the library movement. Educated privately, May had specialized in natural science before emigrating to Canada. The Quebec Literary and Historical Society first employed him in 1853 at £10 a week to catalogue and arrange its collection in mineralogy, geology, and zoology. After leaving this position, May journeyed to Toronto where Ryerson engaged him as Clerk of Libraries and head of his department's museum. May became a permanent fixture in the department for the next half century until he retired in 1905.[19] Only one other contemporary, John G. Hodgins, served for a longer period.

In the political arena, Ryerson, a conservative, was not without his share of adversaries. During his superintendency he opposed "partyism" and excessive use of political patronage. He championed the nonpartisan cause of working for the public good. But an early case of political activism tarnished the impartial image he carefully cultivated. Political reformers, such as George Brown and Robert Baldwin, were reluctant to forgive him for openly supporting the Tory ministry of William Draper and Governor General Sir Charles Metcalfe in the divisive election of 1844. The long-term consequences for Ryerson were serious. George Brown and the Clear Grits were to become a potent force in Upper Canadian politics, and Robert Baldwin's moderate reformers were intent on wresting control from Tories by establishing responsible government.[20] As political parties developed, the growing power and influence of a small cabinet accountable to a majority in the elected parliament increased, a trend that boded ill for Ryerson and the appointed members of the Council of Public Instruction. As for Ryerson's libraries, from the very outset many people were wary of his designs. To some they smacked of authoritarianism or paternalism. No doubt there were many people who believed that the universe of reading was more extensive than the two thousand approved items in the general catalogue, especially for works of fiction that were noticeably absent.

As early as his 1854 annual report, Ryerson was replying to "unseemly objections" emanating from "mistaken booksellers" that were appearing in the press. The book trade, of course, was not enamoured of the education depository's privileged position. The complaint that the "private trader ought not to be injured by government with whom he is unable to compete" was voiced.[21] Ryerson answered the charge in his annual report with a typical mid-Victorian treatise on liberty and good government. First, if the interest of the individual, or of any class of individuals, was placed above that of the community, there could be no system of public instruction. Because the government had deliberately chosen to establish schools and libraries, it followed that it had as much right to supply libraries with a public agency as it did to stock them by private traders. From an administrative and financial standpoint it was more efficient and economical for the depository to supply authorized books at reduced rates. The education department also presented financial data to suggest that the book trade was benefiting from the escalating interest in books.

Secure in the logic of his argument, Ryerson continued to add titles to the depository list until it reached about three thousand items. The *General Catalogue* finally appeared as a separate publication in 1858 and was distributed throughout the school system. It served as a handbook on libraries for more than a decade. It contained the text of the School Act of 1850, its amended sections, and the lengthy regulations promulgated in 1853. At the end of the volume, Ryerson appended some explanatory remarks designed to serve as guidelines. He acknowledged his debt to his American counterparts and issued a brief caution:

> The most of these Regulations – especially those which relate to the forfeiture incurred for the detention, loss, or abuse of books – are adopted from the State of New York, where much experience has been acquired in the management of Public School Libraries. And that experience has shown that a strict adherence to these Regulations is absolutely necessary to the maintenance of harmony among all parties concerned, and to the preservation and usefulness of the Libraries.[22]

He was also careful to emphasize the importance of reading and libraries in general:

> By our system of *Schools*, we are putting it into the power of every Canadian to read, and read he will, whether for good or for evil; and his ability to read will prove a blessing or a curse, according to the manner in which he exercises it. By our system of *Libraries*, we are providing them with wholesome and entertaining reading on almost all subjects, without the poison of publications which are calculated to enfeeble the mind, and vitiate the taste, and corrupt the morals.[23]

Lastly, there was an appendix on public library buildings and bookcases written by an anonymous German gentleman acquainted with recent developments. His brief essay illustrated three basic floor plans. One plan represented the recently opened Bibliothèque Sainte-Geneviève in Paris. Its architect, Henri Labrouste, ushered in a new era of library architecture by placing bookstacks below the grand reading room. Exposed cast-iron columns and arches allowed ample natural light to penetrate the study areas. In keeping with this trend, Ryerson's advisor also recommended a long, wide, well-lit salon as the best possible quarters for a library. The simplest floor plan represented typical thinking about the use and arrangement of space within libraries, and is important in two respects. First, a strict separation of readers and books, divided by railings whenever possible, was recommended. Closed stack arrangements were normal in the nineteenth century. Second, the plan called for housing books around the perimeter of the room against the walls or in short bookcase alcoves or bays that protruded from the walls. Traditional internal arrangements emphasized the library's safekeeping and storage functions and not circulation, consultation, or browsing.

There was heightened interest in library architecture in Toronto and other parts of the colony in 1858. A new library and public reading room were under construction in the east hall of University College under the guidance of John Langton and Frederic Cumberland, two members of the University Senate. Cumberland's architectural firm was also engaged in building the Toronto Mechanics' Institute. Most school libraries in Ryerson's jurisdiction admittedly were humble affairs. This was especially true in rural areas where libraries were housed in small closets, bookcases, or boxes. John George Hodgins' *School House*, published in 1857, included many suggested locations for small libraries along the lines of Henry Barnard's influential American manual, *School Architecture*.[24] But only the more affluent schools in Ontario, like Hamilton's central school, were able to allocate floor space for a library.

Ryerson's belief in the separation of church and state and voluntary support for religious institutions, a typical Protestant viewpoint at this time, led him to support nondenominational schools and the secularization of Clergy Reserves. Such views embroiled him in his first major confrontation over the depository. The Reverend Jean-Marie Bruyère, the rector of St. Michael's Cathedral, issued a pamphlet calling the Chief Superintendent a most unrelenting and oppressive enemy.[25] He objected to the *General Catalogue*'s apparent anti-Christian bias and to the transfer of funds from the sale of Clergy Reserve lands to municipal investment funds to pay for school maps, apparatus, and public library purchases. Ryerson had openly suggested that municipalities use these funds for libraries in a circular dated November 1856.[26]

Bruyère, like many Roman Catholic leaders, disliked rationalist philosophy and disapproved of the trend towards secularization and nondenominational schools. The works of popular writers such as Edward Gibbon and David Hume were anathema to him. He also protested – mistakenly as it turned out – the exclusion of separate schools from the legislative provisions that permitted the spending of generous grants for school prizes, apparatus, and library books. Ryerson was always careful to guard against any political or sectarian interference in school matters, especially with regard to the separate school provisions of the School Act which he was bound to uphold. On this occasion, he was able to diffuse tensions in a series of letters to the press, pointing out that he had shown the Roman Catholic Bishop of London the depository and that he had dispatched the bishop's book orders with the standard apportionment of one hundred percent.[27]

The Superintendent was also successful in his initial encounter with booksellers who were anxious to dismantle his depository system. The two parties now entered into a long controversy that remained unresolved until after Ryerson's retirement in 1876. In April 1858 the recently formed Booksellers' Association petitioned Parliament to enquire into the operations of the depository, which they termed "a useless burden on the public purse."[28] A month later another petition, signed by five book publishers who supported the depository, was presented to the House. Seizing the opportunity to justify his policies and demolish his critics, Ryerson immediately issued a pamphlet, *Special Report on the Separate School Provisions*, to rebut any charges.[29] After a brief investigation, the parliamentary members took no action. Ryerson emerged unscathed and determined to stay the course.

After a decade of departmental support, the public library system was well established. Paradoxically, library sales at the depository were in decline. The distribution of prize books and apparatus was becoming the chief task of the depository (Table 2: Books Sent out from the Depository, 1853-1875). In 1860, the number of prize books was double that of library books for the first time and became the main source of reading for many students and their families. At this time there were 411 common school libraries, 2433 Sunday school libraries, and 347 public libraries categorized as "other."[30] The library system continued to steer an ultra-conservative course in the 1860s while the reading public was turning to the "sensational novel," a term coined for mystery, crime, and horror stories. *Lady Audley's Secret*, by Mary Elizabeth Braddon, released in 1862, was a tale of bigamy, murder and insanity, and typified the excitement and seaminess of this new genre.[31]

To appease new reading tastes, Hodgins, the faithful deputy, convinced Ryerson that more "approved and standard" works of fiction should be entered into the *General Catalogue* in 1868, the same year the Hicklin Rule established the test for obscenity in Britain based on the 1857 Obscene Publications Act.[32] As a result, the novels of Walter Scott, Charles Dickens, Edward Bulwer Lytton, John Galt, James F. Cooper, Thomas Haliburton, George Eliot, Anthony Trollope, and even William Thackeray, at last became available to the public. Of course, many readers had never regarded these novelists as licentious, deprave, corrupt, or immoral. The relaxed ruling had little impact. Almost three thousand works classed as fiction were shipped to libraries between 1868-1875, but the orders always represented less than ten percent of total sales each year. More adventuresome readers seemed to prefer Wilkie Collins' *Moonstone*, redolent of fright and exotic curses, to the standard fare available in school libraries.

In the early 1860s a tide was rising against Ryerson's system of libraries and the central depository. A formal indication of discontent reached the government in 1862 when Bentnick and Glenelg townships in Grey County petitioned to repeal the law respecting school libraries.[33] Neither township council participated in the depository scheme, although school section trustees did purchase books. This protest did not succeed. More damaging was a British report on common schools in the United States and Canada. It was written by the Reverend James Fraser, and it delivered a negative verdict on Ryerson's public libraries. Alluding to the chief superintendent's "mania" for libraries, Fraser proceeded to criticize the system by observing that many complaints in Britain had led to the abandonment of the depository system there, that American district school libraries were not generally successful in serving the public, and that "it is almost impossible, unless under very favourable and exceptional circumstances, to establish in a rural district a successful library," because small libraries were quickly read out by most library users and then neglected.[34] Fraser was more enthusiastic about municipal public library legislation as exemplified by the Massachusetts law of 1851 and the shining example of the Boston Public Library, which had moved into its own new building in January 1858. Boston's library opening generated considerable publicity, even in Ontario.[35]

Critical comments and petitions to parliament did not faze Ryerson. His system was in place and he was satisfied with the *status quo*. He had always claimed that local exertions as well as central direction were essential features. The large number of libraries suggests that both Ryerson and Hodgins were forced to rely on local initiative and school inspectors to maintain adequate collections, suitable accommodation, and careful maintenance. It is difficult to judge how the library system was developing in cities, towns, and villages because the annual report of the education department never tabulated library circulation, and after 1862 it ceased to give statistics on libraries located in individual communities. There were ninety-one larger communities recorded in 1862, but the school holdings were only a quarter of the total reported by other public libraries. Free libraries existed in less than half these places despite the initial enthusiasm for Ryerson's scheme and the attractiveness of the matching grant for books (Table 3: Public Libraries in Urban Centres, 1862).

A major publication appraising development, *Eighty Years' Progress of British North America*, suggested that library service was improving in Canada West. There was emerging "an enlightened literary taste and growing intelligence among the various classes of the people."[36] Hodgins contributed a roseate section on educational agencies and compiled a table of major public institutions possessing libraries (Table 4: Public Libraries in Canada West, 1864). By 1864, the depository scheme had supplied almost 500 common school libraries with close to 200,000 volumes. Sunday school libraries also had benefited greatly from the creation of the depository. It was a remarkable achievement in a province that was still being surveyed and settled. On balance, the policy of maintaining libraries in schools appeared to be well-founded.[37] When George Brown and James Campbell, who coveted a share of the profitable school textbook trade, attacked Ryerson in 1866, it was the depository they assailed, not the free library system. Ryerson survived this confrontation without difficulty by allowing a selection of Campbell's texts to be used in schools.[38]

Subscription Libraries in Mechanics' Institutes

In contrast to the common school libraries, the Mechanics' Institute and literary society libraries, which had predated Ryerson's scheme, were struggling in the 1860s. The institutes in Toronto and Hamilton exemplified the vicissitudes that these organizations suffered: both were facing difficulties with mortgages on their new buildings, despite the fact that by this time Mechanics' Institutes were regarded as a movement within their own right. Walter Eales' lecture at the Toronto Mechanics' Institute in February 1851 is a good barometer of how institutes were regarded in the leading city of Canada West. He commenced his speech by remarking how surprised he was to find only 270 members when by his calculations there ought to be at least 2,000 out of a population of approximately 30,000. Membership offered many rewards:

> The gold mines of California, where thousands go at the sacrifice of health and life, are nothing to that valuable mine which your library contains, – knowledge. By becoming members you will be the means of bursting asunder the bonds of ignorance; and morality, virtue, knowledge, and happiness will find their way into your store, factories, and every dwelling in this fine flourishing city.[39]

Eales eloquently stated the mid-Victorian case that mechanics could develop their knowledge and skills and at the same time contribute charm to social life, support for religion, and purity to politics. Institutes were supposed to devise programs to impart the scientific principles underlying manufacturing, crafts, and natural phenomena to artisans and skilled workers. Lectures, reading rooms, libraries, museums, and evening classes were the main instruments to achieve these ambitious cultural goals. Eales spoke of the pleasant prospects of a better life courtesy of the local institute:

> ... how delightful to the working class, to come in the evening to hear a lecture, with his wife and daughters – for every member has the privilege to bring the ladies free, or the member can go to the reading-room and feast the mind, or

> take a History (or some moral work,) from the library home
> to his family, and read, those long winter evenings by the
> cheerful fire, where his wife and offsprings can listen to truths
> which are the foundation of morality, virtue and knowl-
> edge.[40]

To some people, however, the elevation of the working class seemed to entail the preparation of its members to be obedient citizens. The promise of tranquil politics – a hidden social agenda – appears to have been a priority in the minds of many middle- and upper-class institute directors by mid-century.[41] This class conscious cultural perspective also coloured the British experience. Little wonder then that enthusiasm for the institutes was wanting among the working class in Toronto and the hinterland.

One year after the Common School Act of 1850, the Canadian Parliament passed a statute, the Management of Library Associations and Mechanics' Institutes, to regulate and encourage their operation (14 & 15 Vic., c. 86). Robert Bell, a typical reform member of Parliament, sponsored the legislation. His family had come from Britain and settled at Perth.[42] He was first elected in 1847 to represent Lanark and Renfrew and was obviously interested in libraries, for he had earlier suggested using part of a liquor tax to support school libraries. There is evidence that the members of the Carleton Place Library Association and Mechanics' Institute petitioned him to introduce a bill to allow "libraries and other societies of a kindred nature" to incorporate and receive a public grant on the same basis as agricultural societies.[43] The 1851 act permitted not less than ten persons holding £25 to sign a declaration to form an institute or association. Annual meetings of the membership were to appoint a president, librarian, treasurer, lecturer, and secretary to conduct the business of the corporation, usually for one-year terms. The act made no stipulation for grants-in-aid which Parliament voted during the budgetary process each year. The Bureau of Agriculture, formed later in 1853, became responsible for administering the act.

The same legislation also facilitated the formation of Mechanics' Institutes. Some capable persons, who might have used their talents to strengthen and popularize school libraries, instead swelled the ranks of the new institutes; for example, Dexter D'Everardo, who had corresponded with Ryerson, was instrumental in forming the Fonthill Library Association and Mechanics' Institute in February 1853 and continued to work with this library in various capacities for many years.[44] As the number of institutes multiplied rapidly in the first half of the 1850s, other like minded people followed his example. In effect, legislation and grants encouraged the creation of parallel library systems: the common school libraries and the institute and association libraries. Considering the nascent state of library collections at this time, the process was detrimental to both of them, for it divided valuable energy and scarce book resources.

The first large institute buildings opened at Hamilton in 1853 and at Toronto in 1854. The new edifice at Hamilton was hailed as a credit to the city. It featured a large, well-lit, well-furnished newsroom, a spacious lecture room, and splendid auditorium (100 ft. x 45 ft.) which could accommodate many people for concerts and theater. The chandeliers in the great hall, transported from the Crystal Palace at the London Exhibition of 1851, were dazzling.[45] The cost was approximately £4,000. The interest payments were onerous. By 1864, the directors were forced to make an appeal for public subscriptions and to hold more entertainments to meet interest charges. On one of these occasions, Dr. May (he had graduated with a M.D. from Victoria College in 1863) exhibited the new electric light for a delighted audience.[46] Financial woes continued to plague the Hamilton institute until its closure in 1882.

In Toronto, the architects Frederic W. Cumberland and William G. Storm designed the new institute building (Illus. 2). A handsome and commodious structure, it measured 104 ft. x 80 ft. and boasted a small library (28 ft. x 24 ft.) on the ground floor and a grand music hall and gallery on the upper floor.[47] Its neoclassical exterior was a visual reminder of the institute's educational function. Above the entrance were imposing Corinthian pilasters crowned by a cornice and parapet. Even though the government underwrote almost all of its enormous construction costs, $49,000, between 1854 and 1861, the institute's directors had to wage a constant battle against inadequate operating revenue and working class apathy. Once the building was completed and the lecture hall was furnished, the directors were still unable to schedule regular lecture series until the later part of the decade. Nor were winter evening classes well attended: annual registration fluctuated between 105 to 200, from 1862 to 1867. The President, Frederic Cumberland, lamented in 1866 that even the workingmen who were members did not seem to appreciate the valuable work the institute was carrying on.[48]

The 1860s were a quiescent and trying period for most institutes because requisite financial aid from Parliament ceased in 1859. The 1851 act had not dealt with grants-in-aid, yet the government normally supported any new application made to the Bureau of Agriculture to incorporate an institute provided there were at least ten members holding a minimum value of £25. Between 1851 and 1857, the number of institutes receiving aid rose from ten to fifty-eight while parliamentary control of finances passed through a transitional stage. An Audit Office was created in 1855 with John Langton in charge. When Alexander Galt became Inspector General in 1857, he and

Langton decided to improve control over all public expenditures. In 1858, the Commissioner of Agriculture, Peter Vankoughnet, sent a questionnaire to 143 institutes to gather data on membership, libraries, reading rooms, lectures, classes, and finances. He received only 61 replies (41 from institutes in Canada West): these reported a membership of 4,810 and small library holdings of 31,911.[49] Vankoughnet reacted moderately by trimming the maximum grant to $140 for each recipient in 1858.

During the following year, aid was completely withdrawn without any explanation from the commissioner. The legislative debates suggest that Alexander Galt was concerned with financial retrenchment in his budgetary address of 11 March 1859:

> In the expenditure under the head of 'Literary and Scientific Institutions,' I propose a reduction to the extent of $18,000. The principal item in that account is the donations to Mechanics' Institutes; and, looking to the state of the country the government came very reluctantly to the conclusion that this might be better dispensed with than others of an educational character. I may mention that it is my hope and expectation that the reduction of the grants... will not be permanent.[50]

Of course, Galt's financial measures had to pass legislative scrutiny before any reduction could take effect.

When the House debated the motion of supply later in the month, opponents criticized the measure. D'Arcy McGee suggested appropriate guidelines were necessary to assist the more deserving institutes. The member from Ontario County, Joseph Gould, who had helped establish a local institute at Uxbridge, complained that recently incorporated institutes in his riding would suffer without financial assistance. However, the rationale underlying Galt's proposal carried the day after John Sandfield Macdonald, a rising coalition reform member, criticized abuses in the system of grants.

> There was no question that in more than one county in Upper Canada literary societies had received a double grant, by calling themselves both by the same of 'library association' and also by the name of 'Mechanics' Institutes,' as in the case of Sherbrooke [it had received a triple grant as literary institute, library association and Mechanics' Institute, and Mechanics' Institute]. And he was equally satisfied that many of the societies had been got up with no other purpose than

to receive the Government grant. He was in favour of the grants being withheld from all these institutes.[51]

Consequently, no grants were issued by Parliament after 1859.

The removal of the grant forced many institutes, such as Napanee (a well-documented case), to close their doors because of financial woes.[52] The colony's subscription libraries relied heavily on parliamentary aid, an unfortunate and insecure economic dependence. The majority was struck a severe blow. Stronger ones, for example the historic Niagara library, petitioned Parliament to restore the grant and continued to exude optimism at annual meetings – "this Institute is in a prosperous and satisfactory condition" – but eventually it too reached a "low water mark" later in the decade.[53] By 1862, the minister of agriculture was reporting that many institutes not only lacked a "comprehensive plan of action," but they were also not pursuing activities that would achieve the "objects for which these societies were incorporated."[54]

The department of agriculture itself was not prepared to alter this state of affairs. It had created a Board of Arts and Manufactures by statue in 1857 (20 Vic., c. 32, s. 19-33) to promote the education of the working class in useful and ornamental arts. The government paid the Board's expenses, originally set at $2,000 a year, and provided a few *ex officio* luminaries, such as the minister of agriculture and superintendent of education, to help formulate policies and stimulate programs. However, the board's directors were too few in number and too busy with other duties to perform a useful coordinating role. D'Arcy McGee, the new agriculture minister in 1864, admitted that exchanges between the board members and his department officials "have been heretofore very few in number and very meager in substance."[55] Burdened with weak departmental leadership and parliamentary financial restraints, the Board was destined to be unsuccessful in organizing the activities or resources of institutes.

The agriculture department did not begin to reorganize its own activities effectively until 1864, and even then it continued to administer institutes and literary organizations in the belief that self-help, not state assistance, was the main factor in the success of local agencies. Its policy was "destined to produce a mushroom harvest of local societies and then to wither sadly in the years ahead."[56] The welter of small local agencies mostly ignored opportunities to develop programs, such as evening classes, lectures, or exhibitions, in unison with other institutes or the board. With the approach of Confederation, effective long-range departmental planning was curtailed as politicians turned to matters more weighty than the formation of circulating book collections for the public.

In these circumstances, the Board of Arts and Manufactures struggled during its ten year existence. Any initiative it did display was mainly the work of William Edwards, a sturdy Methodist who became secretary-treasurer to the Board in 1858 and later assumed duties as editor of the Board's journal first published in 1861. Known for his active role in the Toronto Mechanics' Institute, where he served for years in various executive positions (President in 1863), Edwards continued to be active in library affairs long after Confederation.[57] He was the principal force behind the Board's decision to establish a free central reference library on the upper floor of the Toronto Mechanics' Institute and to publish its catalogue.[58] Edwards also suggested a scheme of classification and ledger system of circulation for libraries to the Board and its affiliates, and, in 1864, he contemplated establishing a circulating library that could be "extended to any part of the Province."[59] This latter project never materialized; it was quite beyond the Board's capacity.

Few Mechanics' Institutes chose to affiliate with the Board on a regular basis. Only a select company of delegates from Cobourg, Whitby, Hamilton, Toronto, Dundas, and Ayr could be counted upon to attend Board meetings. On a few occasions (most notably in 1862), the Board petitioned the government to reinstate the grants for institutes on the basis of prescribed guidelines and auditing procedures but without tangible results.[60] Lacking adequate government financing and grassroots support from institutes, the Board of Arts and Manufactures lingered for a decade. When the Ontario Legislature took charge in 1867, it dissolved the Board and vested its assets in the Ontario Department of Agriculture and Public Works. Edwards became secretary of the department and continued his work with the Toronto institute for a number of years.

The Post-Confederation Decade

The end of the Union of the Canadas in 1867 subtly changed the political landscape. Astute Upper Canadian reformers like Adam Crooks knew meaningful political independence and national aspirations would not unfold immediately; in a like manner, a Canadian cultural identity would need time to evolve under new constitutional and democratic provisions.[61] Regional interests and concerns and political loyalties would continue to assert dominance within their respective spheres. Ryerson, detached from the support of federal Conservatives such as Sir John A. Macdonald, found himself dealing with the rising strength of reformers and moderate coalition reformers in the Ontario Legislature. He had to negotiate with the new premier, John Sandfield Macdonald, and the Grit leader, George Brown, both of whom were antagonistic to some of Ryerson's administrative methods and educational ideas.

In a small pamphlet, *The New Canadian Dominion*, published immediately after the first Dominion Day, the superintendent warned citizens about the dangers of unprincipled partyism. Ryerson continued to believe that political parties or factions perpetuated societal divisions, thus obstructing loftier efforts, like his own, which sought unity and the common good. He was joined by those who detested the cruder aspects of party patronage and the impurity commonly associated with the machinations of government. Nevertheless, political parties continued to consolidate and extend their control, the Ontario Liberal party being a particularly noteworthy example.[62] As a consequence, political considerations began to absorb more of Ryerson's time; it took all his vigour to secure passage of the 1871 School Act which enshrined universal free elementary education, introduced compulsory attendance, and improved financing for secondary education.

Affairs in free public libraries received scant attention in Ryerson's annual reports and other publications immediately after 1867. His labours were directed elsewhere. Upon the ascendancy of the Liberals in 1872, it was predictable that the independence, policy-making power, and leadership style enjoyed by Ryerson and the Council of Public Instruction would be curbed. The Liberal government, under the reins of Oliver Mowat, was determined to reorganize the aims and functions of a provincial education system according to its own dictates. Mowat kept an eye on the Ontario electorate when judging the pace of reform. One of the first opportunities for reform lay in the depository. It remained a contentious point between the booksellers and Ryerson, and the government was positioned uncomfortably between the combatants.

The booksellers, supported by the formidable George Brown, returned to the attack in earnest after 1870. Ryerson deflected most of their regular criticisms in a lengthy 1872 pamphlet, *Rev. Dr. Ryerson's Defence against the Attacks of the Hon. George Brown*, to which he appended an earlier report from a committee of the House of Assembly. This report concluded that the depository was financially sound and that books were carefully selected.[63] Ryerson also paraded forth an impressive number of statements from educators applauding the depository system. He published their opinions in his 1872 annual report. Two of his allies were county inspectors who later became education ministers. Haldimand County's Richard Harcourt stressed the need for matching grants: "I know from experience that, did we not get the 100 per cent. grant, I would have a great deal of difficulty in inducing trustees to purchase the requisite maps, &c."[64] To the west, in Lambton, George Ross was also supportive:

> I think it really serves a good purpose and not till the country
> is better supplied with facilities for getting a *good,* cheap and
> wholesome literature (if then) should the Depository be dis-
> pensed with. I believe the money spent by the Government

> in stimulating trustees and others to avail themselves of the
> benefits of good maps, apparatus &c. to be well spent ...[65]

Nevertheless, changing political fortunes resulted in a compromise. The booksellers succeeded in obtaining helpful legislation in 1874. They were now
allowed to forward books for selection by the Council; those selected would
be added to the *General Catalogue* and sold to schools as texts, prizes, or
library books on a public grant basis of fifty percent (37 Vic., c. 27, s. 21).

The same year, 1874, witnessed another critical assessment of the depository. Graeme Mercer Adam, a prominent publisher, attacked Ryerson's system
in a pamphlet, *Reform in the Education Office*. An agitated Ryerson responded
by issuing circulars that refuted Adam's claims and declared his creation to be
the "People's Depository." He prepared documentation to have his case adju-
dicated by the courts, but Mowat refused to allow him to proceed.[66] The conflict reached a climax when the Council of Public Instruction began another
investigation, one chaired by Daniel Wilson, a professor at University College
who had crossed swords with the Chief Superintendent on previous occasions
concerning nondenominational colleges. Hodgins and Ryerson prepared a
detailed defence of the depository in the belief that Wilson's investigation
might be biased in favour of the booksellers. They even prepared a detailed
map showing the location of free libraries and the townships supplied by the
depository. It showed that virtually every part of Old Ontario, particularly
the south-west rural region, had participated in the library scheme since
1850.[67]

Not surprisingly, Wilson submitted a negative report on the depository's
role in supplying library and prize books and, with the assistance of George
Brown, he threatened Ryerson's position. The superintendent reacted vigorously and faced down the challenge. Wilson's report was never adopted officially because of fierce opposition by Ryerson and his supporters on the
Council. For Ryerson, it was a pyrrhic victory. Oliver Mowat made his decision to relieve him of power during this dispute. Early in 1876, the government formed an Education Department under the ministerial direction of
Adam Crooks. The embattled superintendent retired, and Hodgins became
deputy minister.[68] Ryerson's public library system and depository quietly
awaited its predictable fate as a result of this latest shift in the tide of political
fortune.

The decade following Confederation was a more constructive interval for
the Mechanics' Institutes. In Ontario the public library function which the
institutes performed became their major activity. The provincial commissioner
of agriculture and public works resumed grants in 1868 after circulating a
questionnaire to about fifty institutes to ascertain their current condition.

Twenty-two replies were received. As a result, a maximum grant of $200 per institute was apportioned on condition that an equal amount be contributed for evening classes or a library of practical works. It was clear from the outset that a broader public was to be served. The new commissioner, John Carling, noted that many institutes were located in rural areas where "the agricultural-ist as well as the artizan" would equally benefit; thus "all classes of the commu-nity" would support the institutes' activities.

To assist in a province-wide renewal, the Association of Mechanics' Institutes of Ontario was formed by statute (31 Vic., c. 29, s. 24), with William Edwards as secretary. At its first meeting, in Hamilton, attended by delegates from ten institutes, the Association adopted four goals: to act as a centre of action; to prepare a catalogue of books suitable for institute libraries; to arrange for works to be made available at the lowest prices possible; and to promote evening classes, lectures, reading rooms, and exhibitions.[69] Institutes could affiliate with the Association by paying five percent of the government grant – a mere $10. The small annual membership fee ensured that the Association, like the Board of Arts and Manufactures before it, would be seri-ously constrained by its finances.

The number of institutes blossomed under these favourable legislative conditions, especially after the grant reached a maximum $400 in 1871. After this date the government granted two dollars for every one dollar raised local-ly. In 1872, county school inspectors were entrusted with the regular inspec-tion of the institutes to ensure that they complied with regulations (35 Vic., c. 32, s. 6-7). In an effort to establish a uniform classification system, William Edwards proposed the adoption of a system of classifying and registering books for circulating libraries that had been devised by his brother, Robert Edwards, who was Librarian at the Toronto institute. His scheme, using a combination of book size, subject, and library type, arranged books in eleven broad divisions:

I	Biography	VII	Voyages and Travels
II	History	VIII	Miscellaneous
III	Novels and Tales	IX	Religious Literature
IV	Poetry and Drama	X	Reference works
V	Periodical Literature	XI	Illustrated Works, etc.
VI	Science, Art, etc.		

Within each section, volumes were sub-divided by size and assigned let-ters from the alphabet. In Biography, the initial letters for sizes were A, B, and C; in History, the letters were D, E, and F; in Religion, Y and Z; in Reference, double letters were used: AA, BB, and CC. After each initial letter a number, showing the accession, was designated. Books stood on the shelves by size in each section; in the printed catalogue the arrangement in each division was alphabetical. Thus in each division of the catalogue (e.g., Biography) a user might start to retrieve books by noting the call number in the first division:

> B. 294 – Abernety, (Dr.) Life of
> C. 250 – Alexander the Great, Life of
> A. 11 – Arnold, (Dr.) Life of

The book then could be located and charged out.

Edwards was "satisfied that the system of classifying and recording the books taken out or exchanged, is a good one, and is well adapted for either a large or small library."[70] His system facilitated consecutive numbering on the shelves and permitted the recording and charging of loans in a record book divided into two parts – one for an alphabetical list of members with registration number, the other for each initial book letter and progressive number. This circulation ledger ordinarily would be used for six months. The librarian simply had to post a member's registration number beside a book selected for home use and to note the book's call number beside the borrower's registration information. The return date of any circulating book or a member's status could be checked by referring to either section of the record ledger. Both Hamilton and Toronto had adopted this system in the 1860s and reported successful results; it was widely adopted in Ontario after 1872.

Circulating libraries were obviously the most popular aspect of the institutes. In other endeavours, the Association was less successful. It encountered difficulty organizing evening classes and lobbying the government for better legislation. By 1875 the Toronto President, Thomas Davison, was openly critical. Writing to the Association's executive, Davison complained that the requirement for half the directors of local institutes to be mechanics was unjust because in most cases mechanics did not form a majority of members. Davison made three claims: first, the Association failed to serve as a "bond of union" between the institutes; second, the five percent annual affiliation fee was an unnecessary tax; third, he wanted the institute libraries to be the main order of business.

> [I]n my opinion, it would be well that the grant from the Government should not be confined to Mechanics' Institutes, so called or so incorporated, but should embrace one Library Association from each Town or Village, leaving it to the originators to name it Mercantile, Professional, Mechanical Library, or Library Association. So long as its

object was to educate the public, irrespective of creed, nationality or occupation, I think it should be entitled to the grant.[71]

His letter presented a refreshing opportunity to reappraise programs and organization.

Davison's ideas were debated and rejected at the Association's annual meeting in September 1875. A resolution approved unanimously by representatives from twelve institutes recognized the usefulness of the Association as it presently operated. In a more positive response, the Association did try to establish better local contact and improve library conditions. In subsequent years it distributed to each affiliate a set of Andrew Ure's *Dictionary of Arts, Manufactures and Mines* and Alexander Keith Johnston's *Handy Royal Atlas of Modern Geography*. In 1876 it sponsored a prize for the best essays on Mechanics' Institutes: ironically, Davison won first prize. He reiterated the necessity for a library and reading-room that constituted the "sum of attractions in most Institutes."[72] The new minister of agriculture, Stanley Woods, seemed to agree. In his 1877 report on institutes he noted: "The desire among people in towns and villages to possess a public library and the facilities for promoting social intercourse and mental and moral improvement is evidently increasing; the natural outcome of our improved and efficient system of public instruction."[73]

Common School Libraries: "Practically Abandoned"

Adam Crooks presided over the death throes of Ryerson's book depository. The new minister was an experienced member of Oliver Mowat's Executive Council, having served previously as Provincial Treasurer, and he was determined to avert any criticism of the depository's role.[74] When the Booksellers Association again petitioned the government to abolish the depository in February 1876, Crooks appointed James Brown, an accountant, to conduct a thorough investigation of the depository's finances and operations from its very inception. During the course of his investigation, Brown often sought comments from Hodgins or Dr. May.[75] Both men, however, were pressed for time because they had to organize the departmental exhibit for the American Centennial Exposition at Philadelphia in October. Although Brown exonerated the depository of any financial wrongdoing, the evidence gathered from many parties, which was published separately, led Crooks to suspect that there was a need to curtail its operations because the school libraries were not functioning as they originally were intended.

During the government's enquiry, James Campbell's submission on "Village Libraries" had complimented the book selection made by the directors of Mechanics' Institutes, who "appreciate not only good literature, but also the requirements of those for whom they are provided." Of course, many directors relied on the book trade to supply their collections since selection from the depository was limited. Campbell proposed that public school libraries be replaced by village libraries, and, while he did not outline a comprehensive plan, he offered some useful comments for consideration. Four points deserve attention:

> ... it is proposed to establish a library in every incorporate village and other centres of population in the province.
>
> 9. With the establishment of a Village Library, it will be necessary to make it a part of the business of a Public Library Clerk, through the Librarian or Inspector, or otherwise to promote the formation and success of those Libraries, and to report periodically as to their working.
>
> 10. Whether a hall might be obtained as a reading-room to be open at all times, with the attendance of the Librarian at stated times, to give out books; or merely a room, in which the books are kept in a case, and to be given out a fixed times, may be considered. Whether the one plan may answer better in one place, and the other may be more suitable in another, would depend on local circumstances. In some cases the Teacher might undertake the duties of Librarian, with a small salary attached, or when more time might be required a suitable person is usually to be found in most villages.
>
> 11. Among the privileges enjoyed by Mechanics' Institutes, is a certain fund to defray expenses of lectures; this sum might, in the case of the Village Library, be devoted to rent of a hall or room &c.
>
> 12. Indifference, incompetency, and poverty are said to be the great hindrances to the Township and School Libraries, and it would be a work of time to overcome these formidable obstacles, but with the impetus given by the establishment of Libraries in every incorporated village in the Province, and with an energetic Library Clerk in stimulating the trustees of the various schools and townships, a good deal might be accomplished.[76]

Dr. May responded to Campbell's suggestions by questioning the success of the institutes. After examining recent reports filed by school inspectors and the department of agriculture, he discovered that there was no evidence to confirm that some institutes were purchasing new books with government aid as specified in the regulations. Although he did not identify the institutes which were failing in this regard, his revelation was a serious embarrassment, far worse than a charge denigrating the quality of fiction circulating from institute libraries. As for the village library scheme, May was firm: "At the present time villages and towns can procure all the books they require, either as School Libraries or Mechanics' Institutes, and there seems no necessity for a change in the present methods."[77]

Of course, as the education minister's first enquiry had shown, there were still many problems with the common school library system. When George Paxton Young, the Chairman of the Central Committee of Examiners, which began probing the question of selection and prices of library and prize books in 1876, asked John Hodgins for a list of all the libraries ever supplied by the depository and the current holdings in each, the new deputy minister had to admit that many libraries had "long ceased to exist." Hodgins said that a complete list would be unreliable because for some time his department had been emphasizing prize books, not libraries.

> Of late years we have made no special efforts to promote the library system in rural sections, having concentrated these efforts with great success on the distribution of prize books on the merit card system. Under that system good and useful books are sure to get into the families without any of the evils attendant upon personal competition among pupils, while under the library system the books are rarely asked for – they being as a general rule such standard works as are too dry and unsuitable for family reading.[78]

Young's report recommended the continuance of controls on the selection of books and the retention of the depository because of the variety of inexpensive books it offered. This decision predictably led to another booksellers' petition to the Legislative Assembly, in early 1877.

Despite the fact that the depository had received a favourable report on its financial transactions and that the relatively powerful Central Committee supported its existence, Crooks commissioned yet another study. This one was conducted in secret under the direction of Colonel Thomas C. Scoble, a government employee who had previously worked for Dr. May in the depository.[79] Scoble's work apparently was considered an internal, private report; it never appeared in the public record. Whatever the merits of the depository, Crooks realized that the government was essentially funding two public library systems through the agency of two different departments, creating an unnecessary expense he preferred to eliminate discreetly. Ryerson's system of public libraries was naturally the most likely candidate for reform because of its political liabilities.

From available evidence Scoble concluded that the Mechanics' Institutes libraries were more popular. School libraries were faltering. By 1878, the institutes were receiving slightly more than $18,000 in grants-in-aid (Graph 1: Total Grants for Mechanics' Institutes Libraries, 1868 to 1880). Between 1868 and 1878, the total number of books had risen from 22,947 to 94,522 (Graph 2: Total Books in Mechanics' Institutes Libraries, 1868 to 1880). Circulation was also increasing, especially outside Toronto and Hamilton (Graph 3: Library Circulation from Mechanics' Institutes, 1875-1880). By contrast, total funding for common school libraries, which Crooks began to scrutinize closely after 1876 in his annual report, was dwindling. The statistics for free public libraries supplied by the depository between 1876 and 1880 clearly demonstrate this:

> 1876 – 91 libraries – $2,483 legislative grant
> 1877 – 83 libraries – $1,787 legislative grant
> 1878 – 69 libraries – $1,613 legislative grant
> 1879 – 46 libraries – $ 825 legislative grant
> 1880 – 19 libraries – $ 166 legislative grant.[80]

Hodgins' revelations and Scoble's negative report probably did not surprise Crooks. Any misgivings he had about Ontario's common school libraries were anticipated and reinforced by *Public Libraries in the United States of America*, which had been published in 1876 by the United States Bureau of Education at Washington. A perusal of its pages indicated that the development of American district school libraries had been marked by "many changes and mishaps" – for example, state systems in New York, Massachusetts, and Michigan were no longer considered successes, although Ontario's "excellent" system was briefly noted.[81] Generally, by this time American educators considered the public school library to be a prototype rather than a model for contemporary policy making. Municipal free public libraries were the way of the future in the United States,

With Ryerson in retirement, government reports on the status of small school libraries in Ontario tended to confirm the American experience. Ryerson's school libraries had been "read out." They had not been restocked, despite the depository's bargain rates. Furthermore, Ryerson's conception of common schools as the most important source of public education and social activity for local communities was no longer feasible by the 1880s. Now the railroad defined the expanding contours of the country. Rural life centred on self-sufficient school sections – places where instruction was dispensed, meetings were convened, and families gathered for recreation or news – could no longer satisfy eager young minds or clever hands. By this time it was evident that the urban high school had supplanted the local common school as the most important element in Ontario's system of public education.[82]

The department reduced the depository's activities step by step between 1876-80. Crooks preferred to follow a deliberate, conservative course. By using legislation, orders-in-council, and departmental regulations, the minister separated three intertwined issues: school libraries for pupils, prize books for students, and the local public library. The depository's monopoly was ended, then its funding was reduced. In 1879, Crooks removed Hodgins' control over the depository and promoted Dr. May as its superintendent; he also slashed the matching school library grant to one-third the previous amount. The minister's 1879 annual report contains the last mention of free public libraries in schools.

In his budget address of 1880, Crooks noted that Colonel Scoble's private report had verified the minister's suspicions: the library system had been "practically abandoned," prize books were not necessary, and texts for Normal and Model Schools could be procured through general trade channels. He also found that stocking the depository entailed a large expenditure of public money. Crooks concluded severely:

> The operations of the Depository have become smaller since I asked last year for less public money for stock... It is unnecessary to re-stock the Depository, for the schools in general understand that they can be well supplied through the ordinary trade, and any reason for its existence in the former infancy of ours schools, cannot now be successfully urged.[83]

By the end of 1881, the depository was closed, its employees dismissed, and its assets distributed to various educational institutions.[84] Its demise marked the end of a centralized book supply and discount scheme for common school libraries envisaged by Ryerson in 1850.

The turn of the institutes followed. Dr. May's revelations in his brief report had not gone unnoticed. By 1879 there were about seventy-five institutes for which school inspectors had authorized grants. During this year, the government made a decision to transfer the institutes to the minister of education, "to whose department they appropriately and strictly belong," wrote Stanley Woods, the commissioner of agriculture.[85] This administrative shuffle did not receive extensive public scrutiny. At a special convention held at

Toronto in February 1879 to compose a blueprint for the institutes' future, forty-nine delegates from twenty-three institutes drafted proposals for improving legislation, but neither then, nor later in September at the annual meeting of the Association of Mechanics' Institutes held at Ottawa, was there any consultation or discussion about the transfer of institutes to another department.

When he learned of the change, in December, William Edwards wrote to James Young, the long-time association president, that it was be a mistake.[86] However, Young, a Liberal member of the Legislature, felt differently. In the debate on the transfer in January 1880 he expressed satisfaction with the move, possibly because the wording of the legislation was somewhat vague, leaving open different possibilities. By the Act's terms, the education department could make rules and regulations for a variety of purposes: to arrange for evening classes in physical and practical science; to disburse grants; to sanction the purchase of books "in other subjects" (i.e., works of fiction); and to administer inspections and audits (43 Vic., c. 5, s. 1-3). Crooks then appointed Dr. May to do a thorough inspection of the institutes, commencing in the summer of 1880. One era had ended; another was about to begin.

Chapter 2

BRITISH AND AMERICAN
INFLUENCES

By the middle of the nineteenth century there were many forces preparing the groundwork for the formation of public libraries in British North America. Numerous educational groups, a nascent publishing industry and book trade, municipalities, and an expanding reading public were among the leading agents of change. At this stage of development, most citizens did not accept public libraries as rate-supported municipal institutions. A library was considered to be public if it was accessible to all members of a community in terms of geography or group identity; however, as a rule its basic services (circulating collection, reading room, reference service) and ancillary services (lectures and museum) were not free. In the two principal Anglo-American countries, the overall pattern of modern public library service developed along uniform lines, with only relatively minor differences between the two nations. Canadians borrowed freely from both their American and British counterparts, in the process creating a library system guided by outside influences and ideas yet thoroughly suitable for the needs of Canadian government.

In his 1851 report on American public libraries to the Smithsonian Institution, Charles Jewett defined public libraries as those

> which are accessible – either without restriction, or upon conditions with which all can easily comply – to every person who wishes to use them for appropriate purposes. In this sense I believe it may be said that all libraries in this country, which are not private property, (and indeed many which are private property,) are public libraries.[1]

Library collections were available to the public under terms and conditions prescribed by their informal organizations: in the United States, many subscription libraries, lyceums, and athenaeums offered reading materials to those who were able to afford small membership fees; in Great Britain and Canada, Mechanics' Institutes included libraries and reading rooms that were available to artisans, mechanics, apprentices, and the general populace upon payment of a membership charge.

This host of pre-1850 public library types, now usually designated by historians as social libraries, reflected a diverse range of cultural relationships and information concerns. A new literate generation, "The Unknown Public" Wilkie Collins wrote about in *Household Words*, expected more than religious and utilitarian works. It needed, in Collins's words, "to be taught the difference between a good book and a bad [book]."[2] As the diffusion of reading matter for home use, especially inexpensive fiction, turned into a popular feature of public libraries, commercial circulating libraries became alternative sources of reading. Charles Mudie's Select Library was undoubtedly the most successful nineteenth-century circulating library. Mudie's branch libraries, which featured the three-volume novel, expanded into many large English towns where they were patronized by a vast reading clientele.[3] Operations in Upper Canada were less well organized; small local circulating libraries sprang up in a few localities such as Amherstburg.[4]

Very few libraries in Britain or North American were supported by taxes or freely accessible to all residents of a community. The prevailing social attitude among citizens and civic leaders inclined towards voluntary organizations and charges for service. This stance would change dramatically in the second half of the nineteenth century. Schools in several American and Canadian jurisdictions already were offering a tax-supported version of public library service by 1850. Esteemed educators, such as Horace Mann and Egerton Ryerson, and prominent library spokesmen, such as George Ticknor and Edward Edwards, were starting to reorient fundamental views concerning the public library. A second version of public libraries was to arise, one which would eventually supersede its predecessor.

Tax-Supported Public Libraries

In the United States, public libraries in tax-supported schools were the first to diverge significantly from the general subscription pattern. American educators were at the forefront in creating a mass education system in which libraries formed an integral part. Ryerson was obviously influenced by the work of Horace Mann in Massachusetts, Henry Barnard in Rhode Island, and New York State legislators.[5] Mann supported an 1837 law allowing school districts to raise an initial $30 and then $10 in subsequent years to support free libraries, but this law was repealed in 1850, one year before Massachusetts enacted a bill to provide for free town libraries.[6] In Rhode Island, Henry Barnard, the state Superintendent of Education, worked tirelessly in the 1840s to promote a law permitting towns and districts to establish free school libraries. However, the successors to Mann and Barnard neglected these libraries and their original potential was never realized.

New York State had pioneered the idea of school libraries. In 1835 the legislature allowed school districts to raise $20 to establish a library and $10 a year thereafter to maintain it. Improvements in this law continued until, by the early 1850s, there were more than 1,500,000 books in these libraries. This surely impressed Ryerson. However, when New York legislators permitted library money to be diverted to other resources, beginning in the 1850s, rural libraries started to decline and continued to do so into the 1870s, when many knowledgeable library promoters pronounced the experience a prototype or even a failure. This judgement extended to other states, but it was tempered by the recognition that district school libraries had helped elevate the status of the public library as an essential part of public education; they were now rightfully entitled to a share of public taxation.[7]

Community school libraries for adults as well as children contrasted markedly with fee-based social libraries catering to adult interests. Lifelong education, not recreational reading, was the fundamental motive for their foundation. This concept was to play a significant role in the public library movement. Books, especially nonfiction, were to be provided for all ages and all people in order to develop equal opportunities, to raise (or mould) character, to offer antidotes to vulgar novels, and to make information generally accessible. The arguments cited to support community school libraries in many respects paralleled those used to found common schools. Libraries and schools were established within a democratic tradition of religious tolerance and political freedom, and they were linked closely with the functions of government. In this milieu, the library stood as an impartial dispenser of literature judged acceptable by community standards.

Ryerson considered subscription libraries and Mechanics' Institutes inefficient and outmoded civic agencies. From a strictly pedagogic point of view, he believed that they had not achieved their purpose. Indeed, this assessment still prevails, although recent scholarship on British institutes has shown that they were relatively successful as part of a wider popular and scientific culture that aspired to reach the lower classes with modest educational aims.[8] But an even more important factor influenced Ryerson's thinking on the subject of a full-fledged public library system in Canada West: in 1850 there was only a handful of cities, towns, or villages large enough to establish libraries. According to the tabulations of the 1851-52 census, there was not a single urban locality with more than 50,000 people:

Cities		*Towns*		*Villages*	
Hamilton	14,112	Belleville	4,569	Amherstburg	1,880
Kingston	11,585	Brantford	3,877	Chippawa	1,193
Toronto	30,775	Brockville	3,246	Galt	2,248
		Bytown	7,760	Ingersoll	1,190
		Chatham	2,070	Oshawa	1,142
		Cobourg	3,871	Paris	1,890
		Cornwall	1,646	Preston	1,180
		Dundas	3,517	Richmond	434
		Goderich	1,329	Thorold	1,091
		Guelph	1,860	Woodstock	2,112
		London	7,035		
		Niagara	3,340		
		Perth	1,916		
		Peterborough	2,191		
		Picton	1,569		
		Port Hope	2,476		
		Prescott	2,156		
		Simcoe	1,452		
		St. Catharines	4,368		
		St. Thomas	1,274		

A network of common school libraries, then, was the only practical way to extend free circulating libraries to the entire population. The fluctuating fortunes of Mechanics' Institutes during the 1850s no doubt convinced the Superintendent that his policy was sound.

Even in Great Britain, where more than four hundred Mechanics' Institutes existed at mid-century, change was in the offing. The original purpose of providing scientific and technical information for workers had been supplanted by general cultural considerations. In response to this, parliament passed a public act in August 1850 enabling town councils in boroughs of ten thousand inhabitants or more to levy a halfpenny rate to acquire land and buildings for public libraries and museums. The support of two-thirds of the burgesses at a public poll organized by the mayor was mandatory for local implementation of the act. William Ewart, the act's author, had been motivated by an article he had read on public libraries written by Edward Edwards as well as by dissatisfaction with the library services which institutes offered and the fees they continued to collect. Ewart's Select Committee of the House of Commons relied chiefly on Edwards' testimony in 1849 to prepare the way for the Public Libraries Act. Edwards used the term public library to mean "libraries deriving their support from public funds, either wholly or in part; and … libraries as are made accessible to the public to a greater or less degree."[9]

Ewart later amended the act in 1855 to reduce the required number of inhabitants to five thousand; to include parishes or districts; to increase the rate to one penny; and to extend the financial provisions to books and newspapers. Town councils usually managed the library directly, although parish vestries could appoint three to nine commissioners to oversee operations. Ewart's amended legislation remained the principal act for England until a consolidated act appeared in 1892.[10] Manchester was the first large English town to establish a public library, with Edwards, a tireless supporter of libraries for the next three decades, appointed as its first Principal Librarian (1851-58). From time to time, Edwards advocated open access to shelves, Sunday openings and evening service, unrestricted borrowing privileges, and free distribution of some government documents. These were services his contemporaries either disagreed with or considered too visionary.[11]

Only a few towns adopted Ewart's measures during the 1850s, but the public experience with free circulating libraries generally was favourable. This information was publicized regularly in journals, including Ryerson's digest of educational news that was distributed throughout Ontario.[12] In the 1860s, commentators writing in popular magazines, notably *Meliora*, praised the development of free libraries but kept open a critical eye:

> The different circumstances in which our urban and rural populations are placed required certain adaptations to accomplish a given purpose for each, and while we view the free public library as an appliance of the highest value for aiding the mental progress of the people, we cannot help earnestly desiring to see coincident with this movement wide extension of colportage in Great Britain.[13]

Unquestionably, library extension to rural communities was a difficult problem because local self-government operated differently than its urban counterpart. Consequently, there was a need for either voluntary societies – for example, the Religious Tract and Book Society of Scotland – or itinerant hawkers to distribute and sell cheap popular literature. There were more than thirty free libraries in England, Wales, Ireland, and Scotland by the time Edward Edwards published his seminal *Free Town Libraries* in 1869 and about three hundred by the mid-1890s; but rural library service continued to languish in many English villages and parishes.[14]

Edwards' leadership paralleled the efforts of Charles Jewett in the United States. Jewett was well-travelled and conversant with Anthony Panizzi's style of administration and cataloguing rules which the latter had developed at the British Museum.[15] After publishing *Notices of Public Libraries*, Jewett was instrumental in organizing a library conference at New York in September 1853 which attracted eighty-two delegates. This convention enthusiastically discussed his proposal for a national library based in the Smithsonian Institution, a printed centralized national catalogue, and a new system of rules for cataloguing. However, despite plans for the formation of a national librarians' association and a call for another meeting at Washington, nothing substantial occurred at this time because the major participants lacked cohesion and firm institutional bases to continue their work. Only a handful of municipal public libraries offering free services existed at this time in the American north-east.

New Hampshire legislators had passed the first general statute for public libraries in 1849. By its permissive provisions any town could raise and appropriate a fixed sum money for a public library, which was to be open to the free use of every inhabitant. Gifts, donations, bequests, and legacies could be received and administered for library purposes. The New Hampshire law served as a model for other New England states. In Massachusetts, a second library act was passed in 1851. It resembled the New Hampshire provisions with one exception: it set down a maximum tax rate of one dollar for founding a library and twenty-five cents thereafter for its maintenance. The city of Boston had received state approval in 1848 to authorize the establishment and maintenance of a public library but the project was delayed for years. The major personages involved, George Ticknor and Edward Everett, disagreed on fundamental issues, including the question of home circulation.[16] Boston Public Library finally opened in March 1854, then moved into its own building in 1858 with Charles Jewett, who had left the Smithsonian, as superintendent.

The period between 1850 and 1860 obviously was a critical decade for the development of the Anglo-American public library movement. The value and purpose of public libraries was debated thoroughly in Great Britain's parliament; as a result, enabling legislation for municipal authorities spread to England, Wales, Scotland, Ireland, and the empire. In the United States, the Boston Public Library, general state legislation, and the leadership of Ticknor and Jewett – all this helped to lay the foundation for public libraries before the Civil War.

Free Library Bills before Confederation

Initial efforts to establish free municipal public libraries in Canada West did not come to fruition. In fact, the entire system of local self-government for cities, towns, villages, and townships had only been instituted in 1849 by a leading reformer, Robert Baldwin, who was wary of Ryerson's tendency to centralize.[17] In September 1852, a Conservative from Toronto, William Henry Boulton, introduced a bill authorizing cities and towns to establish and maintain public libraries. Boulton's bill was discharged at second reading. Unfortunately no copy of the text has survived, so it is necessary to speculate about the bill's content.[18] From our knowledge of two contemporary American state bills and the Ewart Act, it is likely Boulton drafted what became know later to library advocates as "short" permissive legislation, that is, his bill probably allowed larger incorporated municipalities to set up and operate libraries with the approval of ratepayers. It may also have included a maximum tax rate, a minimum population for a municipality, and reference to procedures for adopting the bylaw.

The first public library bill failed for many reasons. William Boulton had a reputation for appealing to popular sentiment that did not endear him to many of his political colleagues who may have considered his library plan, regardless of its merits, to be premature. Perhaps they thought that Ryerson's depository system and Robert Bell's 1851 act adequately served the needs of the colony given its pioneer conditions. Moreover, there were only a few cities and towns in Canada West at this time that could have taken advantage of Boulton's legislation, and many of them already had a Mechanics' Institute or were in the process of establishing one.

Boulton's 1851 election victory was invalidated in 1853. He did not contest his seat in the House of Assembly, nor did he involve himself with any kind of social legislation once he returned to private life.[19] His place as public library advocate in parliament was taken by a lawyer from Perth, Alexander Morris, who first entered the legislature in 1861 as a Liberal-Conservative. Morris was well-educated, had travelled abroad, and had many connections with libraries, Mechanics' Institutes, and publishing ventures.[20] He had served as vice-president of the Montreal Mercantile Library Association in 1849 and given lectures there and at the nearby Hemmingford Mechanics' Institute in the 1850s. He edited the *Juvenile Presbyterian*, a children's periodical, for a brief period of time. In parliament Morris did not begin to play an important role until after Confederation; however, in August 1866 he did introduce a bill establishing free municipal libraries. It was probably patterned upon Ewart's amended act. The Toronto *Globe* made passing reference to his bill, which was introduced very late in the legislative session and discharged at second reading. The original bill is no longer available, but fortunately John George Hodgins' *Documentary History of Education* preserved its text.[21] It appears as "long" legislation, that is, the composition and election of the library board is set out along with procedures for incorporation, administrative duties and powers of trustees, tax rates, and so on.

Morris's bill allowed cities and towns of five thousand or more inhabitants to establish a free public library after the owners of real estate had given consent by a two-thirds majority at a public meeting. The resolutions passed at the initial meeting were to be deposited at the County Registrar's office. Nine trustees were to direct the library's business: six elected by the ratepayers and three elected by "those who have made donations to the Corporation of books, or money." Two trustees were to be elected at an annual meeting by ratepayers; one trustee annually by the donors. The trustees had the power to levy a tax for library purposes not exceeding one-half cent on the dollar each year. Trustees also were empowered to operate reading rooms, hold land, enter into mortgages, establish library regulations for circulating books, meet monthly, and elect a president or other officers. The library was to be "open to the Public free of charge" subject to regulations adopted by the directors.

The influence of British legislation is unmistakable. In Britain, public libraries were making headway in larger towns: they were being touted as important agents in the diffusion of knowledge, and *Meliora* speculated on the need for classification and cataloguing systems to hasten public accessibility.[22] As a lawyer, Morris could easily refer to the act Ewart had steered through parliament along with its subsequent amendments, and adapt measures to circumstances that suited Canadian municipal life. The necessity for a public meeting, a two-thirds majority of ratepayers, the frugal halfpenny rate, the population limitation, the ownership of land or buildings, and a corporate board of not more than nine trustees – all these were British features.

There was also resemblance to laws in the New England states: the permissive nature of the legislation, the public meeting, the rate limitation, and the power to hold land or erect buildings. One distinguishing feature of Morris's bill was his outright preference for an independent board of citizens operating within the context of local self-governing communities. Clearly, Morris believed that educational needs demanded the attention of a special purpose board. However, the approach of Confederation meant the rapid dissolution of parliament in late summer 1866. Canadian legislators turned to constitutional business. Library matters were ignored in the press of events.

In Britain and American state legislatures, the board form of governance and its role in local government began to receive more attention in the 1870s. Edward Edwards, who continued to recommend many changes after he was dismissed from Manchester in 1858,[23] seemed convinced that boards were more desirable than council committees or parish vestries which many people felt might neglect educational matters:

> But the raising in character and intelligence of the corporations will be question of time. It is sure to come. In the meantime, some of their new functions, under Permissive Acts of Parliament such as that relating to Town Libraries, will be best administered with aid from without. Many men

may be found in most towns whose special qualifications fit them pre-eminently to be members of a Library Committee, but whose aims and pursuits in life make it unlikely that they will ever become Town-Councillors or Parish Vestrymen. In many towns the Clergy have helped, most zealously and most ably, in promoting Free Libraries.[24]

A major innovation took place in the United States when an Illinois state act appeared in 1872. This law featured an independent library board of nine appointed or elected members with staggered three-year terms of office. It also empowered citizens to present petitions to town and village councils in order to establish libraries by means of a simple majority of votes, and it set a claimable mill rate the board could depend upon.[25] The Illinois "long" law became a model for other midwestern states and received praise in many quarters.[26]

Philadelphia and London, 1876-77

In retrospect, the public library movement that arose at mid-century in the British Isles and America embodied important liberal-democratic assumptions about the character of local self-government and public ownership, control, finance, and accessibility that distinguished it from an earlier form of public library service that had been characterized by private-sector voluntary efforts and payment of fees. By 1876, William F. Poole, director of the Chicago Public Library, defined the "public library" this way:

> The 'public library' which we are to consider is established by state laws, is supported by local taxation and voluntary gifts, is managed as a public trust, and every citizen of the city or town which maintains it has an equal share in its privileges of reference and circulation. It is not simply for scholars and professional men ... but for the whole community – the mechanic, the laboring man, the sewing-girl, the youth, and all who desire to read, whatever be their rank, intelligence or condition in life. It is the adjunct and supplement of the common school system.[27]

Poole's statement clarified a number of points and prompted others to follow his lead.

Building upon the community aspect inherent in European and American municipal libraries, as well as experiments with American tax-supported district school public libraries, library promoters began organizing municipal public libraries on a permanent democratic basis after 1850.[28] At a time when educational concerns in Anglo-American countries were resolved locally, and voluntary efforts were an important part of the fabric of government, the authority and legitimacy for establishing libraries normally rested in an enabling act by which political action was necessary at the municipal level to secure majorities for free library bylaws. Current wisdom held that libraries should be publicly funded by local taxes from rateable assessment or by local general funds, and that they should be administered by a board or committee composed of citizens or elected representatives. Finally, free public access for residents should be maintained in terms of local proximity and availability of standard resources: reading rooms, circulating collections, reference departments, and adequate accommodation. All of the above were deemed necessary by advocates and librarians, who were articulating the need for the diffusion of knowledge by free libraries within the structure of local government.

Librarianship as a distinct occupation slowly emerged between the years 1850 and 1875, and it acquired a more definite shape after the 1876 Centennial Exposition in Philadelphia. Exhibitions were common showplaces for new technology, such as Alexander Graham Bell's telephone, and attractive locations for meetings of professional groups. One hundred and three men and women met in conference at Philadelphia, at the beginning of October 1876, to discuss library topics. The U.S. Bureau of Education report on public libraries, prepared for the exposition by its editor-in-chief, Samuel Warren, was well received (the two volumes became a respected library manual for years), and the American Library Association (ALA) was founded. Its notable early leaders were Justin Windsor, Boston Public Library; William F. Poole, Chicago Public Library; Charles A. Cutter, Boston Athenaeum; and Melvil Dewey, who had recently developed a decimal classification system at Amherst College. Shortly afterwards, Dewey, and the publisher Richard R. Bowker established the *Library Journal.* These two men would direct the ALA's course for many years.

One spirited participant, Samuel Green, declared the conference a great success. He later recalled that "The permanent union of librarians effected by the conference also brought together in one body individuals from all parts of the country who could be depended on to work unitedly for the general interest of the library cause."[29] After 1876, the cause would embrace many innovative measures: open shelves, central card catalogues, children's services, improved classification and cataloguing schemes, functional library architecture, branch libraries, state library commissions, and the admittance of popular fiction to circulating collections. American conceptions of public library service would remain at the forefront of international public library development.

The Philadelphia conference stimulated immediate action across the

Atlantic. Edward W.B. Nicholson, Librarian of the London Institution, wrote to the *Times* in early 1877, inviting British librarians and others to an international conference. A number of prominent librarians attended from western Europe, Greece, Australia, and the United States. Neither Edward Edwards nor Anthony Panizzi, the architects of librarianship in Britain, was able to attend. The proceedings were judged to be satisfactory by the conference's 218 delegates. They debated at length classification schemes, open access to shelves, circulating systems, and, on 5 October 1877, they founded the Library Association (LA) for the promotion of libraries and encouragement of bibliographical research.[30] The conference emphasized the need for a general catalogue of English literature, a task which ushered in an era of historical and bibliographical work for which the LA became renowned.

Canadian librarians were not present at either the Philadelphia or London library conventions. The Toronto *Globe* commented on their absence in an editorial on Nicholson's international conference:

> It may be that we take less interest in both the establishment and the maintenance of valuable libraries than do our cousins, either south of the lakes or at the antipodes; if so, one of the best ways of remedying this defect is to see that representative librarians from Canada attend the next Convention, which will be held at Oxford, with a view to bringing away with them new ideas and an increased measure of enthusiasm in their arduous work.[31]

Both John Hodgins and Dr. May were present at the Philadelphia exposition to oversee the Ontario education department's exhibit, which included a prominent display case of prize and library books (Illus. 3). Perhaps they returned home with an expanded knowledge of public library service. Hodgins' commemorative Philadelphia volume does include a few brief comments on American libraries, in particular the acclaimed report on public libraries completed by the U.S. Commissioner of Education. Copies of the report were afterwards forwarded to the education department for distribution in Ontario, and Hodgins wrote favourably about it in the February 1877 issue of *Belford's Monthly Magazine*.[32] The two men must have realized that the public library system they had encouraged for more than two decades was no longer ascendant in the United States.

American library leaders evidently regarded school-based public libraries as *passé* because they stocked books from authorized catalogues issued by central depositories, and this dependency was no longer acceptable. The position of booksellers and publishers was unequivocal. *Publishers' Weekly* carried a caustic review of the Ontario library and prize book display at Philadelphia (reprinted by Hodgins), calling it the *bête noire* of the Canadian book trade.

> This is an institution to which, happily, we have no parallel, except so far as our own Government interferes with the private business of the stationers, by furnishing envelopes below cost. It offers to the schools a selected list of books at one-half off, from which list they are to draw their books for prizes, etc. Naturally, the list is said to be antiquated and otherwise objectionable, for private business is not best done by public departments; but of this the visiting trade may judge for themselves, since in this large case (No. 63), is displayed attractively the full list.[33]

Whatever the effect of foreign opinion, Ontario was proud of its educational system: equality of educational opportunity was supposed to further social mobility and ameliorate the alienation of labourers from capitalists. Many people expected the public library to play a role in this process, and they were ready to offer their services to the cause. For its part, the government had passed legislation and provided small grants, a policy it had pursued for a quarter century.

Ontario Responds

Political conditions at the level of local self-government helped facilitate public support for change in Ontario. There were many reasons why free municipal libraries were appealing. They were open to all community members without direct payment. They ostensibly transcended the division of social classes, and they were to be managed locally by a representative public corporation. The library staff, normally few in number but with specialized knowledge and skills, were trained to render the collection more accessible to all persons allowed to use its resources. The public library movement's founders in Ontario emphasized these democratic features as they distinguished free public libraries from those in Mechanics' Institutes and public schools.[34] While collections in these two agencies were open to the public, they were only one part of each institution's activities and had not attracted extensive patronage for a variety of reasons.

Mechanics' institutes were essentially proprietary bodies with an ambitious educational program using lectures, classes and libraries to teach artisans and skilled workers the scientific principles underlying manufacturing, crafts, and natural phenomena. Reality was more sobering than theory. Novels constituted the major part of many institute lending libraries, a circumstance that was becoming less a liability in some quarters despite the tendentious moral issues. The Toronto *Globe* wrote: "This work of discriminating between things vicious and things merely pleasurable is well done by novelists in general, and thus the writer of fiction has often a valuable educational effect."[35] Others were less kind. Dr. May's landmark *Special Report* clearly demonstrated that the practical value of lectures and evening classes was questionable.[36] In fact, in the Mother Country, the custom of imparting scientific knowledge by means of public lectures was giving way to permanent educational bodies or large-scale exhibitions.[37] Many people – such as Thomas Davison who openly supported provincial grants for public libraries – had grown skeptical of the institutes' potential to reach large numbers of subscribers.

On the other hand, Adam Crooks' acknowledgement that Ryerson's common school public libraries were "practically abandoned" simply recognized the truth. One critic, Alpheus Todd, the parliamentary librarian, stated in 1882 that common school libraries were prematurely forced upon ratepayers and that book selection was too rigidly centralized to suit many tastes.[38] At a later date, 1888, the new minister of education, George Ross, admitted that "the rural libraries, which had been established by Dr. Ryerson, had also done much good, but through the supply of books having fallen short and the books having been worn out and destroyed, the libraries had fallen into disuse."[39] Indeed, the *Special Report* confirmed that in some places – Arthur, Brighton, Collingwood, Oakville, and Scarboro – local institutes had taken possession of the remainder of older common school library collections.

By the mid-1870s, the call for "village" or "town" public libraries, voiced by James Campbell and the booksellers in their struggle against the depository, had surfaced in Ontario. Statements appeared in the press and magazines in subsequent years. Graeme Mercer Adam wrote to the Toronto *Mail*, in 1878, suggesting the formation of a free public library for Toronto to honour the departure of Lord Dufferin, Canada's Governor General for the past six years.

> The few educational and professional libraries we have in our midst, I need hardly say, by no means serve the purpose of a central city library, free of access, and affording to the community the advantages which the wide-spread dissemination of wholesome literature, through such machinery, would provide it with. Neither have we any other adequate provision for securing such a boon to the people as a free library would be, and such as has become so much an 'institution' in the larger cities of England and the United States. The practical matter, however, is, how can an enterprize of the kind be put on foot?[40]

Adam's proposal remained unfulfilled, but evidently libraries in Mechanics' Institutes were no longer considered sufficient for Toronto.

During the following year, 1879, the Reverend W.R.G. Mellen wrote an article for *Rose-Belford's Canadian Monthly* on the subject of endowments which he extended to public libraries:

> Just now, in the City of Toronto, is an opportunity for some rich man to supply an imperious need, and to secure for himself a fragrant memory as enduring as the city. For how pressing is the need here of a free public library, worthy the rapidly growing metropolis of this great and wealthy Province.[41]

Finally, the province's burgeoning urban centres required libraries to supply knowledge. The 1881 census revealed five cities with more than 10,000 inhabitants: Toronto (91,996), Hamilton (36,661), Ottawa (31,307), London (26,662), Kingston (14,091). By the end of 1879, the government decided to transfer the institutes to the Education Department where their performance could be judged according to more exacting standards.

The impression was that Ontario's record in contemporary public librarianship was less than impressive and that the institutes needed invigoration and direction. A thorough inspection was in order. Late in 1878 the deputy minister, Hodgins, forwarded a departmental memorandum on the subject of "Libraries to Mechanics' Institutes," outlining their educational qualities for the minister's attention.[42] The institutes had always been eligible to use the depository, subject to certain restrictions, and they had availed themselves despite the lack of a matching government grant for books and the limited stock. As Adam Crooks wound down the depository's operations, Dr. May became available to conduct a review. He may have been an obvious candidate, but he was unpopular in some quarters. A few commentators called his new office, superintendent of Mechanics' Institutes, a "farce."[43] Others opined that he owed his position more to patronage and loyalty than to capability. One Liberal MPP, Hammel Deroche, stated that "there was a strong feeling in the country that Dr. May was retained in the Department more for ornament than use."[44]

Dr. May began his fact finding tour at the beginning of June 1880 and completed his report in early 1881. He discovered a wide variation in the institutes' conditions and the opinions held by their directors. The new superintendent had to tred carefully. At his first two meetings he observed a division in opinion concerning the government's suggestion to change the title of institutes to "Practical Science Institute and Public Library." Hamilton opposed the suggestion while London favoured it.[45] The fact that many of May's final recommendations called for more supervision by the education department reinforced the institutes' ambivalence toward him and the department. It made dissenters, such as Preston's Otto Klotz, Sr., even more combative about the role directors would assume. In a special report of his own that analyzed May's proposals, Klotz, an influential leader in the Association of Mechanics' Institutes, argued:

> Can it be reasonably expected that ... those same men whom the Report admits to have been chosen from the most respectable and influential representatives of our people, and who are gentlemen of influence and wealth, possessing enterprize, education and intelligence, are nevertheless not to be entrusted with the management of their own joint local affairs, in which the Government of the Province is at the utmost only interested in the small sum of four hundred dollars annually.
>
> Will the public be served better by theorists than by practical men? Are we to have autocracy or oligarchy introduced into our system; or will we in future be allowed to enjoy, as at present, the privileges of self-government.[46]

Dr. May was not overly harsh in his criticism of the work of the institute directors. Indeed, he often countenanced mediocre conditions. Looking at conditions in London, where the collection numbered approximately 2,000 books in a city of 25,000 people, he observed that the library room contained "a fair selection of books, which are kept in locked cases."[47] More discriminating observers were less kind. The London *Advertiser* complained:

> A correspondent yesterday called attention to the lack of a catalogue in the library of the Mechanics' Institute. This suggests the query if the general need would not be better served by the endowment of free public libraries, than by the maintenance of Mechanics' Institutes? These latter have outlived their usefulness, and are no longer useful to mechanics or anybody else... It would be easy enough to say why, but what is the need? We all recognize the fact. Let us have a free public library by all means.[48]

London's executive had just assumed a $15,000 mortgage on its 1877 building and was hard pressed to meet the quarterly payments.[49]

Hamilton was experiencing more desperate problems. Despite May's optimism about this particular institute, which had more than a 1,000 members
and 7,000 volumes, by summer 1882 it was defunct. Its collection was sold by
an auctioneer, and its building was seized by mortgage holders. The directors
had appealed to the public for municipal support without success. A bylaw to
grant the institute $5,000 failed in January 1882 by more than 400 votes.
According to the Hamilton *Spectator*, the new Free Libraries Act offered no
solace: "There are not a few who think the city council ought to take the whole
matter into its own hands and make the library free. The expense, however,
would be considerable, and there is grave doubt that the people would sanction
that plan."[50] Subsequently, the Dundas Institute purchased many of Hamilton's
books and a remodelled business block, the Alexandra Arcade, replaced the old
upstairs music hall and popular library on the ground floor. Hamilton was to
be without a public library of any kind for eight years.

Dr. May's report made clear the rudimentary state of library service provided by Mechanics' Institutes in most communities. Just over one hundred
institutes operated libraries. Usually these collections were in small rooms,
locked in bookcases, and numbered sequentially, and they were used without
the aid of a catalogue. Not many Institutes owned their own building:
London, Hamilton, Toronto, Paris, Simcoe, Garden Island, and Ennotville
were among the privileged few where a library and reading room could be
managed independently.[51] Small rooms in centrally located town halls were
popular (Illus. 4). There were thirteen such libraries, two (Galt and Preston)
of which May singled out for special attention. Galt had "an excellent Library
of well selected books" and was preparing a manuscript catalogue showing
subjects and authors. At Preston, a village of almost 1,500, the 2,676 volume
library had circulated only 2,082 items in 1879-80, yet May remained very
impressed.

> This Institute has a very fine Library; about one-third of the
> books are in the German language. The books are well
> arranged and in excellent condition. The directors have
> splendid book-cases, which are closed when the books are
> not in use. The newspapers are filed and kept for reference.
> There are manuscript alphabetical catalogues for authors and
> subjects, and a separate catalogue showing classification of
> the different subjects, and altogether it is one of the most
> perfect and best arranged Libraries in the Province.[52]

Most institutes leased space in commercial blocks or storefronts: telegraph
offices, banks, book shops, drug stores, and jewellery shops were frequent

sites. A variety of other library locations – an MPP's office, three private dwellings, a high school, a YMCA, and three halls belonging to fraternal orders – also were enumerated by May.

Whatever the accommodation, this type of public library service was lagging behind the circulating and reference libraries found in American states and larger British centres. The *Special Report* noted that, on average, for every volume held British institutes circulated six volumes annually. Dr. May's tabulations (Table 5: Library Volumes Held, Circulation, and Fiction, 1879-80) showed that Ontario institutes had a collective yearly ratio of less than 1:2.[53] Since fiction accounted for slightly less than half the total circulation, there was little cause for satisfaction, and the Doctor perhaps reckoned that inadequate supervision for three decades was responsible for this sorry state of affairs.

At any rate, May could only refer to a few examples of the better class of library. He regarded Brantford's library, which was housed in a YMCA, as "one of the best of its kind in the Dominion" with its "books labelled and numbered," and its magazines "lent to members the same as books." It was open to the public twice a week.[54] The charging system at Dundas was also worthy of praise:

> ... the books are numbered on the outside, and loaned out on so excellent a plan that it is easy to ascertain in whose possession any book may be at any time. In the blank space caused by the withdrawal of a book, a board is placed with the name of [the] member borrowing the book, the date, etc. Of course this arrangement could not be successfully carried out if members were allowed access to the book shelves, but this is not the case; the room is fitted up with counters, and the applicants for books remain outside these counters, the books being handed to them by the librarian.[55]

May was convinced that closed stacks were more efficient and economical, an opinion he held until he retired in 1905.

May seldom mentioned reference collections and thought that the salaries paid to librarians were excessive. He recommended that "women can be employed at a far less cost." His advice probably derived from the Education Department's satisfaction with the rate of promotion of women in the school system after the 1860s.[56] Like many Victorians, May seemed to be obsessed with the popularity of fiction and its contemporary genres, such as the detective novel. His own approach was a pragmatic one: the 1880 regulations which permitted "some light reading" as authorized by the Education Department's *General Reference Catalogue* or approved by the minister were satisfactory. To make the payment of the government grant more "business-like," a euphemism May carefully substituted for greater central control, he suggested that the department begin direct payments to booksellers after institutes had selected their books. He also observed that some uniform system of classification ought to be introduced to all the institute libraries.[57] A few were using William Edwards' scheme proposed in 1872, but May did not specify a preference in his report. The dubious practice of classifying fiction in other categories to reduce circulation figures for novels caused him more concern than the need for a different classification scheme.

After 1876, public library development in Britain and the United States was accelerating in response to the growth of popular and scholarly publishing and the public's desire to read books for educational needs and recreational amusement. "The Unknown Public" of Wilkie Collins was developing a demand for an immense range of reading matter. Improved access to printed materials was becoming necessary. In Ontario there was clearly a need for improvement – the government and a knowledgeable segment of the public recognized that existing conditions would no longer suffice. By 1880, the government had chosen a firmer course of action, first by rejecting common school libraries as the principal public library system, and second by bringing Mechanics' Institutes under the resolute control of the Education Department and the minister, Adam Crooks. However, even after the publication of Dr. May's report in 1881, it was evident that library service required further attention. In Toronto there was agitation for a free library, and in rural areas the Dominion Grange's committee on education began pressing for grants to establish libraries for the agricultural population.[58] The method of moving forward obviously required clarification. "Town" libraries must have looked more promising to the government than the current collection of voluntary societies and Mechanics' Institutes.

The subject of free libraries was receiving serious consideration in some segments of the province, primarily by educators discontented with outmoded practices that lagged behind American and British service. The *Canada Educational Monthly*, edited by G. Mercer Adam, noted: "If municipal honesty were in better repute, we would rather see the Institutes drop their inappropriate title and become Public Libraries, supported by municipal assessment, and free to the people. Some day, when the public mind sickens of party politics, we may see this realized."[59] Antipathy toward "partyism," a residue of Ryerson's era, lingered, but the concept of free libraries also could be harnessed by skillful politicians for political purposes. Once adequate legislation was in place, it would remain for local leaders to step forward, to establish regular communication, and to give the budding movement synergy.

PART TWO

The Late Victorian Transition

Chapter 3

THE CALIBAN OF THE NINETEENTH CENTURY

To many Victorians the cost of a library was trifling in comparison to the advantages it provided. Some civic sacrifice was required if men and women were to utilize fully their natural capacities and enjoy all the benefits of material progress. The editor of the Guelph *Daily Mercury*, James Innes, a former school trustee, was one such enthusiast who followed the free library movement across Canada.

> From old St. John down by the sea to Winnipeg, that latest centre of Canadian enterprise which testifies that 'Westward the course of empire holds its way,' the question of establishing Free Public Libraries is agitating many towns and cities of the Dominion. While we in Ontario have the Free Libraries Act, passed last session of the Local Legislature to govern the maintenance of such institutions, in New Brunswick and Manitoba they have not, and there the movement springs from the people themselves.[1]

The working out of what services citizens wanted government to undertake was a central fact of Victorian politics. Afterwards, experts and professionals would follow and give birth to the twentieth-century administrative state.

Victorian reformers were convinced that social conformity and the political *status quo* were unjust and wasteful if applied too rigidly. They recognized that adverse economic conditions and arbitrary legal impediments could be detrimental to society. By pressing their case for reform they raised many uncomfortable questions. One prominent Canadian historian has remarked that a "Victorian dialectic" was at work during the later part of the century, another has emphasized the lively nature of everyday life.[2] Newspaper publishers and editors of different political stripes, such as Philip Ross of the Ottawa *Evening Journal*, James Innes of the Guelph *Mercury*, Robert

McAdams of the Sarnia *Observer*, and John Ross Robertson of the Toronto *Evening Telegram*, consistently supported libraries. They believed that newspapers and libraries promised Canadians corresponding visions of a bright future: advancement in culture and education, an emerging nationhood, social harmony, unimpeded progress, and economic prosperity.[3]

Public library development touched many people, many communities. Victorian library supporters signed petitions, attended and spoke at meetings, wrote letters to newspapers, and helped organize local committees. It was the duty of voters to approve free library bylaws. Throughout this period in Ontario the municipal franchise was available to most adults, but, it was more restrictive than the federal or provincial requirements. Widows, unmarried women and males twenty-one years of age, who possessed certain basic property qualifications and who were British subjects, were eligible to vote for library bylaws.[4] For these ratepayers, economy and strict utility often were overriding restraints, although they were familiar with some of the arguments used in defense of free libraries. Many of the same explanations had underpinned the rationale for Mechanics' Institutes. At the forefront were educational considerations that linked libraries with Ontario's expanding primary and secondary school system. Many contemporaries, especially those of Scottish or Presbyterian extraction, thought that better education led to more intellectual progress and taught people respect for the boundaries between social relationships.

Educational Qualities

Victorians were confident that educational bodies could help forge a stable culture and political life. Writing on Canadian intellectual life in 1881, John G. Bourinot concluded: "Here there is no ancient system of social exclusiveness to fix a limit to the intellectual progress of the proletariat. Political freedom rests on a firm, broad basis of general education."[5] He was speaking about the Victorian convention of "high culture," the subjective appreciation of what constituted the "best" in intellectual, moral, and social life. Since books were an essential part of education, a portable medium that disseminated knowledge and entertainment extensively, Bourinot regretted that Canada was behind other countries in the formation of public libraries:

> In Ontario there are also some 100 Mechanics Institutes, including nearly 11,000 members, with an aggregate of 118,000 volumes in the libraries; and it is satisfactory to learn that institutions which may have an important influence on the industrial classes are to be placed on a more efficient basis. These facts illustrate that we are making progress

in the right direction; but what we want, above all things, are public libraries, to which all classes may have free access, in the principal centres of population. The rich men of this country can devote a part of their surplus wealth to no more patriotic purpose than the establishment of such libraries in the places where they live, and in that way erect a monument for themselves far more honourable than any that may be achieved by expenditures on purely selfish objects.[6]

Bourinot reasoned that libraries could contribute to the process of mass literacy by disseminating the best grade of literature.

A decade later, the popular historian, William Kingsford, was even more optimistic. He said, "The whole hope of the future of Canada lies in the sound sober sense of community, by which opinion is influenced," and he added, "it is by reading and thought that men of this character are moulded." He confidently predicted that the Toronto Public Library was destined to be one of the foremost institutions on the continent.[7] Libraries disseminated literature; they helped to communicate and make accessible a wide spectrum of ideas to the general populace. Library partisans were fond of citing authorities such as Lord Rosebery, the British Liberal leader between 1894-96, who had remarked that a library was "a temple of reading" where "a fair proportion of thoughtful books are taken and digested," and who had discounted the problem of too much circulating fiction.[8]

It was difficult for opponents to discredit any argument based on the library's fundamental function, which was to circulate general knowledge. Citizens from all classes maintained small private libraries at home and had a genuine affection for reading. In their minds, a desire to learn and a fondness to read formed the basis for intellectual activity and, ultimately, for social progress and stability. Many Victorians would have agreed with Hamilton's chief librarian, Richard Lancefield, who stated in a lecture that, given an educated public, "there is little doubt but that many grave social problems which now threaten us with disaster would be peaceably and speedily resolved."[9] The combination of self-learning and circulating library collections seemed poised to create a better society.

Within this educational context, the circulation of accepted literature, the whole body of books and writing including fiction, was regarded as a public good. Graeme Mercer Adam wrote that a central city library in Toronto should supply "the advantage which the wide-spread dissemination of wholesome literature" provided.[10] The editor of the Brantford *Daily Expositor* wrote glowingly:

We doubt not, that ere long all the cities and towns of Ontario will have free libraries, to which the people can resort, with the feeling that it is a public institution in which they have an interest, and of which they can secure the benefits. The cost is so small in comparison with the general diffusion of knowledge, and its great usefulness to every man, woman and child in the city so apparent that the vote upon it will doubtless be unanimous in its favor.[11]

His prediction was correct: Brantford's library bylaw passed without ado in January 1884 by a vote of 1086 to 275.

Victorians generally concurred that ideas should be communicated as widely as possible and that a unified common culture could be shaped through intellectual, spiritual, and aesthetic development. At this point in time, experts and professionals were still a minority; laymen and amateurs commanded public respect in artistic, scientific, and intellectual discourse. Few would have disagreed with Ontario's deputy minister of education, John Millar, who wrote in a chapter on libraries: "This popularizing of knowledge has, no doubt, increased the demand for higher education. The effect is a national gain, in spite of what the aristocrat may believe or of what the demagogue may proclaim."[12] Popularization was particularly evident in the field of science. Local societies were proliferating; small libraries were building collections; and natural scientists were linked with colleagues in Britain and the United States mainly through periodicals and report literature.[13] Cultural accessibility was highly esteemed. Even difficult works, such as Charles Darwin's *On the Origin of Species by Natural Selection* or James Clerk Maxwell's *Treatise on Electricity and Magnetism*, found large audiences.

Some advocates viewed libraries as an extension of the public school system, as useful repositories for training labourers for the skills and crafts needed in the work place, and as informal universities. At the formal opening of Toronto's library, William Henry Withrow, editor of the *Canadian Methodist Magazine*, described libraries as "the people's colleges, where the poorest lad or the toiling artisan shall enjoy the best teaching in the world. 'The true university of these days,' says Carlyle, 'is a collection of books.' All education that is worth anything must be largely self-education."[14] In 1895, Mary Klotz, whose family was active in the movement, wrote in a similar vein in a special library issue of the Ottawa *Evening Journal*, which Philip Ross helped organize: "The Public Library is an extension of our schools and even of our universities. We may truly call it the peoples university, where rich and poor, old and young, may all drink at its inexhaustible fountain."[15] Indeed, promoters such as John Taylor (Illus. 5) felt that the library was an essential government service.

> Every year hundreds of youths graduate at the Public Schools
> and go out upon the world, drifting about like a rudderless
> ship upon a treacherous sea – without any link between giddy
> youth and sober mankind. That missing link is the public
> library. It is the caliban of the nineteenth century, and the
> only practical adult school which the State can supply us.[16]

A bridge between youth and old age? Quite soon, within its broad span, the
library would lay claim to many functions.

Shakespeare's character, Caliban, had been popularized in Robert
Browning's poem, "Caliban upon Setebos" (1864), and served as the subject
matter of a Canadian publication by Daniel Wilson, *Caliban: the Missing
Link*.[17] The library would contribute to popular education by supplementing
the work of schools and colleges. It was a role that would buttress its claim to
tax-supported status. The *Palladium of Labor* echoed this view of learning by
applying popular Darwinian terminology:

> It is only recently, however, that the public have come to
> understand that the instruction received at school is but the
> foundation of education in its full and comprehensive sense,
> and that to be complete our system must find its comple-
> ment in the means for perpetrating in after life the intellectu-
> al activities which are fostered in youth. The Public Library is
> as truly an integral part of our educational system as the pub-
> lic school, supplementing and turning to account the work of
> the latter, which, for lack of such an agency in times past, has
> often resulted in what the scientists term 'arrested develop-
> ment'.[18]

Popular education was a familiar topic, and free libraries were assuming a distinct role in its activities.

To assist libraries in the cause of popular education, one ambitious independent thinker, George Iles, a former Montrealer, publicized the new philosophy of service some public librarians were promoting. Iles's ideas started to
appear in the columns of a respected magazine, *The Week*, at the beginning of
the 1890s.

> Libraries have therefore come to have a new value in our day,
> and while within recent years this value was being conferred,
> a distinctly new conception of library management has been
> steadily dawning. It used to be thought enough that a librari-

an should be able to get books, guard them trustily, and give them out as desired. He was gatherer and custodian. The new idea is that he shall so vitalize his library that to make his books attractive and useful shall be his chiefest care.[19]

Iles also was developing a scheme called the "appraisal of literature," by which title cards in library catalogues would carry short critical annotations to guide readers.[20] However, libraries and other bookmen were not as enthusiastic about this type of work. Years earlier, G. Mercer Adam had made a more practical suggestion; he had pointed to the need for separately published periodical summaries or abstracts classed by subject to highlight meritorious books.[21] Later, Iles did resort to printed reference bibliographies, which were more suitable aids to readers and students.

The question of technical education cropped up periodically. At a Hamilton meeting, John Hallam referred to "the works of John Ruskin, the Grammar of Ornament, or Smith's Dyeing, or any other of the expensive publications so necessary in the technical education of the artizan."[22] Emmanuel Essery, a London barrister who had been corresponding secretary of the local Mechanics' Institute for more than a decade, had served as a director of the workingmen's library and later became city mayor. He told a small pro-library audience: "Unless the mechanics of Canada were enabled to cope with those of Germany – where they have every facility afforded for a sound technical education – the former would become secondary."[23] In Germany, technical and vocational training was not left to voluntary associations; in the Reich, efficient working skills and training were worthy of state direction. It was an example educationists in Britain and her Dominions were taking to heart, albeit at a tardy pace.[24]

Initially, legislation permitted free libraries to acquire assets or property from Mechanics' Institutes and to continue receipt of the legislative grant that the institute had earned (46 Vic., c.19). This arrangement included evening classes. In one case, in August 1886, the Guelph free library displayed wood carvings at Ontario's exhibit during the Indian and Colonial Exhibition held at London. In 1889, the government formalized the indirect link with technical education. Now libraries could offer evening classes "in such subjects as may promote a knowledge of the mechanical and manufacturing arts" (52 Vic., c.38). By this same act, free libraries could hire and dismiss teachers and instructors; and art schools were authorized to transfer assets to libraries, thus permitting them to assume the government grant for this purpose. Departmental regulations were drafted and approved to include courses in elementary and advanced English and Canadian history, composition and grammar, bookkeeping, arithmetic, writing, drawing, chemistry, botany, and physics.[25]

These additional powers further eroded the work of Mechanics' Institutes; by this time, their reputation had declined precipitously. One Hamilton newspaper ungraciously described the city's defunct institute as a "free roost for aged gamesters."[26] The minister of education, George Ross, was decidedly skeptical about their prospects. He was reported to have said openly in the legislature that "the Mechanics' Institutes had never done any real good."[27] At a December 1888 meeting organized by Ross on the subject of technical education, the following exchange took place with a well-known Ottawa labour leader, Alfred Jury.

> Mr. A.F. Jury said that a feeling prevailed in Mechanics' Institutes that mechanics are not wanted there.
> Mr. Ross – I never thought they were created for aristocrats. (Laughter)[28]

At a subsequent government assembly on university extension, Queen's University Principal, George Monro Grant, quipped, "if you want to go to a place where you are certain not to find mechanics, go to a Mechanics Institute."[29] From the Education Department's perspective, therefore, after 1889 public libraries were evidently assuming a greater priority in popularizing evening classes for adults.

Disappointment attended these aspirations. Drawing classes in art schools were quite popular during the 1890s, although some people questioned the value of the drawing certificates Dr. May issued annually.[30] Evening classes in libraries were less well patronized. The prospective amalgamation of main art schools in Brockville, Hamilton, Kingston, London, Stratford, Ottawa, St. Thomas, and Toronto with the free libraries in each of these cities never occurred. Another approach was attempted in 1897: the government passed an Act Respecting Technical Schools that allowed high schools, boards of education, and municipalities to establish their own schools of art (60 Vic., c. 58). The municipal adult schools were to be placed under the control of the free library board wherever one already existed. If the education department believed that this would remedy affairs, it was to be disappointed again. By 1902, evening classes offered by libraries were almost extinct and were no longer reported by Dr. May. The department would have to seek other remedies.

The Economic Rationale for Free Libraries

The case for technical education overlapped the economic arguments made on behalf of free libraries. Because many conservative-minded citizens were reluctant to tax property for educational reasons alone, a good case for free libraries had to be made on economic grounds for bylaws to pass. An Ingersoll newspaper editor posed a typical argument: "Intelligence and virtue, ignorance and vice are so ultimately connected that the parent, the town and the nation really economize when they spend for the intellectual advancement of those committed to their care." The town voted in favour of a bylaw in 1890.[31] Beyond direct appeals of this kind lay a new type of liberalism. Late nineteenth-century reform liberalism held that the common welfare could be advanced if governments assisted those wishing to improve themselves beyond what private enterprise and the marketplace could efficiently provide. The stability of the nation depended on the subordination of individual interests to the requirements of society.

On the other hand, traditional liberals, accustomed to the Manchester School of thought, believed in limited government activity and maximum individual freedom. The School had attracted a mixture of radicals, businessmen, pacifists, and humanitarian employers who advocated free-trade and *laissez-faire* theories.[32] Liberals of this ilk emphasized the need for strict economy in the provision of new services, and they were less likely to approve government expenditures for libraries because the doctrine of *laissez faire* still loomed large. The decisions of individuals and Adam Smith's "invisible hand" remained the surest guide to economic success and social stability. One Hamilton citizen complained bitterly:

> If making me and others pay for this library against our will is not robbery, perhaps you will tell me what it is. If this is what you call progressing and the advancement of the nineteenth century, I don't give much for such, especially as you have to forfeit principle to attain such… Don't you know that this so called free library act emanated from the same villainous source − a conspiracy to deprive people of their liberties."[33]

But as many library promoters on both sides of the Atlantic delighted in recounting, the home of the Manchester School was also the first large English metropolitan centre to establish a free library. At Manchester library's opening ceremonies in 1852 Charles Dickens wittily defined the Manchester School as a library of books, open for the instruction of all classes, whether rich or poor.[34]

To counter this fundamental difference and to overcome the instinctive objections conservatives raised to new reforms, library promoters pointed out that previous types of public libraries, mostly subscription ones, had failed for lack of a suitable financial basis. They also contended that workingmen were willing to tax themselves for requisite educational materials in order to update their knowledge and skills in changing technological conditions. John Hallam insisted that "the movement being a rate-supported one will render it independent and permanent, and not liable to fluctuations which too often beset many institutions which have to depend for their support on voluntary and charitable contributions."[35] The Toronto *Globe* likewise justified its support:

> In default of private endowments furnishing an income sufficient to pay the salaries of curators, etc., there has never been found any practical way of supporting public libraries except out of the rates. As the libraries are resorted to almost entirely by the poorer classes, there need be no dread of the 'poor man's vote' to stand in the way of improvement.[36]

It was a common sense position.

Modified Utilitarian philosophy and John Stuart Mill's writings were cited to vindicate the library movement. Benthamite thought supplied a rationale for centralized state action and government intervention.[37] John M. Gibson, a MPP who later became Lieutenant-Governor, paraphrased Jeremy Bentham when Hamiltonians voted for a library in 1889: "The by-law was a measure which promised the greatest good to the greatest number." At a meeting prior to the vote, Gibson had urged, "If for no utilitarian object, the fact that Hamilton was singular in being without a public library of any kind should urge its citizens to move in favor of such a project."[38] Of course, Utilitarians of the narrower Benthamite legacy continued to object to raising taxes. In 1896, an Ottawa "Utilitarian" wrote to a newspaper editor opposing a free library.[39] However, the trend towards interventionist government was irresistible. Robert Reid, at the opening of the new library in London, referred to Mill's efforts to broaden the individualistic bent in utilitarian thought in terms of more harmonious integration of economic activity:

> As John Stuart Mill had put it, in his essay on Socialism, the uncultivated masses and their employers must learn to practice to labor and combine for public and social purposes, and not, as hitherto, solely for narrowly interested ones. If our public libraries were conducted on proper principles they could not fail ...[40]

Reid, a longtime trustee in London, assumed that the working class would gain materially with access to library texts and manuals, thus fostering social harmony and the public good.

Businessmen spoke of the potential benefits for workingmen who were organizing on a national scale under the banner of the Knights of Labour and the American Federation of Labor. Augustus T. Freed, a Hamilton newspaperman and one of the chairmen of the federal Royal Commission on the Relations of Labour and Capital in Canada, felt confident that libraries would improve the lot of working-class people. This commission, which began hearings in November 1887, heard testimony from Hamilton workers, and, when Freed returned to Hamilton at a later date, he told an audience that he supported wholeheartedly a free library bylaw.

> As a member of the Royal labor commission he had come into contact with workingmen in Canada from Sydney to Windsor and the fact had been impressed upon him that wherever the working people are intelligent there they were prosperous and vice versa.... [He] was glad to learn that the workingmen are alive to their interests and are taking up this free library movement.[41]

The Chatham Board of Trade circulated a library advertisement to voters, maintaining that "The more intelligent the mechanic or laborer, the higher his wages, and the more comfortable his home. Crude labour is at a discount. Skilled labour is at a premium."[42] Chatham's bylaw passed by a narrow margin, the proposition of markedly higher wages for literate tradesmen apparently being more contentious among the lower orders of the work force than some members of the board of trade had expected.[43]

Ratepayers, trade unionists, and other electors remained to be convinced that libraries were worthwhile institutions. During the last part of the century, the municipal franchise was extensive enough to allow most adults to vote, but property requirements for holding municipal office were more restrictive. Active political life for the labouring classes was usually limited to the "aristocracy of labour," to men such as Henry B. Witton of Hamilton, who was a labour MP for a brief period. He generously lent his support to the Mechanics' Institute and later became a library trustee and donor.[44] Library promoters ordinarily could count on the rising voice of organized labour to boost a bylaw as in the case of London in 1893.[45] But most craft unions, which organized workers in a single trade, had small memberships. Their political influence was limited, and they often shied away from partisan struggles. Many in the industrial work force were satisfied with piecemeal measures such as the federal parliament's 1894 designation of the first Monday in September as a labour holiday.

Even though the principle of utility provided a powerful rationale for government to establish public services – as a noted British economist (also a member of the Library Association) put it, libraries led to "an enormous increase of utility which is thereby acquired for the community at a trifling cost" – local private interests and men of enterprise frequently rallied to the cry of economy.[46] "Economy" was a foe to be respected when ratepayers were confronted by the account sheet of progress. John Hallam, the most articulate leader of the movement prior to 1900, regularly expressed the view that free libraries were profitable investments. At the close of his influential pamphlet, *Notes by the Way on Free Libraries and Books*, he wrote:

> ... they [libraries] must necessarily diminish the ranks of those two great armies which are constantly marching to gaols and penitentiaries, and in the same ratio they must decrease the sums of money which ratepayers have to provide for the maintenance of those places. And even if these libraries effected no saving of money, nay, even involved an ultimate increase in public expenditure (which they will not), then, I say, it would be still wise to have them; for I contend that it is infinitely preferable to pay for intelligence than to tolerate ignorance. I want Toronto to pay for intelligence – for popular education in the free library sense. If she does so fairly and fully, her bill for poverty and depravity will be materially diminished, and with such diminution we shall all be benefited and blessed.[47]

In the Victorian age of social improvement such arguments carried considerable weight, and economic individualism often had to yield to the demands of common civic goals.

Social and Cultural Roles

Intertwined with subjective educational and economic claims about libraries were diverse social and cultural ones. Victorians for the most part believed in progress; they believed that technological and intellectual change would continue to enrich society by advancing knowledge, providing economic prosperity, and improving the human spirit. Literary and cultural melioration was imperative for a growing nation. One social critic wrote:

> Not only is our literary progress evidenced by the larger number of persons who have done permanent and valuable work, but also by the increased yearly output of Canadian books and by the development of Canadian libraries. There

were less than half-a-dozen public libraries in 1837, and now there are hundreds. All these things indicate progress, the nature and extent of which need not here be further discussed.[48]

In an age that revered historical writings and subscribed to theories of evolution, progress formed the essence of history's story.

Societal institutions, such as schools and libraries, were major instruments in this unfolding drama. Alpheus Todd, a respected constitutional historian and parliamentary librarian, told the Royal Society of Canada: "In the machinery of modern progress now in operation, whether in Europe or America, free libraries, accessible to all classes, occupy a conspicuous place."[49] Another tireless champion of libraries, Edwin Hardy, urged the foundation of a rate-supported library at Lindsay in 1898:

> It is true of towns as of business men, that they must be progressive and up-to-date. Towns everywhere are competing: they want factories, mills, railway facilities, and offer greater or less inducements to procure them, hoping thereby to secure increase of population and prosperity. They put large sums into good roads, sewers, police and fire protection, and spend money freely on schools, churches, homes for the aged, hospitals, parks and free libraries. All these things go to attract population, and many a family has passed by one town and gone to another on account of its schools or some other excellent feature.[50]

The doctrine of progress obviously contained certain verities which comforted Victorians.

In Windsor and Hamilton, the appeal to progress was unmistakable. These two cities were unusual because they did not have an existing Mechanics' Institute from which to transfer assets to a free library, hence making the project more expensive. But this liability did not inhibit local supporters. Windsor's library chairman, John Curry, sounded a confident note when he opened a renovated meeting place, Lambie Hall, in 1894: "You are aware that our city is a progressive one. We are blessed with all the modern conveniences which tend to make life happy and this evening we add still another – a Public Free Library."[51] A scant six years afterwards Windsor would be one of the first Ontario communities to seek a Carnegie building on the basis that its library premises were "very limited, very primitive, without ordinary public conveniences, and somewhat dilapidated."[52] Adversaries of free libraries often were labelled as unprogressive or unbusinesslike. Hamilton opponents of the 1889 library bylaw were called "mossbacks," a borrowed American reference to political reactionaries. The *Spectator* welcomed the passage of the bylaw, stating, "The result is evidence that mossbackism is losing its grip upon Hamilton, and that there is really some ambition in the ambitious city."[53]

Religious considerations bolstered the secular faith in progress. Egerton Ryerson had stood firm for authoritative religious principles that would govern the dissemination of literature within the framework of a stable Christian society and government. Victorians were a spiritual people, and religion was held to be the main ingredient in a strong nation. A synthesis of religious beliefs and British conventions, argued Alpheus Todd, enabled Canadians to secure the advantages of freedom while respecting the power of divine providence and the need for political authority and order; this sense of principled loyalism distinguished Canadians from Americans.[54] Books could help spread these doctrines, therefore libraries were rightful public agencies worthy of tax-supported status. This was a passionate, powerful rationale.

Evangelical Protestants – strict observers of the sabbath who read scripture and lived the virtues of trust, piety, and charity – presumed that libraries would embody a strong moral tone. Liberal Protestants also believed that the salvation of souls and the moral regeneration of society were important tasks for the Christian ministry.[55] A Toronto minister advocated a library by asking:

> How much might it do here to attract young men from the 400 dram shops that infest this city? How much to quicken frivolous young women to the perception of somewhat better than silks and jewellery, parties, and flirtations?[56]

William Cochrane, a well-know Presbyterian minister and long-time director of the Brantford Mechanics' Institute, asserted, "In order to remove existing temptations, there must be counter attractions provided, and none better can be found than in the rooms of a free public library."[57] Cochrane emphasized community service in addition to his ministerial duties. His views typified the liberal Protestant synthesis of the sacred and profane which helped fashion Ontario's long-standing moral atmosphere.[58]

Literature and book learning were considered meritorious pursuits because readers could espouse Christian doctrines or liberal virtues such as industry, tolerance, duty, self-help, thrift, liberality, and temperance. Libraries could help to reinforce religious faith and lessen atheistic and agnostic influences simply by allowing shelf space for favourite religious novels such as Lew Wallace's *Ben-Hur*, Henryk Sienkiewicz's *Quo Vadis?*, and Ralph Connor's *Black Rock*. T.K. Henderson, a Toronto compositor, received first prize for his essay, "Free Libraries from a Workman's Standpoint." He wrote that "the perusal of good books would also strengthen and build up his religious character, and as man is a religious animal, it is of no small consequence of what sort his religion may be."[59] Conservatives, as well as upper- or middle-class liberals, were conscious of the need to foster respectability, propriety, morality, family unity, and deference to authority – social attributes the public library could help nurture.

The temperance issue was always close at hand, for public houses were as plentiful as churches on Ontario's streets and country roads. A Baptist minister, Robert G. Boville, warned his Hamilton parishioners –

> Hamilton, it is said by some, cannot afford to support a free library; and yet the people of Hamilton can spend at least $500,000 for alcoholic drink every year. Depend upon it, there will be many an alcoholic vote cast against a free-library by-law; and therefore every temperance vote in the city should be cast in favor of the by-law.[60]

It was a theme repeated in many sermons and newspapers across the province. A Brampton *Conservator* editorial in 1895 concluded that the library would "keep some, at least, out of the barroms [sic], who are now on the road to ruin through barroom influence."[61]

The public library offered assistance in the inveterate struggle against worldly temptation and corruption and contributed to an ordered society. Booklists were prepared to combat the deleterious effects of alcohol.[62] The Ottawa *Evening Journal* cited British statistics from Thomas Greenwood's influential *Public Libraries* to show that vice and crime in the streets might be reduced because institutions, like libraries, were proven "crime-reducers."[63] The nuclear family would be safeguarded. Both the Guelph *Daily Mercury* and the Toronto *Globe* were emphatic on this score:

> When once such a library is established he [a labourer] will not be forced to spend his evenings in listless idleness, or be tempted, in order 'to pass away the time,' to go to the barroom to have a chat and hear the news. The entertaining book from the free library, read aloud by himself, his wife, or one of the children, will interest the whole family, and make the hours pass innocently and pleasantly.[64]

This was a comfortable middle-class convention, familiar to Walter Eales' audience in 1851, but one that seemed to inspire significant numbers in the working class. It helped make the library a public governing entity.

Edwin Hardy also appealed to a sense of family unity in a letter to the Lindsay *Canadian Post* in late 1898.

> It is a serious problem to train up a family, and our streets at night afford only too good evidence that the problem is not being solved in many a home. No doubt home is not as attractive in many cases as it might be, and a large supply of good books, free of access to all members of the family, would go far to make home decidedly more attractive. In more than one case, if a boy had his choice between the streets and a good book he would take the book.[65]

Earnestness had it reward; the Lindsay library bylaw succeeded. Edwin Hardy was to have a long association with libraries; his career had begun on a successful note.

The Democratic Faith

Liberalism, at its noblest, extolled the free dissemination and interplay of opinions and writings. The potential for free libraries to enlighten citizens was a powerful inducement for Victorians to support the movement. They regarded libraries as instruments to strengthen the liberal-democratic foundation of the local community and even of the entire nation.[66] It also gave some measure of reassurance to those who feared the advent of socialism if the rapid extension of federal or provincial franchises were granted. T.K. Henderson's prize essay is instructive once again: "By and by the working classes of Canada will be the actual rulers of the country, and universal suffrage will take its place among our laws. Into whose hands will this power be entrusted?"[67] A second prize essay by another Toronto typesetter spoke about the desirability of workers to have access to books on politics and political economy. "This would enable them readily to see through the specious, threadbare arguments of pothouse politicians and the sophistries of self-constituted but ignorant wire pullers, and would do much to create a more healthy tone in political life ..."[68]

At Stratford, an Anglican minister said that free libraries were a democratic necessity, when the bylaw issue first arose in that city.

> It was the duty of the council to see that they were supplied with proper books. This country... was democratic and whatever statesmen might do the people were the real rulers. The people should, therefore, have the highest possible intelligence. At present books, the reading of which was the best

education, were accessible only to a few rich men. By establishing a free library the highest intelligence would be brought within reach of ordinary people. Besides looking after the material interests of the citizens the council had a higher duty – the promoting of general culture – and the speaker hoped they would not neglect this duty.[69]

If citizens were to lead productive lives and make informed choices, they must be prepared and equipped with knowledge; it was a central fact of a liberal society. The Hamilton *Spectator* put the matter succinctly, "It [the library] will make the people better able to govern themselves."[70]

Associated with this commitment to democracy was the blossoming of civic pride and a stronger, united Canada. For civic boosters, local growth was a guarantee of their community's future. For the lettered, nationhood and a higher cultural attainment were virtually synonymous. George Ross closed a memorable speech at a library opening at London in this idealistic vein:

We hope, round the altar here, that young Canadians will worship with a pure heart loftier ideals of national life; that a broader patriotism will be quickened by higher conceptions of duty, and that in the long hereafter, as was said in the brave days of old, it will be said that there were Canadians made better and stronger men because it entered into the hearts of the citizens of London, in the closing years of this wonderful century, to place at their disposal the treasure-house of knowledge (Loud and continued applause).[71]

Few disagreed with the education minister.

Shortly after 1900, the assimilation of immigrants into Anglo-Saxon Protestant culture began to assume greater prominence in the quest for national unity. Democracy, grounded in the sovereignty of the people, required proper cultivation and direction to achieve stability. Canadian politics could ill-afford an uninformed electorate. The character of Canada's future leaders and their followers must be moulded by educational agencies. Libraries provided resources to educate "our young, our various nationalities, foreign emigrants and social strata" into the "fibrous metal of a unified Canada, a homogeneous greater Britain."[72] Although the ethnic composition of Ontario did not change markedly with immigration during the prosperous Laurier years (more than three-quarters of the provincial population originated in the British Isles according to the 1911 census), in some quarters there was concern about the dilution of British influence.

Public spirit and the provision of civic amenities were evident during the rapid growth of municipal government in late nineteenth-century Ontario, where the strengthening of local solidarity, celebration of community anniversaries, and erection of public buildings and monuments became regular features of civic life. Local boosterism not only promoted town halls, farmers markets, and civic administration, it also encouraged the cause of libraries.[73] Libraries did not escape the attention or fervour of local promoters; even the American term "booming" appears on occasion with reference to the clamour and vigour favouring library bylaws.[74] In this heady atmosphere, a number of public-spirited people contributed property and funds for libraries in advance of the Carnegie building program.

At Uxbridge, a former member of parliament and supporter of the local Mechanics' Institute left money for the town to build the "Joseph Gould Institute" at a cost of $4,200.[75] It was built in an eclectic picturesque style with white brick and red-brick trimmings crowned by a clock tower (Illus. 6). The ground floor was given over to a library which was managed by Sara D. Willis for seventeen years until her death in 1907. The building functioned as a Mechanics' Institute and then as a public library for more than a decade until January 1898, when the provincial library superintendent, Dr. May, appealed to the community to petition for free status. The local newspaper reported that

> He had visited the library here and was astonished at its excellence and delighted with the magnificent building bequeathed for library purposes by the late Jos. Gould. The Uxbridge library had no equal in towns of similar size and out of the 360 libraries (cities included) of the province Uxbridge stood No. 20.[76]

Uxbridge quickly fell into line.

At Napanee, a good-sized library was erected after prominent local men – Uriah Wilson, a member of parliament; John Wilson; and Harvey Warner – donated money and land that allowed the public library board to erect a new building in a small park. When the library board undertook a general subscription for equipment, books, and furnishings to complete the building, the Napanee *Express* supported the activity by suggesting:

> Some public spirited citizen may wish to add to the beauty of the building by the gift of a memorial window to the Canadians who fell in South Africa, or some liberally disposed gentleman may wish to show his loyalty by a gift commemorating the reign of Victoria the Good ...[77]

Napanee did not achieve free library status immediately; however, its building stood as an example for other eastern Ontario communities to emulate.

James Stavely, a wealthy Clinton merchant, died in 1892 without heirs; as a result, his estate reverted to the province. The local council and member of parliament made several appeals to secure some proceeds of the estate; in 1896, a provincial statute gave $10,000 to the town to be used for a hall or other type of public building (59 Vic., c. 6). A library was the main feature of "Stavely Hall," and, upon completion, the ratepayers voted 225 to 121 in January 1900 to create a free library on the strength of an endowment that helped finance operations.[78] The Clinton library opened in early 1900 (Illus. 7). It featured a closed stack library on the first floor dominated by a central librarian's desk. There was a small reading room to the rear which a local source described as "light, airy and commodious, and it is doubtful if another town in the Dominion has its equal."[79]

Some benefactions were less elaborate or were rejected. At Streetsville, in 1901, a resident gave part of a two-storey shop "to the Library Board and its successors in office forever" for a sum of $200 (Illus. 8). This was a small closed stack establishment (24 ft. x 40 ft.) with a delivery desk in the middle of the store and a reading table by the front window. The trustees made the best possible use of their gift. Buoyed up by the donation, the board pressed council for free status. It came into effect on 1 July 1902.[80] A few offers did not materialize because they included qualifications. In 1895, the estate of William G. Perley offered a home for a library in Ottawa provided a free bylaw were passed. However, Ottawa's first bylaw was rejected by the ratepayers despite reports in the press indicating that Perley's home on Wellington Street, said to be worth $70,000, was quite suitable for library purposes and was capable of housing 20,000 volumes.[81]

In spite of its newfound public support at the polls and voluntary donations, the public library in Ontario had yet to achieve a truly vital role by 1895, a shortcoming John G. Bourinot sought to reverse in one of his columns in *The Week*.

> As long, then, as we have the works of Walter Scott, Dickens, Thackeray, George Eliot, Ward, Oliphant and others of note, to delight and instruct the world, I do not think we may fear the establishment of free libraries. After all a free library is an inducement to men and women to spend their time more profitably than is possible in places where one does not exist. Light literature wearies after a while and the mind must in most cases turn to the more invigorating and healthy books that every well-furnished library has on its shelves.[82]

Bourinot represented the opinion of conservative, English-Canadian, Protestant high culture, but in Ontario the library was gaining grudging acceptance by all parts of society – urban and rural, highbrow and lowbrow.

The major problem inherent in the public library concept during this era was its confined role. The enterprise of the public library was circumscribed by its regular client, the reading adult. The library's physical core was a closed access circulating collection, reference room, reading room, newspaper and periodical room, and, occasionally, a meeting room. Its oft-repeated claim to be a "missing link" between elementary school and adult workplace was only partially achieved. The library was beyond the reach of children, adolescents, the elderly, and illiterate adults. The functions of the public library in the Victorian world were narrow by today's standards. The public's ambivalence towards recreational, popular fiction reduced the library's scope even further. In retrospect, the reality of library service, juxtaposed with appealing arguments that assumed societal reforms would be forthcoming if free libraries were established, was hard pressed to live up to its self-promotion. Prospects for reforming society at the community level were exciting but elusive.

Too often, the public attitude toward the free library in many Ontario communities was merely one of apathy. School trustees naturally were interested in literary improvement, but municipal authorities held the purse strings and showed little concern for libraries despite some stirrings among the electorate for the principle of public support. The transformation from libraries managed by Mechanics' Institutes to tax-supported agencies was taking place slowly. The attraction of free use, greater access to circulating collections, better reading rooms, and reference facilities had prompted a few communities to embrace the free library concept. The free library idea had been introduced in Ontario, but arguments on its behalf had not been strongly marshalled. A new generation of library advocates was needed to infuse the movement and refocus its activities.

Chapter 4

THE DAYS OF ADVANCE

When the Ontario Legislature passed the Free Libraries Act in 1882, it commenced the general direction towards free public libraries in the province. Support for the measure was centred in Toronto. In January 1881, two aldermen, John Hallam and John Taylor, announced that they wanted Toronto council to petition the government to allow the city, now more than 95,000 people, to establish a free library.[1] By the end of the year they had secured pledges from leading citizens for financial support and had arranged meetings to have a draft bill prepared for council to forward to the Legislative Assembly at its next sitting in 1882.[2] Hallam was an energetic self-made man (Illus. 9). He had worked in a factory as a child and did not begin his formal education until he attended night school in his twenties. He came to Canada in 1853 and worked at various manual jobs until he set up his own store, a wool and leather business, in 1866. Thereafter, he became more prosperous, entered municipal politics as a representative from the St. Lawrence ward in 1870, and travelled extensively in Europe and the United States on business or personal pleasure.

Hallam was a Liberal of the "Lancashire type," believing in free trade, practical politics, and a love for book learning.[3] He also believed that British civilization constituted the finest organized state of material and cultural well-being and individual freedom. In a short pamphlet, *The Days of Advance*, he documented the progress of municipal water systems, tramways, libraries, and tramp relief and employment in English cities. In Britain all these agencies were coming under public control of a municipal system of management that proclaimed local public service as a high calling. It was a middle-class vision of social action and unity. Hallam ridiculed the "old economically-idiotic plan" of strict economy which passed for mainstream municipal thought, a wisdom that forced people "to stand at street corners, or ramble up and down sidewalks, or steep themselves in drink at nights."[4] He anticipated that Canadian urban development might capitalize on the experience of Britain's local authorities. Foremost on his agenda was the municipal free library.

John Taylor was less prominent, less ambitious politically, but more pragmatic than his counterpart. Taylor represented the same ward as Hallam and was active in the Toronto Mechanics' Institute during the early 1880s. He, too, recognized Toronto's need for more books and better service and diligently gathered information on American and British library progress, in expectation of a bylaw. As events later unfolded, it became evident that unlike Hallam, who favoured erecting a new library building, Taylor was content to renovate the Mechanics' Institute, transfer its book stock, and proceed on a more modest basis for Toronto's public library. Despite their contrasting approaches, both men made valuable contributions to establish the free library. They were active not only in Toronto but also across Ontario.

Plans for library legislation hinged on the provincial government's stance. Oliver Mowat and members of his Executive Council probably preferred general enabling legislation, following the pattern of previous acts for Mechanics' Institutes and common school libraries. However, there was a potential problem: it was clear that provincial direction, especially from the education department under Adam Crooks, would not be appreciated in some interested quarters. Hallam made this point at council meetings and later in his small booklet, *Notes by the Way on Free Libraries and Books*, in which he deplored the "tedious formalities of an education department."[5] Since current legislation in Britain and the United States allowed municipalities considerable freedom, Mowat moved carefully, the hallmark of a cautious reformer.[6] Crooks likewise supported innovations, such as public kindergartens, but, as a rule, he took pains not to earn a reputation as a centralizer.

From the local standpoint, there was the need to transfer property and assets from Mechanics' Institutes to free libraries, thus giving them an existing nucleus around which they could grow and provide leadership at the outset. Graeme Mercer Adam was one advocate who anticipated this process; he remarked rather charitably that "we would look to the proposed Public Libraries Act for the means of galvanizing these moribund institutions into quickened life."[7] After Dr. May's report was tabled in the legislature in early 1881, it remained for Mowat's administration to revise regulations for institutes, to finalize new legislation for the Association of Mechanics' Institutes in consultation with local directors, and to prepare a free library bill for the 1882 session.

Of course, free libraries would eventually drain resources and energy from the Mechanics' Institutes, but the extent of this would be determined locally. Only in Toronto, where the government held a mortgage on the institute building, would the provincial treasury be involved directly. Early in 1882, the education department finally completed its regulations stemming from Dr. May's report and the exchange of viewpoints with institute directors. The total grant of $400 was unchanged; $100 could be used for a reading room, the remaining $300 for a library or evening classes, excluding management costs and salaries. Up to twenty percent of the library portion could be spent on fiction, provided it was authorized by the Department, which eventually compiled two new catalogues for high schools and institutes in 1884/85.[8] To qualify for provincial aid, a sum of at least half the total operating amount was to be raised locally ($400). Adam Crooks also introduced an act to give the Association of Mechanics' Institutes a more generous legislative grant and a slightly modified role *vis-à-vis* the local institutes (45 Vic., c. 4, s. 13-16). Although the department and institute directors continued to talk of evening classes, it is clear from the regulations that a library and a reading room were the government's primary concerns, ones that could be achieved by reasonable local effort and favourable circumstances.

"A Rate So Small"

Having reformed the regulations for institutes, the government turned to the issue of free libraries. Second reading of the free libraries bill took place on 28 February 1882. The ensuing debate clearly illustrates the different perspectives that members of the Legislature held on the subject. Because there is no official Hansard record, we must rely on newspaper accounts. Generally, newspapers did not conflict on substantive matters, but their reporters and editors obviously tailored the news to suit their local audiences. The Toronto *Globe* provided a brief record; the Toronto *Mail* gave a lengthier rendition (condensed in the Hamilton *Spectator*); and the London *Advertiser* relied on another reporter. The three respective accounts of the debate at second reading (reported on 1 March) follow.

> *Globe*
>
> Mr. Mowat moved the second reading of the bill providing for the establishment of Free Libraries. He rejoiced, he said, at the public agitation which called for such a Bill. They provided liberally for the education of the young, yet it was desirable that they should not over-look the education of those who had passed the school age. He hoped they would find the same advantages from this act as had been realized from a similar act in Great Britain. It was proposed to levy a general rate for the support of such libraries after the manner in which the Public Schools were supported, a rate so small to be almost unappreciable.
>
> Mr. [William] Meredith was afraid the Bill would not do much good. He thought that the powers conferred on

Councils by the Bill were too large without a provision for a reference to the rate-payers.

Mr. [James] Young thought the Bill would go a long way towards destroying the Mechanics' Institutes. He failed to see the present necessity for the Bill.

After considerable further discussion,

Mr. Mowat said the object of the Bill was to give the people an opportunity to form an absolutely free library. Those members who had spoken of the libraries being forced upon the people forgot the whole principle of representative government as embodied in the Council upon which rested the responsibility of introducing a free library. The results which the Bill had in view had not been accomplished by Mechanics' Institutes.

The Bill was then read a second time.

Mail

Mr. Mowat moved the second reading of the bill to provide for the establishment of free libraries. He said it was proposed to contribute to the support of these free libraries by taxation. He pointed out that in Great Britain and the United States, wherever free libraries had been established, they had been used by an immense number of readers. It was left to the municipal councils to decide whether the Act should apply to their municipality or not. The bill gave the management of these free libraries to a board composed of the mayor or reeve, three members elected by the municipal council and several members elected by the public and separate school boards. The rate of taxation was limited to a low amount.

Mr. [David] Hay thought the bill should apply to townships.

Mr. Meredith said that he did not think the municipalities would avail themselves much of the provisions of the bill. It would be unreasonable in cities where there were free libraries to continue the grant to mechanics' institutes, which would be a kind of competition.

Mr. [Robert] Bell proposed that a maximum taxation of half a mill might be imposed, but he thought that no such burden should be imposed upon any community without the consent of the ratepayers.

Mr. Young did not believe there was any particular necessity in this country for free libraries. In most of our cities and towns there was a Mechanics' Institute with a library which was practically free, and the effect of the bill would be hostile to these associations. He did not think the municipal councils should have the power of plunging their municipalities further into debt without consulting the people.

Mr. [Abram] Lauder said he would oppose the bill unless the ratepayers were given the right of saying whether they would have a free library or not.

Mr. [Henry] Merrick concurred in the views of the preceding speaker. Under the bill, once the library board was established, they would be free of control from the municipal council, and would send in their estimates, which the council would be obliged to pass. The general feeling of the country would be opposed to the bill as soon as its effect became know.

Mr. [James] Hunter supported the bill.

Mr. [Hammel] Deroche said the bill was in one sense an education bill, and the people were beginning to think that they already paid too much for education. In any case, the question of establishing a free library should be decided by vote of the ratepayers.

Mr. [Andrew] Broder thought the bill would do a good deal of good.

Mr. Mowat said he could not give up the principle of the bill, but would not object to the details being revised at a subsequent stage.

The bill was read a second time.

Advertiser

A motion to read a second time a Bill to provide for the establishment of free libraries.

Mr. Meredith said if the Government established free libraries, then aid to Mechanics' Institutes should be stopped.

Mr. Young said that the Mechanics' Institutes virtually supplied free libraries. The present Bill gave too arbitrary powers to municipalities.

Mr. Lauder said the subject had been broached by Ald. Hallam, but the circumstances of England and Canada in this matter were different. In England the free libraries were established for the very poorest classes. Such necessity did not exist in Canada.

Mr. [David] Robertson supported the Bill.

Mr. Deroche said the Bill was good in principle, but the public should have the right to vote on the question.

Mr. Broder said the library would reach a section (Toronto) which had never had the opportunity of availing themselves of the public school system, but he thought that in the rural districts the law proposed would be a dead letter. He should support the Bill.

Mr. Mowat said the measure would not impose any special burden upon the people, and free libraries were of the greatest importance to the public education. Mechanics' institutes were not well attended. In Toronto, with 70,00[0] of a population only 1,046 belonged to the Institute, which was the best probably in the Province. The burden which the Bill would impose upon any municipality was one of the lightest character. He trusted that in consideration of details the House would well consider the importance of the Bill.

The Bill was read a second time.

The provisions of the bill were relatively agreeable to most parties. One major objection was rectified by making it mandatory for qualified electors to vote on the library bylaw. Also, the number of board members was increased later from eight to nine with the addition of an extra appointment by the separate school trustees.[9] The bill's essential rationale was the encouragement of political activity at the municipal level where majorities for library bylaws would be won. Each community would have to establish a semi-independent board of directors according to terms set out in the act:

1. Free libraries could be established in cities, towns, or villages. The library could include a free newsroom, museum, branch library, branch newsrooms or branch libraries.

2. Upon receipt of a petition from electors, the council had to submit a bylaw to all qualified electors before passing the bylaw.

3. The management of the library was vested in a nine member board ("a body politic and corporate") composed of the mayor (or reeve), three people appointed by the council, three by the public school board (or board of education), and two by separate school trustees. Members of appointing bodies could not serve on the board of management. Appointments

were to be made at different intervals: public school board and council representatives held office for three years, separate school board appointees for two years.

The bill allowed boards to become relatively powerful entities in the evolving status of local self-government. Board governance meant many responsibilities: to elect chairmen; to meet once a month; to keep records of orders and proceedings signed by the chairman; to procure, erect or rent buildings; to purchase and preserve books, newspapers, reviews, magazines, maps and specimens of art and science; to provide fuel, lighting and similar matters; to appoint and dismiss officers and servants; and to make bylaws for the use and management of the library and its property. For financial purposes, boards had to submit yearly estimates to council by the first day of April for interest borrowed, for payments to sinking funds, and for operating expenses. Accounts were to be submitted to municipal auditors. A "free library rate" not to exceed one-half of a mill on rateable assessment could be levied. Debentures could be issued by council for buildings and, in the first instance, for books and "other things," subject to approval by a vote of the ratepayers.

What type of library service was to be provided? How was a free library to be organized by its directors? There were only a few sections in the bill that gave direction on these important questions:

1. All libraries, newsrooms, and museums were open to the public free of charge.
2. Mechanics' Institutes or Library Associations could transfer property to free libraries.
3. Forms were appended that could be used for petitions, bylaws, and debentures.

In this respect the bill resembled American "long legislation," which did not provide many details on the functions of library service. The onus was on local directors to identify functions and determine organization; by default, adult services – a circulating collection, reference department, and newspaper and periodical reading rooms – were library staples.

John Ross Robertson summed up the general sentiment, as he viewed it, in a short editorial on the act.

> The subject of public libraries has been so repeatedly discussed by the press that all must be familiar with the arguments that have been advanced in favour of Toronto doing

what has been done by so many other cities on both sides of the Atlantic – establishing a library open to all without the payment of fees. Such a library would be a great boon to the working classes of the city, who cannot afford to lay in a stock of desirable and useful books. Many men who attained to eminence in various walks of life, attribute their good fortune to the public library, where they found works which implanted knowledge in their minds that brought forth good fruit.[10]

To secure passage of municipal library bylaws, local advocates had to justify the need for free libraries within the emerging sphere of local government. The first two cities to apply the act were Toronto and Guelph. Both were successful in January 1883.

Carrying Free Library Bylaws

In Toronto, Hallam and Taylor spearheaded the effort to present a petition and offer a free library bylaw to the ratepayers on New Year's Day 1883. They orchestrated the printing of thousands of broadsides, 16,000 Christmas cards for school children, and 1,500 posters; they wrote letters to the press and appeals to the clergy; they arranged for public meetings to promote the scheme. Because Hallam and Taylor differed on certain aspects about library service, and the Mechanics' Institute's directors had not tendered any tangible proposal to transfer their assets, Torontonians were unsure of what was being promised. *Grip* joined the fray, printing two cartoons – "Sons of Toil" and "Workingman's Chance" (Illus. 11-12) – that depicted the expectations of the working class. But class concerns were not paramount; the issue was the bylaw's general merits, and defending the bylaw were the two aldermen.

> The free library project is to be voted on at the same time as the civic elections are held. Messrs. Hallam and Taylor, from the very best motives in the world, are doing all they can to carry the by-law authorizing the establishment of a free public library in Toronto. Whether the project succeeds or fails these gentlemen are entitled to credit for all they have done in pressing it upon the public mind.[11]

They succeeded by more than 2,500 votes. Hallam was so pleased he cabled Liverpool to inform British readers and his own correspondents that Toronto had passed its bylaw.[12]

In Guelph, plans were more definite, but the scale of activity was less comprehensive. There was virtually no public opposition to the directors of the Mechanics' Institute, who announced that they were anxious to transfer their 3,000 volume collection and some furnishings to a library board. One director, James Innes, suggested that any additional expenses incurred by the municipality could be easily offset.

> He thought the expense of managing the library could be lessened by the change by utilizing the western stalls in the rear end of the market which could be so altered and fitted up as to form a suitable place. He knew that a considerable portion of these had not been used in the past and would not be for years for market purposes, and by using them $150 or $200 rent could be saved per annum. For every $600 that the Mechanics' Institute expended for books and tuition the Legislature gave them a grant of $400, and under the Free Libraries Act he had no reason to doubt but the same grant would be made, unless the present Libraries Act were repealed.[13]

People in the Royal City took pride in the fact that they shared with Toronto the honour of voting first for a free library.[14] One new Guelph trustee, William Tytler, the secretary of the board, became a close friend of James Bain (Illus. 10), Toronto's chief librarian from 1884 to 1908.[15] Together they hunted in the "Muskoka Club" which Bain, George Paxton Young, and others had founded on an island near Parry Sound in the 1870s (Illus. 13).[16]

How successful was the library movement in putting forth its ideas and achieving its goals in local elections? Prior to 1895, only twelve free public libraries were established in Ontario. The primary interests of most ratepayers (if they cared to vote or speak out on local political concerns) lay elsewhere, on issues such as lighting, streets, and railway bonuses. Few aldermanic speeches referred to the library issue except in unusual circumstances. For example, in 1883, Emmanuel T. Essery, a lawyer and alderman in London, combined a ringing denunciation of corrupt "backroom wire pullers" with a call for a public library.

> He then made a plea for the necessity of a public library, where the citizens of London could he helped to become better educated, and not be handicapped by the Thugs of the Club, who say, 'Money is their God.' He proved the benefit arising from the perusal of good literature, which was now largely in the hands of the rich, and asked why should the poor cringe to these men, when by their votes they can assert their manhood.[17]

London voters delivered a confusing verdict: they supported the library, but Essery was trounced in his own ward. Undaunted, he fought on, eventually becoming mayor in 1893-94 when London finally implemented plans for a free library.[18]

When library advocates were able to include bylaws on municipal ballots, the results were often comfortable pro-library majorities. Moreover, low turnouts suggest that the issue did not interest many voters. Usually, no more than fifteen percent of the total population cast ballots. Election rules enabled ratepayers to vote but excluded everyone else. As a consequence, voter turnouts were not substantial (Table 6: Free Public Library Bylaws, 1883-1895). Perhaps the non-controversial nature of the bylaws themselves encouraged the government to eliminate the mandatory requirement for balloting in every community. In 1895, when the provincial legislature finally decided to reconstitute Mechanics' Institutes as public libraries, it allowed the formation of non-free public libraries by means of council bylaw without ratification by the ratepayers. In exchange for eliminating the need for a vote, this class of public library was ineligible to receive the one-half mill public library rate. As a result, after 1895 the number of non-free public libraries began to increase significantly (Graph 4: Free Library Boards in Ontario, 1882 to 1918).

For the greater part of the decade following 1882, the provincial government was engrossed with matters far more weighty than libraries. Library legislation descended to a low priority as the Mowat administration battled with the federal government on political-economic issues vital to Ontario's interests.[19] Ontario emerged the victor in decisive court decisions issued by the Judicial Committee of the Privy Council. In 1883, *Hodge vs. The Queen* affirmed the principle of provincial sovereignty in its own areas of jurisdiction and effectively struck down the federal power of disallowance. Later, in the bitter dispute over the enlargement of Ontario's boundaries and provincial ownership of natural resources in the north, from James Bay westward along the Albany River to Lake of the Woods, Ontario's land claims, rights, and powers were confirmed. However, Mowat was less successful with industrial and agrarian difficulties after the mid-1880s. His government did enact legislation covering workmen's compensation and arbitration procedures for industrial disputes, but among the farmers, the core of Liberal support, Mowat lost considerable ground in the 1890s to an agrarian political party, the Patrons of Industry. This development foreshadowed the decline of Liberal fortunes in its agricultural base across Ontario.[20]

In these circumstances the public library movement was forced to wait until 1895 when George Ross, the education minister, finally introduced important amendments to the library act (58 Vic., c. 45). These changes were brought about by the movement's unflagging promotion of its political agenda and cultural aims; by the education department's insistence on closer supervision; and by public opinion, which was slow to accept rate-supported libraries as an integral part of government but was receptive to the less expensive voluntary alternative that had sustained Mechanics' Institutes. The government, particularly the education department, realized that free library bylaws were difficult to place on the ballot. Dr. May summarized his two decades of experience with the enabling bylaw process at an Ontario Library Association meeting in 1902:

> ... our adult population did not seem to appreciate the benefits to be derived from municipalities providing good reading for themselves and for their children; another reason which retarded the progress of Free Libraries was that many members of Mechanics' Institutes were very conservative, and preferred paying membership fees, so that they might to a certain extent be exclusive in enjoying the privileges of the Library and Reading Room ...[21]

George Ross identified the substantial cost of "suitable buildings and premises" as a major drawback to library creation in his 1896 school textbook.

> In small municipalities it has been found, however, that while the people may not be willing to incur the larger expenditure necessary for a library building, they are not unwilling to contribute annually a moderate sum for the purchase of books and for contingent expenses. Accordingly, in 1895 the Public Libraries Act was amended, authorizing municipal councils to appoint a board of management for library purposes, even where a by-law had not passed for the erection of buildings.[22]

Of course, from a financial standpoint, libraries were not free, as one Hamilton citizen angrily declared: "It was nonsense to call the library 'free,' because the citizens would have to pay for it in taxes. You might as well call groceries 'free' that you have to pay for."[23]

Obviously, civic economy was a dominate factor confronting supporters who had to weigh the challenges confronting a rate-supported library bylaw at municipal elections. Financial motives influenced liberal, conservative, and nonpartisan citizens. They realized that municipal funding formed the basis of library operations (Graph 5: Local Public Library Revenue, 1882-1914). This obstacle, as well as the disinclination of the Ontario government to improve its own incentives for forming free libraries, contributed to the more relaxed 1895 legislation. Before that year, the directors of Mechanics' Institutes, who could transfer assets to free libraries, realized that there was usually little to gain financially from a library bylaw because most communities were reluctant to levy the maximum mill rate. As well, they knew that the maximum mill rate was often insufficient to provide adequate services, producing less than voluntary contributions or a conditional grant. For example, the village of Seaforth had an 1890 municipal assessment of $365,495, a sum which would yield $188 for the free library. This was twelve dollars short of the $200 government grant. The *Globe* remarked that the half-mill rate was "utterly inadequate for small places."[24]

Five years after the original act was introduced, James Bain, Toronto's far-sighted librarian, suggested two remedies to alleviate the free library's financial penury:

> The problem therefore before us is to convert the institute libraries into free public libraries with sufficient income to pay a regular librarian. Two courses lie before us either by giving them a larger area from which to draw a share of the taxation or by altering the act so as to increase the maximum. To this later proposition serious opposition would arise in the cities, where the feeling exists that it would be dangerous to permit a body not directly elected, power to enforce a higher taxation.[25]

Moreover, as long as the reading public voluntarily continued to pay small fees for library services, Bain's suggestions were unlikely to be enacted.

After 1895, many institutes simply changed their title to "public library" without making any effort to achieve rate-supported free status. Niagara's directors, including the writers William Kirby and Janet Carnochan, passed a simple motion at the annual meeting to the effect that the institute was now a public library. Business proceeded as before. Dundas possessed a small but well-established library (Illus. 14). Its directors were more energetic but indisposed to seek free status. Instead, they approached council to pass a bylaw increasing the municipal grant to three hundred dollars in return for a reduction in the membership fee to one dollar. The Dundas *Star* endorsed this policy: "One dollar is within the reach to any person and the volumes at their command cost many thousands besides the magazines and newspapers on file in the reading room."[26]

The movement's adherents had to rebut a range of practical objections related to the costs involved in library services. This was a crucial test of political wills in the light of the need for bylaw approval by ratepayers. A Hamilton lawyer protested that libraries were not necessities:

> There will not be a book in the library that can be read as a substitute for food, clothing or a warm house. If a public library is not a necessity, it is in the nature of a luxury. The same economy and prudence shown in a family should be practiced in the management of the affairs of a community. No prudent man will purchase a library whilst he is in debt for his cooking stove.[27]

The voters agreed. The 1885 bylaw failed by a slim margin of 189 votes. The Hamilton *Times* reasoned that it failed because "when trade is dull and employment is precarious ... it would be cruel to delude people into expenditures that were not absolutely necessary."[28]

Strict cost consciousness extended to the one-half mill rate, which most communities seemed to find excessive. Consequently, library supporters occasionally predicted that newly appointed trustees would not demand the full rate. This is precisely what happened in Hamilton where a December 1889 meeting concluded with a unanimous motion that the free library rate should be kept to one-quarter mill on the dollar and that "it be impressed upon the city council and board of education charged with the power of appointing the managing board that gentlemen should be appointed who can safely be depended upon not to favor an extreme expenditure."[29] Hamilton's bylaw passed comfortably on this occasion. In 1892, the province reduced the rate to one-quarter mill in cities over 100,000 population (52 Vic., c. 24) to ease electors' apprehensions.

The availability of inexpensive books also emerged as grounds not to form free libraries. Goldwin Smith was among the first to state that cheap printing allowed the public to buy plentiful reading; he suggested at a meeting of the Ontario Teachers' Association in August 1882 that a reference library would best suit Toronto's purposes.

> Not only novels, but works of all kinds, literary and scientific, standard as well as the most recent, can now be bought for a few cents, and everybody can have as much reading as business men or artisans have time for, at the cheapest rate, in his own home. By exchanging with neighbours, the home library may be still further enlarged. The need for city libraries, therefore, seems to be less. What would be a certain benefit in its way is a provincial library of books of reference and

other works not likely to be reprinted in a cheap form, to which students and persons engaged in special researches or in need of special information might resort. It has occurred to me that the Parliamentary Library might be developed into something of this kind.[30]

This was not the last time when Smith would find himself in a minority on library issues.

Concerned with Smith's stance, John Hallam corresponded with William F. Poole in Chicago and Charles Ammi Cutter in Boston. Poole replied that Smith was a bit old-fashioned: "He is behind the times." [31] The presence of low-priced literature usually was not a persuasive argument against free libraries. An editorial in the Conservative Toronto *Mail* illustrated this failing:

We wonder if those who say so ever put themselves in the artisan's place, and calculated how much he could spare in a year, after supporting his family, for books. For a quarter of a dollar in taxes, or less, the library will give him the use of, or choice from, thousands of volumes.[32]

William Briggs, a well-known publisher, agreed, adding, "all that many readers want is the reading, not the owning, of certain classes of books."[33]

Occasionally, in the heat of debate, financial issues could be turned to good advantage against antagonists. The following exchange took place at a Hamilton meeting between Thomas Brick, an active spokesmen for labour and a city alderman, and a well-to-do property owner.

Mr. Anthony Rowan protested that the by-law should not be carried. He said 'I can buy a book for 10 cents and read it.'
A voice [Thomas Brick] – a dime novel.
Mr. Rowan said that the library would impose a heavy tax on property owners.
A voice – Serves you right, for having so much property.[34]

Sentiment for the library carried this meeting, but the bylaw did not succeed at the polls.

In fact, financial considerations often cut both ways, especially when transfer of the assets of Mechanics' Institutes' to library boards was concerned. At Thorold, the town council inspected the Mechanics' Institute and took it over as a free library, primarily because it was a "valuable asset."[35] The ratepayers at Simcoe approved an 1884 bylaw for similar reasons. The town was already paying $200 rent annually for use of part of the institute. It was easy to see that the building's $1,100 debt bearing interest of six percent would be eliminated in a few years and that the town stood to gain. In addition, the building was appraised at $4,500, the library holdings were valued at $4,000, and the directors of the institute had $300 on hand. The library rate would yield about $400 annually, and the government grant for books would be the same.[36] The Simcoe bylaw passed without objection and the transition to free status for the library followed quickly.

However, the general legislative intent that an institutes' assets and book stocks would constitute the useful foundation for a free public library did not always hold true. When the St. Catharines institute came to an end, in mid-February 1888, the municipal corporation had to assume $280 of its liabilities and pay out $200 to cover the new free board's immediate expenses. William J. Robertson, a prominent teacher who was to become the backbone of the St. Catharines' free library, was quick to file papers with Dr. May to receive the institute's annual grant. This was a vital consideration given the circumstances of the transaction.[37] Chatham voters supported a free library in 1890 partly because it became known that the provincial grant to their institute would not be available for library purposes if the directors were forced to close down.[38] Afterwards, a lawyer involved in the exchange admitted to Dr. May that many of the institute's books were "old and of little value and the principal object of the Free Library Board is to secure the Gov. grant which but for this arrangement would go to the Mechanics [sic] Institute."[39]

Another major issue that bedeviled library advocates was the fiction question. Many novels published in the bookselling marketplace were not considered worthy contributions to higher culture; their literary merit was as questionable as their place in tax-supported circulating libraries. One observer noted:

> Probably the chief argument advanced against the adoption of the Free Libraries Act is that because the circulation of fiction is from 50 to 75 per cent of the whole, therefore free public libraries are a snare, a fraud and a delusion, and the general body of ratepayers should not be asked to provide foolish girls and beardless young men with novels to read wholesale.[40]

This was a serious charge. How could free libraries claim to be educational bodies when "light literature" was the chief circulating staple?

From the outset, library supporters met the challenge directly by justifying novel reading and including a generous portion of the "better class" in collections. John Hallam told a meeting: "I can get more true knowledge and real good from such books as the Vicar of Wakefield, Silas Marner, Jane Eyre, Caleb Williams, Adam Bede, and the works of Walter Scott, Thackeray, Dickens, some of Bulwer Lytton's, and those of other great novelists, than I could from nine-tenths of the sermons that were ever preached or published."[41] All groups were in agreement to censor obscene titles which might deprave or corrupt. The distinction between acceptable and unacceptable literature was based on the desired level of polite learning that a work imparted. Literary genres were not a deciding factor. Most library enthusiasts accepted popular recreational fiction and standard didactic fiction, both of which lacked the higher qualities of creativity and imagination found in critically acclaimed authors. They did not yield to rigid evangelical moral strictures or the opprobrium of established literary authorities, who might frown on the lightly-regarded Ouida (Louise de la Ramée) or realistic works such as George Moore's controversial *A Modern Lover*, published in 1883.[42] Thus, the library's mission was relatively liberal: it accepted popular literature, thereby respecting the tastes of a mass readership. This position often drew criticism from a vocal constituency that felt public morality rested on untainted private virtue and that the business of libraries did not extend to the proliferation of entertaining novels.

The debate persisted for decades, with popular fiction gradually gaining acceptance as works of literature despite aesthetic "deficiencies" and "distasteful" content. John Taylor revealed the course of public preference by stating that the public was "too advanced in the nineteenth century to underrate the benefits of good healthy fiction."[43] While dime novels, penny dreadfuls, shilling shockers, romances, railway novels, and most melodramas were obviously frowned upon, "serious" novels were considered a source of moral and social instruction.[44] As long as libraries exercised discretion in book selection, critics might concur with one Toronto bookseller who said that libraries would lead readers in a "proper direction."[45] In his opinion, the higher class of novelists included Dickens and Thackeray. They were followed by best-selling contemporaries – Francis Marion Crawford, William Black, and William Dean Howells.

Many Canadian literary critics and public library spokesmen did not have a high regard for either "inferior" fiction or the fresh trends towards realism and naturalism in novels. Novels that probed everyday human experience typically portrayed people as captives of hereditary or environmental forces and often contained sexuality, atheism, and nonconformist attitudes. These subjects were looked upon with suspicion or distaste. However, by the last decade of the century, public opinion was changing. The Toronto *Globe* sensibly staked out the middle ground, stating the case for both serious and light fiction:

> In Ontario, as in several other civilised communities, the public library system has grown rapidly. The strain in which this is announced is not always wholly congratulatory, there being an undertone of regret at the fact that the novels are well-thumbed, while poetry, science and history grow dusty on the shelves... at an investment of $50 the reader can surround himself with a goodly company of these quiet and unobtrusive friends. To the circulating library he goes for works of less permanent value, for books which are untried, for books which are too expensive to buy. And there is nothing very alarming in the fact that a large part of the borrowing consist of works of fiction.
>
> There is another class of people for whom the circulating library supplies nearly all the literature that they read. The question which arises here is, 'Is such literature better than nothing?' We are told that the young people neglect Scott, Thackeray, Dickens and George Eliot and read 'trash.' But literary people are in danger of becoming just a little pedantic in their selection of authors who are to enter the charmed circle. There are many novels which do not rank as classics, yet the influence of which is decidedly good and wholesome.[46]

The editorial closed with an endorsement of Edward Roe's formula novels.

Most libraries insisted upon better quality fiction, placing their faith in hard-working book selection committees. They relied on standard tools: *The Athenaeum, Publishers Weekly*, and *The Bookman*, which began publishing lists of best-selling fiction in 1895. At one point, the Toronto *Evening News* proposed using the American Library Association's general public catalogue of "best books."[47] However, publication of this five thousand title guide for small libraries was delayed for more than a decade; it was finally released at the Columbian Exposition in 1893. This long delay prompted some American libraries to devise ingenious solutions for improving public reading interests: special reading lists, open shelf collections, book displays, a two-book charging system (one novel plus one nonfiction work), and readers' advisory service.[48] These ideas eventually spread to Canada. Gradually, librarians endorsed the rationale that readers could be weaned from light reading to more elevated works. They did not abandon the role of censor, however, because they felt that they had a duty to control "controversial" titles.[49]

The education department did not issue its *Catalogue of Books Recommended for Public Libraries* until November 1895, and even then it contained only a small section for "standard" novels, most of which were historical or romantic. The Department's respectable novels occupied a spectrum from "light," represented by Rhoda Broughton, Margaret Hungerford, and Mrs. Henry Wood, to "serious," represented by Balzac, Eliot, Hardy, Trollope, Thackeray, and Tolstoy.[50] Detective stories, a growing category, were classed separately. Although the catalogue accepted the legitimacy of fiction, it muddied the fiction issue by incorporating novels in other sections. For example, Annie Swan's *Gates of Eden* and Nathaniel Hawthorne's *The Scarlet Letter* turned up in the section on moral tales, essays, and romances; Jules Verne's *Round the World in Eighty Days* enlivened the category of voyages and travels; and Charles Kingsley's *Hypatia* appeared in historical tales. Juvenile fiction also was classed in different sections.

By the early 1890s, efforts to restrict or discourage fiction reading sometimes suffered the fate of derisive editorials. When word spread that the new chairman of the Toronto Public Library preferred serious novels, the Toronto *Saturday Night* playfully entered the fray.

> And inquiry has revealed the fact that there are shop girls in the city who commit the crime of reading The Duchess [by Margaret Hungerford]. Shall this state of things continue! In this enlightened age are men and women to be allowed to learn something of their fellow-men in the present and past through the pernicious agency of the novel… Thank heavens, the abuse which allows the circulation of thousands of volumes of fiction in Toronto will not long continue, the temple will soon no longer be polluted, for has not D. A. O'Sullivan, LL.D., introduced a resolution for the restriction of fiction reading at the Public Library![51]

But the novel in a variety of forms was to have its way; a mass audience drawn from all classes grew steadily in size and hankered for romance, science fiction, detective stories, and westerns.[52]

On the international scene a few talented Canadian novelists were beginning to receive due recognition. Lawrence J. Burpee, an insightful early critic of Canadian writing, judged their work to be promising, wholesome, and polished.[53] Throughout the 1890s popular writers such as Agnes Maule Machar (*Roland Graeme, Knight*), Sara Jeannette Duncan (*An American Girl in London*), Gilbert Parker (*Seats of the Mighty*), Lily Dougall (*The Madonna of the Day*), and Marshall Saunders (*Beautiful Joe*) expanded the range and quality of Canadian fiction. Didactic and moral purposes were less evident in the hands of these skillful novelists, although some instruction and ethical lessons endured. By 1902, the Stratford trustee, John Davis Barnett, a collector of Shakespeariana, could safely say: "Until I find a non-novel reading community (past or present) which in reforming energy or morals, in manners or charity of judgement, is superior to the novel using community, I intend to claim novel circulation as one of the values the P.L. confers."[54]

Nonfiction also could pose problems. Liberals, of course, believed in freedom of expression, but on occasion freethinking literature, especially atheist or agnostic tracts, could damage the case for libraries. The London Ministerial Association, led by Walter M. Roger, protested against "infidel books" after it learned that the Workingmen's Free Library had requested $500 from council to provide free services in 1892. In effect, the Association was offended by the writings of freethinkers such as the controversial British MP Charles Bradlaugh, an atheist and co-publisher of a book on contraception, *The Fruits of Philosophy*, and Robert Green Ingersoll, the influential American writer and agnostic. The Association claimed:

> We live in a Christian community, whose laws are founded upon the Bible, and whose Government, by repeated deliverances of its high judiciaries, has been declared a Christian Government which will not tolerate for example, the use of its public halls for the propagation of infidel doctrines, and which claims the right to prevent the introduction of immoral or other objectionable books, like those of Bradlaugh and Ingersoll, through its mails and custom houses.[55]

In this case, the London *Advertiser* helped resolve the dispute. It published the complete contents of the Workingmen's library with the prudent opinion: "Our view is that the library as it stands is a very fair nucleus for a free library such as is to be found in nearly all the larger cities in North America and in Great Britain." The newspaper also advised that the Mechanics' Institute library holdings should be included when a free public library began operating.[56]

There was persistent criticism that the working class would not be able to use libraries in their leisure hours. The sixty hour work week being the norm, the Hamilton *Times* explained:

> About the usefulness of a library and reading room as a place of resort for workingmen in the evenings we are inclined to doubt. The workingman, who has to be at his place in the

shop at 7 o'clock in the morning, is not going to have much time to loaf in the evening after he has got his supper and read the daily paper. Professional and commercial men may make the library a place of resort, but mechanics and factory operatives, as a rule, will not.[57]

As well, it was said that optional reading materials existed for the public. One person complained that books, newspapers, and libraries abounded and that "few of us are disposed to yield to the tempter's charms to desert our homes after a day's work to absorb an extra taxed literature collected by a conclave of any designing body of men, whether aldermen alone or in collusion with others."[58] Sometimes support from organized labour could neutralize this criticism; trade unions were trying to become more active in local politics and were interested in securing social benefits for their members.

During the debate on the Toronto bylaw, aldermen Hallam and Taylor attended a Trades and Labour Council meeting in December to recruit support. The Council was not to be ignored. It claimed to speak for about five thousand trade unionists in the city. The audience was a friendly one: the TLC had previously passed a resolution favouring the bylaw. One working-man applauded the two aldermen and spoke out for public control:

He had been a member of a mechanics' institute for twenty years, but when he came to Canada he found a bank clerk at the head of the institution. If there was anything distasteful to a workingman it was patronage. (Hear, hear.) He hoped the library would come into existence, and they would do all they could in favour of it.[59]

A vote of thanks was extended to Hallam and Taylor on this occasion.

Nine years later, in March 1892, Hallam and the TLC were allies again. On this occasion, labour petitioned the legislature in support of the effort of Hallam and the Toronto city council to reduce the library rate to one-quarter mill. Toronto aldermen were upset with the library directors' efforts to establish a museum based on the maximum tax revenue to which they were entitled. The TLC believed that the half-mill rate, which had the potential to raise $75,500 in 1892 (up from $31,000 when the library was established), was "beyond the needs of the free library."[60] The bill passed quickly despite the Toronto library's opposition (55 Vic., c. 47). In general, labour leaders concentrated on collective bargaining, wages, and working conditions, which were crucial issues for the working class, leaving the library movement to other people.

There were times when existing library collections were suggested as fitting substitutes for municipal public library service. In a peculiar instance of *déjà vu*, Hamilton's Central School library, dating from Ryerson's administration, was boldly advanced as a viable alternative during one unsuccessful free library bylaw campaign.

> I repeat that the public do not appear to be aware of the existence of this library, for there have not been a score of applicants for books in the past half dozen years. I refer to the volumes in the library at the Central School. The only expense attending it is the nominal salary of $50 a year to the Librarian. Let this library be divided into four parts and a part placed in each district school...[61]

But the prime candidates for substitution were the parliamentary libraries in Toronto and Ottawa. The Toronto *Evening Telegram* lamented that "We have a splendid library in Toronto, but it is locked up, except to members of the legislature, and even of these very few ever think of using it." It later complained that the "only difference the throwing open of the library would make, would be that there would be more work for the librarians to do."[62] The parliamentary library in Ottawa contained an even more inviting store of literature: "Those who need the more solid class of books already have a collection, not to be excelled in the country, at their service in the Parliamentary library."[63] However, neither the provincial nor federal legislators had any intention of expanding the hours of operation or opening the collections of their respective libraries to the public.

Most of the opposition to free libraries came from adversaries who claimed that existing collections in Mechanics' Institutes were sufficient for their communities. The response to this charge was predictable. Free library promoters appealed to progress. Daniel Wilson reminded his Toronto audience: "The scheme, [Mechanics' Institutes] though well intentioned, and perhaps all that was possible at an early stage, has proved inadequate to the growing demands which a well organized system of education necessarily begets."[64] Fortunately for library advocates, the appeal to progress often carried the day in Victorian Canada and smoothed the way for a free library.

Finally, it was inevitable that local disputes between councils, aldermen, library promoters, and library boards would arise from time to time, especially in larger urban communities. The legislators had said as much when the original library bill reached second reading in 1882. London provided an instructive example for anyone wishing to avoid conflict. London's first library bylaw passed comfortably in January 1884, on the assumption that the Mechanics'

Institute would provide a suitable foundation for a free library. Most London aldermen were not concerned with the library; their interests lay in railroads and water. But one problem loomed large: the three-storey institute building, erected in 1876-77 in the Second Empire style, had become a heavy financial liability.[65] Within five months, the new board members had resigned. They had been unable to reach agreement with the directors of the institute about its debts or a transfer of its property. As well, the council had refused to authorize the levying of the public library rate because the board's estimates were not submitted in time. Shortly thereafter, Judge William Elliott, the board chairman and a long-time supporter of the institute, wrote, "In this situation of matters we have either to engage in litigation with the Council, or remain powerless members of the Board, or resign."[66]

Resignation hardly solved the issue in London. The original bylaw establishing a library remained on the statute books, but no more members were appointed to the board until 1888. In that year, the Trades and Labour Council threatened legal action against the municipal council unless library directors were appointed. Municipal legal advisors confirmed the validity of the TLC's threat, but, the aldermen had other ideas, foremost among them being civic economy. Ignoring the opposition, they submitted a bylaw to the electors at midyear to repeal the 1884 library bylaw. Despite efforts by the Mechanics' Institute directors, who pledged to transfer their assets, the council's efforts succeeded: the library board was officially dissolved.[67] London remained without free public library service until another bylaw passed in 1893, and a new building was constructed in 1895.

New Directions

All these challenges presented serious obstacles to the passage of free library bylaws, especially when the cultural assumptions and benefits postulated on behalf of libraries either failed to match the reality of existing community library services or conflicted with other interest groups. Nevertheless, the movement's encounters with divergent viewpoints helped shape its activities, define its goals, and overcome entrenched opposition. After the provincial government merged collections in Mechanics' Institutes with free libraries and relaxed the free library bylaw process, in 1895, the ranks of the library movement, hitherto small in number, grew steadily as institute directors and municipal participants joined the cause of public libraries.

One exceptional new member was Edwin Hardy from Lindsay. Like James Bain, Jr. of Toronto, he recognized the need for more vigorous organization and additional goals and purposes for the movement. By the mid-1890s, Bain was advocating larger units of service, the inclusion of art galleries and museums in libraries, and improved library funding and organization.[68]

Hardy initiated another change. Writing to the education minister, George Ross, in the summer of 1899, he asked for more centralized direction from the education department; regular publications of library directories, new book bulletins, manuals on management; and a better classification system. Ross encouraged Hardy:

> I think it would be well to have a conference before long of the leading Librarians of the Province and of those interested in Public Libraries, say at the time of the Annual meeting of the Teachers' Association during the Easter holidays, in order that the work of our Libraries may be systematized and the views of those associated with them ascertained. I am glad to see the interest you have taken in the matter.[69]

Formation of the Ontario Library Association followed swiftly.

When the American Library Association met at Montreal in 1900, at the invitation of Charles Gould, McGill University's Librarian, Hardy and eight others from Ontario and Quebec organized a provisional committee to form a Canadian Library Association, on 11 June. Hardy and Bain then met in October at the Toronto Public Library with three other men, Alexander H. Gibbard, a newspaper editor and publisher in Whitby, Hugh Langton, chief librarian at the University of Toronto, and Archibald B. Macallum, professor of physiology at the University of Toronto and former president of the Canadian Institute. These men decided that a provincial (not a dominion) organization was the more feasible strategy. James Bain was chosen as president, Hugh Langton as first vice-president, Hardy as secretary, and Macallum as treasurer. The committee drafted a short constitution and agreed to hold its first conference in Toronto. The government, now led by George Ross, provided the Examiners' Room of the Education Department for the group's inaugural session on 8 April 1901. A firmer organizational basis for province-wide collaboration was finally established. Library promotion would no longer depend solely upon steadfast individuals and small local support groups.

By about 1900, therefore, the public library movement in Ontario was developing along "modern" directions with a stronger level of organization. The establishment of free libraries in individual communities remained the goal of advocates. Free libraries were both an urban and rural phenomenon closely associated with the political culture of Ontario's local self-government. Dr. May's annual report disclosed the amorphous nature of public library growth across the province. Although a number of larger centres (Ottawa, Kingston, Woodstock, Belleville, Sault Ste. Marie, and Peterborough) remained outside the free library ranks after two decades, there was progress in rural areas where several small free libraries were already in existence. The formation of more public libraries at the polls or at council sessions fortified a community's sense of place and helped establish a local identity, vital elements in Ontario politics.

The democratization of reading seemed assured. On a provincial scale, there was a new foundation for cohesiveness among library workers and trustees. In many local communities, there was a structural base on which supporters felt comfortable furthering the interests of the movement and contributing to intellectual enlightenment and material advantage through the municipal process. Unfortunately, the man who had epitomized the movement's progressive spirit for twenty years did not live to see its full flowering. John Hallam died in June 1900 at his downtown residence, "Linden Villa."[70] He had enjoyed an exciting life, rising from an impoverished boyhood in England to campaign for the office of mayor of Toronto. It was his last municipal election and he failed to win. Almost two decades before his death he had written:

> Toronto being the centre or headquarters in Ontario of law, literature, science, and art, ought, I submit, to promptly make a movement in this matter, and set an example to the Province by inaugurating a free library and museum scheme, and school of design.[71]

In time, it was a vision come true, a testament to a "Lancashire" liberal's faith in progress.

The Toronto example prompted other communities to follow suit. A foundation existed. A modern, post-Victorian program of action was about to begin: the founding of publicly funded libraries across the province. These libraries would offer open access to circulating collections, reading rooms, and reference service to the entire public free of charge. Consensus about library services and management would provide a unifying bond and a springboard for collective action. Carnegie philanthropy, better organized cooperative efforts, an expanded range of functions, and modern methods would invigorate the movement and broaden the range of organizational tasks to be undertaken after 1900. Nonetheless, the fundamental spirit of Victorian liberal reform and its optimistic rationale would remain the guiding light for library development in Ontario well into the first part of the twentieth century.

Chapter 5

FROM ONE CENTURY TO ANOTHER

The two decades after 1882 did not pass without improvements in library service and organization. During this period Liberal reformers remained receptive to change. This was especially true of George Ross, who succeeded Adam Crooks as Minister of Education in 1883 after the latter could no longer perform his duties due to cerebral paresis. Ross, a powerful voice in Oliver Mowat's government, continued as education minister until he became premier in 1899. He was consultative but more inclined to direct control. Uniformity and regulations were bywords in the department during his tenure of office. His general view was that the institutes were to provide libraries and, if possible, reading rooms and evening classes. At the outset, the new minister assigned Dr. May to modify the classification scheme inherited from William Edwards. Proofs for a new edition of the Roll and Record Book went forward in 1884, albeit slowly.[1] Coincidentally, Ross's communication with the Association of Mechanics' Institutes was sporadic, even though its mandate had been enlarged by Crooks to include the promotion of arts and manufactures (independently or in conjunction with local institutes), the employment of lecturers, and the publication of works.

Ross began instituting major changes shortly after he became minister of education. He was more vigilant about organizational details which were the responsibility of the institute directors. He consulted with the association about firmer regulations, his usual initial approach to an issue.[2] But, apparently, he did not inform its officers about his own government's intention to abolish the association at the next legislative session.[3] When a short act was introduced to dissolve the association in 1886 (49 Vic., c. 35), no explanation was forthcoming during debate. Instead, Ross disclosed to the legislature that he wanted to "put an end to the irritating uncertainty as to the amount of the Government grant." He continued:

The rule was that 20 per cent. of the Government grant might be expended in works of fiction, but the Mechanics' Institutes, as they had a right to do, had spent on works of fiction a much greater proportion of the amount received from private subscriptions. It was proposed to grant to the institutes dollar for dollar of the amount subscribed.[4]

Surprisingly, there was no significant opposition to the dissolution of the association.

After passage of the act, grants-in-aid were arranged on a completely different basis, the principle being that equivalent amounts were to be raised locally to match provincial dollars. Institutes with fifty members received $25/year; institutes with one hundred members received $50/year. In addition, institutes with libraries were eligible for $150 (the usual twenty percent was allowed for fiction) and reading rooms could receive a maximum $50. Evening classes could qualify for up to $100. For most institutes, the new grants meant a cutback in relation to libraries and reading rooms, i.e., a reduction from $300 to $200 and a decrease in provincial money for fiction. Ross's departmental arrangements necessitated a decrease in the amount of fiction; however, the department was not opposed to novels. It believed that with less income directors would choose fiction more wisely.

As far as the operation of libraries was concerned, the departmental office issued specific regulations that were more comprehensive than those Crooks had hesitated to introduce in 1882. The principal of central control feared by Otto Klotz and others, had been delayed, not discarded, by Ross. Improved standards for library service accompanied conditional grants. Both the reading room and library had to be conveniently situated. The reading room was to be properly warmed and lighted and furnished with suitable racks and paper files; there were to be chairs for at least ten people; it was to be open at least three hours every alternate week day; and it was to subscribe to two daily newspapers, five weeklies, and three magazines. The library itself was to be open at least one hour every week; its books were to be properly numbered and in order on the shelves; and there was to be an accurate record of charges and discharges.[5] No doubt the department believed observance of superior business practices would promote greater efficiency.

Emerging Public Library Leadership

The dissolution of the Association of Mechanics' Institutes was not mourned in the province; even its executive did not create a fuss. At its last meeting in September 1886 in Toronto, the Association's executive simply expressed optimism that another organization would be formed to help conduct the work of institutes. But its disappearance effectively removed any possibility of coordinated voluntary action and ousted from the library field William Edwards, a man who had provided continuity for many years. Edwards deserves recognition for developing a rudimentary classification and circulation system. It drew the attention of Melvin Dewey; it was approved by the education department; and it was used in the late 1880s by ninety-five libraries, including the free libraries in Berlin, St. Thomas and St. Catharines.[6] He had spurred on institute libraries; he had helped manage their functions more efficiently; and he had tried to effect coordinated programs. Now he had to step aside for the less popular Dr. May, who was known for his strong opinions and predilection for rules.

Given that free library direction would normally emanate from Toronto ("Toronto must necessarily lead the way," G. Mercer Adam chimed),[7] the new librarian, James Bain, Jr., and John Hallam naturally assumed the mantles of leadership. Hallam had already established important American contacts. He wrote to the influential library publisher, Frederick Leypoldt, and convinced him to publish a short piece about his proposal to raise money to build and stock the proposed Toronto library. Hallam's article appeared in the March/April 1883 issue of *Library Journal.*[8] Bain began to cultivate contacts with scholars, notably in the Canadian Institute, which appointed him secretary and treasurer. The two men, deprived of a provincial library organization, turned their attention to American Library Association annual conventions. These meetings were held adjacent to Ontario on two occasions in the 1880s, at Buffalo and the Thousand Islands resort.

At Buffalo, in August 1883, Hallam and Bain attended several sessions; they were particularly interested in library architecture and Buffalo's plans for a separate library facility. They also lobbied successfully to host the next ALA meeting at Toronto.[9] This was no small achievement. Their success came in the face of stiff competition from libraries in larger north-eastern and western American cities, such as St. Louis. Hallam's formal invitation included a succinct, cheerful rationale:

> The recent passage of the free library bill for the province of
> Ontario has stimulated many municipalities to action, and
> we have in Toronto already commenced operations. The
> influence of the Association in strengthening this feeling
> throughout the country would be very great, and materially
> assist the cause of free libraries.[10]

The ALA executive was impressed by the Canadian effort and satisfied with Toronto's proximity to the north-eastern states. It hoped that British librarians would meet with the ALA in Toronto, in early September 1884, following the scheduled convention of the British Association for the Advancement of Science in Montreal. However, Hallam and Bain became preoccupied in their efforts to reopen the refurbished Mechanics' Institute by March 1884 and were unable to organize conference sessions. When no other Canadian librarians stepped forward to assist them, the ALA executive cancelled the Toronto meeting in mid-1884 with a short announcement in *Library Journal.* No conference was held in 1884. Not until the Montreal conference of 1900 would the ALA meet in Canada.

At the Thousand Islands conference in New York State, in September 1887, James Bain read a paper, "Brief Review of the Libraries of Canada," and contributed to discussions on extension work for public libraries.

> I went to the heads of various corporations, and got them to invite their men. I had a part of the library opened and lit up. I had men who were engaged in a special branch of manufacture come on a given evening, and had all the things relating to that branch gathered and spread out for use. Then I had one of their number read a paper on the subject. I found it a very profitable method.[11]

That same year Bain compiled a list of public libraries in Canada. It was appended to Richard Bowker's *The Library List,* a handbook recording information on libraries of over one thousand volumes as well as the names of librarians and officers.[12] It is clear from Bain's classed compilation that the term "public library" in Ontario still included a wide variety of institutions. In addition to the free libraries operating under the 1882 statute, he listed Mechanics' Institutes; subscription libraries, and twenty-five libraries in colleges, historical and scientific societies, government archives, theology and law schools, parliament, and the provincial legislature.

James Bain was well qualified to lead the Toronto free library through a series of fundamental changes. He was a skilled bookman-librarian capable of scholarly endeavour, administrative insight, and profitable transactions with the publishing industry. Bain gained his position in 1884 despite stiff competition from Graeme Mercer Adam, who had produced a recent list of books suitable for libraries, and from the publisher-writer, Charles Dent.[13] He had worked for his father, a Toronto bookseller, before joining James Campbell & Son; then he moved to England where he eventually established a partnership in a London publishing firm. It was dissolved in 1882. Upon his return to Toronto, he became manager of the Canadian Publishing Company before applying for chief librarian. His selection immediately raised some eyebrows, but his subsequent career dispelled any lingering doubts about his ability.

The first order of business Bain confronted was the development of adequate reference and circulating collections. To stock the new Toronto city library, Bain and John Hallam travelled to England and the United States, a trip reminiscent of Ryerson's expedition three decades before, in 1850-51. They returned with more than twenty thousand volumes. Fortunately, Bain did not become embroiled in the contentious issue of the new library building; he was free to concentrate on book selection and library organization with the help of his assistant librarian, James Davy, who had served as the librarian of the Mechanics' Institute for many years. The incubus of arranging a new building had fallen on John Hallam's shoulders. In this instance, the weight proved to be too onerous.

Hallam's original plan called for an estimated allocation of $130,000 for a building and $95,000 for books and appliances. The money would be raised by free library debentures. The plan met with a good deal of opposition from the Toronto council, which preferred to spend no more than $50,000. Their alternative was contingent upon the Mechanics' Institute transferring its real and personal property to the city for a public library, by March 1883. John Taylor also favoured this course. Colonel James Mason, the institute president, succeeded in bringing the council's plans to fruition by the end of June 1883.[14] Once the institute was transferred, the library board decided to construct an addition to the rear of the existing institute, which would be the new stack room, and to refit the first floor. When the renovation was completed, the *Globe* cast a studious eye:

> The original promoters of the Free Library scheme had no intention of utilizing this building for the new project, but when the people assemble on Thursday next to witness the formal opening there is every probability that they will be both surprised and delighted to find the city in the possession of so beautiful, so extensive, and so convenient a public institution at withal so small an outlay.[15]

Hallam likely considered the new addition little more than a soothing anodyne.

The converted institute building, entering its third decade, was a typical late century closed-stack free library with a capacity for 50,000 volumes in its bookroom (86 ft. x 52 ft.). There was scant literature on library architecture at this time, an exception being William Archer's statement on the Irish national library at Dublin. He stressed the creation of central reading rooms surrounded by closed stacks not more than eight feet in height to maximize book capacity and access for staff. His plan was acceptable to most librarians.[16] Toronto's design followed conventional wisdom and the practical restrictions imposed by the physical layout of the existing institute. A librarian's counter separated the collection from the large reading room (76 ft. x 53 ft.) at the front, which was subdivided by railings into reference and periodical areas for the convenience of users.[17] The cost was about $12,000. The official opening on 6 March 1884 was a gala affair that celebrated Toronto's fiftieth anniversary; it attracted a capacity crowd eager to listen to Goldwin Smith and William Withrow, and to tour the building in the evening while the band of the Tenth Royal Grenadiers entertained visitors.[18]

Later that year, two branch libraries opened in rented facilities at St. Andrew's market and in the newly annexed municipality of Yorkville, thereby bringing the library into city neighbourhoods. In the next five years two more branches came into operation: an Eastern branch and one in the Parkdale area on Dundas Street (Illus. 15). These smaller branches helped to relieve space problems at the main library and made circulating collections more accessible. Bain's philosophy was to build up a central reference library and have small branches take on the duty of circulating popular books. In an 1898 report to the ALA, he remarked that branches were essentially "a source of recreative reading and not of study" and, further, that forty or fifty percent of the collection should be works of fiction.[19] Branches necessitated more administrative work, but their popularity negated the extra financial outlays.

Toronto's central library and branches were a dramatic improvement in library facilities, but Bain also worked diligently to assemble special collections. Hallam, who continued to communicate with many important library personages until his retirement from the board in 1888, donated his personal collection of 1,600 books and pamphlets.[20] Hallam's offerings formed the basis for TPL's future magnificent Canadiana collection.[21] Bain watched assiduously for book auctions, made a few selective buying trips abroad, dealt actively with second-hand booksellers in North America and Europe, and always was prepared to receive donations during his tenure of office. In a surprisingly short time, by the mid-1890s, he had built a collection that many marvelled at.[22] No less vital were his mastery of government documents and his interest in establishing federal depository arrangements. The latter was a farsighted scheme which he later advocated at meetings of the Ontario Library Association, and in library publications and the *Canadian Magazine*.[23]

Bain was less successful in having a federal duty on books for public libraries removed, despite a special board deputation to Ottawa in 1888,[24] and in promoting a scheme for a museum, a project approved first by a special

board committee which studied the matter at length in 1891/92. When renovations began on the upper floor of the main library, Toronto city council let
it be known that it was not enthusiastic about the idea or the cost.[25] Led by
John Hallam, now more interested in the mayoralty, the council successfully
petitioned the legislature to pass amendments that would reduce the mill rate
to one-quarter for cities of one hundred thousand population and that would
require council's consent for boards to establish a museum (55 Vic., c.47).[26]
Bain, not one to give in easily, later published a paper on the subject, remind-
ing librarians that they "must never forget that the museum is neither a store-
house nor a bazaar, but an additional means of extending and popularizing
knowledge."[27] Under Bain's supervision, Toronto was demonstrating its free
library potential.

Other Ontario communities could only dream about the type of free
library emerging in Toronto. There were only six places – Guelph, Toronto,
Simcoe, Brantford, St. Thomas, and Berlin – with free libraries five years
after passage of the library act. The remnants of Ryerson's free library system
fell into complete neglect in the 1880s. There is little evidence that these collections survived intact after the government finally removed the one-third
incentive grant for school library purchases in 1888. There were exceptions,
of course, such as Wilmot Township, Waterloo County, where old books
from the school library were transferred to the newly formed Baden
Mechanics' Institute in 1889.[28] Free library service across the province was in
a nascent state, especially in rural areas where even the institute libraries were
viewed with mistrust. One farm journal criticized George Ross in 1886 for
the shortcomings of the Mechanics' Institutes and hoped that newly formed
farmers' institutes would be of greater literary benefit to the agricultural populace.[29]

William Wood, a member of the legislature from the rich farming area of
Brant County, asked for a legislative report in 1888 showing the location of
mechanics' and farmers' institutes and free libraries; in addition, he requested
details of revenue related to public libraries in schools and institutes for the
five years leading up to the depository's closure. Wood, like others familiar
with the rural scene, felt that library grants to farmers' institutes would
improve service in country districts. George Ross replied that "the extension
of the system of Mechanics' Institutes was really the best way of meeting the
difficulty."[30] His 1886 regulations had made it easier for the institutes to form
libraries, and a steady rise in the total legislative grant began at this time,
although the average grant for each institute was decreasing compared to the
earlier regulations (Table 7: Grants for Mechanics' Institutes Libraries, 1882-
1895). When Wood's return was tabled in the legislature, it was obvious that
his scheme could not meet rural needs. There were 41 farmers' institutes but

some populous counties (e.g., Bruce and Wentworth) were not represented. The tabulations of the return showed that 143 institutes or free libraries served 35,195 members, received $23,831 from the legislature, and raised $88,547 from local sources. Of this total, Toronto accounted for 14,445 members, $200 from the legislature, and $43,763 from local sources.[31] Free library service worked well in Toronto, but there was still considerable effort needed in the rest of Ontario.

It was not long before the Ambitious City, without library service since 1882, joined Toronto as a leader. The old Mechanics' Institute on James Street was but a memory. Hamilton was faced with the daunting task of building a collection, erecting a library, and hiring a librarian, at the beginning of 1889. One new board member, Henry B. Witton, was a devoted bibliophile and library booster. He and another trustee began searching through catalogues to compile a list of nearly 14,000 books worth $19,000 for the new library, which could not be augmented by any major transfers from other collections. When they submitted their list, changes were demanded, and Witton resigned in anger, never to serve again. His son, Henry, later resumed the connection with Hamilton as a trustee and helped ensure that his father's valuable collection was housed at Hamilton in 1921. Fortunately, Witton's loss was offset by the board's selection of Richard T. Lancefield, a bookseller, as librarian.

Richard Lancefield had worked in Hamilton as an apprentice printer and had operated his own commercial lending library for a brief spell until it failed around 1883. He then lived in Toronto where he was secretary of the Canadian Copyright Association and an editor for *Canadian Bookseller*. He continued these important interests while he was Hamilton's chief librarian.[32] Lancefield's first task was to assist with book selection for the new library, but more pressing was the need to prepare a printed catalogue and to classify the circulating books which would be in demand once the building opened. Lancefield modified the classification system sponsored by the education department; he added book classes for young people, French and German, and useful and fine arts; then published a book catalogue arranged alphabetically by author.[33] After a short trial period, he reclassified the collection, using the Dewey Decimal system (except fiction and juvenile books). Lancefield commented on the "great practical utility" of the decimal system in his annual report for 1891. It is not certain why he chose to use Melvil Dewey's classification, but Lancefield's ideas and practices were far in advance of the average Ontario librarian.

In the same annual report Lancefield mentioned that older students, a group not normally catered to, were beginning to use the central library regularly.

It is a pleasure, therefore, to record the fact that no class uses the Library in all departments – reading rooms as well as books – more than the teachers and students of the various schools, embracing the Collegiate Institute, the Business Colleges and the Art School... the student has use of the dictionaries, encyclopedias and other valuable aids in preparing essays or following up special lines of study.[34]

Hamilton's age limitation for borrowing, set at fourteen years, was relaxed by most standards and would remain in place for many years. Public libraries were for adults; children's libraries were just beginning to become fashionable in America and Great Britain.[35]

Hamilton's building opened to much fanfare in September 1890 (Illus. 16). The architect, William Stewart, had the honour of supervising the construction of the first Ontario building exclusively designed as a free library. It cost about $45,000 – more than twice the original estimate the Ontario Association of Architects had criticized for being unreasonably low.[36] The library interior was just over 5,000 square feet to serve a city of about 49,000, and internal accommodation followed North American experience: a reference room and two reading rooms (one for ladies, one for general readers) flanked a nine-foot corridor leading to a long counter for borrowing transactions and indicators, a catalogue area, and librarian's platform. Indicators were a British invention. They had numerous compartments where tiny cases which recorded the call numbers for books were stored. The ends of each insert were coloured, e.g., red (out) and blue (in), to reveal a book's status. The public could determine the availability of a book from the front side, while staff replaced the inserts from the rear when a book's circulation status changed.[37] Behind the counters was a 33 ft. x 58 ft. stack room, which was closed to the public and fitted up with shelves to hold 50,000 books.

The library's exterior architecture was conventional eclectic, a mixture of late-Victorian Romanesque style, highlighted by an impressive wheelwindow, a feature Stewart also utilized in many churches. To complete the facility, rooms for an Art School and the Hamilton Association occupied the upper floor. In Ontario, at least, the combination of a museum and art school with a library was accepted readily by planners. Ratepayers doubtless found this union cost effective. When the Earl and Countess of Aberdeen presided at the festive opening, the Hamilton *Spectator* boasted that Hamilton had the best arranged and finest looking public library in Canada, and that the ratepayers, who financed the project, should be proud that they, unlike Torontonians, had not patched up an old building.[38]

Hamilton's gala opening was a singular event. Only a handful of small free libraries existed, and many of these were housed in street-front stores like the one in St. Thomas. Library support outside these communities was meagre. Few organized groups actively promoted libraries. Only the National Council of Women of Canada (NCWC), founded in 1893 by Lady Aberdeen, and a few local Boards of Trade headed by businessmen or professionals seemed interested in supporting the cause on a wider basis in the 1890s. The National Council was situated in large cities, and considered temperance and correct morals to be bellwethers for good living. Community boards of trade were flourishing, particularly in the province's southwest; they promoted a host of commercial and economic interests such as trade policy, tariffs, railway rates, immigration, and labour relations.

Boards of trade also dabbled in general social welfare topics. Businessmen realized that improved educational facilities were necessary to train the work force for industrial occupations. At Chatham the board helped form a free library in January 1890, following a December meeting at which its president urged members to prepare literature and assist in canvassing wards.[39] At North Bay, in 1895, a committee of the Board of Trade organized a public library in August with Arthur G. Browning, a solicitor and active member of the board, as president. In the ensuing year library management convinced council to bring the library under municipal control. Browning continued as vice-president. He later became a deputy minister in Alberta politics and typified the progressive attitude many boards of trade fostered during this period.[40]

One of the multifarious interests of the National Council of Women of Canada was the effect of questionable reading matter on the public.[41] Since libraries provided an opportunity to improve the standard of reading, there was a peripheral attraction between library promoters and the NCWC. The first major effort for a free library by a women's local council was a well-financed campaign in Ottawa that fell short of its goal. It was another melancholy lesson in civic politics. As early as March 1895, the local council had presented a petition to aldermen to form a free library. A month later, a special Saturday issue of the Ottawa *Citizen* prepared by women library supporters raised $600. It was a considerable war chest. In the autumn, the women rented an office from which to organize public meetings and circulate promotional literature. However, their campaign failed to blunt the challenge of municipal economy raised by critics. At the municipal elections, on 6 January 1896, the library bylaw was decisively defeated by a vote of 3429 to 1968.[42] Understandably, this thrashing convinced NCWC local committees to discontinue active promotion of libraries and to concentrate on the issue of pernicious literature in schools, libraries, and bookstores.

Only a few free libraries were formed between 1890 and 1895: Chatham, Ingersoll, London, and Windsor. There was a certain satisfaction with

Mechanics' Institutes as libraries that was unmatched outside Ontario; after all, they had provided books for the reading public with the government's active encouragement for more than forty years.[43] A plethora of small, one-room institute libraries with perimeter wall shelving, a few chairs and other bare necessities, took advantage of the departmental grants. A good example was the institute run by James Howe at Southampton (Illus. 17). It seemed to be a time of complacency, a time for measuring success, and not a time for free library advocates to reflect on future possibilities or structures.

The education department under George Ross was basking in the accolades it received at the World's Columbian Exposition at Chicago in 1893, where Dr. May again worked his magic with Ontario's exhibit.[44] At this gala exhibition, surrounded by a giant midway, electrical lights, magnificent landscaped fairgrounds, and neoclassical revival architecture, the Ontario education exhibit celebrated its accomplishments in a separate Canadian pavilion, an indicator of growing national stature. One of the department's wall charts detailed the progress of free libraries and institutes between 1883 and 1892:

Statistics	1883	1892
Libraries and institutes	93	233
Members and readers	13,672	75,425
Reading rooms	59	143
Newspapers and periodicals	1,540	8,949
Volumes	154,093	468,383
Circulation	251,920	1,333,304 [45]

At first glance, these figures were quite respectable to fairgoers, but further inspection would raise uncomfortable questions.

The U.S. Bureau of Education report released in the same year implied that Canadian public libraries might benefit from some invigoration. The report continued to identify "public library" in the traditional sense: libraries available for public use in a variety of institutions and societies, and libraries open to specific classes of people. However, in consideration of the growth of free public libraries, which had larger collections, the report limited its observations to libraries of at least a 1,000 volumes. At one stroke this eliminated about half the Mechanics' Institute libraries in Ontario. The report found 202 libraries met this requirement in Canada – 152 in Ontario. Eleven free libraries were operating under Ontario's 1882 legislation; 108 institutes made up the majority (only one other institute reported in Canada!); thirty-three other public libraries also were recorded. Additional details on thirty-three larger public libraries in Ontario (118 did not report, mostly institutes) revealed that thirteen charged fees and twenty did not; sixteen were strictly for reference; and seventeen were both circulating and reference libraries.[46] These sober figures disclosed that the public library movement had gained a foothold in Ontario, but, as the redoubtable English library champion, Thomas Greenwood, observed the following year, it "has not yet taken deep root inside Canada."[47]

From Free Libraries to Public Libraries

When would beneficial conditions materialize for public library progress? Within two years, significant changes occurred. Although the education department's reports in the first part of the 1890s indicate satisfaction with the prevailing system and the rising level of legislative aid, firmer direction and less government largesse were to become the order of the day. Education had become a public enterprise, not a voluntary one, and a recession had cut into government revenue. The effectiveness of Mechanics' Institutes was in question: a report on technical education issued by the agriculture department in 1893 omitted their mention altogether.[48] Next year, 1894, William Wood again challenged departmental policy by asking for another legislative return showing the location of free libraries and Mechanics' Institutes in cities, towns, villages, and unincorporated villages as well as the electoral districts where farmers' institutes had not been established. But this return was not printed for the legislature, probably because it unveiled no new information.[49] Finally, in spring 1895, George Ross introduced a bill that consolidated Mechanics' Institutes and free libraries into one act.

When Ross tabled the consolidation bill in the legislature, there was virtually no debate. Even in Ontario, the Mechanics' Institutes had become an anachronism; their metamorphosis into public libraries was to receive swift legislative sanction.

> The change of name from 'free library' and 'Mechanics' Institute' to 'public library' was carried, and the bill was passed. Mr. W.B. Wood objected to the decrease in the grant to individual Mechanics' Institutes, which, he said, would bear hardly upon the smaller institutes. Hon. Mr. Ross replied that the number of these institutes had so greatly increased that a decrease of this sort was necessary, as the Government did not care to increase the vote for this purpose. The sum, he said, was distributed in the most equitable manner.[50]

The total grant for public libraries was struck at $46,000 by the Lieutenant Governor. The education department issued new regulations at the close of the financial year in May.

The 1895 Act (58 Vic., c. 45) was subdivided into four main parts. Part I repeated legislation for the formation of free libraries and retained the old mill rate, despite the constant criticism of its inadequacy for smaller communities. Part II brought the older institutes and library associations into the municipal sphere. Local councils were empowered to create a board of management for a public library upon receiving a petition from a majority of directors on the old board of management requesting transfer of assets to the corporation. These were designated public libraries (not free); they were not eligible for the library rate but could obtain municipal contributions of varying amounts. All libraries operating under this section were to be open to the public free of charge; however, voluntary subscriptions were always welcome. Part III allowed at least ten citizens to incorporate for public library purposes, to appoint a board of management, and to receive a legislative grant. These libraries had to sustain a membership of at least one hundred persons: fifty over the age of twenty-one years; no member to be under twelve years old. The Dominion Grange protested in 1896 that these criteria were too rigorous for rural communities.[51]

A concluding section of the act on ways and means introduced a new dollar-for-dollar grant formula: for libraries, the government would give $200 to cities, $150 to towns, and $100 in other cases; for reading rooms, there was a $50 maximum; and for evening classes, the maximum continued at $100. In the following year, the formula changed again – $200 became the maximum for libraries based on the dollar-for-dollar principle, which now allowed local boards to use credit vouchers when applying to Dr. May for a grant (59 Vic., c. 57, s. 2). Libraries that failed to open for two years were to be dissolved, and their books, magazines, and periodicals could be seized by the department for disposal or transfer to other libraries.

Dr. May and the department set to work to prepare some suitable guidelines and regulations. Obviously, stricter expectations were in order for libraries. The "management and control" of public library legislation by the Education Department was formalized in a statute (59 Vic., c. 69, s. 3). Another innovation, a one hundred page catalogue of six thousand books, appeared in November 1895 "for the guidance of Book Committees." Coincidentally, booksellers were doing a thriving business with "bestsellers," such as George Du Maurier's *Trilby*, first released in 1894 to instant success, and Anthony Hope's romantic novel *The Prisoner of Zenda*. In fact, the magazine, *The Bookman*, had introduced a bestselling list in 1895, in which fiction usually predominated. This was always a vexatious statistic for educationalists.[52] On the thorny subject of reading standards, the departmental catalogue, which omitted both *Trilby* and *Zenda*, seemed more concerned with fiction's position on library shelves:

At the present time there is a great diversity in the methods employed in our Libraries in the classification of Fiction: on inspection it has frequently been found, that books of Adventure, Historical Tales, Religious Literature, Moral Tales, Essays, etc., are classified as Fiction. In our classification we enter Novels only as fiction. Books of Adventure are classified with Voyages and Travels. Historical Tales with History, etc.[53]

Dr. May's recipe for fiction classification was bound to attract criticism as readers became more selective.

New and more stringent regulations appeared at the beginning of the financial year in May. Library buildings and reading rooms were to be situated in places convenient to the public. The exterior sign "Public Library" was to be in letters at least four inches long and three inches wide. Rooms were to be properly warmed and lighted. Reading rooms required racks and files for papers, five weeklies, two dailies, and three standard monthly magazines. Seating accommodation for no fewer than ten people was necessary. All libraries and reading rooms were to be open at least three days every week for issuing and exchanging books. Only twenty percent of the government grant for books was allowed for fiction. Books needed to be properly stamped, labelled, shelved, and kept in good order. Librarians were required to keep a stock catalogue showing titles and prices paid for books, to retain a borrowers' register, and to hold a record book detailing charges and discharges. An annual report had to be transmitted to the department.[54]

From George Ross's practical perspective, there were two suitable locales for public library service: cities and larger towns which could support free public libraries by means of debentures which could be used to construct and furnish suitable buildings; and smaller municipalities which were unwilling or unable to finance a building but could afford moderate operating sums for public libraries (not free).[55] The small libraries needed greater direction and commensurately more government money and encouragement if they were to promote free public library bylaws. The consolidated legislation, regulations, and other aids were beneficial public policy changes that exhibited general agreement on the broader, more relevant community appeal of public library service. Compared to the individualism associated with Mechanics' Institutes, the concept of free libraries was more broadly based. Ross himself emphasized the community aspect at London:

> This library is a post-graduate university, at which the citizens of London who have left public and high schools may

take a post-graduate course, which Shakespeare or none of the great writers of the Elizabethan age, or of the early Georges, could avail themselves of. All honor to the municipality for donating the money; all honor to the board for doing their work so well, and to the architect who garnished the building with lines of beauty.[56]

The city's new library building, opened in November 1895, was viewed as a source of community pride, a symbol of progress in late Victorian Canada.

London's red-brick library was designed by Herbert Matthews, a London native who had worked briefly in a New York architectural firm. The Romanesque style and interior design of the two-storey London library represented conventional civic architectural thinking. Its conical towers, rounded arches, and smooth-faced red-brick cladding were fashionable and appealing in the mid-1890s (Illus. 18). Hamilton's library had utilized the same revival style, one which imparted a sense of permanence and strength. Inside, to the left of the entrance, were large reading and reference rooms. The closed stack bookroom was to the right side of the entrance. In the centre were magazines, the circulating desk, and public indicator. The London Historical Society's Museum occupied the second floor. The building with furnishings cost approximately $16,000.[57]

The new librarian, Robert J. Blackwell, formerly a bookseller, commenced his duties in April 1895 (Illus. 19). Blackwell was part traditionalist (the period of the bookman-librarian was still in vogue across Ontario) and part innovator. At this time, the concept of library economy – the administration and management of libraries according to accepted standards and regulations – was pervasive in library organization and activities. It was reinforced by an ALA 1896 publication on good library practices.[58] Blackwell, however, was willing to experiment with new ideas. When the ALA presented the results of a survey of libraries which had children's reading-rooms, at Chautauqua in 1898, Blackwell reported that a juvenile room was "hoped for" in London.[59] He was one of the few chief librarians in Canada, other than James Bain, to frequent annual ALA conventions when they were held within a reasonable distance from Ontario. He also played a supportive part in the formation of the Ontario Library Association in 1900/01 and served on its executive until cancer began to dissipate his strength. He died, still in office, in March 1906.[60]

Blackwell introduced London to free access to all books except novels. Fiction readers continued to rely on the British indicator system for circulation status. Some American and British managers considered indicators obsolete and time-consuming because new cataloguing, classification, and charging improvements eliminated the need for them in an open access collection. Blackwell came to adopt this view. He issued a classed book catalogue in 1897, using the decimal system and a thorough subject index; its appearance, along with a comparable catalogue completed at Hamilton by Richard Lancefield in the same year, showed the advantages of the new decimal classi- fication system for finding subjects.[61] When renovations took place in 1902, Blackwell and the board insisted on a separate ladies reading room to improve decorum. These rooms were popular until the first decade of the twentieth century.[62]

The merging of the two streams of thought on library service – rate-sup- ported free libraries and traditional subscription libraries – immediately made the formation of public library boards easier. After the first year of the new act's operation, 1895/96, there were 54 free public libraries. By the end of 1901, there were 132 free public library boards scattered across the province, serving nearly a quarter of the total population (Map 1: Free Libraries by County or Census District in 1901). Although growth in the number of libraries between 1895 and 1901 was impressive, many recently established free libraries were dangerously dependent on the bounty and goodwill of municipal councils. The legal public library rate was a maximum figure; the actual rate could be reduced by council. Public libraries were popular because it was relatively easy to procure legislative grants and keep local tax levies at a minimum!

There were different opinions about the appropriateness of the half-mill library rate. Some felt that it was too low. Dr. May noted in his 1889 report that the British rate, a penny on the pound, was the equivalent of four mills on the dollar in Canada.[63] However, exact comparisons with conditions in Britain were misleading because the Ontario mill rate followed American practice. Whereas in Britain the library rate was levied on the annual rateable value of a town, essentially its rental value, in Ontario the rate was set on the actual assessed value of real estate and personal property. British municipalities normally operated on lower total assessments. When British and Ontario municipalities of similar size were compared to each other, the Ontario mill rate usually yielded more money for libraries.[64] Perhaps for this reason, Ontario's library directors faced a daunting task when they tried to achieve the maximum mill rate.

In Toronto, where the special rate had been reduced to one-quarter mill, the council usually cut back on the estimates the board requested. This prac- tice became a point of contention in the late 1890s. The board became con- vinced that the erosion of its power had proceeded too far following the 1892 amendment. Its annual reports often included a threat to resist this routine encroachment. Finally, the board, which had the benefit of counsel from lawyer-trustees such as Hugh T. Kelly, sought redress by seeking a court ruling on the matter in 1900. The judgement handed down was in the board's favour: it was within its rights under the law to demand the full mill rate.[65] The directors at least had the satisfaction of budgeting the full amount in their estimates. However, most library budgets were small in relation to other municipal operations and did not grow appreciably in the period 1895-1902 (Table 8: Comparative Statistics of Ontario Cities, 1901). In most cities the total mill rate was barely more than twenty mills. An increase to the public library rate by legislative amendment was not considered to be a realistic possibility. In a few cities – Ottawa, Kingston, Belleville, Woodstock – attaining free status remained the primary goal for library advocates.

Modern Methods

As the nineteenth century drew to a close, new technological, managerial, and organizational changes were transforming the face of institutions across North America. The recognizable Victorian synthesis of ideas and cultural framework was giving way to "radical" modernist thought and the mechanization of technology. Names familiar during the early days of Ontario's free libraries – John Hallam, John Taylor, William Edwards, Emmanuel Essery, William Cochrane – were no longer part of the movement. New leaders, such as Edwin Hardy, were coming to the fore. They were anxious to elevate the debate about library services, popular book collections, and internal organization. They also were interested in new library services and techniques pioneered in the United States. The modern age was touted as an age of betterment; it was an appeal few librarians or trustees could resist.

Some bookmen, such as the author George Iles, magnified the potential that libraries possessed to edify large numbers of people. Iles, originally from Gibraltar, had lived in Montreal before he moved permanently to New York in 1887. For many years, he promoted the idea of literature appraisals by trustworthy authorities. They would choose the best books and justify their preferences to readers by means of annotations. Iles's scheme became better known in Canada after *The Week* published a speech he made at the 1896 ALA conference in Cleveland.[66] He was motivated in part by Goldwin Smith and others who felt libraries should emphasize collections of important literature. Iles followed with another paper on the evaluation of literature at the second International Library Conference held in London in 1897, as part of Queen Victoria's Diamond Jubilee celebration. He was a member of a large foreign contingent that included Hugh Langton from University of Toronto and Charles Gould from McGill University.[67] Subsequently, Iles published an article in *Library Journal* advocating the creation of a central bureau to assess literature. Its accessions would record remarks on catalogue cards as an aid to the general reading public.[68] In 1902, Iles gave the American Library Association $10,000 to support publication of *The Literature of American History* to which James Bain contributed Canadian history reviews. This work became a standard bibliographic guide.

American library practices and ideas were exerting a strong influence by the mid-1890s, despite the feeling in nationalist and imperialist quarters that the brash republican neighbour could learn much from Canada, the elder daughter of the empire, and from Albion, its wise parent. William I. Fletcher, ALA president in 1891/92, commented on Canadian libraries:

> In the Toronto library a librarian from the States would feel quite at home, the arrangement of the library in its different departments and the methods of administration being such as are most approved among us. One exception is to be noted, namely, the use of the 'indicator,' an apparatus quite common in the larger libraries of Great Britain but never a permanent accessory in the United States.[69]

Although Canadian political loyalties remained within the imperial orbit, geography determined that ties with American libraries in northeastern states were easier to maintain than transatlantic bonds.[70]

Despite anti-American sentiment fuelled by strong Canadian nationalism, the imperial tie and British library practices were beginning to wane in Ontario. The Toronto *Globe's* front page might salute Canadian libraries and trumpet national sovereignty with reference to Rudyard Kipling's poem, "Our Lady of the Snows," which dramatized Canada's 1897 decision to declare a preferential tariff for the Mother Country (Illus. 20); Empire Day might be a special school festival inaugurated in 1898 to reinforce the imperial connection; and Richard Lancefield might publish his laudatory biography, *Victoria Sixty Years a Queen*, to commemorate her jubilee year; but in the library world even British librarians were debating the merits of experimental American ideas such as unrestricted open access and very low age limits for all children.[71] Even the terminology "public library" was now preferred in Britain, the term "free library" having acquired such a stigma associated with poor people that Thomas Greenwood was eager to jettison it completely.[72]

By the 1890s, American librarians were serving younger children (both girls and boys), providing innovative legislation for rural areas, and attracting more middle-class patrons in large cities. Improved conditions in library service were quite evident in urban centres where municipal government was expanding rapidly.[73] Business office techniques, supplies, and equipment also were finding a congenial place in libraries: filing systems, catalogue cards, and typewriters were modernizing management theory and clerical systems. Canadian libraries were beginning to take note and experiment accordingly. Support for certain British conventions – indicators, reading rooms for boys, separate newspaper rooms, and limited open access in circulating libraries – was eroding.

Dr. May, a traditional Victorian who favoured orthodoxy and possessed a healthy skepticism about untested ideas, was dispatched by the education department in 1901 to tour library systems in New York, Philadelphia, and Buffalo. Dr. May was past his seventieth year; this trip would be his last major library investigation. Portions of his sober report disclosed that many Ontario libraries were not keeping abreast with American advances in circulation, public access, children's services, and other methods that were modernizing internal operations.

> It is gratifying to state that the Public Libraries in Ontario are conducted at much less cost than the Libraries in the United States. For example, on the 1st January, 1900: [specific accounts for central libraries and branches in New York, Philadelphia, and Buffalo followed at this point] ...
>
> This shows that 280 Libraries, viz, 21 Libraries, 30 School Libraries and 229 Travelling Libraries issued 3,479,975 books. Total expenditure, $321,127.31.
>
> *Ontario.* – 371 libraries loaned 2,043,904 volumes.
>
> *Open Shelf System.* This would not be successful in Ontario; it would require too many assistants, and I am pleased to say that in nearly all our libraries the public are not allowed access to the shelves. It will be noticed that in Buffalo they have 81 employees, salaries $42,092.29.
>
> *Fiction.* The proportion of fiction issued in the United States is much higher than in Ontario.
>
> Children's libraries in free libraries, and school libraries, cannot be too much commended; when inspecting libraries I always try to impress upon the officials the necessity of encouraging the young to read books that will give them information which will be useful to them ...
>
> *Fines.* – the libraries in the United States are stringent in their rules for return of books, and derive quite a revenue from fines. In Ontario this rule could be enforced in free libraries, but in libraries subscribed for by member it is impracticable, ...
>
> *Missing Books.* – The rule in the United States free

libraries is for the loser to pay the price of the missing books. In some of our free libraries, in addition of the cost of replacing books, the authorities demand the amount forfeited for fines;... I do not think that this could be legally enforced, and have advised boards where the matter has been discussed to charge for the missing book only.[74]

The status quo was still acceptable to Dr. May.

If Dr. May was not ready for the quickened pace of change, there were others in the education department who were. Richard Harcourt, a former school inspector, assumed the ministerial duties at the end of 1899 when George Ross became Premier. Harcourt was reputed to be more progressive, to be attuned to the child-centred ideas of the New Education Movement, although he thoroughly approved of the traditional moral strand in education.[75] The *fin-de-siècle* mood, together with the death of Victoria in January 1901, perhaps furthered his desire to give more prominence to the cause of education in the province. He wrote in the department's annual report for 1900:

> Canada may well take a hopeful view of the future if a genuine love of religion and truth permeates the training given to the rising generation. With such a spirit may the reign of the new King be entered upon by all the pupils of our schools. In this way the highest patriotism may be manifested, and that person may be regarded as the best patriot who seeks to aid in all movements that look to the instruction, the elevation and the permanent betterment of all our citizens.[76]

Could library service be refashioned in this manner?

A rising power destined to administer policy in the education department between 1906 and 1919, John Seath, saw a definite need for some improvement in libraries, particularly those in rural areas. Seath discovered that few library boards exercised their authority to organize evening classes and operate technical schools. He recognized that evening classes in libraries might prove popular among school leavers, and he suggested that about $10,000 per annum be diverted from the grant to Mechanics' Institutes (he was still using the old name as late as 1900) in order to finance central libraries under the control of county inspectors. These libraries would use the money to purchase books on manual training.[77] Seath continued to use the term public libraries for libraries in schools, and he obviously was wedded to the older terminology and concepts of public library service harking back to the Ryerson era.

Harcourt himself was anxious to energize school library work and was unimpressed with the tardy progress of small public libraries in rural areas, although he was satisfied libraries were working well in larger urban communities.

Harcourt's and Seath's concerns about rural libraries were shared by others. The involvement of farmers' institutes with libraries remained a lively issue. In 1897, the Prince Edward Farmers' Institute protested the "serious lack of agricultural literature in the Public Libraries in towns and villages." It suggested that five percent of the government grant (ten dollars) be designated for agricultural subjects.[78] An order-in-council was drafted in 1899 using this formula for library books on agriculture, forestry, horticulture, road improvement, and kindred subjects, but it was never signed into law.[79] The Education Department did ease its regulations somewhat by allowing those rural boards which were unable to be open three times a week to open once or twice, but it also decreased the grant in these cases.[80]

James Bain addressed the problem of rural library service at the Canadian Institute in December 1897. His solution was travelling libraries working in conjunction with public schools. These libraries were working successfully in New York and Wisconsin.

> Our school system, by providing school sections of moderate area, each with its school-house and teacher, seems to have placed the machinery ready to hand. In Wisconsin about one-third of the libraries are kept in the postoffice, one-half in farm houses and the remainder in small stores. But with the school master as librarian and the school-house as the distributing post, the most widely-scattered farm population could be easily reached, while the results of the daily tasks would be more satisfactory. By supplying also in this way the smaller existing Public Libraries, which are barely able to add to their collections, boxes of 100 new books every six months, fresh life would be thrown into them and their readers brought into contact with the literature of the day.[81]

Bain advised that some money from the legislative grant be shifted over to travelling libraries. Travelling library service and rural school libraries, a neglected topic after Ryerson's retirement in 1876, were about to emerge as important issues.

There was good reason for Harcourt to be satisfied with the progress of libraries in cities and larger towns. Bain noted that the per capita percentage of books was not unworthy of a province recently "redeemed from the wilderness." However, there remained ample room for improvement. He knew that scholarship required larger collections, better facilities, more qualified staff. The Toronto Public Library, which was housed in the old Mechanics' Institute building on Church street, with its elegant and massive newspaper reading room (Illus. 22), was no longer suitable for special collections and expanded, modernized reference services. With this in mind, Bain advocated a Toronto based provincial reference library at the service of the entire province. He recommended:

1. The Province and Toronto jointly maintain a Provincial Reference Library, free to every Ontarian;
2. The Province erect suitable buildings in a suitable locality for the joint reference library;
3. The Legislative Library transfer its general books to the joint reference library and concentrate on legislative services;
4. The Canadian Institute transfer its books to the joint reference library in return for a suitable meeting room;
5. Regulations be drafted for students in Ontario to share the use of the books.[82]

Bain's ideas were publicized widely in the Christmas day 1897 issue of the Toronto *Globe*.

A number of prominent people in the Canadian Institute formed a provisional committee in December 1898 to promote a provincial reference library and the deployment of travelling libraries. They published a circular in January 1899 to convince the Ontario government of the need for better coordination of library resources. Their efforts, however, were not rewarded. Even though there was no other "English-speaking people as numerous as that of this Province which does not possess a Reference Library,"[83] the education department was not receptive to bearing the costs for any centralized system. Toronto, Hamilton, and London were the only places ready for the type of service anticipated by James Bain. But travelling libraries were another matter. They captured the department's attention because they were successful in American states, notably neighbouring New York. Within a few years, the department would begin its own economical travelling library service for northern regions in "New Ontario."

The state of Canadian libraries and status of Canadian librarians were reviewed in 1902 by Lawrence Burpee (Illus. 21), a civil servant in the Laurier administration. He outlined progress in cataloguing, classification, circulation systems, and the role of the librarian, in a paper to the Royal Society of

Canada entitled "Modern Public Libraries and their Methods." Burpee surveyed twenty-four of the more important libraries in the country. Seventeen of this number were located in Ontario.[84] Almost all of these were free libraries (Dundas and Niagara were public but not free). Burpee found that most libraries were moderate in size. A majority of them operated with one or two staff members. The exceptions were Toronto (16), Hamilton (7), London and Brantford (4), and Brockville (3). Collections ranged from 111,725 books in Toronto to 3,366 in Lindsay. St. Thomas reported the median: 7,293. Dundas had the lowest circulation figures (5,941); St. Thomas the median (21,511); and Toronto naturally was the highest (539,226). Fiction remained a staple in home borrowing. Only four libraries reported that fiction accounted for under fifty per cent of the total number of circulating books.

Technological improvements in the delivery of service were beginning to catch hold in urban libraries. The older printed catalogue, supplemented at intervals, remained the standard device for identifying books, although Paris continued to rely on the outdated manuscript catalogue. Only London, St. Thomas, and Brockville used card catalogues adapted from business enterprises. Libraries were experimenting with "guarded" open access to shelves. Berlin, Elora, Dundas, Hamilton, Niagara, Paris, and Stratford were among the pioneers to implement careful supervision and controlled admittance to certain areas. Since open access allowed people to move more freely among books and periodicals, an easily understandable classification system and systematic shelving arrangements became crucial. If the public were to locate and retrieve their own books, a simple but expensive innovation such as a reduction in the height of shelving units would be necessary. Ladders were no longer practical. Opposition to open access often centred on the costs involved in the transformation.

The education department's classification system was a modification of William Edward's scheme. Over the years it had retained its popularity, but Burpee questioned whether it might be "dignified with the name of a system." Hamilton and London had already adopted the Dewey Decimal Classification with enthusiasm; Toronto's reference department was using modified Dewey. In fact, the department's system had been criticized previously in the legislature by a Conservative member, Arthur Matheson, for failing to reflect accurately the circulation of fiction.[85] Dr. May, however, had continued to issue circulars on "uniform classification" that simply expanded Edwards' scheme. By 1900 the department's entire classification had become a muddled combination of subject matter, printed format, and readers' ages or preferences:

I. History: 1) Ancient, 2) Mediaeval, 3) Modern, 4) Miscellaneous.
II. Biography: 1) Individual, 2) Collective.
III. Voyages, Adventure and Travel: 1) World, 2) Europe, 3) Asia, 4) Africa, 5) America, 6) Arctic Region, 7) Australia, New Zealand, Pacific Ocean, 8) The Ocean, Sea and Sailors, 9) Miscellaneous.
IV. Science and Art: 1) Natural Science (e.g., Zoology, Botany, Astronomy, Physics, Chemistry), 2) Useful Arts (e.g., Agriculture, Electric Arts, Microscope, Architecture and Engineering, Carpentry, General Science), 3) Fine Arts, 4) Domestic Arts, 5) English Language and Art of Teaching.
V. General Literature (e.g., Law and Constitutional History, Moral Tales).
VI. Poetry and Drama.
VII. Religious Literature (mostly Christian).
VIII. Fiction.
IX. Miscellaneous Books: 1) Anecdotes and Short Stories, 2) Detective Stories, 3) Fairy Tales, Fables, etc.
X. Reference Books: 1) Dictionaries and Encyclopedias, 2) Science and Art, Manufactures, etc.[86]

Indicators remained in vogue in Toronto, Hamilton, London, Berlin, Brockville and Collingwood. Loan procedures and records continued to be entered into the ledger book system, the roll and record books William Edwards had promoted for decades until shortly before his death in 1904.[87] Children's departments were virtually nonexistent, but Stratford and Berlin reported space would be available in their new Carnegie libraries. Burpee did not discuss the trend toward functional architecture and more integrated internal arrangements, but this modernist thinking was beginning to displace the Victorian preoccupation with picturesque styles and separate rooms. To Burpee, modern library methods coupled with able direction from educated, well-trained librarians offered almost limitless opportunities for service. He was enthusiastic about the potential of the public library:

> We are merely upon the threshold of a new era in the history of public libraries. What the present century may see, in the direction of increasing and broadening their mission as factors in the educational life of the community, it would be

difficult to foretell, but that influence will be deep and lasting, everyone who has studied the recent development of
public libraries, especially in the United States and England,
must feel heartily assured.[88]

He foresaw the promise of an enlarged library mission in the service of all the
people.

Perhaps the most important contemporary development, one that Burpee
completely ignored, appeared in his own tabulations where the names of
librarians or secretaries were recorded. Several women had risen to the post of
chief librarian in small cities and large towns: Effie A. Schmidt in Berlin,
Carrie R. Rowe in Brockville, Margaret Graham in Guelph, Janet Carnochan
in Niagara, and Eliza Morgan in St. Thomas. This was not an entirely new
trend, but an important extension of the women's sphere of work.[89] By the
mid-1890s, they occupied most positions in urban libraries. For example,
women held all the reference positions in the Toronto library (Illus. 24). A
report on working conditions and wages in 1892 found that the Toronto free
library paid women $300 for their first year and $400 for their second; a head
assistant could make $450 a year. These were relatively low wages, but, there
being no training schools for library workers, the pay compared favourably
with the average annual salary of $296 teachers were making.[90] As a rule, men
continued to hold the key positions in larger cities; only a few women, such as
Frances Staton in Toronto, rose to senior management positions early in the
new century.[91]

Women were beginning to enter the Ontario public library field and
attain a predominance they already enjoyed in primary teaching, nursing, and
similar low-paying positions that required eager, educated recruits: they were
"tender technicians."[92] The library's service mission in society – to educate,
uplift, and improve citizens – was an attractive one reckoned suitable for feminine talents. Burpee briefly hinted at the feminine contribution to the new
librarianship by borrowing a phrase from Minerva A. Sanders, chief librarian
at Pawtucket, Rhode Island: "the librarian should meet the reader in the position of a host or hostess welcoming a guest."[93] Since males encouraged this
outlook, the library was ready to assume a different atmosphere, one more
akin to the warmth of a home. The tendency towards staffing libraries with
well-educated, unmarried women was to continue in conjunction with the
modern office revolution that required women clerks, typists, stenographers,
and secretaries.[94] These trends would feminize most libraries and thrust gender to the forefront in a relatively young profession. From now on, as libraries
increased their service functions, librarians would play a more cordial, inter-

mediary role in the provision of information to patrons. The austere custodial image of libraries, which had prevailed until 1900, was destined to soften.

For the most part, however, neither the appeal of innovative techniques nor the impact of gender constituted a serious challenge to the library status quo. General progress continued to depend on the creation of free library boards, a process that broadened and strengthened the public library movement by adding more communities. A new generation of leaders would emerge and join Edwin Hardy and Lawrence Burpee. A sign of the times was the passage of the Sarnia free library bylaw at the end of November 1899. A small delegation, including a young lawyer, Norman Gurd, and a newspaper publisher, Robert McAdams, presented Sarnia aldermen with a petition for a free library signed by 180 ratepayers. The two men estimated that this service would cost $1000 a year, a small outlay. No determined public opposition surfaced at council or ward meetings in December; the main fear was rejection at the polls because four other money bylaws (water works, drains, sewers, and town hall) would also be on the same ballot. When votes were tallied in January 1900, the library bylaw passed by a vote of 733 to 217 – a majority of 516 – the largest margin for any money bylaw. Meanwhile, the town hall bylaw failed.[95] It was an auspicious beginning for a new public library, which began its existence in the first month of the first year of a new century.

PART THREE

The Modern Public
Library Emerges

Chapter 6

THE ONTARIO LIBRARY ASSOCIATION

It was Easter Monday, 8 April 1901, two o'clock in the afternoon, the Examiners' Room of the Normal School, St. James Square, Toronto. A small group of about thirty men and women gathered to hear James Bain explain the steps taken the year before at the American Library Association conference in Montreal to form a national (later provincial) library association. Edwin Hardy (Illus. 23), who along with Bain and Hugh Langton had worked tirelessly to arrange the first annual meeting, read the prepared draft constitution for the Ontario Library Association.[1] The delegates – including the provisional officers who had encouraged the OLA's formation, William Tytler, Richard Lancefield, William J. Robertson, and Robert Blackwell – signed a register, approved the draft with minor changes, then listened to two papers: "Modern Library Methods and Appliances for a Small Library" by Lancefield and "The Character of Books for a Small Library" read by M.L. Nutting for the Uxbridge publisher, William H. Keller.[2] The first session adjourned at five o'clock; it reconvened in the Department's theatre later the same evening. James Bain opened by reading his paper, "The Library Movement in Ontario." The deputy minister of education, John Millar, offered a warm welcome and encouragement to the delegates, who listened to three more papers before retiring for the night. It was a successful beginning.

The second day commenced with the formal election of the provisional officers: James Bain president, Hugh Langton first vice-president, Archibald Macallum treasurer, and Edwin Hardy secretary. The conference highlight followed. Edwin Hardy's paper, "The Outline Program of the Work of the Ontario Library Association," stressed four endeavours vital to the work of the OLA: assistance to libraries, the public, schools, and Sunday schools. Hardy suggested that a regular book selection guide would benefit all libraries and that bulletins and pamphlets on modern methods – loan charging systems, classification, and cataloguing – would increase a library's utility. Concerning the qualifications of librarians, Hardy proposed summer courses at London,

Hamilton, Toronto, and Ottawa; short training sessions in city libraries; and certification by the Education Department. He also mentioned joint projects which the OLA might sponsor: cooperative efforts in book loaning, prevention of duplication in collections, the retention of periodicals, classification of government publications, and affiliation of special libraries.

When it came to the reading public, the school system and Sunday schools, the OLA could work with citizens, teachers, and various denominations to encourage their patronage of free libraries. The association could stimulate public interest in library formation, help convert subscription libraries to free libraries, and encourage donations. Local history collections, a Canadian bibliography and other bibliographic pamphlets also could attract interested community groups. For Sunday schools and school libraries, the OLA could prepare lists of books suitable to their respective clientele and clarify the relationship between their libraries and free libraries. To initiate these projects, Hardy made three suggestions: all OLA publications should be issued as free government documents to public libraries; voluntary membership fees and a provincial grant should finance the OLA; and the association should encourage the formation of a library commission in Ontario similar to the one in Wisconsin. He concluded on a hopeful note: "that the library movement in Ontario is now entering upon a period of progress, scientifically directed, that will, in connection with her school system, place Ontario among the most highly cultured and genuinely prosperous portion of the world."[3]

By any measure, the OLA had embarked upon an ambitious program. It could count on hard-working delegates like Henry Robertson from Collingwood to advance the association's goals as set out by Hardy at the first meeting. He had been a reliable steward in the Mechanics' Institute for almost a half-century and was now a spokesman for a Carnegie library.[4] Robertson, and many others, would determine the success of activities as set out in the OLA's constitution.

> Its object shall be to promote the welfare of Libraries, by stimulating public interests in founding and improving them, by securing any need of legislation, by furthering such co-operative work as shall improve results or reduce expenses, by exchanging views and making recommendations in convention or otherwise, and by advancing the common interests of Librarians, Trustees and Directors and others engaged in library and allied in education work.[5]

It would be essential to attract more members in order to promote new library methods and services and to end the isolation that had inhibited public library development in Ontario. Dr. May's small branch in the Education Department clearly had not kept abreast with change. The OLA hoped that its missionary ideals would succeed where the government's passive strategy had failed.

The three principals who gave the OLA its initial impetus believed that they had concrete proposals on which to build better libraries. Bain wanted to promote a travelling library system as part of his dream for a provincial reference library; Hardy was totally dissatisfied with library classification ("a scandal"); and Langton was interested in the library commission form of governance that was gaining popularity in the United States. The three men agreed that stronger direction, planning, leadership, and encouragement of better-funded library boards were essential. The government and the legislative opposition fought over these issues until 1909, the year the old 1895 library act was revised completely. Far from being what the *Library Journal* editorialized as a "new auxiliary of the American Library Association," the OLA was to be an regional association in its own right, working for government reform in libraries.[6]

The new minister of education, Richard Harcourt; his deputy minister, John Millar; and Dr. May were ready to accommodate reforms, but they were reluctant to accept the entire agenda put forward by the OLA. In any event, Dr. May's tenure as superintendent was coming to a close; he was a septuagenarian. A Victorian with eclectic tastes, he had divided his time between free libraries, Mechanics' Institutes, art schools, museums, and exhibitions; he had never specialized in library work except at the despised depository; he had never expanded his duties as inspector; and he had never accepted wholeheartedly the new trends taking place in technical education. A transition was underway; it was time to reassess the structure and function of library service in Ontario. While Dr. May's superintendency was reduced in stages, the OLA struggled to attain primacy for its ideas.

A "Proper Footing"

Ontario libraries had need of new ideas and vigorous leadership. The *Canadian Magazine* for one was not impressed with its public libraries: "Our public libraries have never been recognized as part of our educational system; they have been regarded as simply luxuries for those who wished to use them. Who will lead in a movement to place libraries on their proper footing?"[7] Nor were some librarians or trustees satisfied. In response to Lawrence Burpee's panegyric on modern methods, one reviewer wrote in dismay, "I realized that the true library spirit is yet in its infancy in Ontario."[8] Edwin Hardy reported that only twenty-five places could afford to pay the basic $300 salary per annum for a librarian's service.[9]

At this juncture, the OLA was still too young, too diminutive to exert much influence. It needed a firm organizational base; it lacked the mechanics of preparing programs for regular conventions, corresponding with executive members, making travel arrangements, and balancing a small budget. Bain's tenure as president, however, was not uneventful. The OLA's executive received a setback in February 1902 when Richard Lancefield, a member of the founding committee and an OLA councillor, fled Hamilton after defrauding the library of thousands of dollars.[10] No charges were ever laid, but his disappearance became a *cause célèbre* in the local newspapers. Lancefield moved to Toronto, and an awkward silence enveloped his past career. This embarrassing episode coincided with Bain's failure to arouse much enthusiasm for a central reference library and with a revival of the debate over a mandatory library rate. In the wake of Lancefield's dishonor, Henry Carscallen, the Conservative member from Hamilton East, introduced a bill that proposed to allow councils to revise board estimates and limit the rate to a one-quarter mill on the dollar for cities with fewer than 100,000 inhabitants, i.e., all cities except Toronto, which already operated under this condition. Fortunately for Bain and the OLA, the government blocked Carscallen's private bill.[11]

On the positive side, forces outside the OLA were working hard on Bain's suggestion concerning travelling libraries. Reverend Alfred Fitzpatrick, a Presbyterian minister, and Walter Brown, who had recently returned to Canada after working for the YMCA in Chicago and St. Louis, were lobbying the government to establish this service.[12] Fitzpatrick's main interest lay in the lumbering camps of northern Ontario where reading matter was meager at best. This type of work suited his missionary temperament and led ultimately to the formation of Frontier College. Walter Brown was more concerned to erect libraries in rural agricultural districts and to develop popular education in voluntary associations, such as farmers' institutes. The department of agriculture also had contacted Richard Harcourt about the role of farmers' institutes.[13] Brown was embarking upon a career in the field of adult education that would eventually take him to the University of Western Ontario.

Walter Brown wrote Richard Harcourt at the outset of 1900, outlining his ambitious plan, which was based on his experiences in Chicago and St. Louis. In Brown's words, the department should establish

> a 'Travelling Library Bureau', which would undertake to select the most popular and most helpful books on a wide range of subjects, and place them in cases (100 in each case), and so distribute them that every school section and neighborhood in Ontario might have the use of an up-to-date library. The Bureau should encourage, by adequate supervi-

sion, the formation of literary societies, debating clubs, and
magazine reading circles; conduct essay competitions, orator-
ical contests, and debates, by counties, districts and for the
Province. Subjects might be assigned, and awards made in
the form of medals, college and university scholarships, etc.
The Bureau might also co-operate with existing institutions
and movements that the people may have advantage of the
largest number of lectures and talks possible.[14]

Brown suggested dividing Ontario into sixty districts and starting fifty
libraries in each district – three thousand libraries in total! Rural postmasters
could serve as librarians and guardians of the book cases. Families and individuals could purchase cards to charge out books. Brown estimated that $25 for
each neighbourhood would produce an annual revenue of $75,000 towards
the cost of his scheme.

The enthusiastic correspondent continued to write the department about
his plans. During the spring he sent Harcourt information on American state
laws and agencies. Brown discussed his ideas with James Bain, who felt it was
overly ambitious to encourage societies, contests, and other activities.[15] Brown
even offered his services as manager of the program. But, by mid-summer, the
deputy minister replied that the department could not arrange anything in
the near future and that Brown was "at liberty to undertake any private enterprise in connection with the project."[16] Perhaps the magnitude of the scheme
dissuaded the department from adopting his proposals. When the department
finally commenced its operations later in 1901, only $1,200 was spent to ship
boxes of fifty books per box to lumber camps in the first year. The amount
increased to $2,000 in the second year. Brown's experience with the depart-
ment was not a happy one, and he later complained that he should have
approached the agriculture department first.[17]

By August 1900, Alfred Fitzpatrick was writing to Dr. May about travelling libraries. He had "come to the conclusion that small libraries may be put
into lumber and mining camps, and that a series of lectures and sermons may
with success be arranged for."[18] Unlike Bain or Brown, however, Fitzpatrick
was able to use his contacts in the new north – at Little Current, Nairn
Centre, and Algoma – to pressure the department into activity. In September,
Fitzpatrick sent a circular to lumber firms seeking support for three recommendations: the appointment of a travelling library commission and an
appropriation from the province to purchase libraries; legislation to grant
library boards, particularly Little Current, the power to send small collections
into camps; and the organization of a camp library club to organize the work
of churches and library boards until the commission was formed.[19] By

December, Harcourt was supportive; in fact, he went on record as "desirous of aiding you [Fitzpatrick] in every way in my power."[20]

During the 1901 legislative session, the department gathered information on travelling libraries from many sources. Melvil Dewey, the New York State library director, was approached because he was a recognized authority.[21] A letter was circulated to prominent citizens, soliciting lists of books appropriate for travelling libraries. There was some understandable delay on this point, book lists being a time-consuming business, but James Bain's response was immediate.[22] He knew an opportunity when it presented itself. In the first year, the department managed to organize several small travelling libraries and to issue regulations stipulating that the program was for "new and sparsely set-tled portions of the Province."[23] The government also advanced Fitzpatrick $100 for his good work in the reading camps. By April 1902, Harcourt could say that "our short experience, in sending out these libraries, is very satisfacto-ry."[24]

It was during Bain's presidency that Andrew Carnegie announced grants for fifteen libraries; the Carnegie building program had reached Ontario. To this end, Bain helped Hardy organize talks on library architecture for the 1902 OLA conference at McMaster University, Toronto. They arranged for William R. Eastman, superintendent of libraries for New York State, to speak on library buildings.[25] A resolution was also prepared to spur the education department into more vigorous activity:

> Resolved, that this Association, recognizing the growing magnitude of the Library question in Ontario, involving as it does a large number of problems regarding the supervision and direction of Travelling and Public Libraries, the question also of the provincial grant for Public Libraries, respectfully requests the Lieutenant-Governor-in-Council to appoint a Commission to examine into and report on the whole ques-tion of the Library System of this Province.[26]

Since an election was imminent, it was left to the executive officers to press Richard Harcourt (or his successor) for the creation of a commission.

The OLA's first major venture into politics was a failure. George Ross's Liberal party barely salvaged a victory at the polls in May 1902 and was pre-occupied afterwards by a series of election irregularities and by-elections. Although Bain and Hugh Langton, the new OLA president, pressed Richard Harcourt for a commission at a meeting near the end of October 1902, they were unsuccessful; the government was not about to adapt the commission style of library administration to Ontario. Harcourt discussed the matter with the premier and reported to Langton: "It is not at all likely that he [George Ross] will be able to appoint one in the immediate future."[27] The only solace gained by Langton and Bain was Harcourt's recognition that Dr. May would have to be replaced and that the efficiency of library inspection required upgrading.[28]

In fact, the education minister's immediate concerns lay elsewhere. A departmental memo to Harcourt in the first part of 1900 had resurrected the issue of rural school libraries, an enterprise the department had abandoned under Adam Crooks. Harcourt was ready to give these libraries priority status which meant the expenditure of $4,000 to $5,000.[29] Consequently, his enthusiasm was absorbed in building up school libraries, a subject revisited in the minister's annual report for 1900, in which he noted that the requirements of children were often ignored in public libraries. Harcourt, like Ryerson and Ross before him, believed young minds needed guidance to avoid the effects of ubiquitous light literature; good books provided proper direction.[30] John Seath's article on manual training and his suggestion to divert $10,000 from public libraries to school libraries also appeared in this report. During 1901, the department was prepared to finance the school library system without regard to the needs of adult readers. In 1902, a legislative apportionment of $3,000 was made for rural libraries. Regulations and a catalogue of approved books were issued. Reading matter included biography, history, geography, travel, mythology and fables, elementary science, and citizenship. Fiction was relegated to a minor role. School trustees would receive a grant amounting to half the amount expended from local revenue for books purchased from the new catalogue. The grant was not to exceed ten dollars. Principals were required to make the selections.[31]

Harcourt also was scrutinizing grants to public libraries because the legislative apportionment of $46,000 set by the Lieutenant Governor in 1895 was no longer sufficient to provide a full grant to every single library that submitted an application. As a result, the government was forced to make unpopular *pro rata* reductions. It came in for some criticism on this score because it was not paying "dollar for dollar" as the act apparently stipulated. Trustees were often frustrated when preparing estimates: "We have to expend the sum called for by the regulations...in order to qualify for the grant, and when that grant is afterwards cut 20% you can readily realize the shape it leaves the Board in."[32] The problem surfaced when George Ross had allowed Palmerston and Clifford to use promissory notes or borrowed money to match the legislative grant for books in 1896. This dubious use of credit spread until Dr. May became concerned about the financial welfare of public libraries that were not rate-supported. After 1895, the liabilities for this category of library had doubled. The superintendent wrote Harcourt to suggest that the minister amend the act or issue a circular stating that grants would not be allowed on borrowed money after a certain date.[33] Harcourt did nothing.

Two years later, May sent another memo on the same issue, informing the minister that sixty libraries might not be able to pay their incurred liabilities even if the grants were paid in full.[34] It was evident that a large number of smaller libraries were dependent on provincial revenue and borrowed money (Table 9: Public Library (Not Free) Revenue and Expenses, 1895-1910). This time Harcourt acted. The department received an ingenious legal opinion that reinterpreted the phrase "one dollar allowed for every dollar" to mean that it would pay only half the total amount spent on books and newspapers locally to a maximum of $250. Not many boards were able to spend $500 locally in order to receive $250 from the province. However, the legislative grant in 1902, which paid for 1901 expenses, actually increased by more than ten percent.

The following year Harcourt introduced a bill to abolish the use of credit. A memorandum from Dr. May estimated that "if grants are not allowed on Notes, etc. a large number of Libraries will not in future expend $100.00 for Books."[35] After the bill became law (3 Edw. VII, c. 23), the effect was dramatic and immediate for many small libraries – as provincial revenue plummeted there were concomitant drastic cuts in expenditure and a dramatic rise in liabilities. The legislative grant paid out in 1903 was almost halved. More ominously, Harcourt had told the legislature that "this bill was intended only as a temporary one, until a thorough public library act could be introduced, which he hoped to be able to do next year."[36] Harcourt apparently had become convinced that many public library boards in rural Ontario were not working satisfactorily. In fact, farmers' institutes were now operating circulating libraries with the assistance of the *Farmer's Advocate*, which described these institute libraries as "a movement of a self-helpful character, based on the diffusion of useful knowledge – the safest of foundations."[37]

Harcourt's judgement was shared by the new president of the Ontario Educational Association, John Seath, whose April 1903 presidential address dealt with the relationship between school libraries and public libraries in a predictable manner.

> To secure this eminently desirable relation throughout Ontario, one board should control the public library as well as the schools; they are all parts of the provincial system of education. But, until public opinion justifies the step, the principals of our Public, Separate, and High Schools, or at least one of each of them, if there are more than one in a

locality, should be members of the Public Library Board; and, to them, when practicable, the Public School Inspector should be added. These school functionaries should be members *ex officio*; and if they are what I trust our principals and inspectors always are, enlightened and forceful men, our public library statistics and our public morals should tell a different tale before many years went by.[38]

Dr. Seath's conception of library administration was at odds with the idea of a library commission, but he was in good company. Harcourt, in a confidential note dated the previous month, had agreed that the inclusion of school principals as *ex officio* members on library boards was an excellent suggestion.[39] James Bain's protest in a Toronto paper that Seath's proposal held no "distinct advantages" was ignored.[40]

The new OLA president, Hugh Langton, chief librarian at the University of Toronto, made the formation of a Provincial Library Commission the subject of his presidential address in April 1903. He considered the OLA's initial (unsuccessful) attempt the year before to persuade the government to create a commission merely "a preliminary skirmish." Furthermore, he scolded the government's complacency:

> It is not enough to have the existing abuses reformed or regulations amended; we shall always lag behind at that rate. What is needed is systematic stimulation of public interest in libraries through the efforts of a central authority that shall influence as well as regulate – a body with missionary, not administrative ideals. No ordinary Government department can supply these essentials, and therefore recourse must be had to extraordinary measures and we must demand the establishment of a Library Commission.[41]

There was faint praise for previous government efforts in his speech.

Langton expanded on the conditions and duties vital for a successful commission style of governance for his OLA audience. Regarding commission structure, he said the appointment of five or six knowledgeable members representing different geographic areas would suffice. The members should serve without remuneration. Regarding commission functions, Langton placed priority on the promotion and establishment of free and not free libraries and travelling libraries. As well, the commission should assist small libraries with book purchasing and book selection, and classification of collections. Advice on library techniques and management (e.g., cataloguing and book charging) and the formation of courses of instruction (e.g., a summer school) should also form part of its mandate. Unfortunately, the plan Langton put forward was not widely publicized in newspapers. Instead, the press was feasting on the latest Liberal misfortune, the Robert Gamey affair, which allegedly involved financial payments to a Conservative member of the legislature in return for his political support.

The Ross government continued to be plagued by scandal and absorbed by plans for the Ontario Power Commission during the 1903 legislative sitting. Consequently, there was little opportunity for library reform. Commission style governance was fine for the management of hydro-electricity, but for libraries it was a non-issue. Undaunted, Harcourt continued to propose his own modifications. In his 1903 annual summary, the education minister surmised that perhaps no grant should be given to a library that was not free to the public. He added that it would be best for school trustees in sections and small communities to operate libraries directly. There was no need to have special purpose boards to maintain small libraries because public libraries could be placed in schools and teachers could act as librarians.[42] Moreover, there was a definite need for technical libraries, improved evening classes, and a new syllabus for art school examinations; in fact, Dr. May's handling of art schools was now under critical scrutiny.[43] Whatever Harcourt's plans were, they obviously did not include a library commission.

When the 1904 legislative sitting resumed, it became apparent that the minister intended to reduce Dr. May's responsibilities for technical education and, by extension, reduce the role libraries had assumed in this field. Art schools were transferred to the new Inspector of Manual Training and Technical Education, Albert Leake, and the syllabus for art exams was completely revised. Leake was to remain in the department until 1935. He was the author of highly respected publications on vocational training.[44] In the same year he was appointed, he reported that evening classes conducted by public libraries were practically nonexistent outside of Toronto, Hamilton, and Brantford. "The old Mechanics' Institutes," he wrote, "have entirely disappeared and nothing has been done to fill the place they occupied."[45] He hoped to revive adult evening classes which had languished in the later years of Dr. May's superintendency.

The government also introduced a bill to allow the amalgamation of library, high school, public school, and technical school boards into a single board of education on a majority vote of the municipal council.[46] The proposed amendments were circulated to some libraries. Norman Gurd, a Sarnia lawyer prominent in OLA circles, responded negatively to the amendment in a letter to his member for Lambton West, William J. Hanna.[47] Hanna was an influential Conservative who may have had a hand in changes to the bill at second reading. The clauses pertaining to libraries were withdrawn in advance of the OLA meeting at the Canadian Institute in Toronto. On another positive note, an amendment to the Public Libraries Act that would allow councils, upon a two-thirds majority vote of aldermen, to increase the public library rate to a maximum of three-quarters of a mill, quickly became law (4 Edw. VII, c. 10, s. 55).

At the Easter 1904 gathering of the OLA, delegates came to realize that "little has been accomplished" to bring the idea of a library commission for Ontario to fruition.[48] Langton, Bain, and the treasurer, Archibald Macallum, who was active in the Canadian Institute and a member of the advisory provincial educational council, still felt that the matter was of prime importance. Macallum spoke to the issue with some humour:

> ...the committee appointed had waited on the Government, but had been told that a commission was not in keeping with the genius of the constitution. Personally he had not met the genius of the constitution – (laughter) – but he inclined to think it consisted of a disinclination to allow the matter to pass from the direct control of the Government.[49]

Delegates also remembered the recent appointments to the commissions governing Queen Victoria Niagara Falls Park and the Temiskaming and Northern Ontario Railway. The government's logic in denying the OLA a library commission escaped them. They decided to continue their campaign. Clearly, the unproductive consultation with Harcourt and departmental officials was disheartening. The library commission committee shouldered on for two more years. Immediate prospects were not bright, for many people expected the next election to end the long reign of the Liberal Party in Ontario.

At the same conference, McGill University's Charles H. Gould, who along with Bain had stirred Canadian interest in the *International Catalogue of Scientific Literature*, announced the opening of Canada's first summer school classes for library workers at his university.[50] The precarious position of small libraries operating under the department's new fifty per cent interpretation also came up next for discussion. It was agreed to leave the issue with the executive because the deputy minister, John Millar, reported "no hope of any change." William J. Robertson, the new first vice-president, gave a paper on library certification. He had been active on many educational fronts: teacher in St. Catharines; writer of mathematics texts for Ontario's high schools; senator of Victoria University; and president of the Ontario Historical Association. While he did not think that there was any need for the government to establish special schools for librarianship – business colleges and private institutions could provide this training – he did believe that certification by the department should be linked to grants in order to maintain desirable public standards.[51]

Accredited training and government certification were becoming important issues. Robertson, aided by two other delegates, delivered a report on training and certification at the next day's session and made a motion concerning these two items:

> That the librarians of public libraries receiving not less than
> 75% of the maximum government grant shall hold Junior
> Leaving (or its equivalent) English standing, and in addition
> be required to pass a professional examination in library
> work, under the control of the Education Department. This
> regulation not to apply to present librarians.[52]

His small committee was directed to consult with the minister of education on the issue. Prospects seemed encouraging because the new president for 1904/05 was William J. Tytler, a long-time library trustee and a school inspector from Guelph who had a bent for practical matters (Illus. 25).[53]

William Tytler had supported pursuit of a library commission. However, in the face of political uncertainty and Harcourt's antipathy, the new OLA president and his executive officers turned their collective attention to the issues of grants, library architecture, and classification. To these ends, they expended most of their energy in 1904/05. They arranged for A.W. Cameron, from Streetsville, to conduct an open session on the fifty percent grant interpretation. Hardy canvassed libraries for information on library buildings. As well, they invited Melvil Dewey to the 1905 annual meeting, and asked Miss Effie Schmidt, librarian at Berlin, to speak on classification. She already had applied the decimal system to her library collection without incurring undue financial expenditure.

Expectations for incremental change were now more encouraging. Two months before the 1905 OLA annual meeting, the Conservatives scored their long-awaited victory at the polls, smashing the remnants of Liberal rule founded by Oliver Mowat. New men, unburdened by the past, pledged themselves to honest and efficient government under the leadership of Premier James Pliny Whitney. In February, Dr. Robert Pyne, a physician from Toronto, emerged as the surprise choice for minister of education. One of his connections with educational affairs was his chairmanship of the Toronto Public Library Board in 1891. Dr. May's position was no longer secure; the old civil service veteran realized where he stood. Patronage was an important consideration in government appointments. Only Dr. May and

John G. Hodgins, now the department's librarian and historiographer, remained from the Ryerson era.[54]

The 1905 OLA meeting illustrated some internal divisions on fundamental concerns that existed in the library community. The introduction of decimal classification was still contentious in Ontario. The afternoon discussion that followed Effie Schmidt's talk on "Classification" was pointed. Robert Blackwell recommended the decimal system, saying that he had noticed "long delays" in Toronto because the old class system was still in use.

> That brought Dr. Bain to his feet in defence of his library. In the first place, he said, the Toronto library was the oldest in the country, and still held to the old system, but he did not know any better one. The most ignorant man could find three or four numbers. The object of the public library was to reach a number of people in the quickest way, and that they succeeded in doing in Toronto... The same system was in use in Chicago and other western towns.[55]

Dewey disagreed. He responded that no one "had any right to run a library on the idea that the 'old plan did very well.'" Afterwards, Hardy presented his findings on library buildings. He spoke on selection, children's rooms, exteriors, heating systems, bookstacks, and domes.

In the evening session Dewey spoke on the library's relation to home and higher education. Dewey was not necessarily a "commission man" at heart, for he had spent many years as the director of the New York state library and was in the midst of departmental reorganization at Albany. He recognized that an educational bureaucracy could impose constructive measures leading to standardization. The type of service he described entailed acting as a bureau of information, promoting library interests, founding and reorganizing libraries, selecting and purchasing books, advising on library methods, inspecting libraries, organizing travelling libraries, training librarians, and publishing reports and bulletins.[56] The next day, A.W. Cameron spoke to the 1902 fifty percent ruling. Not surprisingly, the convention decided to approach the new government about that unpopular decision.

With Dr. Pyne as the new minister, the OLA sensed the possibility for cooperation and progress. Premier James P. Whitney's party had repeatedly criticized the Liberal government's handling of the grant applied to fiction and its unwillingness to extend services to agricultural districts. During the previous year, two Conservatives from rural ridings had introduced a house resolution: that "the Government should take an early opportunity of establishing libraries in farming communities for the dissemination of useful information on agricultural topics."[57] An opportunity to improve travelling libraries and library organization was at hand. But who would emerge as head of the department's library branch? One candidate, who was unknown to OLA members, Thaddeus W.H. Leavitt, had applied for the library post shortly after the Conservative election victory.[58]

Leavitt, age sixty-one, had been a newspaper editor for many years and was an author of note; he had written a history of Leeds and Grenville and *Kaffir, Kangaroo, Klondyke*, a travel book about his days in South Africa, Australia, and New Zealand. He was also a Conservative Party organizer and had worked for Dr. Pyne in the 1902 election campaign. Pyne recommended him for the position.[59] There the matter rested over the summer. In the autumn, Pyne had to chose a new deputy minister to replace the deceased John Millar. Finally, in early November, word reached the press of Dr. May's fall from grace and Leavitt's appointment as Inspector of Public Libraries, Scientific Institutions and Literary and Scientific Societies.[60] Dr. May's long service was not acknowledged in library circles; most people felt that he had stayed too long. They were more interested in the policies his successor might initiate.

The inspector's 1905 report to the minister was not very revealing, but change was clearly in the offing for the entire department. In early 1906, Arthur H.U. Colquhoun, a writer, newspaper editor and friend of federal and provincial Conservatives, was appointed Deputy Minister, a position he would hold until his retirement in 1934.[61] For library enthusiasts it was a welcome selection – he was an author, a book collector, and earlier had written a tribute to his close friend, James Bain.[62] Less welcome was John Seath's appointment as Superintendent of Education. He would oversee and develop departmental policies in accordance with Pyne's announcement on 10 April 1906 that the government would amend and consolidate the two acts on high schools and public libraries at the next sitting of the House.[63]

Towards a New Act, 1906-09

Thaddeus Leavitt did not have a library background, but he did have sound administrative experience. He was convinced that public library development in Ontario needed better direction. Travelling libraries had been introduced, but improvements were obviously required. The issue of a library commission remained unsettled. For the new inspector, working with the OLA was a sensible course because it provided a ready source of advice for the department. However, not everyone accepted Leavitt. James Bain, for one, told Hardy that he was "unfitted" and "unsatisfactory" for the position.[64] But Bain's influence was waning because he was reluctant to adopt decimal classification, and he was not a proponent of children's libraries. Hardy, who was emerging as the principal organizer and heart of the OLA, was more disposed to accept Leavitt and work for change. William Robertson, the president for 1905/06, knew that the department could play a more central role in library matters – this meant working with the new inspector. The vice-president, Norman Gurd, inclined to agree.

An opening for cooperation came immediately. After the 1905 OLA meeting, Norman Gurd and two librarians, Effie Schmidt (Berlin) and Carrie Rowe (Brockville), agreed to compile a catalogue of books suitable for children. Gurd felt that it was essential for libraries to serve a broader public;[65] better provision for children was one of his chief aims.

> The library must meet the competition of the dime novel and the sensational story paper, and for this purpose nothing is more effective than the sound wholesome fiction of Henty, Strang or Macdonald Oxley. The librarian should not attempt to force any book on a child. He should take an interest in each child and endeavor to ascertain the child's taste, so that he may tactfully influence the reading of the child for good by easy steps.[66]

The education department was an obvious choice as publisher; it agreed to print the booklet, which was a list of nearly one thousand books. Each title was selected to stir the imagination, broaden the horizon, and add to the knowledge of children. A new working relationship had been forged within a short time.

The government also was willing to assist small libraries, although it refused to reconsider the fifty percent ruling or restore promissory notes for grant applications. The Conservatives believed that smaller libraries deserved support only if they could demonstrate self-reliance. To help matters, Dr. Pyne guided an unusual bill through the legislature in 1906. Leavitt discovered that some unscrupulous booksellers had gotten word of the abolition of credit early in 1903. They had approached smaller libraries with the following scenario:

> 'We are rather hard-up this year, could you not, as the Chairman, or as the Secretary, or as a member of the Board, sign a note that we could put in the bank?' In most cases they got the notes and when the law changed they had the individuals pretty tight. The signers of the notes had to pay.[67]

To complete the financial transaction, the booksellers gave some of their creditors invoices for $200 to submit to the department. After investigating, Leavitt concluded that "They never sold them the books at all, not one of the books were ever in a public library, and yet they drew money out of the Government on invoices of that kind, and some chairmen of Boards in the Province swore to the truth of the statements."[68] Pyne's act allowed boards which had purchased books, periodicals, or newspapers in 1903, prior to the abolition of credit on 12 June, to receive their original grant.[69] Claims had to be filed within six months.

There were mixed feelings towards the government at the 1906 OLA annual meeting chaired by William Robertson. The association was small in number and the opinions of a few counted heavily on some issues (Illus. 26). Leavitt attended the first session and said classification, travelling libraries, and rural school libraries were immediate departmental concerns. With Dr. Seath's appointment in mind, the OLA passed a motion cautioning against the union of library and school boards. The main business featured Robertson's presidential address; it highlighted the possibility of establishing library institutes across the province, an idea which Hardy had raised in 1901 in his outline program and had elaborated upon in 1903. Institutes would bring together library workers and trustees for one or two days on a regional basis, thus promoting public interest in libraries and providing better instruction to librarians and boards. They would be forums for discussion and the dissemination of community interests, new ideas, and better management techniques. Teachers' Institutes had existed for many years and had been a success, so there was an expectation that the department would finance a similar arrangement for libraries.[70]

Leavitt's appointment energized public library affairs. He was receptive to Hardy's and Robertson's push for institutes. Before the end of 1906, he had accepted a proposal to stage a small convention or round table somewhere in western Ontario.[71] He was interested in children's services and the removal of age limitations in public libraries. He also realized that libraries could play a supportive role in the field of technical education. He augmented his staff in 1907 by hiring an assistant, Walter R. Nursey, another Conservative fund raiser with a temperament for travel and adventure, to help manage travelling libraries. Nursey's foremost qualification was literary; he had published several histories and was working on a biography of Isaac Brock for William Brigg's "Canadian Heroes Series."[72] Most importantly, Leavitt was able to work with the new OLA president, Norman Gurd, who presided over consecutive OLA meetings in 1907 and 1908. The link between the department and the association was formalized in 1906 by an annual grant of $200 to the OLA and by agreement to fund the publication of its annual proceedings starting in 1907.

Leavitt began an immediate reorganization of the travelling library system along the lines James Bain had laid out almost a decade before. New regulations appeared in 1906 that extended the service and changed some conditions:

1. book cases could be lent out to small public libraries;
2. boards were responsible for losses;
3. transportation charges for receiving cases were to be paid by boards;
4. cases were to be loaned for three months;
5. librarians were responsible for circulating the books.[73]

The department redesigned physical storage for the books to facilitate transportation as follows:

> Each case contained a movable shelf, thus providing for books varying in length. The cover was hinged and fastened with a lock. When the case is opened the cover forms a small table upon which the books can be examined, while all of the titles are immediately exposed at a glance. Locks with duplicate keys are used, one key being retained in the department the other sent by mail to the borrower. A simple register is included in each case for recording the circulation.[74]

The inspector successfully increased the grant for travelling libraries in 1907, a trend that continued for several years (Table 10: Provincial Expenditure for Libraries, 1902-14).

Both Dr. Colquhoun and Leavitt attended the 1907 OLA conference as speakers. The deputy minister's talk was non-committal and informal. Privately, however, he had already told Hardy that the government was no longer contemplating the management of libraries by boards of education.[75] Leavitt offered more clues to departmental plans when he outlined his ideas on travelling libraries and submitted a series of questions concerning legislative matters, to which delegates responded favourably. Travelling libraries remained his immediate priority. Leavitt earmarked $3,000 for them in the 1907 estimates. Library institutes would be improved and extended to more regions. A new conditional grant formula was necessary. To this end, the OLA passed a motion favouring a grant of $275 for libraries.[76]

Commencing in 1907, the old classification scheme, devised for Mechanics' Institutes by William Edwards, was another casualty of Leavitt's reforms. The inspector originally had decided not to promote one classification system at the expense of another. But, in a March 1907 circular on grants, the education department openly recommended either the Dewey Decimal Classification (DDC) or Cutter System.[77] This was the death knell for the class subjects used in circulars and departmental reports since the mid-1880s. From now on, all novels were to be classed as fiction, and a separate juvenile section was encouraged. Furthermore, the percentage of fiction upon which the grant was paid was increased from twenty to forty-five percent of the total sum paid for books. When the matter of estimates for libraries was raised in the legislature, the Premier stated that public libraries had hitherto been circulating too many "slushy novels."[78] The change, therefore, aimed to balance the amount of fiction purchased and to rationalize the division of fiction, nonfiction, and juvenile literature in libraries. After a delay of one year the OLA officially endorsed the DDC with Cutter author tables.

Leavitt favoured the development of children's libraries and the lifting of age restrictions for youngsters. Anxious to implement these reforms, he hired Patricia Spereman, librarian at Sarnia, in the first part of 1908. Her duties, as initially conceived, were taxing.

> Miss Spereman will be sent out to libraries to establish children's rooms in the libraries, separating the books for the children from the adult portion, and to show how to catalogue and classify them. She will try to begin the story hour. She will have about two hundred pictures with her. The object of these is educational and also to attract the children to the public library. She will also have a couple of children's libraries, and I hope to put her into the places where they had the rule that they would not lend books to children.[79]

Library boards had to apply for her services and then wait their turn. She would visit for a short time and provide basic training for staff and volunteers.

Like most people entering Canadian librarianship, Patricia Spereman at first did not possess any formal library training. She began working at Sarnia after graduating from the Ursuline Academy in Chatham. The new Carnegie library was nearing completion, and she was part of Sarnia's successful introduction to free access, decimal classification, and children's work. Her story hour for children was a pioneering effort in Canada (Illus. 27). A year of library training at the distinguished Pratt Institute Library School in Brooklyn, which featured technical subjects and a semester of practical work, prepared her for more rewarding opportunities. Her address at the 1908 OLA meeting on children's work articulated the need to reach out to all children – "little newsboys," "street arabs," and the "studious" – and was well received by most in attendance.[80] Her practical experience with decimal classification proved to be a valuable asset. She would oversee its adoption in more than one hundred Ontario libraries over the next several years. Patricia Spereman remained with the department in various capacities until her death shortly after the end of the Second World War.[81]

Leavitt's auspicious beginning was cut short by the news of James Bain's death at the end of May 1908. His passing stunned the Ontario library community. In his final years, Bain's ideas were not accepted by everyone. Advocates of decimal classification, like Robert Blackwell, found him adamantly opposed to any acceptance of the DDC on the part of the OLA When Bain openly took issue in the Toronto *Telegram* with Norman Gurd's remarks on the need for better children's libraries – saying that small libraries had been turned into "kindergarten schools" – Gurd privately complained to Hardy that "there is certainly no library on this continent the size of Toronto which is so badly administered."[82] Gurd responded publicly in a letter to the editor: "Unless a library wishes to become a home of lost causes, it must keep pace with the movement towards freedom which after all means the greatest good to the greatest number."[83] Nevertheless, Bain remained highly respected. No one in his lifetime had done more to raise the image of libraries or librarianship. He continued working right up until the time of his illness, having arranged by early May for another $50,000 Carnegie grant for two more Toronto branch libraries.[84] Eulogies flowed freely on the day of his funeral, 26 May, and some of his old friends in the Muskoka Club served as his pallbearers.[85] The Toronto Public Library was closed during the afternoon to honour his memory.

The long awaited new legislation – An Act Respecting Public Libraries and Art Schools – came into force in 1909 (9 Edw. VII, c. 80); its features reflected the Whitney government's desire for better public control of libraries by means of more scrupulous regulation.[86] This policy meant that legislation for free libraries remained mostly unchanged. Boards of management continued to be responsible for libraries, reading rooms, branch libraries, and museums; and for purchases of books, magazines, newspapers, maps, "specimens illustrative of the arts and sciences;" and fuel, lighting, accommodation, and buildings. Their authority to conduct the operation of art schools and evening classes for mechanical and manufacturing arts also remained untouched. The library rate could be increased to three-quarters of a mill upon a vote of two-thirds of the council members, except in police villages and cities of 100,000 or more where the half-mill and quarter-mill rates were already in operation. Public libraries (not free) founded between 1895 and 1909, which lacked the right to receive a mill rate, now were eligible for the public library rate; part II of the 1895 act was repealed.

Part II of the new act established Public Library Associations. This type of library could be formed by the incorporation of no fewer than ten people under twenty-one years of age. The board of management was to be elected at annual meetings each January; membership on the board ranged from five to nine persons. Children over the age of twelve could be members, but no one under twenty-one could vote at annual meetings or hold office in the association. Municipal councils could pass bylaws assuming the assets and property of associations in order to establish a public library under part I. Evidently, the government felt a continuation of the subscription public library was the most suitable means to reach rural residents in the province's southern counties.

Leavitt's changes to the grant system were introduced in Part III. The maximum legislative grant was set at $200 for books, bookbinding, and cataloguing/classifying materials; and $50 for magazines, periodicals, and newspapers. This grant was only $25 less than the amount the OLA executive had requested.[87] It could not exceed fifty percent of the total local expenditure on these materials; nor could it be paid on an expenditure on fiction in excess of forty-five percent of the amount expended on other books. Part III also provided supplementary grants ranging from five dollars to twenty dollars, based on local receipts, for reading rooms open for a specified number of hours. Legislative appropriations were authorized for travelling libraries, schools for training librarians, library institutes, and employment of departmental officers as special instructors for boards and librarians. The membership requirement for association libraries, which was tied to a library's eligibility to receive grants, was reduced by half to fifty persons over twenty-one years of age. This was a welcome relief to many small rural communities. Art schools continued to be eligible for $400 annually. The department had to approve library rules which prohibited free access "to the books of the library or of a section of the library" and stipulated age restrictions for children. Two controversial issues were effectively settled. The OLA approved the concepts of free access and children's reading rooms when it reviewed the act at its 1909 convention.

Some OLA members, however, were less receptive to Leavitt's ideas on technical education, which were aired at the 1909 meeting.[88] The Inspector had devised a plan whereby travelling libraries would be used to promote technical instruction among mechanics and artisans with the support of participating public libraries which contributed $100 in the first year of the program. He proposed that certificates or diplomas be awarded upon successful completion of a departmental examination.[89] A centralized plan meant more formalized control by the department and raised questions among members, notably George Locke, who was Toronto Public Library's new chief librarian. Locke preferred to design and coordinate programs at the local level.

Although he was a newcomer to OLA, and it was unlikely Toronto would make use of travelling libraries, his basic philosophic arguments on the library's mission in adult education carried considerable weight.

> Its [the public library] courses are elective and it aims to make them attractive; it is practical because it gives what you think you want, not what a learned body of men think you want…This helpfulness ought not to confine itself to books; it ought to, in a visual and in a tangible way, show what may be learned from books – in other words, there ought to be lectures and practical demonstrations of the difference between an artisan and an artist in any trade, and how the artisan may become an artist.[90]

Since the public library's role in technical and manual education had a checkered history, a special OLA committee was struck to study the issue with Leavitt.

The potential for change in the field of technical education, as conceived by Leavitt and the OLA, was never realized. The inspector was unable to attend the association meeting in April 1909, and he died in June at his summer residence in Bancroft. In his will he left a private collection of five hundred volumes to the Athens High School. His assistant, Walter Nursey, became inspector. Nursey was the first to admit that his predecessor had "left many unsolved problems behind him."[91] In his short term of office, Leavitt had swept away years of inaction and introduced a modern public library act to Ontario. He recognized the provincial government's role in encouraging free access, children's libraries, library institutes, travelling libraries, library training, and technical education. He had not shied away from any major issue. His work was not complete in 1909; but there were many associates ready to follow his lead.

"Growing in Interest and Power and Influence"

Ten years had passed since Edwin Hardy had written to George Ross proposing a library conference; the OLA had matured steadily over this time. The new president, Judge Alexander D. Hardy, a Brantford trustee who would remain active until the end of the Second World War, summed up the accomplishments of OLA's first decade in his 1910 address:

> Along with Mr. Carnegie's splendid work, our own Government have been aiding library work in a very practical way, and have been on the lookout to follow up suggestions

that have been made from time to time. We are grateful for that assistance. Then this Association has been growing in interest and power and influence yearly. We find now that the question of public libraries in Ontario is a living one. We may be said to have created a public imagination as to what the library should be. At least this desideratum is in process of formation, and this is the first thing for us to obtain in order to have behind us that educated and solid body of public opinion which will back up the work of this Association by reason of its appreciation of the work we are doing. It is not necessary now to justify the public library.[92]

Yet there was still much to be done. While it might be said that the public library had "come of age," the OLA still had an agenda crowded with unfulfilled issues.

B. Mabel Dunham, chief librarian at Berlin (now Kitchener), exemplified the new spirit of forward thinking. A former teacher and graduate of the University of Toronto with a B.A. in languages and history, she had taken Gould's summer school course at McGill before accepting her position at Berlin as a library assistant in the summer of 1908 (Illus. 28).[93] Colleagues immediately noticed her ability; she became chief librarian within a short time. It was not long before she was invited to address the OLA on modern lines of work. Dunham delivered an entertaining paper about a visiting Utopian gentleman who conversed with her on the requirements for successful libraries. There was much to be learned. According to this gentleman,

> The public library is one of these unfortunate creatures of circumstance with no law but the gentle rule of moral suasion and no power but what she herself creates. I have come to believe in the old adage that human nature is much the same the wide world over, but, in her helplessness the Canadian library instinctively trusts to architectural grandeur, to improved methods of classification and charging systems, to its books, and lastly, to the librarian and the board of management, whereas the Utopian library puts her confidence in the same means of attraction though in exactly the reverse order.[94]

Dunham's entertaining comparison of Canadian libraries with those in Utopia has remained a classic to this day.

Immediate attention was focused on technical education. Dr. Pyne agreed to provide $300 towards a tour of American libraries in the north-east: the State Library in Albany, New York; Boston Public Library; Worcester Public Library; Providence Public Library; Newark Public Library under John Cotton Dana's direction; the Pratt Institute in Brooklyn; Buffalo Public Library; and Niagara Falls Public Library. E.A. Hardy, David M. Grant, Judge Alexander Hardy, and Walter Nursey left during February 1910 for a one week tour. In their report, they concluded that Leavitt's original proposals on technical education were sound, but they also had a few reservations:

> As to the matter of instruction through the public library by any such scheme as Correspondence courses and examinations and recognition of such work by Government certificate or diploma, the committee do not feel at present able to offer any definite suggestion. They quite realize the possibilities of such a scheme, but they also realize the difficulties...[95]

Their report, which abandoned a centralized arrangement for evening classes, was presented and quickly approved at the 1910 OLA conference.

Later in the same year, John Seath issued a comprehensive report on technical education. Seath, who favoured vocational training in high schools and specialized industrial schools, scarcely mentioned libraries. He was concerned with formal courses, qualifications of teachers, legislation, and departmental programs. The superintendent showed no interest in the supplementary resources which libraries were best equipped to provide workingmen. Educators realized that voluntary self-help could not succeed on a broad scale. Reading books, attending lectures, and browsing book collections were not enough to impart a thorough knowledge of a trade. Regarding art schools, Seath felt they needed invigoration; his recommendations completely ignored the role of libraries.[96] It came as no surprise, then, that the Industrial Education Act of 1911 rescinded previous legislation that allowed art schools and libraries to conduct evening classes. The new act established two-year general industrial schools, specialized schools, and vocational training in high schools (1 Geo. V, c. 79).

In June 1910, the Dominion government established a Royal Commission on Industrial Training and Technical Education. Hearings were held between July 1910 and February 1911. Ontario librarians and the OLA made presentations emphasizing the library's role. Justice Alexander D. Hardy stressed the usefulness of libraries for many workingmen who did not have the time or financial means for special training:

> The technical school, college or university, it is true, provides adequate training for the young man who has the time and means at his disposal to attend there; but there is no provision made for the ambitious married man who has a wife and family to support, and who is unable to give much of his time for the purpose of equipping himself for the needs of his handicraft. It is for such that the public library, with its technical side fully developed, may prove of great benefit.[97]

The commissioners acknowledged the good work conducted by library boards, but their final report, issued in 1913, never developed specific proposals integrating library work with other educational programs and institutions.

While the OLA struggled to retain its place in technical education, a positive advance during these years was the realization of a summer school for librarians in Toronto. By this time, systematic school library training was becoming the norm rather than the exception. In his 1910 OLA presidential address, Alexander Hardy spoke of the need for trained librarians and an Ontario library school. The era of the bookman-librarian, exemplified by Adam Hunter in Hamilton, was ending. By 1908, more than twenty Ontarians, most of whom were from the eastern region, had attended the two-month summer library school at McGill. A few ambitious people had enrolled in American library schools for one- or two-year programs. The OLA initially had supported minimum qualifications and provincial certification of librarians without however proposing the type of schooling it preferred. After Walter Nursey attended McGill, the department approached Charles Gould in late 1908 about the feasibility of opening a permanent library school in Toronto. Gould felt that there was no urgency for two Canadian schools; he suggested holding a summer school in alternate years at Toronto and Montreal.

> This plan was really suggested to me by Dr. Bain during his last visit to our Library School. He said 'When the new building for the Toronto Public Library is finished and the Library itself has been re-organized we will furnish you with the requisite rooms and lend you what books you need, and then you can bring your school up here every other year, running it alternately in the two places.'[98]

Following these conversations, the 1909 act went a step further; it allowed the province to finance a school for instruction.

Inspector Nursey and departmental officials obviously believed that the McGill University school was too distant for most prospective Ontario students. They understood that money for training was a scare commodity in small libraries and that promotions often depended upon local acquaintances, not education or training. William Robertson's OLA speech in 1904 had given a good description of how local patronage worked. Moreover, the public perception of librarians was still unflattering:

> The librarian in the village is usually a respectable old gen-
> tleman who has held a series of secretaryships and who
> declines into the keeping of the library with a gentle resig-
> nation, which later on becomes a certain intellectual pride
> in the treasures of the shelves...He wears garments of a sub-
> dued shabbiness and looks dubiously over his spectacles at
> the High School student who demands the latest novel or
> the young woman who asks for the recent number of the
> *Woman's Home Companion*. He is frequently appointed as
> judge in the debates of the local literary society and is capa-
> ble of weighing nicely the arguments as to the relative dev-
> astating power of war and intemperance.[99]

Nursey was determined to undo this general caricature of librarians as he set about organizing library training in Toronto.

A one-month summer school for librarians opened at the Education Department's Model School in June 1911. B. Mabel Dunham, who had impressed Walter Nursey with her work at Berlin, was in charge. The Inspector had worked hard to receive departmental approval from his superiors, and he forged ahead as soon as funding became available. The department provided books and supplies from its Educational Library, which had been reclassed using the decimal classification, and also from its travelling libraries. Nursey obtained the services of several people as lecturers, including Dr. Colquhoun, and arranged visits to several Toronto libraries, such as the reference department of Toronto's new College Street central library. The school's primary purpose was to raise the standard of librarianship in smaller centres. Accordingly, entrance qualifications were set at the high school level or its equivalent and no admission fee was charged. Thirty-one candidates were admitted the first summer (Illus. 29).

Under Dunham's direction, the school offered seven main areas of instruction. Dr. Lewis E. Hornung from Victoria College, a regular visitor at OLA meetings, taught a general literature survey course. He had collaborated with Lawrence Burpee to produce the first systematic bibliography of Canadian English fiction.[100] The school offered instruction and lab work in new library methods for book selection and purchasing, accessioning, book preparation, charging systems, book repair and binding, patron fines, and accounts. Mabel Dunham, Hester Young, chief cataloger at the University of Toronto, and Grace Andrews, of the Educational Library, directed classes in classification and cataloguing using the decimal system. Inspector Nursey and E.A. Hardy taught library administration – acts and regulations, publicity, building arrangement, equipment, and library services. Considerable emphasis was placed on reference work, a subject of growing importance. William Carson, chief librarian at London after 1909, and Toronto's Frances Staton and Elizabeth Moir were the instructors. Nursey stressed the use of travelling libraries and the importance of library institutes. Patricia Spereman and Bessie M. Staton, Toronto Public Library's children's librarian, conducted classes on juvenile libraries and story hours.

The school's curriculum stimulated new thoughts about the status and training of librarians. A decade earlier, E.A. Hardy had provisionally divided library work into two service components: mechanical and trained service. His mechanical duties (routine circulation or supervision of books and rooms) required no special expertise. Trained service involved acquisition, selection, and purchase of materials; accessioning, classification, and cataloguing; library publicity; coordination with schools, study clubs, and individual patrons; and local history. Hardy suggested summer library training courses be organized by the government.[101] Now, according to William Carson, who spoke to the issue at the 1912 OLA annual meeting, librarians were expected to possess experience, natural ability, a broad education, and professional training. On the subject of library related working experience, Carson had little to add; he seemed to assume that apprenticeship was necessary above all else. Natural ability included personal qualities such as resourcefulness, progressive attitudes, and common sense. These practical attributes were not unique to librarians, of course, but they did constitute the ideal type which boards and administrators were willing to hire.

Carson was cautious when speaking about education. It was not merely formal academic achievement but applied knowledge that counted in librarianship; business training might be considered the equivalent of certificates, diplomas, or degrees. On strictly professional training, Carson was specific. He included three classes of work: bibliographic skills, administrative knowledge, and technical training. Bibliographic work encompassed the subject of bibliography, book selection, and reference work. Administration took in legislation, governance and management of libraries; buildings and equipment; secretarial work; library publications; history; and children's rooms. Technical training concerned classification, cataloguing, accessioning, bookbinding, and routine work (e.g., borrower registration). He described professional training as a "scientific system" that underpinned organization:

> [T]he public library offers unlimited opportunities for the
> exercise of judgment and initiative. But the knowledge and
> training in the subjects embraced in library science are essen-
> tial to the librarian if he is to exercise his powers to the best
> advantage.[102]

As for instruction and training, Carson considered the new summer school
suitable for those who did not have time to attend a one- or two-year library
school, but he also acknowledged that the summer school needed to be supplemented by advanced training. In some larger libraries, like his own,
apprentice classes were organized for promising assistants with senior matricu-
lation. These library subordinates could benefit most from in-service programs.

By all accounts, the first school was a success for everyone, from the experienced hands to tyros. It attracted considerable talent from the Ontario
library field, mainly those people with close connections to their communities. However, conditions were not always conducive to study. There were the
long hours from Monday to Saturday plus the excessive heat of late June and
early July which on occasion reached about 100°F. One participant, Mary T.
Butters, chief librarian at Niagara Falls, spoke at Port Colborne in September
about the taxing hours: "We put in a very busy month, for after school hours,
which sometimes lasted till five o'clock, we were expected to write up our
notes taken during the day."[103] Butters already had succeeded in arranging for
free access, the DDC, and children's services at her library; she continued as
chief librarian until retirement in 1923. Two new chief librarians also attended. They were Mary J. Black, who commenced her duties at Fort William in
January 1909, and Fred DelaFosse, appointed in January 1911 at
Peterborough. They were to serve their respective libraries for more than a
quarter century.

Mabel Dunham's efforts on behalf of the school were recognized by everyone connected with its operation. She modestly summarized her experience
for the 1912 OLA conference by saying that the school had "justified its existence."[104] She returned as instructor-in-charge for 1912 and 1914, using her
vacation time on each occasion. After the first year, the school ran from the
end of May to late June to avoid intemperate, sweltering weather; classes were
held in the women's reading room at the University of Toronto Library. In
1912, McGill's Charles Gould gave a brief guest lecture on library training.
Hester Young, another McGill school graduate, was appointed instructor-in-
charge for 1913. She was joined by Patricia Spereman, Adeline Cartwright, a
graduate from the Pratt Institute, and Lillian Smith, a University of Toronto
graduate and Toronto Public Library's recently appointed children's librarian.

Smith had trained for two years at the Pittsburgh Carnegie Library Training School for Children's Librarianship and afterwards worked for a short time at the New York Public Library. Examinations were held at the conclusion of course work and certificates, graded in three classes, were awarded. There were thirteen graduates in 1912, twenty-six in 1913, and thirty in 1914. No school was scheduled for 1915, the last full year Inspector Nursey held office.

As improved apprentice school training was reshaping librarianship in Ontario before the Great War, the OLA developed regional sub-groups and expanded into many communities. Regional library institutes were the instrument of the association's advance. Executive OLA officers realized that the number of delegates in attendance at annual meetings was small in proportion to the total number of library boards in the province; between 1901 and 1906, the number varied between a low of 25 and a high of 38 delegates from a host of well over 350 public library boards. To remedy this situation, the OLA organized a demonstration institute at Brantford in July 1907. It was hosted by the chief librarian, Edwin D. Henwood. Twenty-one libraries, the majority from surrounding counties, took part in the all-day experiment.

Brantford's Edwin Henwood was typical of the kind of recruit the OLA was hoping to enlist.[105] He had administered the library since 1901 and helped supervise the Carnegie expansion. He was quite willing to participate in OLA matters, becoming a member of the committee on binding in 1907. When the Brantford board invited trustees and librarians for an institute on 11 July, Henwood naturally agreed to help organize the program and stand on the local executive. The meeting covered a variety of topics: library cooperation, small libraries, book selection, children's work, and finances.[106] The institute was an unqualified success and another one was planned. The following year Henwood spoke at the OLA convention on in-house binding. He so impressed the assembly with his system that the education department published his short treatise for distribution in Ontario and directed Patricia Spereman to train staff according to his recommendations.[107]

Three institutes were arranged in 1908, at Chatham, Niagara Falls, and Brantford. Legislation followed in 1909. The education department would assist with funding, and the OLA would continue to administer the institutes with local executives in charge of programs. The avowed purpose of the institutes was threefold: a community of interests could be fostered by assembling librarians and trustees on a regional basis; departmental officials, especially the inspector, could discuss library conditions and speak directly with participants; and participants could join round-table discussions and receive instruction on library methods, economy, new issues, and procedures.[108] While everyone was conscious of the need for training and local organization, recreation and socializing were not ignored. For example, at the 1908 Niagara

Institute chaired by William H. Arison, the delegates took an evening side trip on the country's busiest electric railway to the new St. Catharines Carnegie library.[109]

Following the new act of 1909, local response to the institutes was crucial. By the end of 1910, representatives of 234 libraries attended twelve regional institutes; this compared favourably to the 55 libraries which sent delegates to the OLA convention that same year. This encouraging trend continued (Table 11: Libraries Represented at OLA and Library Institutes, 1907-14). On a regional basis, the twelve groupings were Brantford, Chatham, Niagara, Eastern, Belleville, Georgian, Guelph, Lindsay, London, Orangeville, Stratford, and York. The autumn 1909 Eastern Institute meeting, hosted by Lawrence Burpee at Ottawa's new Carnegie Library, was particularly important (Illus 31). Twenty-three libraries were represented; it was the largest institute to date. It included the Montreal librarians Charles Gould, the current president of the American Library Association, and Mary S. Saxe from Westmount. Otto Klotz, Jr., presided as chairman. Obviously, institutes were a viable way of reaching many libraries with news, ideas, and practices.

The Education Department considered the institutes essential because Walter Nursey's small staff could not possibly hope to inspect and direct library progress from Toronto. To encourage participation, the department covered the entire cost of travel for delegates and extended the sessions to two days, an arrangement which made possible elementary library instruction. Attendance by librarians was considered essential. Nursey liked to point to Ridgeway, a small hamlet of six hundred people, as an example of the institutes' influence in the process of elevating the status of libraries. Dr. George Snyder and another Ridgeway trustee attended the institute at Niagara Falls in 1908 and came away excited about the prospects of building a new library. By year's end, Ridgeway's building committee was hard at work. The goal for 1909 was to find property, raise $1,100, and launch an up-to-date library service. The trustees erected a small bungalow, thirty-six ft. long by twenty ft. wide and hired Effie Schmidt, now employed by the Library Bureau in Toronto, to recatalogue the collection with the help of a few young ladies (they did not know that Patricia Spereman's assistance was available through the education department). When Dr. Snyder recounted his story at the 1910 Niagara Institute, Ridgeway was applauded as a model for small libraries.[110] Shortly afterwards, Snyder became president of the Niagara district executive.

There were, however, few Ridgeways, as the findings of Snyder's own local survey of twenty-five libraries in the Niagara district confirmed in 1911. Only five libraries owned their building. Most libraries purchased too much fiction, thereby reducing the maximum government grant they could receive if they budgeted the "right" proportions. Municipal grants ranged from $1,700 in Niagara Falls to nothing at Cheapside. Half the boards failed to collect overdue fines, partly because circulation records were deficient. As a remedy, Snyder favoured annual reader's cards that would limit to twenty the number of books (half fiction, half nonfiction) a patron would be allowed to borrow.

> New cards must then be taken out for the new year, and in
> this way extra proceeds are added to your library funds and
> every reader is more careful of his card. By the use of such a
> card non-fiction is encouraged to be read, for the card is a
> constant reminder that non-fiction is supposed to be read,
> and also a person does not care to thrown away his card
> when it is only half used up.[111]

Classification varied from library to library. Some devised their own scheme; others used the old departmental system; six had changed to DDC and Cutter. On the matter of librarians and trained assistants, Snyder advised small boards to choose a young lady with a good education who would work part-time for $30 to $75 a year. The diverse conditions in Niagara pointed to a genuine need for increased library promotion, cooperative efforts, and training by institute executives.

As the OLA organized additional institutes, it became more apparent that they served two different constituencies, trustees and library workers. This was cause for some soul-searching because of its potential consequences for long-term planning. Although organizational meetings usually were held in Toronto each year to draft generic programs, some participants were dissatisfied with district offerings. Mabel Dunham complained to E.A. Hardy about the undue attention trustees received:

> The one thing I feel strongly about in this institute work is
> the way the trustees attend and make the librarian stay home.
> It makes me wrathy. I can't believe it. I do not feel that the
> two-days session is long enough time to hope to give the
> trustees any idea of the Dewey Decimal Classification and
> Rules for Cataloguing. The librarians, in some cases would
> benefit more I am sure. If this elementary school is to be car-
> ried on again this year, I suggest that Miss Spereman do the
> instructing in all places...[112]

Admittedly, local committees often were unable to strike a balance between the needs of trustees and staff. Walter Nursey, who approved the bills and tried to oversee the work of all the institutes, often grumbled to Hardy about the suitability of program arrangements, the merit of printed brochures prepared in advance, or minutiae like the omission from circulars of any reference to the Department of Education.

While Mabel Dunham's criticism was justified, it was equally difficult to deny the need for trustee education and lay leadership. Public entities depended on public opinion and the guidance of appointed representatives. Trustees such as Otto Klotz in Ottawa or Robert McAdams from Sarnia, who worked mostly outside the circle of the OLA executive, provided needed regional energy and encouragement. Klotz and his wife, Marie, had been associated with the free library project in Ottawa since the mid-1890s. He spoke at the Eastern Institute and had a paper read at OLA in 1910 on the role of trustees and the library's value in a community.[113] Robert McAdams, the Sarnia newspaperman, was less prominent, but his views were still important. He emphasized the vital link between trustees and the public. McAdams told trustees at the Chatham district institute that they should develop policies to keep the public in touch with the activities of the library: "The idea is to get the public to realize that the Library is their Library; that the books which it contains are their books; and that the employees and members of the board are at their service for any information or assistance which they may require."[114] The subordination of the trustee's management function was an important new direction. Better trained librarians now were poised to assume a greater administrative voice in library work.

"Quite a Big Boy Now"

By 1913, after the addition of three more institute districts, two in the north and one in Toronto, there were fifteen regional institutes in operation (Map 2: Library Institute Districts in Ontario, 1913). With the sudden enlargement of the "library community" to many parts of Ontario which were unaccustomed to free service or modern lines of library work, it was evident that library extension and collective efforts demanded even more attention. Small public libraries, which formed an overwhelming majority in the province, led a precarious existence. Andrew Denholm, a trustee from Blenheim, reckoned that a "small" library was one that could not earn a legislative grant of $100. Using his definition, only fifty-six free and seventeen association public libraries were earning more than $100 in 1910. For Denholm, reaching all persons was a necessity because "the welfare of our Canadian nation demands that every unit of the population should be given the largest opportunity for mental expansion."[115] The OLA executive agreed with his assessment. In their view, the 1909 act had improved the fortune of the small library, but it had not solved the problem of inadequate services in many rural areas.

Inspector Nursey undertook to investigate the provincial dimensions of library service in 1911. It was the first extensive survey of library progress since the introduction of service in 1882. By grouping the 355 reporting service points into urban and rural categories, Nursey was able to chart the successes and problems of uneven library development.[116] His figures have been reworked with a computer program (Table 12: Public Library Service in Ontario, 1910/11). In urban Ontario (cities, towns, and villages), 92.6% of the population was served by a free or association library board. In rural townships, a mere 7.4% of the population received library service through boards organized in police villages or association hamlets; the remaining 92.6% was unserved. There were 377,170 people in townships who were not served by any type of library board; 552,418 people lived in townships which were contiguous to library boards and indirectly received service by payment of non-resident membership fees. These two totals accounted for 91.8% of the number of persons unserved by public libraries in Ontario and 40.5% of all the people in the province!

The spatial extent of library service (based on Nursey's survey) is shown in Map 3: Municipalities in Southern Ontario without Libraries in 1911/12. The unshaded portion (377,170 people in townships without any access to service) represents 16.4% of the provincial population; the shaded area represents a further 27.7% of the provincial population (635,909 persons) situated in towns, villages, or townships who were served indirectly by neighbouring library boards. In sum, 55.9% of the entire populace (1,283,068 people) was being served.

There was an obvious need for collective action to reach the forty-five percent of the populace who were without direct library service, but opinions varied on how to achieve this goal. Lawrence Burpee spoke on library cooperation at the Eastern Institute in 1911, saying that the 1909 act was a tad paternalistic with regard to some rulings: "if some of the mandatory clauses could be cut out, and room found for one or two broad policies, such as a county library system, the act would be as near perfect as any reasonable librarian could desire."[117] County libraries were being formed in the United States as an alternative to local municipal incorporation; in some cases, county systems were established only for those localities without an existing library. But rural Ontario, eager to guard its heritage of local political control, was not yet ready for this development. Inspector Nursey summarized the situation this way: "I think it is possible to make things too easy."[118] William Arison, who was beginning his lengthy tenure as chairman of the Niagara Falls library, outlined in more detail this self-help and self-promotion attitude that prevailed locally, when he spoke at the Niagara Institute held in Beamsville in 1912:

> *Getting results is the main thing!* Before entering into exten-
> sion on county lines, *let us make the fullest use of what we
> have.* The principal of efficiency is to-day recognized as all-
> important in business management and is no less applicable
> in library work...Good advertising brings results, and it is
> regarded as of so much value that experts are employed to do
> it by many business concerns.[119]

Clearly, the extent of local initiative and freedom was the central issue to be
addressed in any rural library scheme.

Proponents for change were divided on how to introduce a plan that was
practicable. One proposal for the general organization of extension services
drew upon the idea that James Bain had made fifteen years previously: the
need for a central provincial library. A.W. Cameron, OLA president for
1910/11, felt that such a library was a necessary foundation on which to
develop rural library service.

> There is need then of a Provincial Library whose volumes are
> accessible to everyone in this Province; a system of County
> Libraries to supplement the smaller libraries and to exercise
> judicious supervision over them and such provision as will
> make it possible for townships and even sections of them, to
> organize so as to secure free Public Library facilities. Free
> education will not be wholly attained in this Province until it
> is possible for every sincere student to obtain the material for
> his legitimate study and research from some of our Public
> Libraries.[120]

Cameron proposed an amalgamation of the Legislative Library, the Law
Society library at Osgoode Hall, the Department of Education library in the
Normal School, and the Library for the Blind at Markham. But there was little interest. Even Hugh Langton, who had returned as OLA's treasurer for one
year, said that he failed to see the benefit.

In fact, Cameron's suggested amalgamation competed with another major
proposition by Lawrence Burpee, the incoming OLA president for 1911/12.
Burpee wrote to Hardy in February 1911 to say that he had called for the cre-
ation of a National Library at Ottawa, in the pages of Andrew Macphail's
University Magazine. He asked Hardy to "support it by an article in one of the
Toronto newspapers, or wherever you think it would have most weight."[121]
Burpee conceived a central library in the nation's capital which would collect
resources from the whole range of human knowledge, serve as a reference

library, and interloan books to colleges, universities, and provincial and public libraries across the country.[122] The OLA membership unanimously endorsed his concept at the 1911 meeting, calling for a royal commission to investigate the establishment of such a body. Hardy forwarded the resolution to the federal government in May 1911. Although a number of prominent newspapers and magazines, including *Saturday Night*, backed Burpee's argument, national politics followed its own agenda.[123] A federal election was underway by midsummer; it resulted in the defeat of Sir Wilfrid Laurier's Liberal party in September. The plan for a national library lingered for many years thereafter. Burpee resumed his lobbying in 1918 with a proposal to combine a national war memorial with a library, but nothing concrete came of his efforts.[124] Burpee was not to live to see its creation in 1953.

To rouse support for library extension, Lutie Stearns, an outspoken advocate from the travelling library department of the Wisconsin Free Library Commission, was invited to speak at the 1913 OLA conference. She was a success. Stearns spoke of the "library militant," its need for aggressiveness to disseminate "the right ideas and ideals," even if it meant barring certain magazines or authors. The practice of censorship in libraries had yet to be squared with the public's democratic right to read. Comparing the work of her own commission, staffed by seven workers, with the efforts of Walter Nursey, she frankly stated, "I think he ought to get a Carnegie Hero Medal."[125] Stearns was a good judge in these matters: she had helped establish 150 libraries, 1400 travelling libraries, and 14 county systems since commencing her work in 1903.

The OLA finally was in a position to develop a province-wide consensus on library extension in 1912. By this time, library institutes were attracting representatives from more than 250 libraries, which was four times the number in attendance at the OLA annual meeting. The success of the district programs meant that a more accurate gauge of grassroots opinion could be made; thus the OLA's standing legal committee sought resolutions between 1912 and 1914 on a better system of rural extension. The committee considered and rejected a proposal for obligatory library grants by county councils. It then entertained rival plans for a "free rural library" system based on township or county boards. Opinion was divided in the institutes: Guelph and York favoured the county as a unit of service; Lindsay and the Eastern institute advocated the township; Belleville, Niagara, and Chatham did not have a preference; the other institute districts made no comment. In 1914, the legal committee recommended the township as the next logical step.[126]

In fact, neither the OLA, nor rural delegates, nor the Inspector's office could decide on the issue: a clear-cut verdict was impossible in the face of so many options. County system advocates, such as Edwin Hardy and William

Carson, ran the risk of infringing the principle of local autonomy, despite pleas for "a co-operative scheme so that the public money is expended for every part of the public."[127] The Chatham district put forward its own solution: it would allow any city, town or village library board to be taken over by the municipality in which it was geographically situated, thus creating a free library. By this measure, surrounding township residents would be entitled to use libraries free of charge and to receive a grant from the county. Andrew Denholm stated the case at the annual OLA meeting in 1915:

> Let the County Councils see that the people are getting the benefit outside of the towns and villages and there will not be any material objection from them. To adopt this proposition means you are placing a burden on all the County Councils in this Province, probably $50,000.00 a year. It is not a considerable amount at all, and by so doing you put the people of all the townships in the position to go to their nearest town and have library privileges, ...[128]

To some delegates, though, Denholm's option trespassed on the autonomy of cities and towns.

There were other remedies. Bolstering provincial aid or relaxing grant regulations for smaller libraries were familiar themes, ones popular with the grassroots majority. However, Walter Nursey was quick to point out that Ontario's financial aid took second place to none and that legislative aid was not likely to be increased. This being political reality, some old library schemes were revived. For example, following the 1914 recommendation, one of the members of the legal committee, Norman Gurd (Illus. 30), who had resumed his activity in OLA after writing *The Story of Tecumseh*, must have startled his audience at the Eastern Institute when he suggested that the rural schoolhouse could function as a free public library. The school section board, then, would constitute the library board. He was aware that this system "was tried years ago in Ontario and was not a success ... but much water has run under the bridges since then."[129]

However, there could be no turning back to Ryerson's free public library system in public schools. Urban life and communications were transforming the regional bastions of Ontario. Toronto was the hub of the province's industrial life. As the pace of society quickened, the interconnections between farmhouse and city factory became more binding. Now more than fifty percent of the populace lived in urban centres according to the census of 1911; farm communities were suffering the effects of this exodus. Highways were about to replace railways. According to a 1912 automobile guide, close to twenty thousand automobiles were now registered in the province, several clubs had been formed, and a concrete highway from Toronto to Hamilton was under construction. By 1914, the transmission lines of the Hydro-Electric Power Commission of Ontario, formed in 1906 under the direction of the ambitious London politician, Adam Beck, connected dozens of southern cities with generating stations at Niagara Falls. Farmers were promised the convenience of lighting, electric farm tools and house appliances. Telephone lines crisscrossed the rural landscape and competed against rural free mail delivery. The old school section, Ryerson's centre of rural life, was dwarfed in the process.

But these changes being so recent were not necessarily pervasive. In rural Ontario, there was no base on which to build a library system. The number of police villages which had adopted free libraries since 1898 was negligible, and smaller communities, where association libraries thrived, could not possibly muster the tax resources to support free libraries. Permitting townships to form free library boards was a simple, logical course, but the government always had been reluctant to use this arrangement. A decade earlier, it had blocked a private member's bill sponsored by Thomas Lennox, a Conservative from York North riding, which would have permitted free libraries in townships.[130] Presumably, the government felt more study was required before a complete revision of the library act could be issued. When the government finally did act in 1916, it was mostly in response to the township of South Norwich, which wanted to secure a $6,000 Carnegie grant for a library in the police village of Otterville. In this case, the member from South Oxford prepared legislation to allow townships to form free libraries (6 George V, c.45). The act solved Otterville's problem; it seemed logical; and it reflected the desire of rural residents to keep decisions for rate-supported services close at hand. Self-help and local autonomy were integral partners in the success of library extension, although it was an uneasy coalition to maintain in any type of cooperative scheme.

If the OLA was unsuccessful in defining the kind of library extension best suited to rural Ontario, it was able to boost the image of library service by hosting the ALA annual meeting in 1912 at Ottawa. Executive members had talked for years about such a meeting; however, they had never taken any definite action. There always seemed to be too few people to act as a local organizing committee or participate in programs. For example, OLA efforts to promote a "Canadian Day" at the July 1910 ALA meeting on Mackinac Island, Michigan, had failed for want of speakers and financial support. Walter Nursey declined to become too involved in any plan to host ALA, but he did agree with Hardy that "it would be an admirable idea to try and get the American Library Association to hold their annual meeting say in 1912 in Canada."[131]

Three days after receiving Nursey's letter, Hardy read a missive from Burpee.

> My dear Hardy:
> A formal invitation has just been sent from here to the A.L.A. to meet in Ottawa in 1911. I have been trying for several years to arrange such a meeting, but hitherto the lack of satisfactory hotel accomodation [sic] has stood in the way. Now however we have the promise that the Chateau Laurier will be completed next spring. I shall be very glad if Cameron and yourself would formally endorse the invitation on behalf of the O.L.A. You could either write direct to Hodges, or send me a letter that I could submit at the meeting this year.
> I hope that you and Cameron and at least a few others will manage to get to Mackinac.
> Yours sincerely[132]

Burpee was the right man to organize the meeting. He had many contacts in the Eastern Institute, the government, and national organizations in the capital, which allowed him to put together an energetic local committee of approximately forty politicians, academics, librarians, teachers, judges, trustees, and organizational representatives. For their part, both Nursey and Hardy were to become principals in rousing other libraries to make the convention a success.

After the ALA executive considered Ottawa's proposal, they chose 1912 as a suitable time for their second visit to Canada. Burpee, Hardy, and Nursey all worked tirelessly to organize a strong Canadian contingent. Dr. Pyne agreed to allocate $900 towards the meeting; most of the money was reserved for travelling arrangements. Hardy compiled a list of one hundred libraries and mailed a memorandum in January 1912 requesting boards to send a representative, preferably the librarian, and to underwrite hotel accommodation for five days. Delegates were asked to fund their own registration and membership fees, which were set at $3.00.[133] The April OLA gathering, attended by sixty members, was another opportunity to discuss the advantages of registering for the ALA conference.

This undertaking occupied Hardy and Nursey for the first six months of 1912. Some boards were reluctant to send the librarian; others had to be prodded to attend. In the case of Palmerston, Miss Adeline Kopp asked Hardy to write the board's secretary again, suggesting that the librarian be allowed to attend. The board finally responded to Hardy's follow-up letters and permitted Kopp to go to Ottawa.[134] These day-to-day maneuvers on Hardy's part eventually spelled success. By the beginning of June, Nursey was anxious about costs – he had fewer than $700 to pay transportation expenses all round. He asked Hardy to close the invitation list because "we won't have money enough."[135] Then a preliminary list of about seventy-five delegates, along with railway and hotel arrangements, was published.[136] Eventually, one hundred and twenty-five people from Ontario registered for the ALA conference. This was more than any single American state, including nearby New York. When one considers typical attendance figures at the OLA annual meetings in Toronto, this turnout was a well-organized Canadian showing.

ALA delegates travelled to Ottawa at the end of June by special trains from the east and mid-west states. The western travellers stopped at Toronto where they were guests at a round of local receptions and dinners. Mary Ahern, the editor of the Chicago-based *Public Libraries*, described them as cordial and pleasant but tiring.[137] The conference opened on 26 June; the outgoing president, Herbert Putnam, from the Library of Congress, declared, "we are free to indulge in reciprocities that will be complete, mutual, and enduring."[138] On Dominion Day, Sir Wilfrid Laurier, now leader of the opposition in the Commons, spoke to the assembly about Canadian-American ties, extolling the undefended border as an ideal friendship between two nations worthy of emulation by others. Laurier's sentiments were shared by Richard Bowker, the editor of *Library Journal*, who replied that "American" should be used in a broader sense: "We may almost hope that there shall be no Canada library association, but we hope that Ontario, with its library association, will be the pioneer to lead its sister provinces into the fellowship and affiliation in which our other [state] associations stand in the American library association."[139]

Ontario representatives actively contributed to the proceedings. Canadian offerings dominated the Trustees Section held on Friday evening, 28 June, in the private dining room of the Chateau Laurier. Otto Klotz prepared a paper on board members' duties, and Walter Nursey spoke about the role of trustees.[140] The Americans were surprised (or amused) by frequent references in the local press to the sizeable number of women at the conference, and they found the number of male trustees from the host province unusual.[141] At the conclusion of the general annual meeting, a resolution was passed supporting the establishment of a National Library "at the earliest possible moment." By all accounts, the conference was deemed successful. It was proof of Ontario's growing stature in the world of librarianship. The ALA would not return to Canada for another fifteen years, and when it did, George Locke, a minor official in 1912, would host events at Toronto as ALA's president.

By 1914, the OLA had unquestionably matured. The president, William F. Moore, summed up the general sentiment: "This is the fourteenth year of our existence and we are getting to be 'quite a big boy' now, and we should pause and take stock of our proceedings."[142] He remarked that the association had secured some impressive achievements, notably summer training schools and library institutes. But the promotion of modern methods in local libraries seemed foremost in his thoughts:

> Before we organized, every Library stood as an isolated unit with very little influence even locally. The great majority of them were Mechanics' Institutes with a membership fee and a very high age limit. I do not think there were ten libraries in the Province with open shelving and probably not more than the same number have a standard system of shelving. Many of them have at least the card system of cataloguing and nearly all of the towns and cities have the Dewey Decimal or Cutter System. No possible help could be given as to systematic purchasing of books or of repairing them.[143]

Moore also stressed that improved government support after 1905 and Carnegie benefactions had helped position the library closer to the centre of local concerns.

In Ontario, library service had improved dramatically within a brief span of time. The provincial population had reached two million after 1900. Meanwhile, the number of volumes held and circulated by free libraries had doubled (Graph 6: Free Library Volumes and Circulation, 1882 to 1918). As well, the OLA was gaining national and international recognition, an impressive feat for so young an organization. In Canada, dedicated alumni from OLA were now helping to organize in other provincial jurisdictions. The ex-president, A.W. Cameron, and Alexander H. Gibbard, one of the original organizers, were instrumental in establishing the Saskatchewan Library Association, which lasted from 1914 to 1918.[144] American librarians conferred recognition upon the OLA at the Ottawa meeting; subsequently, Canadians were invited to speak at state association meetings in New York and Michigan.[145] More American contacts also were made because the OLA shared similar international interests. For instance, in 1914, Matthew Dudgeon, from the Wisconsin Free Library Commission, spoke in Toronto on the universality of library service. It was a goal shared by most trustees and librarians across North America. Like his Ontario colleagues, Dudgeon felt victory depended "upon the people engaged locally in the work, and upon nothing else."[146]

The dimensions of OLA's leadership can be gauged by its position on the thorny problem of book selection, particularly "respectable" fiction. At the first OLA meeting in 1901, William Keller, an Uxbridge publisher, had tapped into mainstream thought when he gave his opinion on the selection process by library board members.

> Therefore we attach a great deal of importance to the charac-
> ter of the books intended for promiscuous readers, and rec-
> ommend directors or purchasing committees of a library to
> exercise as much care as they can in selecting books, and a
> parental censorship. With the greatest care possible some
> trash will creep in, and a lot of light stuff will be read. In fact
> we have to buy a certain amount of it knowingly. Selections,
> however, can be made with a view to lead the readers of the
> lighter fiction into the realms of historical tales, biography
> and voyages and travel, which are a good substitute.[147]

Keller's acceptance of the stepladder theory of reading was not uncommon. It came at the same time when new literary genres were emerging, such as the espionage novel and American western fiction. Erskine Calder's *The Riddle of the Sands* (1903) was an excellent example of the former, and Owen Wister's *The Virginian* (1902) became a benchmark for the latter. As well, the censor's role continued to be an integral part of librarianship before 1914.[148] On the censorship issue, OLA leaders were hardly enthusiastic proponents for more lenient standards.

The inhibition of thought was an ingrained part of the Edwardian men-
tality. After William Sykes, Ottawa's new chief librarian, set about the task of developing a retrospective list of about two thousand fiction titles for Canadian public libraries, he spoke on the subject of trustworthy selection guides at a session of the 1914 OLA conference. For current books, he recommended the American Library Association monthly book list, the OLA's year-
ly book list, and the English *Librarian and Book World*; for current reviews, he suggested the Chicago *Dial*, the New York *Nation* (both termed "fearless" for their independence), and the London *Athenaeum* ("a stern watchtower"). For retrospective buying, he favoured the *A.L.A. Catalog, 1904* and its supple-
ments, the H.W. Wilson Company's *Fiction Catalog* published in 1908, and Ernest. A. Baker's *Guide to the Best Fiction in English*.[149] Sykes' own work, *Selected List of Fiction in English* (1914), supported the status quo: along with the 1904 *A.L.A. Catalog* and the 1908 Wilson *Fiction Catalog*, it declined to include controversial novels. Gustave Flaubert's *Madame Bovary*, Emile Zola's *Germinal*, Thomas Hardy's *Jude the Obscure*, George Meredith's *Lord Ormont*, Oscar Wilde's *Picture of Dorian Gray*, George Moore's *Esther Waters*, Arthur Morrison's *Tales of Mean St.*, Henry James' *Turn of the Screw, The*

Ambassadors, and *Awkward Age,* and Frank Norris' *McTeague* – all these significant works of literature were absent from the three lists.[150] Librarians and trustees believed that there were limits to public tolerance, and the OLA did not explore the boundaries.

The first years of the Great War fortified traditional social beliefs and values. It was a time for self-reflection on the part of Ontario library workers. At the Ashbury Park, New Jersey ALA annual conference, on 1 July 1916, Edwin Hardy lectured on the special features of Ontario's library system.

> First, the public library is an integral part of the educational system of the province. Second, voluntary co-operation, organized as the Ontario Library Association, is a driving force of increasing power. Third, the joint activity of the official staff [the education department] and the unofficial organization makes possible many things that neither could accomplish by itself. Fourth, the development of the trustee has kept pace with that of the librarian. It may be that this is our most distinctive feature ...[151]

The Ontario library movement was riding a crescendo of applause and self-congratulation. A good deal was justified. The system's merits outweighed its faults, and Ontario's librarians had a right to radiate enthusiasm and energy.

The worthy accomplishments of the OLA were interrupted abruptly by the outbreak of war in Europe. All public energies were urgently channelled towards the swift subjugation of the Central Powers. In every community across the province, patriotic work and enlistment became the order of the day. Almost a quarter-million Ontarians would shoulder arms for Empire and Country in a struggle the magnitude and ferocity of which no one imagined in August 1914. Library trustees and other officers were no exceptions. Inspector Nursey, a veteran of the North-West rebellion, canvassed libraries to find that forty men and women already had joined military ranks by the first months of 1915. Their names immediately were published as an honour roll.[152] Patriotism and heroism were still noble virtues in spring 1915.

However, as the conflict escalated with no decision in sight, a noticeable change of public mood transpired as the grief, horror, and ultimate futility of warfare came to be better comprehended. Many readers saw the truth of the matter in H.G. Well's *Mr. Britling Sees It Through,* a realistic wartime novel which portrayed a young American recruit in the Canadian army who dreamed not of conquest but of a lasting peace. The Great War came to signify not another imperial interlude in the nation's history, but a psychological watershed, a coming of age undertaken in a brutal baptism of fire at obscure infernos: Ypres, the Somme, Hill 70, Vimy Ridge, and Passchendaele. Once the soldiers returned home, politics and private life were changed forever. The library movement was no different. Its many pre-war achievements were pale memories by November 1918.

Illus. 1 Egerton Ryerson [AO, S-623]

Illus. 2 Toronto Mechanics' Institute entrance to Music Hall on Adelaide Street, n.d. [AO, S-1178]

EXHIBIT OF THE EDUCATION DEPARTMENT, ONTARIO, AT THE CENTENNIAL INTERNATIONAL EXHIBITION 1876

Illus. 3 Ontario's prize and school library book display (front row, far left) at the Philadelphia Exhibition, 1876

[J.G. Hodgins, *Special Report on Ontario Educational Exhibit* (1876)]

Illus. 4 Waterloo Mechanics' Institute in Town Hall on Albert Street, n.d. Entrance on right side. [Waterloo Public Library]

Illus. 5 John Taylor served on Toronto library board, 1884-99 [MTRL, T-3061]

Illus. 6 Joseph Gould Institute built of white brick with red brick trimming, completed 1887 [*RME* for 1907]

Illus. 7 Stack room and delivery desk in Clinton library [AO, S-2031]

Illus. 8 Streetsville Free Public Library after 1 Nov. 1901 [AO, S-16035]

Illus. 9
Merchant, alderman, library
chairman: John Hallam,
1833-1900 [MTRL, T-13698]

Illus. 10
James Bain, Jr., 1842-1908
[MTRL, T-13648]

Illus. 11
Grip cartoon, 2 Dec. 1882,
"The Workingman's chance":
Scene: a gentleman's house
Tom Plane – Jack, how long do
you 'spose it will be before you
or me owns a library like this?
Jack Square – Not long. I
expect to have something finer
than this early in the new year.
Tom – Nonsense! What do you
mean?
Jack – I mean that I'm going to
vote for the Free Public Library
at the same time that I mark my
ballot for John Taylor as
Alderman.

Illus. 12 *Grip* cartoon, 30 Dec. 1882, "A chance for the sons of toil":
Santa Claus: Vote for it, my dears, and you shall have it.

Illus. 13 The Muskoka Club: the OLA presidents are James Bain (4) and William Tytler (7). [MTRL, T-15202]

Illus. 14 Dundas Public Library in the old Elgin House Hotel on King Street, c. 1896 [AO, S-6934]

Illus. 15 Toronto Public Library's branch on Dundas Street, c. 1900
[MTRL, T-30605]

Illus. 16 A quiet place to read: Hamilton's reading room, n.d.
[Hamilton Public Library]

Illus. 17 James Howe with his captain's hat in the Southampton Mechanics' Institute library, n.d. [Bruce County Museum]

Illus. 18 London's old red brick library, n.d. [London Public Library]

Illus. 19
Robert Blackwell, chief
librarian 1895-1906,
London Public Library
[London Public Library]

Illus. 20 *Globe* cartoon, 26 Jan. 1899: "Our Free Library." What Uncle Sam doesn't known about governing a nation would fill several volumes – and we have the books.

Illus. 21
Lawrence J. Burpee believed in modern methods
[NAC, PA-110839]

Illus. 22 Standing room only: Toronto Public Library's central newspaper reading room, c. 1900 [MTRL, T-12006]

Illus. 23
Edwin Austin Hardy,
OLA secretary 1900-25.
[E.A. Hardy, *Public Library*]

Illus. 24 Toronto reference staff, c. 1895. *Standing l. to r.*: Eva Davis, Rose Ferguson, Elizabeth Moir, Hattie Pettit, Margaret McElderry, Margaret Graham, Frances Staton. *Seated l. to r.*: Teresa O'Connor, Mina Wylie.
[MTRL, T-12007]

Illus. 25
William Tytler, one of the OLA
"originals"
[E.A. Hardy, *Public Library*]

Illus. 26 OLA conference delegates, 16 April 1906. Seated in front row:
Norman Gurd (third from left), William Robertson, president (centre),
James Bain (far right) [Ontario Library Association]

Illus. 27 After the story hour: Sarnia Public Library, 2 March 1907
[AO, S-2058]

Illus. 28
B. Mabel Dunham, chief
librarian 1908-44, Kitchener
Public Library
[E.A. Hardy, *Public Library*]

Illus. 29 First Summer Library School, 1911. *Top row l. to r.:* Inspector Nursey, Fred DelaFosse, Lewis Hornung. *Centre row l. to r., third,* Patricia Spereman, *fifth,* Mabel Dunham. *Front row far l.:* Mary Black. [*RME* 1911]

Illus. 30
Progressive ideals: Norman Gurd, Sarnia Public Library 1900-43 [E.A. Hardy, *Public Library*]

Illus. 31 Eastern Institute meeting, Ottawa, 17 Nov. 1909. Otto Klotz (1), Charles Gould, McGill (2), Lawrence Burpee (3), Mary Saxe, Westmount P.L. (4), Walter Nursey (5) [Ottawa Public Library]

Illus. 32 Andrew Carnegie (to left of the mayor of Ottawa wearing the chain of office) at the opening of the Carnegie Library, Ottawa, 30 April 1906

Illus. 33 Pedimented Beaux-Arts style: Lindsay Public Library, c. 1905
[AO, S-2037]

Illus. 34 Columned Beaux-Arts style: Guelph Public Library, c. 1905
[AO, S-2035]

At the Opening of the Library.

Illus. 35 Ottawa *Evening Journal,* 28 April 1906: "Wake Up! We're Going to Open the Library."

Illus. 36 Children's department at Ottawa, c. 1909 [Ottawa Public Library]

Illus. 37 Reference library on College Street, Toronto, 13 March 1915
[NAC, PA-61384]

Illus. 38 Reading room, Toronto Public Library, 11 March 1924
[NAC, PA-86499]

Illus. 39 Adam Hunter (and library staff?) at the laying of the cornerstone at Hamilton, 1 Aug. 1911 [Hamilton Public Library]

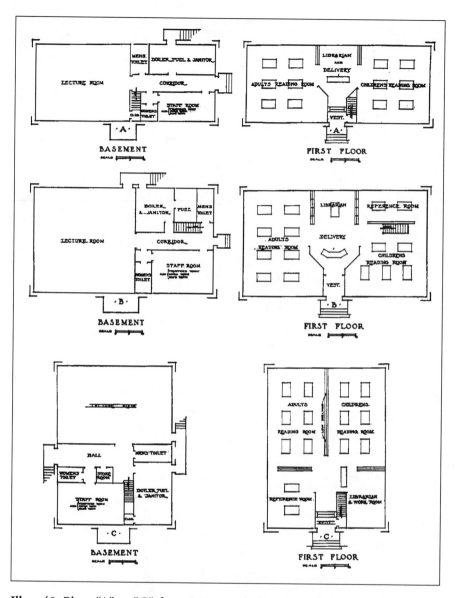

Illus. 40 Plans "A" to "C" from *Notes on the Erection of Library Buildings* by James Bertram

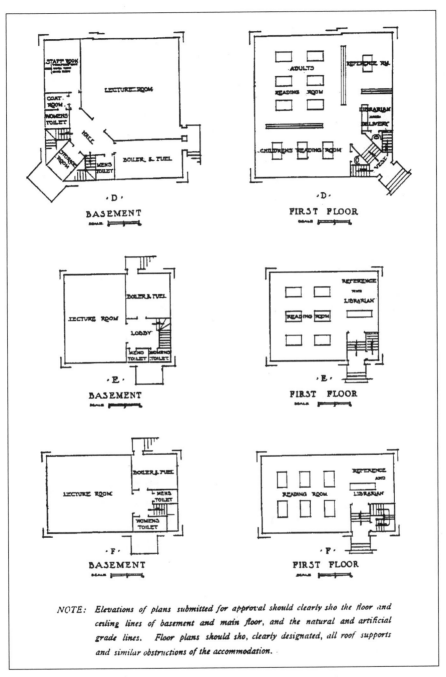

· D ·
BASEMENT

· D ·
FIRST FLOOR

· E ·
BASEMENT

· E ·
FIRST FLOOR

· F ·
BASEMENT

· F ·
FIRST FLOOR

NOTE: Elevations of plans submitted for approval should clearly sho the floor and ceiling lines of basement and main floor, and the natural and artificial grade lines. Floor plans should sho, clearly designated, all roof supports and similar obstructions of the accommodation.

Illus. 41 Plans "D" to "F" from *Notes on the Erection of Library Buildings* by James Bertram

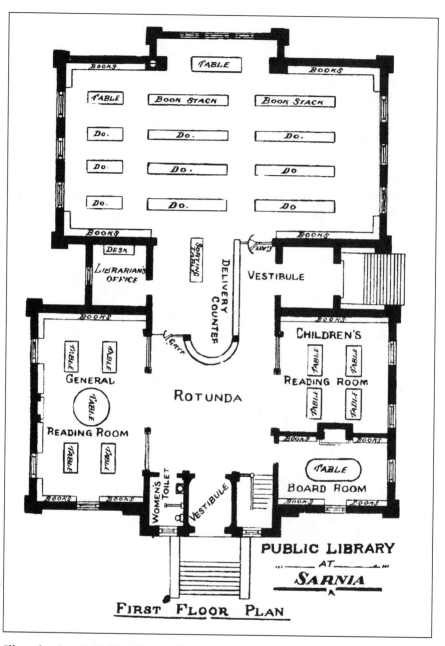

Illus. 42 Sarnia Public Library floor plan [*RME* for 1906]

Illus. 43 Public Library, Victoria Park, Sarnia, c. 1907 [NAC, PA-60700]

Illus. 44
Mary J. Black, chief librarian at
Fort William 1909-37
[E.A. Hardy, *Public Library*]

Illus. 45
William O. Carson,
1874-1929 [London Public Library]

Illus. 46
George Herbert Locke, c. 192-?,
chief librarian, Toronto Public
Library, 1909-37 [MTRL, T-13722]

Illus. 47 Toronto Public Library branch on Church Street, 8 Feb. 1924
[NAC, PA 86436]

Illus. 48
William Sykes, OLA president
1921/22 [NAC, C-27771]

Illus. 49 Boys' and Girls' House, St. George Street, c. 1922 [MTRL, T-30604]

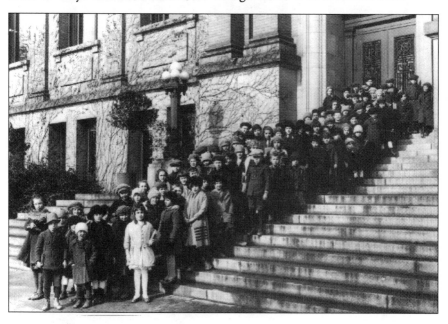

Illus. 50 Waiting for the story hour at Toronto Central Library, c. 1921 [MTRL, T-12141]

Illus. 51 Main floor of Kingston Public Library, c. 1925 [Kingston Public Library]

Illus. 52 Passing the Carnegie Brantford Library entrance, 7 May 1922
[NAC, PA-84804]

Illus. 53 Ontario Library Association executive officers, 19 April 1926:
l. to r.: E.A. Hardy, F. DelaFosse, William Briden (St. Catharines),
James Steele (Stratford), George W. Rudlen (Arnprior), Fred Landon,
Winifred Matheson (Brantford), Aimee Kennedy, Mary J. Black,
David Williams (Collingwood), George Locke [AO, 1018]

Illus. 54 Foreign delegates at ALA conference, New York's Hotel Plaza
ballroom, 9 Oct. 1926. George Locke seated third from right at head table
[MTRL, T-13643]

Chapter 7

CARNEGIE PHILANTHROPY

When Andrew Carnegie retired from the business of steel in 1901, he formally offered a program to fund the construction of public library buildings in English-speaking countries. His fortuitous munificence accelerated the transformation of library service in Ontario. Leaders in the OLA provided ideas and energy for action, and the Education Department encouraged and regulated developments; however, Carnegie grants were the necessary catalyst in the rapid expansion of public libraries during the Edwardian era. Carnegie's generosity made possible the erection of public edifices specifically designed as libraries, supplanting the ill-suited halls and cramped, rented rooms that had passed for libraries since 1882. In some instances, the metamorphosis was swift. Robert Nixon, the son of a Liberal premier and a former leader of the Liberal party in Ontario, said, "The founder of our library system was Andrew Carnegie, an American who was born in Scotland. He did more for the library system of this province than this Legislature ..."[1] Nixon's judgement, far from being hyperbole, accurately summed up the lasting impact of Carnegie philanthropy.

The steel magnate from tiny Dunfermline possessed a simple philosophy about libraries. He was uninterested in almsgiving. As he noted in his essay, "The Gospel of Wealth," his fortune was directed to those who demonstrated the indispensable ethic of self-help: "No millionaire will go far wrong in his search for one of the best forms for the use of his surplus who chooses to establish a free library in any community that is willing to maintain and develop it."[2] Carnegie's faith in libraries stemmed from his belief that they were an integral component of local self-government. Municipal government, particularly the American variant, was a feature of the democratic genius of the Anglo-Saxon race. It was a political convention which citizens in other nations should adopt to their own advantage. Writing in *Triumphant Democracy*, an industrial captain's paean to the American republic and its industrious citizens, Carnegie stated, "her members are readers and buyers of books and reading matter beyond the members of any government of a class."[3] Years later, in Ottawa, Carnegie still held to this belief: "The free library flourishes only under free institutions. It is the child of triumphant democracy. Within its walls there is perfect equality."[4]

Carnegie was like John Hallam: he had an abiding respect for book-learning and self-education. It was a panacea he had adopted when he emigrated from Scotland to America and began working as a bobbin boy in a cotton mill near Pittsburgh. He never abandoned his faith in libraries; it became a lifelong commitment. On 11 March 1915, he wrote William Carson, the president of OLA, summarizing his thoughts on the value of the library as a social force.

> The library has become an essential part of the useful and intellectual life of the community. Its work begins with the children, in many cases before the school. It follows the pupil through the school years and helps him in his study hours. It follows him in his business and profession and helps his wife at home. In fact, it furnishes instruction, recreation, solace, help and inspiration.[5]

If knowledge was power, people of all ages from every station in life, who availed themselves of the library's resources, might benefit from its civilizing force.

The terms for receiving a grant directly from Carnegie or the Carnegie Corporation (between 1911 and 1917) were straightforward.[6] Two businesslike commitments were required from local municipalities before funds for a building were released: a suitable site and a promise to provide at least ten percent of the total grant for annual operating expenses. Most architectural arrangements were made locally; not until 1908 were communities required to forward building plans before grants were authorized. Carnegie and his personal secretary, James Bertram, who handled library correspondence, both insisted on dealing with elected officials and library trustees on this score, thereby eliminating voluntary associations from the philanthropic process. The standard Carnegie formula for awarding grants was approximately two dollars per capita. In Ontario, grants ranged from $275,000 for Toronto's central library to $3,000 for Kemptville. Most grants were not sizeable. Only three places – Toronto, Ottawa, and Hamilton – received $100,000 or more before the Carnegie building gifts ceased at the end of 1917.

There was also a third requirement, one that boosted the social standing of public library service: the library must be free to its citizens. Society or association libraries which charged membership fees were excluded from Carnegie's largesse. In 1900, there were 126 free library boards and 263 public libraries classified as not free for a total of 389 boards in Ontario. This was a remarkable increase over two decades. Free libraries were mostly of recent origin; they had come into existence after the revised 1895 legislation had broadened the meaning of free status and eliminated the necessity for a local bylaw vote. However, some large cities, such as Ottawa or Kingston, had not made the transition to free status; their communities could apply for Carnegie grants but were not eligible to receive them until they adopted those procedures in the provincial act which refashioned the power, funding, and governance of their boards. The American millionaire's program strengthened the ranks of free libraries, and provided an important asset for local organizers who were attempting to improve library conditions.

What then were the major consequences of Carnegie philanthropy in Ontario? Ottawa's civic address of welcome for the New York celebrity, who personally opened its library in 1906 (Illus. 32), proclaimed a lasting debt: "In your generous support of the public library movement you have earned not only the gratitude of the present generation, but the gratitude of generations to come."[7] Beyond the rhetoric, Carnegie funding was a pivotal moment in the province's public library history. There is ample evidence that it provided a strong incentive for libraries to attain free status. Since the local interplay among individuals, library boards, municipal councils, and aldermen usually resulted in acceptance of a proposed gift, libraries generally profited from these debates. Even in difficult circumstances, any increase in public support furthered the cause of free libraries. Tavistock is a good example. It received Carnegie approval in April 1914 shortly before the Great War; it passed its free library bylaw in May 1915 by a vote of 123 to 20; and then it proceeded to erect its building while public energy was devoted to the war effort.[8]

The Carnegie program of library building undoubtedly stimulated and reinforced the library movement. Free library service and the popular use of books grew steadily during the Carnegie years. The public perception of the library changed at the same time new library methods, building techniques, and architectural concepts were introduced. Trustees, librarians, and architects experimented with open access; shelving arrangements which accommodated books classified according to the decimal system; less imposing circulation counters which used more efficient charging systems; children's sections; and improved floor layouts which reduced the number of halls and passageways. The emphasis in library design evolved from a priority on storage to user convenience and preference. As a result, the public library's service programs garnered increased public respect; its institutional base in the community was strengthened; its ranks were swelled with new recruits; its goals were redefined with the object of catering to the convenience and perceived needs of users. The Carnegie boom of the first two decades of the twentieth century helped create a shared vision of the library as a busy centre of community intellectual life.

Mr. Carnegie's Canadian Reception

Carnegie funding was often a source of contention in many Ontario communities. Carnegie spoke freely on many issues; his name was associated with many causes and viewpoints, some less palatable than others, which transcended national boundaries.[9] The conflicts that surfaced when library gifts became available provided a valuable opportunity for library boosters to explain the important role libraries served and to attract more supporters. A great awakening was slowly taking place. Many local allies, who otherwise would not have served as library trustees or have been associated with the OLA, came forth and successfully altered the status quo within their communities. Obviously, additional backing was crucial, for a community's alleged fondness for book-reading by itself would not convince many aldermen to accept the responsibility of erecting a library and providing subsequent maintenance.

Although opposition to Carnegie funding arose on numerous occasions, the opinions of local elites and the general public converged to actuate a high degree of acceptance. The various reasons for acceptance underscore the complexity of local political culture and the growing strength that the public library movement was achieving in the age of Carnegie. Recent American research on local or regional responses to Carnegie benefactions indicates that pro-library arguments may have been similar across the nation but often were voiced in terms of dissimilar local cultural settings; also, variations could exist within regions.[10] The Ontario experience suggests similar conclusions, that is, a resemblance of surface events with underlying structural differences. It also demonstrates, in a Canadian context, that pro-Carnegie considerations boosted the public library movement during this critical period, even though Carnegie's opinions and his image clashed with some of Canada's national goals.

Andrew Carnegie was the son of a Chartist weaver. He loved to invoke his Scottish roots and sometimes recalled that his father had organized a circulating library in his home town. The Union Jack sewn to the Star Spangled Banner flew over Carnegie's holiday castle at Skibo, described by an Ontario writer-poet, Wilfred Campbell, as ancient Scotland with American touches.[11] But in Canada the steel king was regarded as a foreigner, an American capitalist who did not know (or care) about Canadian aspirations and the country's material and social conditions. On the question of Canadian nationhood, Carnegie claimed that Canada's destiny lay with the United States, that the British connection would falter in a world where all colonial linkages were weakening.[12] In *Triumphant Democracy* he wrote:

> But why talk of Canada, or of any mere colony? What book,
> what invention, what statue or picture, what anything has a

colony ever produced, or what man has grown up in any colony who has become know beyond his own local district? None.[13]

Naturally, this drew the ire of strict Canadian nationalists, who were opposed to continental union, and imperial thinkers, such as Premier George Ross, who felt that Canada had to evolve within the British orbit. Another serious liability was Carnegie's decision to champion American style republicanism – "the march of the Republic" – over British political institutions at a time when Canada was still proud to be the eldest daughter of the empire and when Canadian Clubs were forming in major cities.

Many Canadian imperialists believed that Canada's national character was unfolding within a British imperial federation that was strengthened by the young nation's vigour. In fact, the phrase "splendid isolation," often used to describe Britain's *fin-de-siècle* diplomatic situation, originated in Canada's parliament. It was coined when American pressure on Britain heightened during the Venezuelan crisis of 1895-96. Its terminology applied not only to Britain but also to the great Mother Empire itself to which Canada belonged by choice and which Canada was destined to transform as its stature and influence matured.[14] The imperialist sentiment thrived in Ontario. Sara Jeannette Duncan's *The Imperialist* was an accurate barometer of this mood. However, as Canadian nationalism grew, the British tie weakened. Common sense dictated a middle course. Canada was the United States' best neighbour, a partner in the world's longest undefended border. It shared a continental culture; for example, in 1904, Canadians competed as a separate team at the third Olympiad held in St. Louis. A growing number of people were inclined to think that Canada could live peacefully with both powers as a completely independent nation.

Some Ontarians refused outright to accept any Carnegie assistance. To them, self-help meant carrying out good works at home; charity from abroad was denounced as demeaning and enervating, especially when they read Carnegie's pronouncement that "Canada has no future except as part of the United States."[15] The Conservative federal member for West Toronto, Edmund B. Osler, characterized Carnegie's $350,000 offer to Toronto as "a piece of impertinence." He felt that Toronto was able to govern its own education and should not submit to Carnegie's arbitrary terms. Lieutenant-Colonel George T. Denison, an old "Canada Firster" and ardent imperialist, stood his ground: the outside offer should be resisted, Toronto was able to pay its own way. But other staunch supporters of Canadian independence disagreed. John McConnell, the assertive manager of *Saturday Night* who advocated increased national autonomy, wanted to accept the money to build up

Canada; he reasoned no one would refuse money from Canada if it were offered abroad.[16]

A Methodist clergyman, A.H. Going, issued a typical nationalist expression of disfavour at the beginning of 1902. Going told his Stratford congregation that an important reason for refusing Carnegie's money was the issue of his comments on Canadian nationality.

> Carnegie was a foreigner and a foreigner who aimed at the subverting of our relation to the mother country. 'He would touch money from no man who would aim to pull down the British flag from over the Dominion, to replace it with the stars and stripes.'[17]

When Going's remarks were attacked in Stratford newspapers and rejected by the municipal council, he repeated his earlier criticism and proudly asserted, "I'm a Canadian. I'm not a great man, but I want it understood that a colony has produced one man who spurns his proffered gold, and who would feel himself less a man if he did not say so."[18] His stand drew support from many quarters, and the Stratford council only accepted the gift by a narrow vote of five to four after three months of debate.[19] Stratford became one of the first Carnegie libraries to open its doors in Ontario, in September 1903, but the name "Carnegie" did not appear above the entrance.

Opponents, including Going, were at a serious disadvantage when they were asked to propose alternative sources of funding. They had to admit that there were no donors close at hand as generous as Carnegie. The public libraries built at Clinton, Napanee, and Uxbridge, which were built before the Carnegie program, were exceptions. Why did Ontario not produce men such as Carnegie or his English counterpart, John Passmore Edwards, who funded about thirty free libraries before his death in 1911? A contemporary columnist in the *Canadian Magazine* wrote, "It is largely a question of a lack of ideals both on the part of the giver and the town."[20] From the perspective of hindsight, perhaps it was simply a case of having fewer millionaires.

For whatever reason, benefactors in Ontario usually did not find the public library worthy of attention. Only a few communities drew substantial support from local donors; for example, Belleville received $25,000 from Senator Harry Corby. Kingston, a city that refused library gifts from foreigners, had to make do with a butcher shop donated in March 1911.[21] Regardless of one's opinion about the man, Andrew Carnegie was forthright in his financial support; once an agreement was struck, the Carnegie Corporation would fulfill its promise if local elected authorities performed their tasks. As a result, philanthropy became divorced from the realm of local paternalism. The direction of Carnegie library benefactions established the modern pattern for foundation grants based on regular, rational, transnational policies.[22]

The absence of bountiful individuals, the woeful condition of some libraries, and the unlikelihood of municipal debentures for a building left no alternative in many cases. In 1903, James Bain, who had gone on record about the need for a revitalized central library in Toronto, and who had spoken about the need to add branches in the last part of 1902,[23] made a strong case on behalf of accepting Carnegie's proposal.

> … the Public Library building, having been erected in 1854, had become so rotten that on Saturday last three men were required to bail out the water which leaked through one section of the library. To place the library in anything like a safe condition would necessitate an outlay of at least $15,000. The heating apparatus had been put in 1872, and such was the condition of the pipes that sufficient heat could not be driven through to keep the temperature about 55 degrees on a cold day.[24]

The librarian's predicament carried the day in a *Globe* editorial that pronounced in favour of Carnegie's intelligent style of philanthropy: it was simply a matter of replacing an unfit and unsuitable library in order to open up "a new era of progress and usefulness."[25] In due time a promise was secured, land was designated for a site, and before the end of 1906 a cornerstone had been laid by the board chairman, Chief Justice William G. Falconbridge.

Some of Carnegie supporters had difficulty dealing with the nationalist charge that he was an American alien, a scheming plutocrat, who could not to be trusted. These same people found comfort in one of the philosophic ideas Carnegie encouraged, "Anglo-Saxon" racism. He believed that the civilization of the two major English-speaking nations, Great Britain and the United States, was racially superior.[26] This vague sentiment softened Carnegie's foreign image to a degree. Since the racial bond between Britain and America made the countries appear to be natural allies, a rapprochement between the two powers became more plausible. Some Canadians, notably Goldwin Smith, a loyal friend of Carnegie, had promoted this convergence theory for many years. It conveniently smoothed the way for British withdrawal in the Americas and recognized the inevitable American expansion in the hemisphere.[27] Even the conservative-minded Toronto *World,* a newspaper ready to scold anyone critical of British tradition, seemed to find elements of nobility and grandeur in Carnegie's global vision.[28] As Anglo-American friendship slowly supplanted the long held hostility between the two nations, Canada's position as a younger member of the Anglo-Saxon family sparked discussion on both sides of the ocean.

Anglo-Saxonism connoted different things to different people. Most knowledgeable Canadians realized that the possibility of a formal alliance between Britain and the United States was unlikely.[29] For some, Anglo-Saxonism implied not so much a racial convention as a cultural aptitude for liberty and self-government. At times, Anglo-Saxonism was evoked as a potent vision of destiny and greatness. Its civilizing mission was, after all, linked with progress. The retired millionaire, who was sometimes inconsistent on many points, eventually revised his stance on Canada without retracting his previous contention that ultimately it would be absorbed by its southern neighbour. When he visited Toronto on 26 April 1906 to address the Canadian Club, the city newspapers reported favourably on Carnegie's declaration that Canada's immediate task was to bring together Great Britain and America, thus reuniting the major English-speaking nations in the beneficial process of "race imperialism." His revision was welcomed. Canada's function as a mediator between the two powers was a familiar theme with prominent imperialists, such as George Monro Grant.

Carnegie's espousal of Anglo-Saxonism coexisted conveniently with Ontario's latent xenophobia concerning its major partner in Confederation, Quebec. Most Anglo-Saxon proponents held that Quebec was inhabited by the predominately Catholic, less gifted French-speaking Latin race (the positive aspects of Norman lineage were acknowledged by more discriminating racial theorists). Even though the idea of racial superiority was shot through with the internal contradictions and intellectual shortcomings of Social Darwinism, there were library boosters in Ontario who could not resist recounting the case of Montreal. In their view, Montreal had declined $150,000 from the American millionaire in 1902 mainly on language and religious grounds, and to their way of thinking, this was folly on a grand scale. When Toronto debated its own offer a year later, the Loyal Orange Lodge counselled aldermen to accept immediately, for it objected to any Roman Catholic ecclesiastic or adherent "attempting to prevent this great Protestant city from enjoying the benefits offered by Mr. Carnegie."[30]

Ontario's anti-French atmosphere, and the posture of its Conservative government, stiffened over time. In 1912, the government considered severely limiting instruction in French in its schools, a course it finally adopted with the infamous Regulation 17.[31] At the same time, *Saturday Night* came to the defense of Carnegie when a Quebec journal, *L'Action Sociale*, attacked him for financing educational services that could erode the strength of Catholicism. The Toronto editor was puzzled and outraged:

... as for Carnegie libraries they [Quebec] have long passed them over, with the result that there is not to-day a decent public library in Quebec city, Montreal, or in any other centre of the province of Quebec where the Catholic church holds sway.[32]

Toronto, on the other hand, had chosen wisely and was reaping the blessings of its earlier decision to accept Carnegie gifts. Obviously, the power of Anglo-Saxonism aroused strong emotions and tended to strengthen Canadian ties with the American benefactor.

A more positive political factor weighing in Carnegie's favour was his belief in progressive social reform fashioned by idealistic individuals, municipal governments, and organizations. Here he was on an advantageous footing, not only in terms of local self-help or personal improvement, but also in general terms regarding social equality, civic and municipal reform, and liberal improvement. These were transatlantic bonds shared by Canadian reformers, American progressives, and British liberals.[33] Stephen Leacock might satirize the bumptious face of businesslike reform in "The Great Fight for Clean Government," published in his *Arcadian Adventures with the Idle Rich*, but reform and boosterism remained a potent force in municipal life. Such was the fervour of local resourcefulness that Lawrence Burpee applauded Carnegie's decision to turn down St. Catharines' request in 1905 for an additional grant of $5,000 to buy furnishings. This city, he alleged, by its attempt to exploit a generous donor, had discredited a principle that all Anglo-Saxon communities ought to possess: self-reliance and self-respect.[34] Both Carnegie and James Bertram doubtless agreed: the Secretary simply rejected St. Catharines by stating, "he [Carnegie] does not see his way to add to the amount."[35]

The pursuit of Carnegie money sometimes introduced the suspicion of opportunism. In Sault Ste. Marie, a new town of the north blessed with pulpwood mills and hydro-electric potential, a local architect, H. Russell Halton, sought a grant and planned a library as part of a larger civic complex that included a fire station, magistrates' court, city offices, and a spacious public hall underneath the library.[36] When the library gift was announced in December 1901, hyperbole in the local newspaper heightened the perception that aldermen were too anxious to grasp a one-time windfall.

Andrew Carnegie, who has so much money he feeds his bull pup on fruit cake the year around, has promised to let go of $10,000 for a free library building for the Soo. Andrew gets four freight car loads of money dumped into his backyard at

> No. 5, West 51st street [sic], New York, every morning,
> whether he will or no, and the thing has got to be a nusance
> [sic] … So he heaved a sigh of relief when Mr. H.R. Halton
> came forward and asked him for a free library building for
> the Soo.[37]

Whatever the local intentions, municipal expense was kept to the absolute minimum. After fire destroyed the uninsured Sault library in 1907, a second grant, this time for $5,500, had to be secured from Carnegie.[38]

Not everyone was ready to acknowledge that libraries deserved lavish sums of money. Goldwin Smith, corresponding with Carnegie, continued to doubt the merits of popular circulating libraries two decades after downtown branches opened in Toronto.[39] Smith wrote to a friend:

> In my humble judgment, Carnegie is making a very doubtful
> use of his money, by multiplying popular libraries, which will
> multiply fast enough of themselves, and which circulate
> about seventy-five per cent of novels. But if I were to tell him
> this, I should run the risk of impairing our friendship.[40]

Part of Smith's unwillingness to offend Carnegie stemmed from a recognition that his friend's philanthropic habits were a positive force for local improvement in many different countries.

Carnegie poured sizeable sums into respectable causes outside the municipal realm that diffused his adversaries' criticisms and attracted support for his personal philosophy of giving. His library giving introduced him to Melvil Dewey, the influential American librarian, who was among the first to endorse the wisdom of Carnegie donations, in an article for the respected *Journal of Social Science*.[41] Carnegie later corresponded with him on many occasions and gave considerable sums to Dewey's efforts to simplify English spelling. The attempt to make simplified English a common world language, which was assisted by well-intentioned luminaries, notably President Theodore Roosevelt, enticed Carnegie to fund Dewey's campaign. However, as time passed and the efforts of the National Simplified Spelling Board yielded few results, he withdrew his annual $25,000 support in 1915.[42] The outbreak of war in Europe dispelled Carnegie's optimistic opinions concerning human nature and the viability of progress. It also ended the immediate prospect of international peace, another cause he held dear to his heart.

Carnegie's involvement in the prewar peace movement was perhaps his boldest initiative in world scale humanitarianism. He often denounced the bellicosity of foreign nations and the ineffectiveness of international diplomacy.

He liked to point to the peaceful boundary shared by Canada and the United States. On his 1906 Canadian trip, Carnegie lauded both the undefended border and Sir Wilfrid Laurier's pronounced distaste for European militarism. The Canadian-American relationship was an illustrious precedent for the rest of the world to imitate: two Anglo-Saxon nations demonstrating the power of peaceful coexistence! It was difficult to argue against Carnegie on this score. Even Laurier himself admitted that the two of them held many ideas in common.[43]

At first, Carnegie elected to exploit his own influence with international figures, but, upon further consideration, he decided to spend his money for peace on a modern corporate plan.[44] After he allocated ten million dollars for the Carnegie Endowment for International Peace in 1910, the prospect for creating worldwide organizations and tribunals to adjudicate disputes between hostile nations seemed auspicious. Carnegie's concern for peaceful endeavours, coming as it did midway in the library program, earned him some credit, but Canadian pacifists were still on the political periphery during these years. Only a handful of people associated with libraries, such as Lewis E. Hornung, supported the peace movement or seemed concerned about international efforts to stem the tide of militaristic jingoism.[45] Nonetheless, Carnegie's exploration of mediative ways to achieve peace conveyed a constructive force in world affairs.

If one ignores Canadian nationalist aspirations, one might view the Carnegie image in Ontario's political culture in a positive light. But that light was diminished by the charge of tainted money. The steel baron had not made his fortune without confrontations with his workers. The most notorious episode occurred in Homestead, Pennsylvania, in July 1892, while Carnegie was abroad. The Carnegie Iron and Steel Company hired three hundred armed Pinkerton agents to deal with a workers' strike organized by the Amalgamated Association of Iron and Steel Workers. It was a perilous situation. After negotiations had reached an impasse, the union strikers seized the steel works and refused to leave. As soon as the Pinkerton guards arrived in Homestead, gunfire erupted. During the course of the fighting, 145 were wounded and 11 workers and 9 agents were killed. When order was restored, the union cause was smashed, and the strike was terminated. Many observers held Carnegie directly responsible for the violence; labour leaders vowed to remember the bloodshed.[46]

Although labour organizations and trade unions were a growing power in Ontario's cities, union membership rolls were not swollen by any means. Less than ten percent of the non-agricultural work force was unionized in 1911.[47] Working class parties and trade unions were struggling to assert their place within the framework of municipal, provincial, and federal politics, and they were striving for effective legislation on collective bargaining. Allan Studholme first represented Labour at the Ontario Legislature in 1906 for Hamilton East. Labour membership on library boards normally was restricted to one person, so its ability to influence decision making was limited. At Toronto, T.W. Banton was serving as the designated labour representative when the Carnegie offer came in 1903. His was the only vote cast in opposition. Obviously, labour leaders were at a disadvantage when aldermen or library trustees voted on Carnegie offers.

The memory of the Homestead strike became an albatross lurking over Carnegie gifts in the United States and Canada. At the rhetorical level, at least, labour organizations recommended that the public oppose his gifts. In many large cities, labour organizations usually were quick to disparage Carnegie's generosity. In 1903, the Toronto Labor Council voted seventy-seven to seven to protest the $350,000 promise because "Workingmen had not yet forgotten the tragedy of Homestead."[48] In Ottawa, J.W. Patterson, a long-time labour organizer and former candidate for Parliament, lamented: "Build a Carnegie library in Ottawa and when workers pass it they can bow their heads in memory of the martyrs of Homestead and the humiliation of the Canadian capital."[49] It was a powerful image to invoke. At Welland, where the Trades and Labor Council openly opposed a Carnegie grant, the library bylaw was defeated by a small margin (144 to 83) in May 1914, but, the result was partly attributed to poor organization rather than labour intransigence.[50]

On balance, labour unanimity across Ontario failed to materialize on the Homestead issue. Not all labour officers or rank-and-file members wanted to decline Carnegie offers – at least publicly. Some were genuinely alienated by the tragic events at Homestead, but they chose to accentuate the positive aspects of Carnegie libraries. The president of the Ottawa Allied Trades and Labour Association, A.J. Kelly, did not place any stock in Patterson's prose; he felt that the workers needed the benefits of a library more than the satisfaction of spurning the offer.[51] Some newspapers, which adopted a pro-Carnegie stance, often interviewed labourers to demonstrate the troublesome division. The Guelph *Mercury*, for one, found an ironworker transplanted from the Pittsburgh mills who believed Carnegie's philanthropy was worthwhile because "the Pinkertons [not Carnegie] were responsible for the deplorable and fatal riot which occurred at Homestead in 1892."[52]

Another labour-inspired obstacle the pro-Carnegie forces worked hard to counter was the general attitude that the canny Scott had made his fortune on the backs of workingmen. Big business had a reputation for manipulating tariff barriers, underpaying its employees, and securing handsome subsidies. Carnegie's capitalistic skill in these fields was legendary. The *Canadian*

Magazine helped buttress this argument in a 1905 editorial on people and affairs. After noting that Carnegie had made $450,000,000 within a short lifetime, it suggested that

> [t]here must be something inequitable and unjust in a state of industrialism which allows men like Carnegie, Rockefeller, Strathcona and Macdonald to amass millions when a large percentage of the population of this continent is in actual want.[53]

The editor of the piece was encouraged that some cities had chosen to refuse library offers.

The Guelph *Mercury* pointed out an obvious flaw in the criticism of the robber barons in one of its frequent editorials waged on behalf of acceptance.

> So long as the people support protective tariffs, railway subsidies, municipal bonuses, and systems of taxation, legislation and administration which inevitably tend to the benefit of the strong and wealthy, and to the detriment of the weak and poor, we do not see how they can set up a higher standard of conduct by refusing his money, or can even consistently attack Mr. Carnegie, who had only done, to the measure of a high ability, what hundreds and thousands have done to the measure of a lower ability, but all using the same conditions.[54]

The exploitative capitalist system, rather than the visible Carnegie symptom, should be the object of reform. In a democracy the people should rule; they also should accept responsibility for societal failings.

A few union leaders discovered for themselves the quandary which grant proposals presented. When Toronto's Thomas Keilty, an organizer for the American Federation of Labor (AFL), sought counsel from the AFL's Chicago-based president, Samuel Gompers, he was advised to take Carnegie's money. Gompers admitted that the steel king's fortune undoubtedly had been amassed at the expense of labouring men, but he insisted that Toronto workers should bargain for a reduction in working hours. Fewer working hours meant more leisure time to use the new central library.[55] His recommendation was consistent with the AFL's practice of avoiding partisan political activity. It is fair to say that Canadian labour, which was mostly non-unionized during the Carnegie era, was divided on the issue and disagreed on the tactics to deal with it. Consequently, labour's influence on the outcome of local decisions usually was negligible.

Community acceptance of library promises periodically became entangled with local matters. In these circumstances opposition groups, aldermen, individuals, councils, library trustees, and trade unions, intervened in a variety of ways. Reticence, delays in construction, or adverse local conditions (such as a fire at Thorold in March 1915[56]) sometimes accounted for a protracted delay between the promise of money and its receipt. In one unusual case, the city of Toronto annexed the town of Toronto Junction before Toronto Junction's library came into operation and its status as a free library could be realized.[57] It was left to George Locke to complete the details of Toronto Junction's incorporation as a branch library into the Toronto Public Library system.

Trustees on non-free boards ordinarily were eager to receive a promise from James Bertram, yet many such boards delayed changing status for several years. Examples were Owen Sound, Dundas, Dresden, Beaverton, and Teeswater. At Teeswater, a village experiencing depopulation (930 people in 1901; 854 in 1911), a bylaw to accept a generous $10,000 Carnegie promise was defeated in January 1908 by a margin of 128 to 35.[58] Five years later the ratepayers relented. In March 1913 they voted for a free library bylaw at which time the grant application was resumed by the local council.[59] At Owen Sound a handsome offer of $17,500 arrived in June 1904, but the ratepayers declined to establish a free library in January 1905, partially owing to anti-Carnegie sentiment.[60] The library board continued as an association for several years until it was in a stronger position to revive the offer and open its Carnegie building in February 1914.

At Lindsay, the Central Committee of the Allied Organizations endorsed the objections of a few local aldermen who said that council should make all appointments to the library board. Dissatisfaction with appointees from bodies other than the elective council was always an issue in Ontario community politics. A few Lindsay aldermen resented their exclusion from the library board; they felt that "according to the present arrangement they are not good enough to be associated on the Library Board."[61] But on this occasion, the council was reluctant to use a special act of the Ontario Legislature to override general legislative provisions. In the end, the Lindsay council accepted $13,500 from Carnegie, continued its purchase of the market site at Queen's Square for the building, and allowed the board to continue as constituted by provincial legislation (3 Edw. VII, c. 61).

A similar scenario had unfolded in Ottawa in 1902, but the results were far different. A free library did not exist in Ottawa prior to the Carnegie proposal. Ottawa aldermen decided to use a special act to authorize receipt of the Carnegie grant of $100,000, to specify the location for the library, and to enact a clause to retain the right to control all library board appointments. By resorting to special legislation, council kept complete control of the grant process and the formation of a free library board. Despite protests from long-standing library supporters, such as Otto Klotz, the Ottawa council established a local board composed of the Mayor, eight aldermen, and three citizens. Council made all the appointments and limited the term of office for members to one year (2 Edw. VII, c.55). The legislation eventually was repealed.

At Palmerston, a small town of 2,000, the Carnegie offer of $10,000, promised in February 1902, became embroiled in the politics of turn-of-the-century reform. It was a confrontation with the old way of thinking which John Hallam had pilloried in the early 1880s. As recounted by one participant, a few determined reformers created a slate for mayor and aldermen who were pledged to modernize the town by building a lighting plant, a public library, water works, and sewage system.

> The 'Old Guards' put up a challenge, using the cry 'Don't use Carnegie's money for a library!' and some joker issued cards, and spread them over the town. These said: 'The steamer 'youngster' will start out 1st of January, 1903, for the City of Destruction, and arrive at its destination at 6 p.m. unless wrecked before on Carnegie Rocks.' The 'youngster' slate, however, carried by a huge majority.[62]

Opponents sought an injunction to block acceptance of the grant by the new council and library board but later withdrew their complaint. The reformers, successful on this occasion, added $2,000 from local revenues to the original Carnegie grant and housed the library in a modest civic complex.

At Orillia, the Carnegie offer became ensnared in a contentious dispute that raged for six months. The town initially received a letter in April 1909 pledging $12,500; however, as a first step, it had to establish a free library board. As a result, the vote on the proposed bylaw assumed a dual character: it was a vote on the legal precondition for a free library and, indirectly, on public acceptance of the offer. One local newspaper summarized the dangers inherent in this procedure:

> It seems to us that in the interests of the library by-law, the Council would do well to separate the questions as to taking over the present Public Library, and changing it into a free library, and the totally distinct issue of the desirability of accepting Mr. Carnegie's offer of $12,500 for a building.

> There are undoubtedly a number of ratepayers who would
> heartily support the former poposal [sic], who are either
> lukewarm over, or opposed to, the Carnegie building. But as
> the matter stands at present, once the by-law is carried, the
> Council and the Library Board will be free to do as they like
> about the Carnegie building, without consulting the ratepay-
> ers further.[63]

The bylaw campaign continued with each side expounding the pros and cons
of Carnegie giving.

Both Orillia papers promoted the bylaw; their support may have tipped
the scales in the closely fought contest. The Orillia *Times* conscientiously
declared that the public should show "the same spirit of Christianity and liberalism that prompts the donor of the gift."[64] The library board and a majority of the aldermen also supported the bylaw. The board actually had touched
off the drive for a free library and Carnegie grant in January, three months
before a promise from Bertram arrived. The Council received a boost when
the Deputy Minister of Education, Arthur Colquhoun, responded positively
to its request for information about the advantages of free libraries and suggested contacting Norman Gurd, the OLA president. Gurd forwarded a
lengthy letter supporting free libraries.[65] But a combination of people who
opposed a free library and those who wanted to decline the $12,500 left reso-
lution of the issue in doubt to the very end. Finally, on 14 June 1909, the
ratepayers spoke: the bylaw passed by a slim majority of thirty-four, 335 for
and 301 opposed. Shortly after, councillors voted to locate the library on a
corner of the market square.

A common concern which surfaced during discussions about grant offers
was the location of a new library. The Carnegie Corporation insisted that
localities assume responsibility for the provision of suitable sites. Central locations were highly desirable, but they were expensive to obtain. Moreover,
councils tended to be parsimonious and did not appreciate that location was
vital to the success of a library. The temptation to acquire donated property or
to build on municipally owned land was difficult to resist.[66] The real estate
motive also extended to ratepayers. At Lindsay, bylaws to raise $2,000 for a
site were defeated twice.[67] Site selection often provoked public reaction
against acceptance, prompting questions about the potential value of the gift
to a community. St. Mary's and Goderich were typical cases in this respect.

St. Mary's was, by all accounts, a strong pro-library community. A free
library was instituted in January 1896 by a vote of 433 to 254, or almost sixty
percent in favour.[68] Carnegie's offer of $10,000 passed in council in March
1904 without discussion. As it turned out, the real problem was finding a

good location for under $800, a relatively low price for property in the central business district. When council decided by a close vote of four to three to build on its own property, on the north side of the town hall, where it kept its steam road roller and watering cart in a shed, nearly a hundred people signed a petition, protesting

> that such a site is entirely unsuited for any such purpose not being near the centre of the population of the town, inconvenient of approach and surmounted by cattle yards, town scales, stables and other buildings being more intended for a general market and traffic business and insecure title if not absolutely worthless, while there are a number of suitable sites on Water street and Wellington street, east or west side.[69]

After council voted four to three to uphold its original decision, a group of citizens directed a firm of barristers to write Carnegie, cautioning him that legal action might ensue because council had acted "irregularly" and the library idea had become "unpopular."[70] Nevertheless, the project proceeded and a handsome stone library was erected on the site.

A similar dispute arose in April 1902 at a public meeting in Goderich convened to discuss the Carnegie offer of $10,000. The audience generally favoured approval, but the proposed location of the library remained controversial because it involved transfer of the marketplace, a convenient service for surrounding farmlands and townsfolk. The mayor explained that council intended to build on the market grounds, a few blocks from the main square; this option involved removing the market to the fairgrounds, a less central location. There were questions about whether the market or a library was more suitable for the site; whether there was a prior claim on the lot for a hospital; and whether there was a lease on the site's grain warehouse. In the end, the library emerged victorious. Council resolved to move both warehouse and market and authorized a building contract for the proposed library.[71]

Not every community's Carnegie experience was rewarding. In a few cases, opposition, lethargy, inflation, unusual circumstances, and changing local priorities united in various configurations to postpone library construction for lengthy periods or even to prevent its start altogether. Gravenhurst, a free library since 1897, received $7,000 in April 1906. Years of delay followed. Different committees were established to investigate the suitability of different sites and to raise funds locally, in 1910 and 1916, but essentially nothing was accomplished. When war ended in Europe, the Carnegie Corporation enquired about Gravenhurst's progress. The problem at this point was not indifference but inflation. It had seriously eroded purchasing power during the intervening period. Fortunately, the education department offered assistance with floor plans. After seventeen years of procrastination, the Gravenhurst library opened on 1 May 1923.[72]

Other communities were not so lucky. Smaller places were usually in a more precarious financial state. Tilbury's original $5,000 grant, approved before the First World War, was rescinded by the Carnegie Corporation in the mid-1920s. The entire project was beset by a perplexing series of false starts at the tendering stage, a reluctance to submit a free library bylaw to the electors, requests for additional money, delays because of municipal funding problems, a prohibitive rise in costs, and bitter local rivalry over site selection.[73] Otterville, a police village situated within the Oxford County township of South Norwich, was first considered by Bertram to be too small for a grant; instead, he promised $6,000 to the township in March 1915. Special legislation permitting townships to form boards was duly arranged in 1916, but the war effort scuttled any further movement in this direction until January 1923, when the township electors refused to pass a free bylaw. Consequently, the award to South Norwich lapsed.[74]

Even a few cities and larger towns encountered problems. Port Arthur received three promises: a grant of $10,000 in 1902, an increase to $30,000 in 1909, and an additional $10,000 in 1910. Despite some delays with building plans, the city was ready to erect a $40,000 building by early 1912. However, Bertram reduced the grant by $10,000 in March of that year because revised population figures released by the Dominion census indicated fewer people than the official application, which was based on municipal assessment. As a result, everything collapsed; the library board and council preferred a larger building and the project was lost.[75] Trenton received a promise for $10,000 in April 1911 and passed a free bylaw; however, when local library efforts flagged, Inspector Nursey rescinded the board's free status in 1913, and Bertram judged the endeavour finished. Efforts to revive the Trenton pledge after the war failed. Bertram testily advised that a proposal to construct a library as a war memorial should be financed by a local community, not an "outside agency."[76]

In sum, then, despite the cropping up of a variety of objections, Ontario's communities proved to be fertile ground for Carnegie endowments. No political, national, ethnic, or class opposition blocked the building program. Eventually, 111 Carnegie libraries valued at two-and-half million dollars were constructed in Ontario, an unprecedented building program never replicated again. The province's share of the Carnegie bequests compares favourably with the three leading American states: Ohio, California, and Indiana. Libraries were erected in 104 communities (seven branches were built in Toronto and

Ottawa). Of these 104 places, 56 already had free libraries in 1900; another 48 achieved this rank by 1918 when the building program ceased. In that year there were 183 free boards, an increase of 57 since 1900 (Graph 4: Free Library Boards in Ontario, 1882 to 1918). Naturally, there were deletions and additions to the free list not attributable to the building phenomenon during this eighteen year time span, yet a significant segment of the increase after 1900 – 48 boards – did partake in the Carnegie scheme. Local library boards realized that the Carnegie program was indispensable to the erection of modern library structures, and that free status was a small price to pay for Carnegie generosity.

The formal acceptance of a grant, the attainment of free library status, and the completion of construction did not always unfold smoothly for every community, despite favourable conditions during the economic boom between 1900 to 1913.[77] Nevertheless, most grants and building arrangements took place expeditiously under the watchful eye of James Bertram, local communities, and enthusiastic councils and boards which desired modern library quarters. Oshawa was an excellent case in point. The mayor, Frederick Fowke, corresponded directly with Bertram, arranged a vote of the ratepayers in June 1906 to purchase a site at the corner of Simcoe and Athol streets, and had the Toronto branch office of the New York firm, Carrère & Hastings, draw up architectural plans in advance of the promise of $14,000 which was offered in November.[78] Carnegie's philanthropy, coupled with general economic expansion and public approval, presented a strong inducement to amplify, redevelop, and democratize library services. It was a constant, dynamic force that aligned people with free public libraries at a time when modern library service was changing rapidly. The public image of libraries improved vastly in all parts of the province. The library was now associated with progressive forces which were modifying the face of society.

In the decade leading up to 1914, Ontario was being transformed into an urban, industrialized province with Toronto as its leading metropolis.[79] The city was replacing the farm as the centre of economic activity; its aspirations would dictate socio-economic changes. Urban expectations for future development were shaped by businessmen, clergy, doctors, lawyers, educators, journalists and other professionals. The members of this relatively homogeneous stratum of society shared many local interests through voluntary organizations, met regularly, and shared common career or work conditions. They recognized that urban growth and technological advance required better organized social services. Their decision to include libraries in their reform agenda for making local government more efficient, effective, and accountable to the general populace was crucial to the well-being of libraries in the Edwardian era.

For the municipal elite, the Carnegie name symbolized many desirable things: progress, self-help, Christian generosity, idealism, business knowledge, and educational advancement. Progress was perhaps the most important of these symbols and, of course, progress meant growth. At some stage the local library would have to modernize. Why not start with a new building? Mr. Tomlinson, the wealthy donor in Stephen Leacock's "Arrested Philanthropy," discovered as much after he was led to a university library said to be in urgent need of financial assistance – it was too old at the age of twenty! This humourous episode in *Arcadian Adventures* mimicked real life. Progress and reform were the order of the day in many municipalities. People viewed Carnegie grants as beneficial, as a stimulus to a better future, and they were willing to shoulder the necessary tax burden. Ideally, the public good would be served, for the library was an exemplar of public ownership at the service of all citizens. From a practical standpoint, a splendid opportunity to inject new and vital life into public libraries could not be dismissed out of hand.

Ontario's cities, towns, and villages were in good company. Carnegie had financed promises for 2,500 libraries in English-speaking countries. So impressed was H.G. Wells that he included a chapter on public libraries in his popular social commentary, *Social Forces in England and America*. This short article, reprinted from a British magazine, succinctly captured the essence of the Carnegie legacy. Wells told the story of a philosopher seeking to create a better society, one which happily included public libraries. How would the sage establish his library? Wells's philosopher would first draw up a catalogue of holdings, then offer to construct a suitable building. And what of future upkeep?

> He would try to make a bargain with the local people for their co-operation in his enterprise, though he would, as a philosopher, understand that where a public library is least wanted it is generally most needed. But in most cases he would succeed in stipulating for a certain standard of maintenance by the local authority.[80]

That is how Wells's rich philosopher would obtain efficient libraries throughout the country "at minimum cost." It was a plan well suited for the temper of the time.

Library Architecture

The construction of new libraries enabled local library boards to shape the type of service they felt best suited their own communities. The proper arrangement of space for the needs and purposes of library buildings was a tremendous opportunity. It also was a frustrating task because there were no authoritative manuals on library architecture at the turn of the century. No clear-cut consensus existed on what constituted conventional library services, uniform administrative practices, and proper staffing. There were no library standards set by governments or professional bodies in the United States, Great Britain, and Canada to help determine overall building size or space for collections and staff. Most articles or booklets were content to put forward general recommendations: secure a large site, make room for future expansion, keep an eye to economy on building size and staffing, consider local needs. Very few architects or librarians were prepared to give explicit guidelines dealing with general building size, interior layout, or functional relationships.

A growing body of literature had appeared since the 1890s on basic library architecture. Charles Soule, a Boston bookseller and publisher who was an active ALA trustee, was the author of an introductory architectural booklet published by ALA in 1902. He suggested twenty volumes per square foot for the capacity of a book room (an area 30' x 40' would hold 24,000 books). He also urged a trefoil grouping of functions: the stack room to be located behind the central delivery counter and the catalogue area to be flanked on either side by a public reading room and a reference area.

> With this theme, with subdivision of each department, proportioned to the size of the library, with provision made for enlarging each department as the library grows, the architect may plan a building which will stand all tests of library science, which can be built within the desired limit of cost, and which will also be an ornament to the town in which it is situated.[81]

Too often in the years before 1914, Soule's sensible advice was ignored by architects, builders, municipal councils, librarians, and boards.

A lengthier, illustrated British manual by Frank Burgoyne, the librarian of the Tate Library in the London suburb of Brixton, was balanced but permeated with caution. This book addressed the merits of two conventional building designs – the traditional perimeter/alcove book hall system that could be accessed directly by users and the closed stack system of more recent vintage with its delivery counter and adjoining reading rooms – but it avoided making a preference or giving standardized rules about building types or sizes. Burgoyne believed that the most frequented areas would be the newspaper and periodical rooms, the boy's room, the lending library, and the reference department. British experience in the closing decades of the nineteenth century demonstrated the suitability of the two-storey library for most large cities.

The lending library, newsroom, and boy's room were on the ground floor, the reference department and bookstacks were upstairs, away from the noise and traffic of less studious users.

Burgoyne's *Library Construction* advocated the assessment of local needs prior to the assignment of space for basic services and optional, specialized features. The former included reference and lending departments, a reading room, and staff work area. The latter included separate rooms for girls, boys, and women, lecture halls, museum and art gallery, and restricted areas for incunabula and local collections.[82] On the question of free access, which was becoming commonplace in smaller public libraries, especially in the United States, Burgoyne instructed his readers that "a large public library should have the bulk of its books shelved on the stack system, in book stores adjacent to the readers' room; but this may have a wall case around it for the most popular works, open for use without the formality of filling up a reader's ticket."[83] This was a popular option in a few of the larger British cities where busy home circulation departments were on lower levels.

Statistical tables which correlated library income with building accommodation were not available until 1903, with the appearance of James Duff Brown's *Manual of Library Economy*. The British library community considered Brown, the librarian at Clerkenwell Public Library in the Finsbury district of London, to be something of an iconoclast. He championed the "workshop concept" of public libraries: they "should be constructed and stocked with the view to constant revision, and that their size should be limited by the number of *live* books likely to be wanted at any period."[84] He outlined the following relationship between local funding for yearly maintenance, and suitable building sizes, book capacity, and accommodation of readers.

Income £	Size in Sq. Ft.	Capacity in Vols.	Readers Accommodated
1,000	4,412	34,000	200
2,000	8,824	68,000	400
3,000	13,236	102,000	600
4,000	19,200	136,000	800
5,000	24,000	170,000	1,000
10,000	48,000	340,000	2,000[85]

Brown's tabulations were formulated for British conditions (Canadian equivalents can be calculated at the prewar exchange rate of $4.80 to the £1). They may seem rudimentary today because he rejected population as a factor in his calculations. This shortcoming, however, was compensated by his progressive ideas which have prevailed over time: the correlation of building size and local funding; free access to collections; the use of decimal classification; and the adoption of children's libraries.

On one point there seemed to be unanimity: exterior features and ornamentation should remain simple. The interior plan should be designed first, keeping in mind the principles of good lighting, convenient public access to rooms, ease of supervision, and proper ventilation and heating. Decoration in a "high" architectural design should be tasteful and discrete.

> The exterior may properly be embellished to any degree, if the windows are grouped and planned as interior lighting requires; and of the interior, the halls and stairways, if located so as not to separate or interfere with the service-rooms, offer opportunity for effective ornament.[86]

Many of these guidelines departed from the typical Victorian library which gave prominence to eclectic revival styles for the exterior, newspaper rooms with mandatory stands, lofty ceilings, heavy furnishings, a separate women's reading area, and closed stacks. Library architecture was entering a period of transition. Modern library service was maturing slowly. It was characterized by the open design concept, an expanded range of public services, and additional technical requirements for interior floor plans (e.g., electric lighting, security, heating, and fire prevention).

The chief characteristics of Carnegie library buildings in Ontario were the ubiquitous neoclassical style associated with the École des Beaux-Arts in Paris and the rigidly planned interiors which restricted flexibility. The World's Columbian Exposition, held at Chicago in 1893, had ushered in the Beaux-Arts style and captured the imagination of the architectural profession. Consequently, traditional Graeco-Roman orders – Doric, Ionic, Corinthian, and Tuscan – graced many processional library entrances built in the first two decades of this century. There were two basic categories of neoclassical style: 1) a columned temple entrance with a triangular pedimented roof; 2) a columned arch entrance divided into one or more bays which supported the roof line (Illus. 33-34).[87] Although this monumental style prevailed in most Ontario localities, it was not universal: Victorian revival (e.g., Tudor in Toronto's branches) and modest vernacular exteriors ("cottage" or "street front"), which incorporated aspects of "high" styles, also were employed by local architects and builders.

The interiors of early Carnegie libraries usually were delimited by means of permanent walls or partitions which denied the possibility of expansion or alteration. While not every Carnegie building exhibited a fixed compartmental make-up, it remains largely true that flexibility in relation to function seldom was given priority. This changed in 1911 when the Carnegie Corporation, under James Bertram's firm hand, issued a small pamphlet, *Notes on the Erection of Library Bildings* [sic]. Bertram was assisted in part by the New York architect, Edward L. Tilton. The publication was aimed at the small library. Its leading recommendations stressed simplicity and the use of movable bookcases in place of permanent partitions. Bertram's pamphlet came too late. With the exception of Hamilton, the Carnegie libraries in major Ontario cities already were built. Form, not function, determined the character of most Carnegie buildings.[88]

Canadian library architecture remained a quiescent field compared to its American and British counterparts. Before 1900, neither architects, nor librarians, nor trustees disputed ideas bearing on architecture. William Langton, a Toronto architect and brother of the University of Toronto librarian, Hugh Langton, did contribute a piece on library design to the *Canadian Architect and Builder* in 1902. He helped generate dialogue on some major issues by distinguishing between small and large libraries. Langton ruled out open access – it was still serving a trial period – except in small libraries where all major activities could be confined to one floor in the usual perimeter/alcove arrangement. For smaller libraries, Langton followed the trefoil plan by illustrating the new library at East Orange, New Jersey: the bookroom and working rooms were at the back; the delivery area, library staff, and the reading rooms were at the front. He felt that the announced design for New York Public Library represented "the best that is known on the subject" for large libraries.[89] Thus, a closed bookroom on the lower level with a reading room on the second floor above the stacks would serve as a good model for Ontario's principal libraries.

Langton discussed the most efficient ways in which Carnegie's gifts could be applied to smaller libraries.

> We may then perhaps assume not less than: 1. For the public; a reading room for the grown up people, a reading room for children, and ample space apart from these for the coming and going of borrowers. 2. For the librarian; a delivery desk and a private room in connection with it; ... There should be also working room for unpacking, marking and cataloguing the books. The unpacking room would be best in the basement, but the other work should be done on the ground floor, in close connection with the librarian's office. 3. For the storage of books; plenty of room now and an opportunity to grow.[90]

The Toronto architect also expressed his preference for a floor area subdivided by open screens of columns; this sensible method would reduce noise and provide a sense of seclusion in various rooms without the necessity for permanent partitions or walls.

Naturally, the OLA stressed the need for improved library design; at its inaugural meeting, Dr. Lewis Hornung, from Victoria College, moved that a committee be appointed on library architecture. The next year, 1902, Hugh Langton, the committee's chairman, reported on the state of Carnegie grants. Reiterating an idea aired by his brother William, he suggested that only small libraries should resort to open access. In 1903, Gordon J. Smith, a Paris trustee who was engaged with the development of his town's Carnegie building, offered practical advice for smaller libraries which presaged Bertram's *Notes* by eight years:

> The building should not be more than one story, using part of the basement, which ought to be well lighted, as a small public hall for holding meetings for literary or scientific purposes. The general design of the building should be artistic, with enough distinction to set it apart from the general run of buildings one encounters in a small town. All the accommodation for the public in the way of reading-rooms, etc., should be on the main floor with in the range of vision of the librarian.[91]

Smith eagerly supported acceptance of grants, his only proviso being the omission of the Carnegie name at the entrance.

Edwin Hardy made three valuable contributions to library architecture at annual OLA meetings from 1904 to 1906; his first presentation summarized Carnegie donations to date; the second explored merits and defects of contemporary Ontario libraries; the third dealt with general arrangement – plans, elevations, and sections. The 1905 annual meeting stimulated a lively discussion about sites, open access, and technical points such as heating and space requirements.

> The unanimous testimony was that a hot-water system of heating was the best, superior both to steam and hot air. Anyone could work a hot-water system, but steam required an engineer. The annual cost for coal, with a hot-water system, was put at $120 by delegates from some of the new libraries. Other ideas made clear were that a dome should not be built on small library buildings and that the stack room should be made large.[92]

Similar views were gaining ascendancy in the United States and Great Britain, but regional or local experiences were more germane to the Toronto audience.

As more Carnegie libraries opened, Hardy continued to collect information which he passed along each year for the benefit of trustees. In 1906, he condensed his findings on Ontario libraries and advised not to overbuild. Smaller structures and simple designs were in order.

> The trefoil arrangement of the reading-rooms and stack-rooms was [s]hown to be generally adopted. The open supervision system was shown in an illustration of the proposed Yorkville branch library. It was stated during the discussion that the Carnegie libraries had been found expensive to maintain, so that less money was available to buy books than formerly.[93]

The OLA's industrious secretary published a selection of his data, illustrations, and blueprints in the education department's annual 1906 report; this served as an important guide to the first five years of Carnegie building in Ontario.

The popular press and general interest magazines seldom described the design problems architects faced. Contemporary reports usually focused on the personalities involved in securing grants. Architectural analysis was not in demand. One exception to this was the praise the *Sault Star* conferred on H. Russell Halton, an architect who pursued a grant for his community in 1901:

> Mr. Halton deserves a deal of credit for the way he has stuck to the library scheme through thick and thin. When he first broached the idea last fall [1901], the council poured cold water on it, and the property committee could not see the advantage of getting a gift of $10,000.[94]

When the merits of Halton's architectural plans were appreciated more fully, the Sault Ste. Marie council accepted them as part of a combined municipal centre.

> The library is a large, airy and well lighted room in the west wing, 40 ft. by 50 ft. It contains a separate reading room for ladies, librarian offices, extensive accommodation for books and board room for the library board. It will be fitted up with reading tables and every library convenience and finished in oak.[95]

Two interesting details about this library were ignored: it was quite small for the size of the city, and it opened in 1904, when separate women's reading rooms were beginning to vanish because of space restrictions and changing attitudes about the place of women in society.

In the early period of Carnegie building, 1900-1908, before James Bertram required the inclusion of architectural plans during the approval stage, Ontario communities had a free hand in designing their own libraries. This led to concerns about the poorly planned libraries. Goderich's triangular shape made it impossible for attendants to supervise the reading room from the main lending desk. Guelph emphasized its ornamental exterior, especially its dome, and neglected requirements for adequate interior space.[96] Bertram deplored these preferences. By the time Andrew Carnegie accepted invitations to visit two of his benefactions, Ottawa and Smith's Falls, in 1906, the OLA and the education department had accumulated so much documentation on new buildings that they began to loan their material to libraries. This timely collection, supplemented by experience, was used in planning many buildings. Disagreement on library design was closely linked to the debate on library service. Consensus was difficult to reach on many matters: open access to shelves; an age limit and separate room for young children; the need to reserve space for a separate women's reading room; catalogue access to collections and the use of indicators; and a classification system for public retrieval and browsing. These were fundamental service questions, the resolution of which would affect the optimal size and interior design of a community's library building.

Questions of appropriate building size and the amount and arrangement of functional space to be devoted to library purposes remained unsettled before the Great War. Normally, the library proper did not occupy every square foot of space. Additional rooms for museums, historical and scientific societies, art schools, and auditoriums were common in Carnegie libraries because a close relationship between the public library and other local cultural agencies had existed during the previous era of Mechanics' Institutes and literary societies. Prior to 1914, separate stack rooms and reading rooms were standard features in Ontario. The public usually was unable to browse the shelves directly. Confronting them were large desks or wicket booths for charging/discharging books – the barrier system. Even when admission to the shelves became policy, most people did not understand the classification scheme. The process of erecting Carnegie buildings taught many boards the wisdom of integrating books and readers; simply enlarging closed stack rooms or adding more reading rooms would not solve crowding or satisfy public demand for direct access to literature.

A few generalizations can be made about the Carnegie libraries based on information concerning more than thirty buildings erected between 1882 and

1914 (Table 13: Functional Space in Selected Ontario Libraries). The census population of a community divided by a library's dimensions gives the square footage per capita. The average square footage per capita for the sample was one half square foot, a figure library planners considered insufficient for communities under 10,000 population by the beginning of the 1940s. Only a handful of small places – notably Burlington, a non-Carnegie structure – exceeded the more suitable figure of one square foot per capita.[97] This lack of space contributed greatly to the reputation of Carnegie libraries as inefficient and overcrowded buildings. The usual Carnegie building was rectangular; it presented architects and planners with more possibilities than squares. One notable exception was the "T-shape" (multi-tier stack room at the rear with reading rooms forming wings at the front) adopted by Brantford and Ottawa. A closer examination of Ontario's three largest libraries – Ottawa, Toronto, and Hamilton – indicates the diversity of ideas and the evolution of design that took place prior to 1914.

Construction on the $100,000 Ottawa library, designed by Edgar L. Horwood, who later became a federal government architect, commenced in 1903.[98] When the library opened in April 1906, after well-publicized delays which the press gleefully caricatured (Illus. 35), it was a blend of old and new, and not necessarily a prescription for the future. It was a two-and-a-half storey "T" library with the stack room along the stem. This was a popular plan introduced in the closing years of the nineteenth century, but it was too small for the number of patrons and too large and too subdivided for the library staff. The stack room was designed to hold three tiers and was heated with hot air. The heating system was criticized from the outset. The basement was large enough for a bindery, newspaper room, and auxiliary services. Located on the main floor were a reading room, children's library, circulation area, cataloguing room, general reading room, reception room, and librarian's office. On the second floor were the reference room, board room, and studies. A museum completed arrangements. The exterior, finished in Indiana limestone, was fashioned in a classical style.[99]

Lawrence Burpee, Ottawa's new librarian, assumed his duties in 1905 as construction drew to a close, too late to make any substantive contribution to its design. This man of modern methods held conceptions about library design that were obviously different from the original building committee. That committee, which included James Bain and Otto Klotz, had looked to New York and Washington for guidance.[100] In a 1904 paper concerning small libraries, Burpee had stressed the need for a self-contained children's department: "If the plan of the library makes open access to all the books impracticable or inconvenient, a selection of standard works, with a few of the best new books, may at least be placed upon shelves an alcove or other convenient place ... "[101] Not surprisingly, within a few years the Ottawa library took on a new look. Burpee installed Snead Company stacks from New Jersey to double the book capacity, added island shelving and a catalogue to the reference room, installed a separate desk and catalogue in the children's department (Illus. 36), and converted the ladies' reading room into a browsing collection where patrons could charge out books without having to go to the central delivery desk.[102]

Lawrence Burpee left the library board to take up a position as Canadian secretary of the International Joint Commission in 1912. His successor, William J. Sykes, realizing that space was restricted, tentatively approached the Carnegie Corporation in 1913 to fund an extension to the central library. The proposal would have cost the Corporation about $25,000. James Bertram's reply was firm: no![103] Bertram disapproved of grants for additions to central libraries, and Ottawa wisely embarked on building branches. One branch, situated in the former municipality of Hintonburg, was sufficiently large enough to warrant a Carnegie gift of $15,000 in 1917.[104] The west end branch had the distinction of being the last Carnegie library grant promised in Ontario. It opened at the end of November 1918. Carnegie was invited to attend, but he was unable to be present.

The largest Carnegie library built in Ontario, Toronto's central reference library and circulating branch on the corner of College and St. George, was opened in October 1909 (Illus. 37). It served a dual purpose and reflected the emphasis placed on branch libraries by Carnegie, who spoke of the need for an alternative to showy central edifices on his 1906 Toronto visit. On that occasion, he remarked, "it is the mass of the people we should try to reach."[105] The building committee sponsored an architectural competition which was won in 1906 by Alfred H. Chapman and the firm Wickson & Gregg. The committee had issued a pamphlet which contained guidelines for the competition; it drew heavily on James Bain's experience and contained detailed specifications and heretofore unprecedented dimensions. For example, concerning the main floor, it stipulated the following:

1. Main Reference Library Reading Room, about 6,200 feet area, having a width of about 50 feet.
2. Patent Room (separated from Reading Room by rail and columns, area about 1,800 feet).
3. Newspaper Room, Area about 1,800 feet
4. Map Room[,] Area about 900 feet
5. Art Room, Area about 2,250 feet
6. Board Room, Area about 440 feet
7. Librarian's Office, etc., Area about 440 feet

8.   5 Study Rooms,   Area about 84 feet each
9.   Cataloguing Room,   Area about 600 feet
10.   The balance of the space to be allotted to entrance, corridor, staircases, halls, sanitary accommodation, etc.[106]

Upon completion, the reference and patent rooms took up 7,980 sq. ft. on one side of the main floor (Illus. 38). People had direct access to selected volumes of the research collection, and they were allowed to work in an area almost as large as the total area of the old central library on Church Street.[107]

Alfred Chapman was a young architect embarking on a prestigious career. He did not follow exactly all the preconditions, but he did plan a L-shaped library that placed the stacks and working areas in the centre, separated reference and circulating functions, and allowed for ample future expansion which eventually took place under his supervision in 1928-29.[108] It was a highly functional library for its era. On the main floor, the circulation area linked five tiers of Snead Company bookstacks (located directly to its rear) to the reading room in the College Street wing; also on this level were administration, newspaper and art storage areas in the St. George Street wing. The Art Museum of Toronto was on the upper level: Bain's preference for a connection between libraries and museums had finally materialized! On the ground floor, below the reading room, a circulating library of 10,000 books was available through a separate west end entrance on College Street. This convenient arrangement had proved successful in three large British libraries in Birmingham, Edinburgh (a Carnegie funded building), and Newcastle.[109]

The magnitude of the new library often left many users, as well as librarians, in awe. The reference library became a showcase for knowledge, and its schedule of regular evening hours was a novelty. A Toronto *Star* reporter commented in a short piece about the new facility:

> Entering the big roomy hall, after ascending the steps outside, you stand in an enormous room, with high ceilings, and into which a flood of light pours from the immense windows on the south. Looking west, parallel with College Street, there extends reading table after table in a double line. Shaded lamps are placed generously on each table to provide for the evenings or for dull days. Along the south wall are alcoves, containing books which are classified, as well as human intelligence can classify them under various subjects. Art or literature, history or philosophy, mechanics or architecture – these and more are the classifications. In these

alcoves are four thousand out of the seventy-five thousands volumes. With these one is permitted to step up, pick out the book one wishes, look at it, standing there, and return it or take it to a table. If taken to the table the book must be left there, so that the attendants can put them back in their proper places.[110]

The library offered new freedoms, a new spatial ordering of tasks and interactions, and new vistas of knowledge.

Toronto's central library was not the last word on library planning. Hamilton completed the trilogy of large buildings erected during the Carnegie era. It too served a double function: a central city reference library and a lending library for its citizens. After receiving a $75,000 promise in March 1909, Hamilton formed a building committee, issued a small pamphlet of instructions, and organized an architectural competition. Fortunately for the committee and the librarian, Adam Hunter, ideas about interior arrangements were now more consensual. A new British manual on library architecture by Amian Champneys had appeared recently. The authorities in Hamilton were wise to heed most of its recommendations.

> The first necessity in connection with the disposition of the various parts of a library is that it shall be adapted to the work of the library according to the methods employed.
>
> That is to say, that while both the human occupants and the contents of the library must be afforded every protection from unsuitable and harmful conditions, the convenience of the public on the one hand, in their use of the library must be studied: on the other, every facility must be given for the easy and efficient performance of their duties by the staff.
>
> To these must be added another consideration, namely, economy in cost, maintenance, and working, ... [111]

Although Hunter and the Hamilton trustees were not very active in OLA, they seemed no less knowledgeable about buildings than their contemporaries. In their original specifications, they called for a "most modern system of open shelves."[112] And events would prove how fortunate they were to be with architects.

The Hamilton architectural competition was a convoluted and hotly contested process. In the end, Alfred W. Peene, a local man, was selected. Tenders were called. Then, Edward L. Tilton, trusted advisor to James Bertram, was contracted to supervise the final architectural drawings in April 1911.

Bertram now was exercising control over plans before final approval by the Carnegie Corporation. Tilton and Peene devised an open concept interior with a restrained exterior.[113] Tilton's outstanding architectural career was launched at a time when his ideas about library design were considered advanced. He published an article in *Library Journal* in 1912, which developed a formula for library size based on library income and suggested using twelve foot modules as flexible units of space. He also espoused the "open plan," that is, free access on the main floor to a large collection of the most popular books with infrequently used books relegated to storage. Tilton's main public area would not be partitioned by permanent walls. Instead, divisions between departments would be created by columns, bookcases, small counters, or tables.[114] As a result, Hamilton's free standing bookshelves and the reference room were located on the main floor; the reading rooms, special collections, and children's department were on the lower level.[115]

The Hamilton cornerstone was laid in late summer 1911 (Illus. 39). A year and a half later, in May 1913, the Lieutenant Governor, Sir John M. Gibson, officially declared the new library open. He was an old friend of the library who had campaigned for a free library in the 1880s and travelled to New York to acquire an extra $25,000 grant from Carnegie. Hamilton's modern design was immediately popular. A local paper trumpeted that the library authorities were being more trustful with the circulating collection.

> Under the new system, a reader will merely have to take the book he or she wants from the shelf, take it to the desk and have it registered, and walk away. Instead of a slip being filled out, a permanent card is kept in the book, on which the number of the reader's card is written and kept until the book is returned.[116]

This was a progressive step indeed! The open concept, while not entirely original with Tilton, was best expressed by his library work until the Second World War.

While Hamilton was under construction in 1911, the primary architectural document that would shape the future of Carnegie libraries was issued. In the leaflet, *Notes on the Erection of Library Bildings*, James Bertram introduced the open library concept to every library board wishing to receive a promise of funding. The *Notes* were intended for buildings in small communities or city branches. Simplicity was a primary concern. Rectangular, one-storey buildings, undivided rooms, low ceilings, few restrictions that separated readers from books, and unpretentious exteriors were recommended. These plans were an expression of the changing social logic of space, and were in accord with the open access revolution, which stressed services to groups previously neglected, standardization of the decimal classification system, and better circulation procedures.

Six outline plans accompanied by a brief text were developed for one-storey libraries in the *Notes* (Illus. 40-41).[117] These open concept schemes were rather austere, mixing talking and reading areas by screening off areas with bookcases or ranges of shelving on the ground floor. Plans "A" and "B" were simple "Carnegie rectangles" with central entrances on the long side, an open interior, librarian's working area to the rear and separate adult and children's areas to the sides. Plan "B" was intended for a larger community because it contained a separate reference room. Plan "C," also for a larger library, located the entrance on the short side, reference room and librarian's area to the front, separate adult and children's libraries to the rear. The right/left symmetry of these floor plans allowed some flexibility. Plan "D" adapted the first three plans for a site at a street intersection with the entrance on one corner. Plans "E" and "F" considered arrangements for small places – the form was square or oblong with off-centre entrances, and the library was one-room supervised from the side by the librarian's desk. All plans located the lecture room, service facilities, and washrooms in the basement. Plans "A" to "D" also located the staff room in the basement. Domes, fireplaces, or skylights were not recommended despite their popularity with architects and trustees.

Bertram's *Notes* were firm about the open-plan concept, but his leaflet had little to say about exteriors or ornamentation, save to put monumentalism in disrepute. If Carnegie funds were to be used for building a library, then pomp had to yield to restrained grace. Three branch libraries in Toronto built under George Locke's careful scrutiny epitomized the new trend toward simplicity, openness, and charm. Locke and the architectural firm, Eden Smith & Sons, completely abandoned Beaux-Arts classicism by shifting to the open concept in the design of the Beaches, Wychwood, and High Park branches. Eden Smith, working during the Great War, adapted a seventeenth-century English collegiate grammar school style to please users. He kept the interiors uncluttered by returning to perimeter shelving and comfortable by adding stone fireplaces and open timber trusses supporting the roof. As well, the landscape architect, Alfred Hall, contributed imaginative arrangements of shrubs, flower gardens, walks, and trees to beautify the approaches and to increase the library's appeal to passers-by and regular patrons. The reformed style and pleasant nature of these libraries received deserved attention from Ontario library planners.[118]

The free access and open design concepts, as well as better children's work, contained many ramifications for planners involving the liberalization of interior space. If readers and children were to be permitted to move freely among collections and rooms, public space would have to be increased and designed differently. Efficient, effective work space for library staff also was a desideratum. Proper heating, lighting, and ventilation demanded more technical knowledge. Better thought needed to be given at the design stage to the placement and selection of shelving, furniture, and collections. The practical division of floor space and intelligent stationing of islands of stacks arranged for easy supervision or browsing were absolutely necessary. High perimeter shelves were inconvenient; lower bookshelves were becoming standard. Circulation desks were to be carefully constructed for new bookcard methods designed to speed up the process of charging out books. Charging and discharging operations could be located at entrances or in subject areas next to stacks for control purposes. By these means, free access could be safeguarded, and its critics assuaged.

Caution prevailed in Ontario library design because the new concepts of service and open concept buildings did not immediately win the day. After all, most of the early closed-stack Carnegie libraries were a vast improvement on previous accommodations and were less than ten years old. Many librarians genuinely feared for the safety of circulating and reference book collections. Possibly the public might steal or misplace valuable items and wear out collections faster. The deportment of users, young and old, was another contentious issue. How were librarians to handle disorder and disturbances in reading rooms? Should separate ladies' reading rooms, now less popular even in Great Britain, be abolished? Equipment and furnishings would have to be reconsidered and replaced in some cases. And the introduction of decimal classification, a task both labour intensive and expensive, was a questionable undertaking in view of the fact that many librarians were unacquainted with its intricacies.

The OLA, as usual, was instrumental in promoting new ideas, especially better classification. It recommended Dewey's system, because it had the great virtue of allowing relative locations for books and providing superior access to printed subjects. At the 1908 conference on classification delegates learned that

> It allows an almost unlimited intercalation of new books on the shelves and makes very easy the introduction of new subclasses on the shelves without the use of shelf labels. If we have a number of books in 517 (calculus) but only two or three in 517.2 (differential calculus) which we wish to keep together, we can label the books 517.2 without needing to write a long shelf label.[119]

Modern methods prevailed with the help of OLA's library institutes and support from the education department. The advantages of allowing people direct access to better classified circulating collections became more apparent over time. Card-charging systems and card catalogues eliminated cumbersome ledger systems, printed dictionary catalogues, and indicators. Librarians were successful in developing popular programs for children. Their work was highlighted at the 1913 OLA conference on children's work led by Lillian Smith (Toronto) and Clara Hunt (Brooklyn). Boards began to abolish separate women's reading rooms and agree with a British architect who commented, "The truth is, that most of them do not care to be considered as creatures apart."[120] Of course, planners welcomed fewer demands on space.

A summary of transitional features from available sources on buildings in Ontario shows that the acceptance of new ideas was belated in some cases (Table 14: Interior Features of Carnegie Libraries). In more than two dozen Carnegie libraries opened between 1903 and 1913, the trends toward controlled open access, the abolition of age limits, separate children's quarters, the elimination of reading rooms for women, and use of card catalogues proceeded gradually. Perhaps 1908/09 marks a new beginning. The OLA formally adopted the DDC in 1908 and Ontario's revised library legislation went into effect in 1909. The regulation of age limits and free access prompted the education department to begin working in earnest to formalize these landmark changes. Patricia Spereman began giving instruction in the use of decimal classification system, card cataloguing, children's department services, and the installation of card charging.

Only about half the Carnegie libraries surveyed in Table 14 operated controlled open access to books beginning on the first day of operation. Sarnia, where Patricia Spereman began her career, was among the first to embrace this practice despite the fact that the building originally was designed for closed stacks. One of its trustees, Norman Gurd, never hesitated to publicize the open concept.[121] Other reforms followed. The directors eliminated the age limit, set up a children's room, and changed over to a card catalogue and decimal system. The general design and services were often cited by Inspector Leavitt as an example for others to emulate (Illus. 42). Sarnia was rectangular in form with the stack room at the rear, circulation control at the centre, and its reading rooms to the left and right at the front of the building. Possessing a dome, considered extravagant by some librarians, the library was somewhat larger than most structures and was set in a park area which bestowed a graceful surrounding (Illus. 43). Many judged it almost ideal for library work, and the contributions by Patricia Spereman and Norman Gurd enhanced its reputation.

For several years, Patricia Spereman's work took her to more than one hundred cities, towns, villages, and hamlets across southern Ontario (Table 15: Libraries Organized by Patricia Spereman, 1908-16). Many places possessed a Carnegie building, but their library boards and staff were not as knowledgeable about the full extent of change in children's work, cataloguing, classifying, and circulation as the education department expected. In Ontario, until the 1909 act, children's departments were the exception rather than the rule. Age limits of twelve or fourteen years had been the norm for decades, not because librarians or trustees were biased against children, but because they were indifferent to modern librarianship devoted to giving up-to-date service for residents of all ages. Inspector Nursey and Patricia Spereman set out to refashion these ingrained attitudes.

Spereman's interesting reports sketch the struggle to redefine library service and to adjust interior space in the years before the First World War. Brockville, a closed-access building completed in 1904, was typical. She wrote in 1910 that

> In this library there are about 13,000 volumes. I gave instructions in the cataloguing and classified all the library, as well as establishing a Children's Department. The Library Board at that time were not very favourable to having the children become members of the Library, and an *age limit* existed of *14 years*. Gave one "Story Hour," with an attendance of about 80 children. This Library is very fortunate in having a good librarian, who is not afraid of work.[122]

Brockville obviously was not completely in tune with progressive change.

Windsor, a larger city, was another library where inertia and resistance to children's work, modern cataloguing, and adequate staff training persisted. Andrew Braid, the long-time board secretary, was unsuccessful in his attempt to solicit Carnegie money in 1910 for a proposed extension which included space for a children's department.[123] As a result, Spereman noted that improvements were at a standstill.

> Free access is allowed to all the shelves, but an age limit varying from 14 to 16 exists for the children. In a library as large as this one is [19,500 books] I think a children's room should be provided, and also more attention given to the children's department. The library was in a very bad condition as regards the classification and the card catalogue, so much so that my visit had to be extended two weeks in order to give

the necessary instructions. A thoroughly competent head librarian and also harmony of the working staff would soon place this library where it rightly belongs – one of the first in the province.[124]

Conditions at Windsor must have tried Spereman's patience, for this report followed her second trip there.

Sometimes an older Carnegie library could be reorganized and space converted to better use. St. Mary's, built in 1905, was a good case in point. Spereman wrote:

> There are about 7,200 vols. in this library; some of the best books were upstairs in an unused room, these were brought down and classified and catalogued with the rest of the books on the shelves. The stack-room was not at all suitable for free access, so at my suggestion one of the large reading rooms was made into a stack-room and free access is now allowed to all the shelves. The old stack-room is to be used as a children's room, and I am sure when the alterations are completed it will be one of the best in the Province.[125]

Patricia Spereman was an unheralded catalyst in transforming service.

As Spereman's work proceeded and slowly produced desired results, there was a consequent reduction in the number of client libraries requiring her talent. With the onset of war in Europe, departmental funding for her work diminished and, by 1916, the new inspector, William Carson, decided to reduce her duties in classification and children's work. Most of the major libraries had abandoned the ledger system; they were using the decimal classification and were moving towards children's services. Many libraries had gained experience in proper planning through participation in the Carnegie building grant program. Carson decided that only libraries willing to purchase supplies, take instruction, and continue the work locally would be considered eligible for Spereman's time on site. This meant a drastic reduction in the range of her work and the end of the education department's direct participation in this basic but vital era of library management.[126]

For adults and children the new, invigorated Carnegie library was a refreshing experience.[127] The modern library of circa 1918 was a quite different place than its immediate, less hospitable predecessor. The predictable neo-classical exteriors conveyed a fundamental Western intellectual tradition, one seemingly appropriate to house book collections and to maintain public custody of a proud literary heritage. Inside there were new freedoms, new principles, which were beginning to democratize services and liberalize space for users. No longer would readers be separated from books by a barrier system, no longer would age or gender restrict users' activities. For many communities, their Carnegie libraries were successful architectural edifices given what had existed before.[128] Writing in 1912, Edwin Hardy emphasized the need for congenial features in smaller libraries: "... a library should be a one-roomed building, as spacious as possible, with bookcases all around the walls and a fireplace and cosy corner somewhere to give a touch of homelikeness, and the."..librarian's desk to give another touch of the same kind."[129] This type of thinking was a revelation compared to John Hallam's advice to Hamilton trustees twenty years before that only standing room should be allowed in newspaper rooms to keep the idle away.[130]

The Carnegie program of philanthropy, in conjunction with changes in library design and advances in the philosophy of library service, heralded a new era of self-improvement and community involvement. It also established a powerful role for libraries in shaping reading tastes and assisting the cause of continuing education. The library, with its new physical presence, was in step with the pace of societal change. The opening of the Carnegie library at Renfrew on 1 October 1921 typified the esteem in which many communities held their library.

> Shortly after 2 p.m. the civic parade started for the library from the Dominion House corner. The Citizen's Band led the way followed by automobiles containing the guest of the day [Dr. Bruce Taylor, principal of Queen's University], members of the Board, the Town Council, and the School Boards. Then came the Girl Guides, the Boy Scouts' Band and the two troops of Boy Scouts.[131]

Addresses by the mayor, the president of the board of trade, board members, and Dr. Taylor stressed the importance of books and reading for individuals and the promotion of good community spirit. These were qualities the public library could dispense in abundance.

The Carnegie renewal, as a physical construct, announced a more active community role for libraries. These libraries often included lecture rooms, museums, art galleries and other municipal services – they were more than just libraries. It also announced that, far from being an elitist institution that only larger tax-supported communities could afford, libraries were now within the reach of residents in the smaller towns and villages. To critics who complained that "overbuilding" by Carnegie might be an incubus to some communities, his defenders answered that they missed the whole point, for the

American millionaire had assisted those who were willing to help themselves. Far from being an isolated community experience, a venture inimical to the finances of local communities, the Carnegie program was conceived as a bold collective stroke to strengthen the values of Anglo-American civic life and demonstrate how taxes could work to the benefit of everyone. Free books for all could make a difference in people's daily lives.

Most importantly, the Carnegie era established new physical structures, ones which possessed a style and sensibility less rigid than before and conceptualized social relationships differently within an architectural setting.[132] Bertram's *Notes* emphasized the principle that publicly funded libraries should exhibit modest form and utilitarian functions. The Ontario library landscape created by Andrew Carnegie was a creative modernist synthesis, an enduring demonstration of the power of one man's imagination and the dedication of hundreds of people and groups scattered across the province. Carnegie grants were the axis upon which the public library movement turned, gaining a purposeful, opportune impetus. By the time the last Carnegie libraries opened in Ontario during the first part of the 1920s in smaller communities such as Renfrew, Glencoe, Norwood, and Gravenhurst, their benefactor had died (1919) and the Carnegie Corporation had abandoned the original library program. The flurry of building had passed, but the public library would continue to prosper on main street because it had been strengthened immeasurably by Carnegie's singular faith in its future.

Chapter 8

A PROVINCE TO BE SERVED

During the upheaval of the Great War, profound changes affecting men and women, young and old, rich and poor, swept Canadian society. Governments promised freedom, better administration, and precious victory, but simultaneously they tightened their grip on people and intruded into economic, social, and cultural matters.[1] A federal income tax, conceived as a temporary measure, was imposed in 1917. Prohibition, a provincial reform with many purposes, arrived in 1916 with passage of the Ontario Temperance Act; the federal government rigorously enforced it under the authority of the War Measures Act in 1918.[2] In Ontario, women received the vote in 1917, dramatically broadening the electorate; the Dominion franchise was extended to them the following year. Conscription took effect in 1917; this legislation was extremely divisive, but most Ontarians stoically accepted the harsh law in order to make the world safe for democracy. In the same year, as inflation steadily eroded the wages of disgruntled workers, the Ontario legislature agreed to finance Adam Beck's gargantuan undertaking (estimated at $20,000,000) for the world's largest hydroelectric generating installation at Queenston-Chippawa, near Niagara.

By Armistice Day 1918, the old colonial, individualistic society of nineteenth-century Canada was giving way to a firmer national consciousness and the gradual collective intervention of state action in the service of mass democracy. The comfortable conventions of pre-1914 were not to be perpetuated. Prewar colonial status and imperial ties with Britain could no longer satisfy the country's national interests. When Germany signed the Treaty of Versailles in June 1919, Prime Minister Robert Borden insisted that Canada be a signatory, a condition which bestowed membership at the first meeting of the League of Nations at Geneva. Later, in August, at the first convention to select a national party leader in Canada, William Lyon Mackenzie King became the federal Liberal leader. King was the author of *Industry and Humanity*, a study advocating improved industrial relations and adequate national social welfare programs. In December, the federal government took steps to form the Canadian National Railways by the merger of unsuccessful private railway lines nationalized during the war. These events, coupled with increased provincial reliance on federal subsidies, signalled the arrival of big government.[3] People sensed that the power and resources of the state had superseded the credo of self-help when it came to improving society.

While public attitudes towards the role and functions of government were unsettled, Ontario retained familiar links with its past, a half century after Confederation. The 1921 Dominion census revealed that more than three-quarters of the province's 2,933,662 residents had been born and raised within its borders. Although many immigrants came to Canada after 1900, seventy-eight percent of Ontarians claimed British ancestry; the only significant groups from outside the British Isles were of French and German extraction. Two-thirds of the populace worshipped in Methodist, Anglican, and Presbyterian churches. These were solid demographic attributes that had given "Empire Ontario" its character and strength to resist the encroachment of American culture. There continued a rich, voluntary participation in small-town life that even extended to some established neighbourhoods in larger cities. But the census also indicated that change was in the offing. Although the province continued to be the economic heartland of Canada, rural depopulation was a disquieting trend: in 1921 fifty-eight percent of the population lived in an urban setting. Farm youth were being drawn ineluctably to the city.

Improved transportation, electricity, and communications were beginning to diminish distances and replace familiar regional economic patterns with ones tightly linked to metropolitan centres. Planning for a system of paved provincial highways from Ottawa to Windsor was underway. By the end of the 1920s, concrete and asphalt highways would link major cities in the southern counties, allowing ever increasing numbers of people to travel by automobile, bus, and truck. Highways would displace rail service as the major means of transporting people and goods. Adam Beck's ambitious plans for electric transmission lines brought domestic conveniences to working families in cities and also to the farm family. Local authorities were adding more users annually to telephone exchanges. Radio sets were finding a place in most homes, receiving news, advertisements, and broadcasts from Toronto or adjacent American border cities.[4] Household radios and local town cinemas instantaneously spread the culture of metropolitan centres at the expense of traditional rural culture. Rising standards of living were altering the expectations of labourers and eroding farmers' isolation.

By the end of the war, both farmers and labourers were thoroughly disenchanted with party politics at Queen's Park. The Liberal party remained in disarray after its progressive leader, Newton Rowell, decamped for federal politics in 1917. The provincial Conservative party, in power since 1905, now personified the status quo: it stood for conscription, patronage, and business interests. The impetus for reform stirred by James P. Whitney had ebbed under his political heir, William Hearst. New parties were canvassing for the support of returning soldiers, women, farmers, and industrial workers. The political influence of the United Farmers of Ontario (UFO), the successors to the Patrons of Industry, and the recently formed Independent Labour Party grew daily. When more than a million Ontarians went to the polls in October 1919 – twice the turnout of any previous election – William Hearst's Conservatives were crushed: the United Farmers, supported by Independent Labour, swept into power.[5] After Adam Beck declined offers to lead the UFO, Ernest C. Drury, who had not even stood for office, agreed to lead the coalition at the next Legislative session in spring 1920. Both the voters and the Farmer-Labour politicians envisaged a new and better society.

Wartime Library Planning

Library conditions during wartime also mirrored the equivocal public mood that rejected Victorian/Edwardian societal conventions and struggled to find acceptable surrogates. Mary Joanna Louise Black of Fort William (Illus. 44), the north's best known librarian, became the first woman president of OLA in 1917/18.[6] She invoked the gender issue with some pride in her closing remarks at the 1917 OLA annual meeting: "I realize, in the first place as the first woman President of this Association, that the Association is making a very great innovation – I would not like to say a step in advance – but a wonderful innovation that I think could only have been introduced in this great democratic country of Ontario."[7] Mary Black's ideas were fashioned by progressive library thought current on both sides of the Atlantic.[8] Her motto was "Service!" She was not satisfied with complacency.

> I think that there is no question in the mind of almost every one associated with the public library, but that the fundamental object of the institution, is to carry the right book to the right reader at the least cost. Is there not, however, a very general fallacy held by us, that in having defined our work, we have accomplished it? This, in spite of the fact, that many of us know perfectly well, that with the money expended in Ontario in the aggregate, very much better service could be given?[9]

The OLA President felt that improved training for library staff and librarians and larger, better-funded cooperative systems might advance the condition of free libraries more rapidly, especially in New Ontario, the area north of Lake Nipissing, where library development was still at a rudimentary stage.[10]

Transition also was noticeable in the Department of Education. Walter Nursey, saddened by the death of his wife and approaching seventy, left the public libraries branch suddenly in early 1916 without an obvious successor in place.[11] Even though patronage continued to be common in civil service appointments, now there were persons with library credentials who were qualified for the position of Inspector. Edwin Hardy wrote, "My great hope is that they will appoint some one who will be in complete sympathy with the OLA, and I believe that will be a factor."[12] His cautious prediction was confirmed early in April when Dr. Pyne appointed William Carson inspector. He had reasonable Conservative credentials as well as ten years of requisite library experience at London.[13] Later, in 1918, Dr. Pyne retired from politics. He was replaced briefly by Canon Henry J. Cody before an Ottawa native, Robert H. Grant, assumed charge for the UFO government. In 1919, Dr. Seath died. His position as Superintendent was left vacant. Successive premiers and education ministers chose to wield more direct influence over the department.[14]

The new inspector, although physically frail, was a persuasive man whose personality and ideas provided a suitable touchstone for those who wished to improve library services (Illus. 45). He was a vigorous promoter of the free library. Carson introduced many reforms at London Public Library. He inaugurated free access, revamped reference service, replaced a ladies' reading room with a separate children's room, and established in-service training. His paper on the Canadian library as a social force, delivered at the 1915 OLA conference, amply demonstrated his views:

> The future greatness of Canada depends upon the intelligence and virtue of its people. The Canadian public library can perform a great service in making Canadians a better, wiser and happier people. The public library is a social force of the highest order for the reason that it gives nothing for nothing; it provides literature which helps the reader to help himself, and in helping himself he learns how to live this life well.[15]

Unlike some Canadians, notably the expatriate Gilbert Parker, who was working secretly with British intelligence to spread Allied propaganda in American libraries during the war,[16] Carson subscribed to high principles. For him the library stood as a trustworthy nationalist force for the continuous dissemination of useful information.

One of Carson's immediate concerns, which received support from all quarters, was to organize more effective war camp libraries for Canadian soldiers-in-training before they departed to the battlefields of Europe.[17] Toronto Public Library had organized small libraries at the commencement of the war, but permanent training camps for Canadian soldiers were not commonplace until midway in the war. It was, therefore, difficult to establish effective libraries. To stock the camps the inspector solicited books from libraries, utilized volunteers to prepare donations for circulation, and organized a simple loan system for camp use. About ten thousand books were distributed by mid-1918 to camp libraries at Niagara, Petawawa, Deseronto, Leaside, Fort Henry, Camp Borden, Camp Mohawk, Camp Rathbun, London, Beamsville School of Aerial Fighting, Armour Heights, and Brockville. After the armistice, the books were redistributed to military hospitals.[18]

Carson spent the war years studying various library problems. He perceived that improved planning would result in efficient, better utilized services. Library finances, the need for better staff training and education, the reorganization of library institutes, and amendments for postwar legislation – all these were foremost on his mind. He reminded OLA delegates at the 1917 conference:

> I do not think we should even contemplate assisting schools
> or doing other kinds of extension work until we have got our
> own houses in order. I think we should look after fundamen-
> tals first, and subsequently, when everything has been
> brought up to date, we can take up other matters.[19]

No doubt he was aware of important changes taking place in Great Britain and the United States, but he concentrated on issues relevant to the core of local service. To his way of thinking, the quality of existing library work in Ontario's cities, towns, and villages would have to be improved measurably before the OLA ventured on fresh initiatives.

The war necessitated reassessments in all sectors of society. Libraries were no exception. Although Andrew Carnegie's library benefactions had given the library movement an enormous boost,[20] in the United States and Great Britain the utility and impact of Andrew Carnegie's program of grants were coming under greater scrutiny. Carnegie had formed a Carnegie United Kingdom Trust in 1913 with £2,000,000 which emphasized library improvement, not library building. Were bricks and mortar to be more effective over time than better organizational systems? An Oxford professor, William G.S. Adams, criticized "overbuilding" and recommended U.K. trust officials shift their attention to rural county areas.[21] As a result of the Adams study, British efforts were renewed to eliminate the penny rate clause and to empower county councils to form boards serving all (or parts) of rural counties. These fundamental reforms came into effect in England and Wales in 1919. In the United States, a Cornell University economics professor, Alvin Johnson, submitted a report to the Carnegie Corporation in 1915 that favoured phasing out building grants and establishing library education as a priority.[22] When building grants came to an end in 1917, it was not a complete surprise. Library planners had already begun to concentrate on adequate local funding, larger units of service, and library training and education.

William Carson was not alone in his desire to formulate a new agenda for action, but, of course, he had to contend with different circumstances and rely on native resources. A Carnegie corporation or trust to fund library planning and stimulate experimentation did not exist in Canada. One of Carson's first ideas was the *Ontario Library Review and Book-Selection Guide*. Established in autumn 1916, it served as an organ of communication and a selection aid for libraries. This journal was immediately popular. The OLA's book selection guide, commenced by James Bain in 1902 and printed sporadically over fifteen years as an annual or in parts, served as a model.[23] Carson was determined to improve the quality of book selection across the province. His new publication, financed and produced by the government, would ensure timely reviews and would "enkindle responsive minds and hearts, and enlist them into the glorious work."[24] In addition, the quarterly would keep abreast of important issues bearing on libraries. It did this during the influenza outbreak of 1918-19.[25]

Carson also proposed an extension of the departmental library school program to two months, commencing in September 1917. Carson aimed to elevate the standards of librarianship: "The time has come when librarians of our free libraries should possess qualifications and credentials. The usefulness of public libraries is determined to a greater extent by the personal and professional qualification of the librarian than by any other factor," he wrote in 1916.[26] Winifred G. Barnstead, from Toronto Public Library (TPL), took on responsibility as the chief instructor; her students studied at Toronto's elegant Dovercourt branch library.[27] Barnstead was well qualified. She had prepared a Canadian history section to supplement decimal classification in 1912 and was on the verge of publishing filing rules for a dictionary catalogue with the assistance of Carson's departmental branch.[28]

A third reform, the reduction in the number of library institutes and standardization of their programs, was not expected in some quarters, but it happened in 1917 in accordance with wartime austerity and Carson's own observations concerning their ineffectiveness.

> I am inclined to believe that the average library fails to put
> into practice the ideas gained at the institutes. This is proba-
> bly due to the fact that in at least two-thirds of the libraries
> amateur management prevails, and that the whole library
> board of a small library is not influenced sufficiently by the
> one delegate who attends the institute.[29]

The inspector's agenda dictated that his efforts should be directed to long-range planning; the creation of better training programs for library staff; and expansion of the departmental office for inspection, travelling libraries, and book selection. He maintained this focus during the immediate postwar period. As a result, the institutes declined in relative importance.

The department of education under Carson began serious reconsideration of the public library rate which had remained at one-half mill – "unappreciable" in Oliver Mowat's words – for almost four decades.[30] The inspector analyzed variations in local assessments, the costs of modern library requirements, the impact of Carnegie building grants, and the relationship between population served and income necessary to provide what he considered a reasonable service. He was the first Canadian investigator to detect that deficiencies in local assessment bases and the increased costs in maintenance for Carnegie libraries often put many community libraries in an adverse situation. The Ontario mill-rate restriction left smaller boards unable to generate the annual revenue equal to their Carnegie pledge to provide ten percent of the original grant. In one instance, Carson advised Tilbury's beleaguered town clerk that it would be "better to take less and maintain the honour of the town than to get more and not keep the pledge."[31] As early as 1917, Carson began to advocate a per capita municipal rate for libraries, an innovative, controversial, point of view: "If a library's income is below thirty-five cents per capita, either the patronage is below what it should be, or the quality of service is not good, or, which is more probable, the demand and the service are below a reasonable standard."[32]

The crux of the matter was the standard of service Carson expected to establish. Simply put, modern library operations covered a wide range of activities and required more income. In his 1919 report, Carson estimated that only a third of the 425 public libraries in Ontario could be judged as "first-class, good, fairly good." He was specific about what he judged to be reasonable service arrangements.

> Five kinds of service are usually given by the modern library:
> (1) Reference service, from the answering of simple but not
> unimportant questions to furnishing extensive information;

(2) lending books for home study; (3) lending books for recreative reading, from which there is a greater educational value as a by-product than is generally supposed; (4) special service to children, including the story-hour; (5) providing reading rooms with periodicals and newspapers.[33]

Following Carson's analysis, temporary amendments were set in place during the spring 1919 legislative session to increase the minimum public library rate to one mill for places under 100,000 people (a half mill, exclusive of debt charges, for Ottawa, Hamilton, and Toronto) and to allow boards to honour Carnegie obligations (9 Geo. V, c. 25, s. 26-29). However, hesitation on the part of William Hearst's government to sanction thoroughgoing reforms and his party's preparation for an election delayed any meaningful changes. This postponement made inevitable another round of discussion and revision.

The Modern Public Library

Carson's war time administrative initiatives helped create a proactive orientation for progressive librarians. Cooperation between the OLA and the library branch had made possible many improvements under inspectors Leavitt and Nursey and had heightened awareness of the library's potential. During the war the number of free libraries increased, and the editor of the *Catholic Record* noted that the public library "has a sphere all its own, in which it offers equality of opportunity to every citizen capable and desirous of taking advantage of it."[34] After the war Carson was poised to accelerate reform. To aid reference work in the province, the public libraries branch published *Reference Work and Reference Works*, a list of three hundred useful reference books. As Carson put it, "No phase of a public library's work is more important than reference work."[35] The various aspects of this service were described in detail. This work was a valuable contribution to the then embryonic state of Canadian library science. To assist smaller libraries with circulating collections, the branch encouraged a simple book-pocket loan card system adapted from the Newark charging system.[36] If libraries were to become active forces within their communities, there was obviously much work to be done.

Perhaps the best perspective on the library's postwar mission was delivered by Sir Robert Falconer, President of the University of Toronto, at the 1918 OLA convention.

> When the war is over there are several questions that are going to demand more and more from us. One is education as a whole...

There is another change coming which is linked up with the industrial development of the country. Two points seem to me to deserve our attention in this respect. The first is the fact that labouring men of all kinds, of all classes, will probably have shorter hours, and shorter hours of labour means longer hours for self improvement, ...

There is another point to which I desire to refer. If one reads the situation aright there is going to be a demand more and more after this war for the opportunity of each and every one to realize himself and herself in a fuller liberty...

These three facts, then, seem to me to place the library of the future in a far more influential position than it every held before. Education from the childhood up, the longer hours for self development and the newer sense of liberty in which the individual is to realize himself intellectually and morally as never before.[37]

Falconer's appeal for intellectual and moral regeneration, which was explained at length in his publication *Idealism in National Character*, was a frame of reference shared by others in the library field.[38]

In early 1920, Carson recommended a course of action to strengthen service, a program that he was confident would shape future events. First on his agenda stood a series of revisions to the act governing public libraries: an improved library rate; an easier way to establish free libraries in rural areas; regulations governing qualifications for librarians; more powers to the minister of education to promote the library movement; as well as several minor changes. By using the full range of power and authority of the office of inspector, Carson hoped to provide effective, ongoing leadership from within the corridors of the provincial civil service. Second, a permanent training school for librarianship would be necessary to instruct and encourage qualified librarians. Carson firmly believed that a library's success depended upon the librarian. Finally, if expanded accommodation for the public libraries branch could be secured, three additional matters – the expansion of the travelling library system, central assistance for small libraries to purchase books, and more staff to carry on the provincial leadership role – could be managed more readily by Carson.[39]

The London native's philosophy of service and his methods to achieve it impelled the public library movement towards institutionalization, the process by which modern library service would be sanctioned and maintained in societal structures. This was, of course, a fundamental goal that the movement's organizers and adherents always had laboured to attain – that the public library might become an integral part of the ordinary citizen's world and that its goals might be embodied in stable local organizations seeking to ameliorate the conditions of life. The public library movement had not been an unchanging entity. It was open to change and adaptation. As it developed across Ontario it had freely borrowed ideas from an Anglo-American venue in order to achieve its various reform objectives. Now the political and societal setting that had nurtured the movement was ready to absorb it completely. In all sectors of society the Farmer-Labour government under Ernest Drury was attempting to satisfy rising expectations by undertaking an expansive range of duties between 1919 and 1923.[40] Farm credit legislation, a minimum wage for women, the Mother's Allowance Act, a civil service pension plan, strict enforcement of prohibition, and major highway construction exemplified the UFO's progressive aspirations. Provincial expenditures spiralled steadily upward until the Great Depression: in 1910 outlays were $12.6 million; in 1920, $82.8 million; in 1930, $212.8 million. Consequently, the public service, ministries, and government departments quickly expanded.[41]

By 1921, sixty-four percent of Ontario's residents lived within the area of a library authority; they enjoyed the services of free or association libraries. Ninety percent of those people who received library service resided in communities where ratepayers had approved free library bylaws or a local council had acquired the assets of a library association (or Mechanics' Institute) and assumed the minimum annual library rate. Since the Carnegie program had transformed their physical persona, libraries generally put forth an attractive modern face, featuring improved public access and a clearly defined administrative system. These facets contrasted favourably with conditions before 1900. Wartime patriotic committees, which based their activities in libraries between 1914 and 1918, further strengthened the library's democratic appeal.

> As a result the public library has become better known in the community, and in its case to be better known is to be better appreciated. Library grants were not cut by the municipal councils except in some isolated communities handicapped by poor library boards who had little or no influence in the community.[42]

The war effort, initially a potential obstacle to library advancement, contributed measurably to its maturation.

Library users discovered that circulating collections were larger and normally directly accessible, and that the scope of available literature was more universal. Educational publications continued to be a priority. As William Sykes wrote, "I venture to say that every large library has its experiences of trained progressive men in every walk of life resorting to its shelves to find the latest work on their particular vocation."[43] And the day had passed when the entire genre of the novel could be dismissed. Good fiction, a Brampton trustee affirmed, was "the encyclopaedia of humanity," a source of stimulus to the imagination, a solace during weary hours, a reader incorporating all phases of life.[44] The nationalistic magazine, *Canadian Bookman*, first published in 1919, and the Canadian Authors Association, established in 1921, also boosted the standing of Canadian writers, magazines, and publishers at every opportunity. Single works of fiction might arouse the ire of moralists, but censorship in the library was now less overt.

The majority of citizens recognized libraries as legitimate public organizations designed to provide information or entertainment, including fiction. A Toronto *Mail and Empire* editorial appraised the situation in the first part of 1919.

> The modern library has an important place in community education – more important, in many respects, than secondary schools. If the proper books are available, it becomes a source of technical instruction to ambitious men and women. Practical subjects are taken up as a means of promoting commercial success. The librarian can reach people whom the churches and colleges never touch.[45]

The Conservative education minister agreed. Before his party's electoral debacle in 1919, Canon Henry Cody was prepared to investigate and act on issues that William Carson raised, an activist course that Dr. Pyne had avoided for the most part. Given rising public expectations, the province was willing to recognize the need for coordinated efforts and more forceful direction.

The Farmer-Labour coalition introduced a revamped library act in the spring of 1920 (10 Geo. V, c. 69).[46] As usual, there were three parts to the legislation – a section for free libraries, one for association libraries, and one for general terms. Free libraries were now extended to local school sections with the expectation that libraries would profit from the stronger public support enjoyed by school boards. No vote needed to be held in this case; a petition signed by a majority of school supporters would suffice. Provision for union boards and contracts for service by two boards were introduced. The process of creating and disestablishing rural boards in adjoining police villages and townships was clarified. But for the most part, association public libraries operating under section two of the new act predominated in rural areas. The new legislation allowed their transfer to a municipality without the necessity of submitting a bylaw to electors. The age stipulation for association library members was abolished. In terms of creating larger rural units of library service, a process being promoted in American counties and by the Carnegie library trustees in the United Kingdom, Ontario legislation was uncreative and uninspiring. Nevertheless, province-wide praise was immediately forthcoming. Mary Black was most enthusiastic. She wrote that the act "may well be considered as the most progressive and practical Library Act that has ever appeared in any statue book, the world over."[47]

The real genius of the 1920 legislation was the realization of Carson's per capita public library rate, which was fixed at a minimum fifty cents. The originality of this arrangement attracted American and British interest. To a curious American audience Carson said, "We believe that our principle of taxation will stand the test of time," and he estimated that this rate might, on average, permit a tax revenue increase of two-thirds for libraries.[48] One Michigan librarian familiar with Canadian and American conditions, Samuel Ranke, using a survey of one hundred U.S. libraries, figured $1.00 per capita would be more suitable, but there was no disputing Ontario's enterprise in the matter. Ranke recommended that the ALA conduct a study to determine a reasonable minimum per capita standard which would encourage growth. His recommendation for a guideline was adopted in 1933.[49] Editorial support for the new measure flowed from many Ontario newspaper columns. The library community regarded the minimum fifty cent rate as a panacea, particularly after the *Ontario Library Review* published comparative rates for the old and new systems.[50] Some enthusiasts were so impressed they cautioned against requesting the full rate from council!

Part three of the new act empowered the education minister and the library branch to implement and modify regulations which would satisfy changing requirements for conditional provincial grants. Flexible regulations could be issued for travelling libraries, library institutes, library training, librarians, and the administration of public libraries; government grants would be withheld if boards failed to comply with the regulations. The new grant regulations restricted the total sum payable for books, periodicals, and newspapers to a maximum of $250 and effectively stiffened conditions for opening reading rooms.[51] Special sections on library training schools and a bureau of home study also were included because courses for home study were part of the developing field of adult education and the need for permanent library schools was gaining greater credibility. Inspector Carson was determined to promote these priorities.

The 1920 library act, unlike the legislation of 1882, 1895, and 1909, retained its essential structure for a prolonged period; in fact, it served as the basis for public library service until 1966. Future library progress in Ontario would depend on basic ideas and attitudes quite unlike the ones which characterized the public library movement's heyday from 1880 to 1920. Voluntary linkages and personal ties were replaced by more formal organizational connections that were defined by legislation, regulations, inspection, communication, and initiative supplied by Carson's public libraries branch. Library training would improve the proficiency of staff members in communities across the province, building expertise and competence in library work, especially in the crucial domain of book selection. Formal programs for librarianship would establish professional norms at the administrative level. Librarians would begin to displace lay leaders from the traditional leadership role they had assumed by default for the past forty years.

Inspector Carson himself often reckoned that a librarian accounted for the major part of the success of any library. On a transnational basis, the discipline of library science, bolstered by the establishment of American degree granting schools in an academic setting, created and expanded consistent standards for undergraduate curricula and teaching that ultimately led to graduate level programs. In the United States, the Carnegie Corporation was scrutinizing library education in the 1920s, demonstrating its concern with educational and administrative arrangements even before the release of Alvin Johnson's seminal report.[52] Canadian practice was to follow the same pattern. On a provincial scale, Carson's long-range plans included standardized library education and departmental certification of every librarian's qualifications. As a result of his work and the program of the Ontario Library School, a reinvigorated leadership, espousing new ideas, would emerge in the 1920s.

Carson preferred to extend library training and education to three months. Approval for his plan came in 1919. Students from smaller libraries were given a one-month course. Those who desired more intensive study continued for an extra two months. The 1919 program was held at Toronto Public Library; Gertrude Boyle, from TPL's cataloguing staff, was chief instructor. TPL remained the home for the Training School for Librarians (renamed the Ontario Library School in 1923) until 1927, with Dorothy Thompson, from the public library branch, in charge from 1920 to 1927. After 1921, an entrance examination in literature, history, current events and general information was necessary for candidates who did not possess a university degree. No fees were charged, texts and supplies were provided, and, to attract potential candidates, a large portion of students' travelling expenses was reimbursed.[53] Guest lectures and hands-on practice comprised the course work.

The three-month Ontario Library School had three main purposes: to improve librarianship, to provide training for currently employed but inexperienced assistants and librarians, and to serve students who filled junior positions in public libraries. Persons over thirty-five were advised not to apply.

Forty percent of the time was devoted to lectures, sixty percent to practice. The main course subjects were book selection, modern literature, reference work, administration, classification and cataloguing, circulation and readers' advisory work, children's work, Canadiana, and special subjects, e.g., library history. By all accounts, the short course in training satisfied the limited need for appointments in libraries during the 1920s. While this arrangement was acceptable for most libraries, Carson believed a one-year course was the ultimate solution. It took the inspector many years to convince the department of education of this wisdom.

In September 1928, the first students entered the one-year academic library program at the Ontario College of Education in arrangement with the University of Toronto. The Department of Education continued to finance and supervise the school's operations. Winifred Barnstead became the school's director with professorial rank at the University of Toronto. The university granted diplomas to graduates; the education department issued certificates. Field work was provided in conjunction with TPL.[54] The replacement of vocational training by a professional program meant that professional leaders and personnel were recognized as crucial to the welfare of libraries. From the standpoint of many full-time workers, libraries continued to be part of a larger social movement. However, the immediate local organization in which they were employed demanded primary consideration and allegiance. The institutionalization of education, training, and employment was changing fundamental perceptions of the public library and the librarian's role therein.

Carson began to strengthen the administration of the public libraries branch after the war with expanded quarters for his small staff. During the 1920s the departmental branch grew to seven people: Dorothy Thompson was hired as a librarian to assist the inspector; Patricia Spereman remained as library assistant; Samuel Herbert was senior clerk; and there were two other clerks and a stenographer. The small number of persons obviously curbed the branch's work. For the most part, it regulated and dispensed grants to public libraries, rural school libraries, and other cultural agencies (e.g., the Ontario College of Art, Boy Scouts and Girl Guides); organized library institutes; superintended the library school; inspected libraries; and managed travelling libraries. Concerning this last function, Carson admitted: "The Department's best efforts are unlikely to be directed toward giving more than a limited service." He cited problems arising from sparsely populated districts and the tremendous cost of serving rural communities.[55]

A mid-1920s library study by an Ontario Agricultural College undergraduate compared Ontario to the state of Wisconsin in terms of travelling libraries. Ontario fared poorly beside Wisconsin, which was recognized for its work in this field across North America.

It is estimated by Mr. W.O. Carson, the Inspector of Public Libraries, that to do Ontario as Dr. Locke does Toronto would require an outlay of between $800,000 and $900,000 annually. A Wisconsin inspector estimates that if Mr. Carson were to do Ontario as they do Wisconsin it would take him fourteen years to get over the province once.[56]

At this time, there were 50,000 volumes circulating in about 425 cases which cost the department $5,000 annually. The program was relatively successful, but its application was uneven. A good deal of the branch's activity was centred on Women's Institutes, a strong organization with extensive roots throughout rural Ontario.[57] A travelling library bookcase loaned to an institute usually was the prelude to the formation of an association library and then a free library.[58]

One particular reform was destined to fail. From the very beginning of his appointment, Carson had advocated better book selection in public libraries. In 1918, he proposed the establishment of a "Department of Education Book Room" as a means to create a representative book stock of "recommended" or "acceptable" titles. This way he hoped to encourage better book selection and purchasing. Carson reasoned that small libraries could buy at low rates without paying duty on imports and could capitalize on publishers' remainder sales. Publishers would have the advantage of selling in quantities, thus increasing sales volume. He expected a startup cost of $40,000 and annual sales of $100,000. Carson explained his proposal this way:

> The nature of the business would hardly justify an estimate for a 'turnover' of more than three times a year. First cost plus twelve and a half per cent. [sic] would be a sufficient charge for books to cover cost of books and of handling, etc. After the establishment of a book-room it should pay its own way; the only expense to the Government should be the invested capital, and the furnishing of rent, light, and heat.[59]

Although Carson advanced credible arguments to justify the establishment of a "book room" for smaller public libraries and school libraries, his solution was unacceptable. Forty years prior to his administration, the education department had abolished Egerton Ryerson's book depository. And the rationale for its abolition in 1881 prevailed over arguments for its resurrection in 1921.

Underlying the 1920 act, which enhanced library education and training and increased departmental work, was an expanded library service mission catering to all segments of society. Ideally, libraries were to encompass all age groups, and librarians were to offer users a greater variety of reference information, educational advice, and recreational programs. A new attitude ruled. As Mary Black had asserted, the right book could be put into the hands of every reader with a little forethought and effort regarding public need for reading materials.

> If this modern [librarian] were asked to enumerate the qualifications necessary for successful librarianship, he would surely put the spirit of service and knowledge of people even before a knowledge of books and all three would precede an acquaintance with library technique and business training.[60]

These were uplifting ideals that community librarians often failed to realize immediately after the Great War. Nonetheless, these ideals retained their power to motivate and sustain the profession in the days and years ahead.

The changing ethos of service spelled the end of Victorian moral didacticism and the library's custodial image. The trend in libraries was towards the design and delivery of more public services and away from sculpting the moral qualities of library users. The librarian might be a scholar, a custodian, an administrator, a booklover, or a feeble failure, but the community's diverse needs were more important than character building or social engineering. Mary Saxe, the long-time Westmount librarian who was active in the affairs of the Ottawa-based eastern Ontario institute, accentuated the new service role:

> Librarians must make their minds elastic enough to cope with any subject, no matter how distasteful. They must learn to accept people's beliefs and religion, just as they accept people's dispositions. Both are usually the result of inheritance. It is not the librarian's duty to change a leopard's spots.[61]

To be sure, the librarian-as-custodian continued to perform an important educational role. Collection building and the arrangement and retention of information in a variety of media formats was a task which was becoming more demanding each year.

Censorship issues still plagued the library, but librarians no longer felt that one of their routine roles was to exclude literature at the selection stage, although the long-standing Hicklin Rule of 1868 still pertained to works in the category of James Joyce's *Ulysses*. Mary Ingraham, a Maritime librarian, accented a fresh, impartial role to obscenity and distasteful literature that suited a democratic society.

The true censor will not forbid the sex novel, but he will have that novel of so high a class that it will not attract the weak and salacious. Shakespeare is obscene, but so great is he that his obscenity will never harm. Moreover, the librarian shows small respect to the thinking public if he, for religious scruples, denies to them the works of the great unbelievers.[62]

While censorship problems continued, chiefly in regards to a little used 1926 amendment to the library act (16 Geo. V, c. 56), the banning of books in libraries was a subtle business in Ontario. In the United States, the ALA was adopting a code of ethics, and liberals in the profession were beginning to rally to the concept of freedom to read. This decade surely witnessed a "critical shift" in the way trustees and librarians thought about censorship on the open shelves of libraries.[63]

The general populace seemed to accept that publicly funded libraries, which embodied shared democratic and educational values, were capable of accomplishing certain societal functions which otherwise would be neglected. Concerning the library of tomorrow, Mabel Dunham boldly predicted at the 1919 OLA conference:

Some day the general public will waken up to realize what it has a right to require of its public library and of the librarian in charge. It will demand the service and it will pay the price. Then the day of promissory notes and overdrafts will have passed, for each library board will have the privilege of stating as school boards do now, how much money will be needed annually for the maintenance of the institution they represent. Then the public library will be as ubiquitous and as far-reaching in its influence as the little red school house.[64]

Although library governance would fall short of her elusive target, her words were a fairly accurate forecast of the increased political and financial support libraries were to enjoy.

A potent factor working in favour of urban libraries was organization. Generally, after 1920, they developed in a more structured way, emulating the successful Toronto library system, which was governed by a lay board of directors and managed by professional librarians. It was an exemplar forged by the trustees of the TPL and George Locke, the chief librarian. The policy/administration dichotomy between trustees and senior administrators (usually chief librarians) was gaining credence. The *Ontario Library Review* helped promote this convention:

> The larger the library the more the trustee confines his attention to policies and the larger administrative problems. The smaller the library the more the trustee is obliged to penetrate into detail. In the larger cities trustees have fairly large problems to face and they have qualified librarians to advise them and to develop the library's organization and services.[65]

Board members received their authority from provincial law; they were representative of the social fabric of their communities; they were above the strife of local politics; and they participated in a broader educational movement serving society. This was an orthodox view of trusteeship and librarianship conceived during the first quarter of the twentieth century.

In cities, where board members might justify their policy-making role by referring to the detailed nature of their deliberations, the politics/administration canon suited urban reformers and progressives who were seeking to shield the mechanisms of government from objectionable political interference. Twentieth century bureaucratic practices were nourished by the theories of scientific management or Taylorism (named after its founder, Frederick Winslow Taylor) and later by the human relations school. These techniques already were operating in large North American libraries, where pragmatic directors were successfully introducing sound business methods.[66] The tenets of scientific management and the primacy of the urban professional combined to embrace libraries as well. Efficiency, economy, and technical expertise were the new bywords in the public library lexicon.

Public relations also had a role to play in the operations of libraries in towns and villages remote from the its expanding base on Madison Avenue, New York. One newspaperman, David Williams, a long-time Collingwood trustee who served OLA in many capacities, dealt with the need for a good relationship with the press in his 1917 presidential address. In a follow up article in the *Ontario Library Review*, he wrote about the library's wise use of publicity to contend with competing pleasures and distractions.

> In this age, when the public library has so many competitors, special efforts must be put forward to maintain it in its proper place with the public. The movies, comfortable and attractive, must be counteracted. The automobile, which in the warmer months gives ease, comfort and pleasure to those fascinated with outdoor life, must be combated. The summer camp with the accompanying merry making and 'loafing' is another detracting force that may not be overlooked. These,

and other forms of amusement, equally free from condemna-
tion, must be given consideration by library workers.[67]

Traditionally, libraries had used regular columns in local newspapers to promote their recent acquisitions; now radio broadcasts could be used to encourage listeners to "Be a library fan as well as a radio fan."[68]

New educational outlooks spread across the province's library landscape
during the prosperity of the 1920s. As the cause of technical education reced-
ed, the demand for adult education surged. William Carson wrote, "the
library seems to be one of the few if not the only educational institution that
deals with its patrons as individuals."[69] The inspector played an important
role in this new movement when he became the Canadian representative on
the ALA's commission on adult education. Established at Saratoga Springs in
June 1924, it was a project financed by the Carnegie Corporation. The commission's 1926 report included a special chapter on Canadian library work:

> Canadian people believe in public libraries as a means of pro-
> moting popular education and good citizenship. Several of
> our libraries have gained a reputation outside the Dominion.
> Speaking generally the principal libraries of Canada compare
> favorably with those in municipalities of like size in the
> United States and Great Britain.[70]

The scope of adult education – continuation classes, extension lectures, correspondence courses, study groups, institutes, summer classes, and programs
with clubs and organizations – gave the public library a potentially prominent
role to play after 1925. However, it had to rely on government and private
organizations for financial support, which withered rapidly after the October
1929 stock market crash.

Did library growth satisfy Ontario's public demand during William
Carson's inspectorate? Unadjusted annual statistics from his office, between
1916 and 1929, showed that within a brief time the free library system was
more secure, that it had become a network serving almost two-thirds of the
population. There were impressive percentage increases for free libraries during the 1920s: 81% for circulation, 44% for volumes held, 102% for book
expenditures, 68% for expenses, and 30% for population served (Table 16:
Ontario Public Library Growth Under Inspector Carson, 1915-1930).
Comparative figures for association libraries were less heartening, but there
was no denying minor improvements. Even retrospective figures show reason
for enthusiasm when expenditures, adjusted for population increases and the
changing economic fortunes of two decades, are recalculated (Table 17: Public

Library Finances, 1920-40). In quantitative terms, progress was moderate but sustained prior to the onset of the Great Depression.

The period commencing with the 1920 library act enacted by the short-lived Farmer-Labour alliance and ending with the stock market crash was a comparatively buoyant interval for Ontario libraries, although there were minor problems. Inflation eroded revenue gains, book circulation did not increase every year, few new buildings were opened, and the unserved population remained too numerous. However, measured library progress was steady in the exuberant twenties. During Carson's inspectorate, the departmental library component expanded considerably; in fact, its size, duties, and budget were not surpassed until after the Second World War.[71] Across Ontario, institutional development was marked by the maturation of modern library service in larger towns and cities. At the centre stood Toronto, a provincial resource, surrounded by smaller libraries which were emerging in their own right under the capable direction of a new generation of professionally oriented leaders.

One only had to consider the Toronto Public Library to appreciate what could be accomplished with a deft administrative touch. Canadian librarianship in the 1920s was dominated by the brilliance of George Locke (Illus. 46), who was developing a dynamic metropolitan branch system with the capable assistance of his staff. He served as OLA president in 1918/19 and was an active participant in Toronto's influential Arts and Letters Club and the Canadian Authors Association. He was also the popular author of *When Canada was New France* (1919). Locke had never taken formal library training, but his administrative ability, as the Toronto *Globe* noticed shortly before the First World War, was formidable.

> Conventionality is not a conspicuous characteristic in the make-up of Toronto's Chief Librarian. Traditions were shattered when he was appointed, and customary usages have gone by the board ever since. He has completely upset the popular conception of what a librarian should be, and has, for Canada at any rate, established a new idea of the duties of the office. He stands to-day the impersonation of a vigorous, up-to-date administration of a highly important public service.[72]

For the Beamsville native, the library was a business proposition to be run on the general lines of efficiency, economy, and usefulness.

Locke's philosophy of libraries and librarianship depended on the utility of the book. "A public library is the great world of books where only the vicious and needlessly vulgar are excluded. The ordinary rubs shoulders with the 'high-brow' and one is sure in such a cosmopolitan crowd to find some of his friends," he wrote after the war.[73] At the 1930 convocation of the University of the State of New York, he told his Albany audience that people should be able to find reading material worth reading in any place or region, that getting people to want to read books was a fundamental educational goal, that education, learning, and reading were a lifelong process.[74] The library was a central organ in this evolutionary journey:

> There is a large, and what ought to be an influential, division of education known as the public library, an educational institutional with no entrance requirements, no fees, no instructors and no examinations. It has books and trained persons whose duty it is to help people to help themselves.[75]

If there was an inherent weakness in Locke's philosophy, which he developed prior to 1920, it was his stress on the informal, personal nature of library service. Locke seldom expressed interest in developing formal working relationships for libraries within government levels.

Under Locke's command Toronto became a major North American library system in the 1920s, personified by imaginative, appealing, functional buildings.[76] Locke "got the evangelic idea of free books for all Toronto in the greatest cycle of branch libraries (designed by sundry Club architects) ever built anywhere in one decade," enthused Augustus Bridle in his 1945 recital of accomplishments of past presidents of the Arts and Letters Club.[77] Eight major branches opened on Toronto's busy streets between 1921 and 1930: Earlscourt on Dufferin (1921), Eastern on Main (1921), Boys' and Girls' House on St. George (1922), Northern at Yonge and St. Clement's (1923), Gerrard (1924), Downtown at Adelaide (1927), Danforth on Pape (1929), and Runnymede on Bloor (1930). The Danforth Street branch, surrounded by retail stores and situated near a street-car intersection, was considered at the time to be a "shopping centre" branch that suited the life of its neighbourhood and provided an innovative way to reach the public.[78] The new Downtown branch marked the end of an era – it meant the closing of the original central library inherited from the Toronto Mechanics' Institute (Illus. 47), an event which left many of TPL's staff and clientele with a distinct sense of loss.[79] The Boys' and Girls' House adjoining the central library was a large renovated private home. It had an upper apartment for exhibitions, library room furnishings, and books suited to different age groups, ranging from early elementary school to upper-level high school students (Illus. 49-50). Under Lillian Smith's guidance, this department quickly received international recognition and hosted visiting librarians eager to view its work firsthand.[80]

Of course, Locke could not have built this system without the aid of reliable – perhaps remarkable – librarians. Frances Staton was an old hand from the Bain era. As head of the reference division, she publicized TPL's prize collections in *Books and Pamphlets Published in Canada up to the Year 1837* (1916); *The Rebellion of 1837-38* (1924); and *The Canadian North West* (1931). In 1924, she gave a paper to the Canadian Historical Association on her absorbing bibliographic work and research.[81] Her scholarship culminated in TPL's *Bibliography of Canadiana*, a book she co-edited with Marie Tremaine; this work served as a fundamental source of information on Canadian publications prior to 1867, and supplemental editions continue to be published. In the children's department Lillian Smith made important contributions to librarianship that were to percolate far beyond Toronto's central library. From the very beginning of her career, Smith knew that she wanted to "put into the hands of boys and girls, books that make for higher ideals, good citizenship, and a love of the best in the world of books."[82] Upon her retirement, she would distill her knowledge in *The Unreluctant Years; A Critical Approach to Children's Literature*. Published in 1953, it remains a standard work today. Another departmental mainstay, Winifred Barnstead, head of technical services, was a creative and powerful force in the training of personnel throughout the Toronto system. She introduced many improvements in cataloging and classification before she left to head the library school at the University of Toronto in 1928.

"The Libraries are Progressing Rapidly"

After the war, Toronto was considered a nucleus around which other libraries could build. There remained cities without free service, Kingston being the most conspicuous, and there were still a few incumbent directors without library credentials. However, by the early 1920s, William Sykes in Ottawa, Mabel Dunham in Kitchener, Fred Landon in London, and Mary Black in Fort William were well respected throughout Ontario. New appointments presented opportunities to transform the character of local service in larger cities. The challenge in Ontario was to move forward under better leaders and to promote an active role for libraries succinctly described by Mary Black's phrase, "the right book to the right reader at the least cost." Leaders could exercise great influence. Across Canada the 1920s was marked by the exertion of small, elite groups of intelligentsia who promoted various forms of cultural and national progress through a network of formal organizations.[83] Public library development in Ontario was a regional drama, played out on a smaller geographic stage, with a remarkable cast that created a new image of public librarianship.

Naturally, Toronto's library was held in the highest esteem; in fact, most librarians conceded that it would be impossible to duplicate Toronto's enterprise in their own communities even on a proportionate scale. However, as the twenties unfolded, local library improvement was the order of the day. As Carson optimistically reported in *Library Journal* in 1925:

> The libraries are progressing rapidly, their use having increased by one hundred and twenty-five percent in the last decade, the expenditure for library purposes by one hundred per cent. and the number of trained librarians from a score to three hundred and seventy-five – all in the same period. Library leaders in the Province are keeping in constant touch and are in active participation in the advances that are being made in the study and application of adult education, standardized library training, library extension, work with boys and girls, etc.[84]

It was a road not travelled without its share of difficulties. A crucial trial for Carson's version of library service – indeed his very ability to influence change – arose in Hamilton just after passage of the 1920 legislation.

Adam Hunter, approaching seventy and one of the last of Ontario's book-men-librarians, had been director in Hamilton for the past sixteen years.[85] By most criteria, Hamilton's female staff were underpaid. Hunter and the board attempted to deal with this problem in the first part of 1920, but they were not successful. As the year wore on, questions about the general management of the library surfaced in the city press. Finally, the Hamilton board of control and the city council took up the matter and asked the minister of education, Robert Grant, to investigate. Grant answered their request by passing it along to Carson, who wrote the library board shortly before the end of November, telling them that the library was below desirable standards.

> The Hamilton public library as an institution for serving the people of the city is below the reasonable level of merit as judged by modern standards. It is capable of giving its patrons a fair amount of satisfaction, but it is only realizing a small fraction of its possibilities. The weakness and defects of the library are so manifest as to be obvious to anyone well versed in librarianship.[86]

Carson suggested that he conduct a two-week examination of the library's overall operations. His reasons for a thorough inspection were obvious: Hamilton's personnel were not adequately trained, qualified, or compensated; the library's financial management for many years had been lax; and its future depended on "complete reorganization."

Publication of the inspector's criticism in the city press renewed interest in the need for a full-scale, independent investigation. Robert Grant refused to initiate this course of action in mid-December.[87] After some procrastination, Carson personally surveyed Hamilton in the early part of 1921. The inspector interviewed staff and prepared a detailed report on the failings of the library and its employees. It was not happy reading for the harried board of directors. Carson did not spare the staff, the collection, or management.[88] He concluded that most staff were poorly qualified, that the salary schedules should be revised, and that new people should be hired to provide competent direction. More money had to be expended on books; some subject areas in the collection were seriously deficient.[89] The chief librarian, Carson contended, should be responsible for book selection and ordering; the board members, even respected collectors such as Henry Blois Witton, should be concerned with outcomes, not administrative procedures. As well, the library's classification and cataloguing required the services of a skilled head cataloguer so that books would no longer be "dumped" into general class areas.

The Carson report meticulously dissected Hamilton's operations and pointed to the rewarding potential that new directions posed. Surprisingly, unrest among staff was not as contentious as originally suspected, perhaps because Adam Hunter revealed to Carson that he wished to step down as chief librarian; he was willing to take an assistant's salary and provide continuity while a new director assumed charge. The inspector recommended several remedial courses of action. He stated in his report that a qualified librarian should replace Hunter, who could continue as the new director's assistant; that specialists be engaged for the catalogue, circulation, and children's services departments; that assistants receive better training; that a revised salary structure be adopted; and that two more branches be added within the next five years.

The personnel and administration at Hamilton changed dramatically during the next three years as a result of the Carson report. Adam Hunter received a leave of absence and an allowance for health reasons in the autumn; he died in May 1922.[90] Hunter's absence and the board's immediate quandary apropos to staffing persuaded Carson to recruit professionally educated American librarians. This was an unprecedented step in Ontario. William N.C. Carlton, who had recently reorganized American war library collections into a free public library in Paris, was temporarily available at the end of 1921 and the first part of 1922 to help reorganize Hamilton.[91] Carlton quickly established new management doctrines at Hamilton: the board was to make policy decisions related to finance, books, and administration, and to select its librarian; the librarian was to take charge of the details of management and administration.[92] Another American, Earl Browning, succeeded Carlton in early 1922; he had extensive public library experience. Browning completed the application of major recommendations arising from the Carson report, and, under his tutelage, Hamilton adopted the progressive mode of management and service which Carson was anxious to impose.[93]

Foremost in Carson's mind was the establishment of viable salary schedules that would attract (and retain) competently trained people to an identifiable professional career path. Using his knowledge of personnel grades in the recently reformed Ontario civil service, Carson suggested entirely new ranks and levels for salary schedules: an unstated, negotiable amount for a chief librarian; a maximum $1,800 for department heads; $1,300-$1,500 for heads in larger branches; $1,000-$1,300 for smaller branch heads; $1,100-$1,400 for senior assistants; $720-$1,250 for intermediate library assistants; and $720-$1,000 for library clerks.[94] Carson realized that salaries had to keep pace with economic realities if graduates from the Ontario Library School were to remain within the province. He was not, however, expecting inexperienced graduates to advance at the expense of senior workers or other specialists. He retained the rank of senior assistant for these people and assured them that there were places for those possessing "a broad cultural background with training in some other fields than librarianship."[95]

Realizing that advancement in Ontario was unlikely, Browning left Hamilton at the end of 1926. A search for his successor took an unusual turn. The appointment of Lurene McDonald, the first woman to hold a position as chief librarian in a major Ontario city, was announced in January 1926. This was a milestone, but everyone realized that she was as qualified as any Ontario director. A native of Tillsonburg, she was educated at the University of Toronto and Columbia University Library School, and she had worked in the New York Public Library system. Lurene McDonald was a careful administrator who preferred to stress the educational facets of librarianship, particularly reference work.[96] She was president of OLA for two consecutive terms in 1933/35, an unusual accomplishment.[97] She also held the absolute confidence of the Hamilton trustees. After her marriage in 1928, she was permitted to continue working, an unheard of arrangement that did not become standard in public libraries for another three decades. Her tenure at Hamilton, from 1926 to 1940, was a period of steady advancement, despite the difficulties brought on by the Great Depression and poor health which finally forced her to retire prematurely.

Compared to the startling adjustments taking place in Hamilton in the 1920s, other principal library centres were relatively stable. At Ottawa, William Sykes was midway through a lengthy career which lasted from 1912 to 1936 (Illus. 48). A former high-school English master at Lisgar Collegiate,

Sykes loved to speak and write about English literature and to publicize the library's collection. Adult education was a particular interest to him.[98] He compiled a selection of good reading fiction in 1914 and edited a scholarly anthology of Wilfred Campbell's poetry in 1923.[99] Under his guidance, Ottawa made systematic progress during the 1920s, although the library board often protested that municipal levies were inadequate to meet the spirit of the fifty cent per capita standard. In ten years, the bookstock increased from 77,524 in 1921 to 115,324 in 1931; about twenty percent of the collection was French language publications. Circulation also kept stride with acquisitions. In 1921, total circulation amounted to 287,446; in 1931, it was 378,123, an increase of thirty-one percent. Sykes proudly proclaimed that adult fiction accounted for less than half his library's total circulation: "Any library can make its circulation rise at will merely by providing unlimited fiction of a sentimental and mediocre type – oceans of Zane Grey and Ethel M. Dell, of detective and mystery stories."[100] English and French circulating collections also were loaned to city classrooms.

Sykes headed a small staff. Approximately twenty regular employees comprised the full-time complement; of these a quarter were university graduates. After the west end branch (financed with Ontario's last Carnegie grant) opened, funds for larger capital projects dwindled. Nevertheless, during the 1920s the central library interior walls were removed to make more space for readers and study areas; a residence across the street was purchased and remodelled as a Boys' and Girls' House (following Toronto's example); and smaller quarters were rented for an east end ("Rideau") branch and a south side branch. Since part-time assistants outnumbered the permanent employees, Sykes conducted an three-month program to train assistants every autumn. He preferred in-service training for recruits on the British style. He felt that potential library workers were not served very well by library schools; they "should not fly so high that they lose touch with actual everyday library work."[101] However, the American style of library education, similar to other influences from the United States, had won the day.[102] By the time Sykes retired in 1936, the University of Toronto was granting a Bachelor of Science degree in library science and restricting its admissions to university graduates.

In London, two librarians attempted to incorporate modern methods, but inadequate buildings hampered their efforts. Fred Landon was city librarian from 1916 to 1923. He had been a journalist for ten years with the London *Free Press* before he replaced William Carson.[103] Under his leadership, the public library system expanded: an eastern branch opened in 1916, a southern branch (housed in Victoria Public School) in 1918, and a southeastern branch in 1922.[104] Landon strengthened the children's and reference departments and emphasized local history and regional collections. The latter were subjects to which he devoted a lifetime.[105] He helped secure John Davis Barnett's collection of English literature for the Lawson Library at the University of Western Ontario.[106] Shortly after the Great War, Landon began to campaign publicly for a new main building. The old red-brick central library, built in 1895, was no longer adequate for the demands of modern service: "London's needs in the matter of a public library consist of a fireproof building situated in the most accessible location for London citizens, with accommodation for 100,000 books, reading rooms, several private study rooms and adequate accommodation for the work of the library staff."[107] Following his appointment as university librarian and professor of history at the University of Western Ontario, Landon continued to promote library education and to be active in OLA, serving as its president in 1926/27.

His successor, Richard E. Crouch, was another city native and the husband of Hazel Tanner, London's children's librarian. Although he lacked library experience, he had worked for two important agencies in the field of adult education, the Y.M.C.A. and the Workers' Educational Association. His appointment depended on his youthful vigour, earnestness, and promise. Crouch remained director for almost four decades.[108] His foremost concern was to erect a modern building, a desideratum for the continuance of good service. To this end, Crouch and London trustees mounted a concerted campaign. They made their plight evident to the press and public: the old building was too small, too crowded; it was a potential fire hazard; and some library departments, such as the binding section in the basement, were completely inadequate for efficient functioning. Keeping in mind Crouch's broader concerns for adult education, the board pressed for an ambitious combination library, museum, and art gallery.

Late in September 1926, the board initiated the lengthy debenture process which would be subject to a vote.[109] The cost in debentures, over twenty years, was estimated to be $240,000. The municipal council was reluctant to act on a request of this magnitude. After a potential site on Queen's Avenue was selected, the board was fairly confident that the bylaw would pass. Inspector Carson even delivered an address to a Kiwanis Club meeting declaring his old library quarters inadequate.[110] However, in spite of vigorous promotional advertising, a crushing defeat for the library proposal was delivered in all four wards by a margin of 3630 votes (2929 yes, 6559 no) in December 1927.[111] This summary verdict appeared to demolish hopes for a new building, but in his annual report Richard Crouch refused to acknowledge defeat.[112] He knew that the library's problems would not vanish so easily. Perhaps additional effort with extra information might persuade the public of the library system's dire needs.

Another bylaw was submitted in 1930, the first year of the depression and poor timing for any kind of local improvement. Richard Crouch and Fred Landon adopted an optimistic stance. Landon wrote to one newspaper, "The costs of building are not likely soon to be lower than at present and the expenditure upon building will have its effect in relieving unemployment and in stimulating business conditions generally."[113] The bylaw went down to a second defeat: this time the library project was pronounced dead. Crouch, soon to become president of OLA, was disappointed, but now he faced even worse prospects as depression budget retrenchment forced the closing of London's modest branch system. By 1933, all of London's branches were shut. The London *Free Press* complained in an editorial that the library was being "severely crippled" by budget cutbacks.[114] Crouch and the library board ultimately prevailed; but a new London central library did not open until 1940, two decades after the initial campaign for its construction began.

Aimée Kennedy, a graduate of the 1916 library school at Toronto, was another librarian who began her career in cramped library accommodation. Until her appointment, the Kingston library had lagged behind other major Ontario cities. When Kennedy started working at the association library atop a drug store, her first priority was to convert it to free status. It was a strenuous process, and she faced many years of frustration. It was not until 25 March 1920, after the registrar of Queen's University, George Chown, a longtime library supporter, offered $20,000 to purchase and renovate a building at the corner of Brock and Bagot Streets, that city ratepayers approved a free library. The vote was 827 to 217.[115] This bylaw marked the end of an era: it was the last free library bylaw passed in a major Ontario city. Eligible voters were attracted, in part, by advertisements in newspapers depicting plans for a new library:

> … a general reading, reference and stack room on the main floor. In the basement the Children's room, and the newspaper room where the men may read and smoke, and in the top flat a lecture hall seating about 300 with platform and two small rooms, either side of platform, where committee meetings of all kinds may be held.[116]

When the issue of municipal ownership of the property and additional costs for renovations threatened this scheme, Aimée Kennedy helped organize a money bylaw for $35,000 in December 1924. It too passed. Finally, after more than five years, Kingston's two-storey library opened in December 1925. At the opening ceremony the mayor formally acknowledged Kennedy's leading role when he remarked that "a good deal of the credit for the new building belonged to her."[117]

The gray limestone Kingston library exhibited many features that had become conventional with the passage of two decades. The adult section on the main floor was one large, unpartitioned room with an attractive dark oak circulation desk in the centre, steel bookstacks on one side and reading tables, reference, magazines and papers on the opposite side (Illus. 51). The upstairs children's department had a big fireplace and its own separate entrance.[118] Kingston's collection reflected Kennedy's insistence that readers of all ages have access to a wide range of published works, including controversial matter. Normally, she opposed the practice of censoring books at the selection stage and refused to condemn disagreeable works if they passed serious scrutiny. Kennedy advised her colleagues:

> If a book is immoral, place it aside, but first be sure it isn't deemed so merely by prejudice. Unless you can enter into the feeling and experiences of people of other lands and manners, why should you say their point of view is bad? Youth, and I mean the present generation looks upon many things from a viewpoint different from ours. Are they wrong, or are we only inflexible?[119]

After the formal Kingston opening, Kennedy was free to become more active in OLA. She served for a number of years as councillor on the association's executive and later as president in 1930/31. She did not retire until 1949.[120]

In Fort William the industrious Mary Black served as a model chief librarian for a smaller city: she "belongs to no unions and does not work an eight hour day. Her day is a twenty-four one."[121] She was renowned for putting people at ease and making the port-city library a hospitable place. A journalist friend marvelled at Black's attachment to Fort William and her passion for public service.

> I believe it is because her heart is here, and that it is on account of this very thing she has made such a success. The library to her is not just a place where she spends so many hours per month to receive therefor a certain number of dollars. She could retain her position and receive her salary with the expenditure of half the effort. It is to her an expression of her personality – in the truest sense of the word a 'life-work.'[122]

This was genuine praise shared by others who knew her service philosophy. Mary Black believed that librarians should possess a love of people. In her opinion, the ideal librarian realized "that books without readers are of no avail; that catalogues and call numbers are only means to an end; and that the most perfect charging system in the world becomes a curse if it makes membership numbers more important than people, and circulation records more essential than happy and satisfied readers."[123]

Mary Black was undoubtedly the Ontario summer library school's most famous and successful graduate. Her broad education was self-driven; she never attended university, although her father was a professor. From 1909 until her retirement in 1937, the Fort William library prospered in her capable hands. Her administrative ability was unquestioned – her Carnegie library, opened in 1912, was known as a marvellously efficient public institution easily surpassing its predecessors, the Canadian Pacific Railroad library and an association membership public library.[124] To accommodate Fort William's heterogeneous population, she established multilingual collections. In 1919, she opened a small branch in rented quarters for the convenience of residents in the western part of the city. She was a member of the Carnegie Corporation enquiry on Canadian library conditions. The commission's report, issued in 1933, was one of the most important studies of Canadian libraries ever made. Black was the first woman president of OLA; she was also active in the ALA's extension work program. From time to time, she was mentioned as a possible Liberal candidate for parliament, but she gracefully declined on each occasion. Shortly before her death in 1939, a branch library bearing her name opened in the western part of her favourite city; it was a fitting memorial.[125]

Mabel Dunham was another outstanding librarian. She began her career at Berlin (renamed Kitchener in 1916) in 1908 and remained there until retirement in 1944. She was among the first in Ontario to be trained at the McGill summer school administered by Charles Gould. From the outset, Dunham seemed to possess the instinctive qualities necessary for librarianship. Shortly after graduation from Victoria College, she made an insightful (and playful) contribution to the college magazine about her easy transition to librarianship.[126] During her stewardship, the Kitchener library received two Carnegie grants. The first doubled the capacity of its stack room in 1909, and the second built a south wing in 1915. Her priority, though, was services, notably for children and youths. In 1912, she began a children's story hour in the upstairs hall of the Carnegie library; in 1923, she organized an adolescent section. Contributions to librarianship and libraries came early in Dunham's career. She was the chief instructor of the Ontario summer library school on three occasions (1911, 1912, and 1914), and she was the second woman president of OLA, in 1920/21. Her presidential speech, characteristically forthright, dealt with some problems library work posed to women.

> ... although there are good positions in library work in
> Canada, there are few openings and advancement in the pro-
> fession is slow and uncertain. There are too many instances
> of University women who have taken library courses but who
> have failed to get a footing in the library world. When vacan-
> cies occur, preference is usually given to local applicants
> without any special regard for educational or professional
> qualifications... This fact cannot be gainsaid, the majority of
> women engaged in library work in Canada began in their
> own home town and have not departed from it.[127]

Dunham recognized that there were limited opportunities for librarians in
Ontario and that some women (and men) failed to provide the type of leadership necessary for the survival of the relatively young profession.

Mabel Dunham also found time for writing, an avocation she enjoyed for
many years. Like many Canadian writers during this period, she was attracted
to the genre of historical fiction. According to Dunham, it had the potential
to make history "an animated, pulsating, enthralling story of humanity."[128]
The Trail of the Conestoga, her first novel published by Macmillan in 1924,
told the story of Pennsylvania Dutch settlement in Waterloo County and the
hardship and satisfaction of pioneer life in the first part of the nineteenth century. Another novel, *Kristli's Trees*, was completed in retirement and published
by McClelland & Stewart in 1948. It won a Book-of-the-Year award for children's literature, which was presented by the newly formed Canadian
Association of Children's Librarians.[129] Altogether, she authored four novels
and a history of the Grand River. Her contribution to Canadian literature
clearly belongs to the tradition of regional writing. Of course, Mabel Dunham
and her hardworking staff epitomized devoted community work too: the
1933 Carnegie Commission of Enquiry wondered if Kitchener, with its fine
German collection, might serve as a valuable regional centre.[130]

Fred DelaFosse, another early graduate of Inspector Nursey's summer
school, also was disposed toward the calling of libraries and writing. Born in
India during the British Raj, he arrived in Peterborough from England at the
turn of the century and was appointed chief librarian in 1911 for the new
Carnegie library then nearing completion. DelaFosse stayed until 1946.[131] In
some respects, he was a throwback to the nineteenth century. In his mind,
Samuel Smiles' popular mid-Victorian manual, *Self-Help*, epitomized the best
type of reading for young people. Imbued with the qualities of a Victorian
gentleman, he contended that public libraries should provide children (and
adults) with "competent and willing mentors," who could dispense advice and
direction on a suitable course of reading.[132] It was a point of view he main-

tained staunchly for the duration of his professional and administrative career.

Using the pseudonym, Roger Vardon, DelaFosse wrote *English Bloods*, a Englishman's dramatic account of an ill-fated farming settlement in the Muskokas at the turn of the century, when the Canadian government actively encouraged immigration from European countries. This novel appeared in 1930; it was followed by a book of poetry, *Verses Grave and Gay*, in 1937. Neither work made DelaFosse wealthy or gained him prominence in Canadian literature. His true forte, as he wrote later, was dedicated service to the community.

> I have been in library work for many years, and can lay claim
> to a sincere regard for service, and Service with a big "S."
> Library work is so important and so vital to a community's
> welfare that it calls for sacrifice of time and energy and above
> all for a sincere desire to help one's fellow-man.[133]

DelaFosse put in long hours and never lost his yearning to oblige Peterborough's library users; his work ranked Peterborough among the finest of the small city libraries of the province.

Agnes Lancefield, the daughter of Richard Lancefield (who had prematurely left Hamilton in 1901 under suspicion of fraud), was one chief librarian who had to endure a strained relationship with members of her board. George Locke hired her in 1909 for the Toronto system, and she progressed quickly through the ranks, rising to librarian-in-charge of the Riverdale branch by 1913. She came to Windsor in 1919, where she faced the formidable Andrew Braid. A long-time trustee who had originally handled the successful Carnegie application, Baird was reluctant to yield any management functions, particularly book selection. His selection knowledge was grounded in the older concept of literature's higher character; he was no friend of the "popularizers."[134] Lancefield, who had attended the departmental library school in 1917, took charge of day-to-day operations and preferred a popular touch. She clashed with Braid on many occasions; eventually, in 1923, Braid resigned, but not before he widely publicized his difficulties with the new librarian.[135] It was a trying time for Lancefield, but she continued as chief librarian until her marriage in 1929 led to resignation. During her short term of office Windsor progressed rapidly.[136] She opened two branches, reorganized the main Windsor library, and founded the *Canadian Periodical Index*, the first issues of which she printed in mimeographed form. In "retirement" her library career was far from finished. She was influential in trustee circles and participated for many years in the Canadian Library Association after its foundation in 1946.[137]

In nearby Walkerville, a town of 8,500, another librarian was beginning to establish credentials that would ultimately gain her the presidency of the OLA (1940-41) and of the Canadian Library Association (1954-55). Anne I. Hume received a B.A. from Queen's University in 1914 and was an Ontario library school student in the class of 1919. She directed the Walkerville library between 1920 and 1936 at a time when it was the envy of many smaller (and larger!) communities. The library was the former home of E. Chandler Walker and the gift of his estate. An elaborate and luxurious mansion, it was built in the Elizabethan style on sixteen acres of parkland called Willistead. Walkerville was an exemplar for smaller centres across North America, and Anne Hume served as its progressive librarian: "Miss Hume is conducting the library according to the best standards of modern librarianship and is serving well as guide, philosopher and friend to the patrons of the library."[138] After the Border Cities (Windsor, Walkerville, East Windsor, and Sandwich) amalgamated in 1935, the libraries were consolidated into one system. Hume became Windsor's chief librarian and its secretary-treasurer in 1937.[139] The service ethic was Hume's strongest point. Toward the end of her career she wrote, "a great responsibility falls on the librarian to see that they [the public] have all the services they need."[140]

Dorothy Carlisle, who had worked briefly at London and Saulte Ste. Marie, arrived in Sarnia in 1924 to take up the position of chief librarian. Her motto was "I have always maintained that to have a successful library, it is necessary to promote the library as much in off-duty hours as in regular office hours." Her record was impressive: thirty years as chief librarian at Sarnia and a guiding spirit of county library systems (Lambton County was the first county library association formed in Ontario); president of OLA in 1936/37; and a chief promoter of interprovincial library association cooperation resulting in the joint Quebec-Ontario library conference at Ottawa in 1937.[141] Of all these accomplishments, she was best known for her advocacy of county libraries. Cooperation and sharing were central to her thoughts. Carlisle vigorously encouraged the coordination of centralized book purchasing and rotation of collections among the smaller libraries in Lambton through her own library in Sarnia.[142] She breathed life into this system as early as 1931, five years before the province passed legislation permitting formal county library associations (1 Edw. VIII, c. 55, s. 19). Due to her determination, for the first time in Ontario, plans for regional-based library service received serious consideration.

Amidst this array of talent, Angus Mowat, the grand-nephew of Oliver Mowat, was the most popular and admired librarian of his generation in Ontario.[143] A veteran wounded at Vimy Ridge, Mowat became chief librarian at Trenton, which had rejoined the ranks of free libraries by 1922. People took notice of his congenial manner and administrative dexterity when he spoke on reading and libraries at the 1923 OLA annual meeting. Mowat reminded his audience that a sense of humour was a great asset. He recounted his adventure with an older man he thought was browsing for a meditative book but who was really looking for "a nice little love story."[144] While at Trenton, Mowat attended the three-month library school in Toronto before moving to Belleville (1928) and then to Windsor (1930) to replace Agnes Lancefield. He often spoke about the ways to improve service to adults, and the need to devote more attention to reference and personalized service.[145] After a stint in Saskatoon, he returned to Ontario where he was appointed Inspector in 1937, a position he held until retirement in 1960.

Mowat, and the cadre of chief librarians in centres outside Toronto, realized that they could not always live up to the high expectations held by many in their emerging profession. Nevertheless, the progress they made in the 1920s toward better service created new benchmarks for their successors. With Toronto acting as their beacon, urban libraries, which served the majority of Ontarians, achieved a substantial degree of uniformity in the delivery of services. While it was true that rural residents did not benefit to the same degree from the application of new standards, the overall quality of work in modern public libraries was superior to service offered in 1900. It was grounded on open access, the Dewey Decimal classification, the card catalogue, the book-pocket charging system and reader's card, reference work, and public programs. Reader services had become a crucial ingredient: emphasis now was placed on lists of recent additions, books of topical interest, and best sellers.

Normally, the development of management skills in local libraries coincided with the development of modern techniques. After the war, chief librarians were able to introduce new library procedures and equipment. Internal office procedures were modernized step by step: unnecessary registration and accessioning schemes were eliminated, and a variety of more sophisticated equipment was used, such as typewriters, adding machines, and telephones. Although the public perception of libraries often hinged on external features, regular clients no doubt were impressed by many innovative improvements to the interior of their favourite library. The fact that by 1930 libraries occupied a variety of buildings, large and small, old and new, converted and purpose-built, which permitted modern methods and services to function more smoothly, had powerful ramifications. The functional legacy of *Notes on the Erection of Library Bildings* was significant. The trend was towards simpler, more functional routines, which allowed staff and patrons to interact more effectively.

Reprise: The Pioneer Spirit

Much of the library growth that took place at the municipal level proceeded methodically in contrast to the rapid change and social flux of the twenties. The exterior grandeur of Carnegie buildings conveyed a classical image of libraries that recollected an era overwhelmed on the battlefields of Europe. But, by 1925, only a shadow of the library's Victorian splendour remained; it was struggling to keep abreast of contemporary changes (Illus. 52). As the postwar depression gave way to economic prosperity by mid-decade, Canadian culture and the public mood were shifting perceptibly. Canadians were rethinking their cultural identity in tangible political expressions, supplanting traditional narrow ethnic, religious, and class definitions of culture which had predominated prior to 1914. A new nationalist wave was eclipsing conservative Victorian colonialism. Upstart Canadian publications, such as the *Canadian Magazine, Maclean's,* and *Chatelaine,* competed against the mass circulation, American-based *Saturday Evening Post* and *Atlantic Monthly* for a popular audience that had emerged in recent years. Novelists were encountering this same phenomenon.

Celebration of the Diamond Jubilee of Confederation in Ottawa and the provincial capitals, in the summer of 1927, aroused a wholehearted national sentiment. That same year, Mazo de la Roche's *Jalna*, which romanticized the colonial-imperialist era, won the prestigious $10,000 *Atlantic Monthly* prize, touching off an outpouring of nationalist literary pride. During the twenties, the Canadian cultural milieu was enriched by the Group of Seven. The Group's exhibitions depicted Canada's rugged northern landscape with an original perspective unfettered by European tradition. But clouds were gathering on the horizon of this new landscape: Canadian popular culture was beginning to encounter the formidable and ubiquitous American presence in popular radio programs, Hollywood films, literary publishing, and the mass periodical industry.[146]

The immediate postwar political outburst of class, region, feminism, and prohibition had been superseded by the search for normalcy. In Ontario, the brief Farmer-Labour partnership was demolished in the 1923 summer election by George Howard Ferguson, the hectoring Conservative boss and an acknowledged master at brokerage politics. His support lay not with the forces of reform but with the vested interests of the marketplace. Ferguson recorded three impressive election victories by wrestling successfully with formidable social issues and by moulding a strong provincial Conservative apparatus. He effectively harnessed the impulse towards dramatic change that people had craved. By 1927, prohibition in Ontario was no more; in its place the Liquor Control Act provided government controlled retail stores, as well as local option for bars, hotels and restaurants, and it generated welcome revenue for provincial coffers. In 1929, the Supreme Court had blunted the federal government's challenge to the development of hydroelectric power along the St. Lawrence and Ottawa rivers by negating Ottawa's long held claim to the ownership of streams and rivers. Ferguson's support of provincial rights played a pivotal role in the creation of a potentially enormous provincial water-power utility. By the end of the twenties a modern province had emerged. Northern Ontario forests and mines were being exploited on an unprecedented scale, and southern farmland was linked to cities by a 2,500 mile network of paved provincial highways stretching from Quebec to Michigan.

The application of business methods and the advancement of industry were Ferguson's concerns. He catered to the public's desire for prosperity by promoting private enterprise and permitting cautious government intervention.[147] Only reluctantly, on the verge of the 1929 provincial election, did the province join the new federal scheme for old age pensions; this adroit move helped elect ninety-two Conservatives and keep the opposition to twenty members. As for education, the Premier held the cabinet portfolio himself, implementing few reforms between 1923 and 1930. He was not a minister to encourage initiatives, although he promoted the goal of equality of educational opportunity. He personally favoured the formation of rural township school boards as replacements for weaker school sections, but he let the matter rest because it stirred fierce local opposition. Similar thoughts about rural library systems were not contemplated. Supported by Arthur Colquhoun as deputy minister and Dr. Frederick Merchant as chief director of education, Ferguson skillfully circumvented the lingering odium of Regulation 17 and made provision for French instruction in those schools where it was considered necessary. By 1927, the contentious language issue which had beset Ontario schools for fifteen years was resolved for the most part. But, aside from this major challenge, the department made few forays into the sphere of education policy.

No major library legislation was forthcoming under the Ferguson administration. One curious 1926 amendment to the Public Libraries Act, which required proprietors of private circulating libraries to obtain a permit from the education department, reflected Ferguson's private moral code and tendency to use autocratic procedures. He wrote to one owner about the need for higher standards in commercial circulating collections:

> Under this method, where it is found that an objectionable book is being circulated, the attention of the proprietor will be drawn to it, and I think in ninety-nine per cent of the cases the book will be withdrawn and that will be the end of it. On the other hand, if a man persists, his permit can be withdrawn from him and he will be subject to penalty on summary conviction.[148]

When his legislation appeared, it specified penalties of $10 to $100 for every day (or part day) private owners were in non-compliance with the statute (16 Geo. V, c. 56). This amendment was short-lived. After Ferguson left office, his remedy was repealed in 1931 (21 Geo. V., c. 71, s. 17). This limited intervention, unopposed by the public library sector, seemed to be the extent of Ferguson's library concerns while he was minister.

Efforts to curtail censorship were not yet a primary resolve of librarianship. Librarians had not developed a coherent and consistent strategy on the subject. Expressions about the folly of censorship might appear in the pages of the radical *Canadian Forum*, but these occasions were rare.[149] As moral standards were gradually liberalized, however, ingrained habits concerning book censorship slowly crumbled. No less an authority than George Locke spoke defensively about the need for censorship by librarians. He argued that the librarian was duty bound to select "quality" books from publishers; readers could purchase what they pleased, subject to legal strictures. For Locke, respectable community tastes rather than broader societal moral values dictated the content of library book collections and the librarian's role in book censorship.[150]

The Premier thought that the library system was working well under William Carson's able jurisdiction. Ferguson directed his attention to small railway-car schools (and their library bookcases) which travelled the CNR and CPR tracks north of Sudbury after 1926.[151] When William Carson died in 1929, the government did not replace him immediately.[152] The proficiency of one man had dominated provincial planning, and the changes he brought to the provincial library office overshadowed even the many accomplishments of the OLA. During the 1920s, the OLA gradually refashioned its role and influence through a skein of events. No longer was its presidency dominated exclusively by trustees; after 1926, it became customary for librarians to preside over annual OLA meetings. There was some initial interest in pursuing the ALA's "enlarged program" immediately after the war. The complimentary ideas of broadening the base of library support *vis-à-vis* an integrated program aimed at the community, and of improving library education, training, and public relations techniques were appealing, but the failure of the enlarged program in the United States doomed an Ontario effort before it could begin.[153] Edwin Hardy also tried to revive interest in county libraries, making an argument analogous to the provincial highway project, but to no avail. Projects on this scale depended on provincial endorsement and financing, requirements beyond the OLA's power to influence to any great degree in the 1920s.

The arrival of Canadian Book Week in 1921 offered a fine opportunity to publicize Canadian authors and to allow the OLA to reformulate its own image and agenda.[154] Its annual meetings began to assume a different character. Every effort was made to feature themes of broad appeal. As a result, more emphasis was placed on literature, adult education, rural extension, reading, and international library development. In 1924, Jesse E. Middleton, William S. Wallace, and Robert J.C. Stead spoke on different aspects of Canadian literature; in 1926, Augustus Bridle, the Toronto *Star* art and music critic, talked about his successful novel, *Hansen: A Novel of Canadianization*; in 1928, Alice Chown recounted her work for the League of Nations Society.[155] In 1925 and 1926, Lieut.-Col. J.M. Mitchell, secretary to the Carnegie Trust, and Charles F.D. Belden, ALA's president, lectured on library promotion in the United Kingdom and the United States respectively.[156] Liaison with other organizations, however, remained sporadic because the size and influence of the OLA did not change substantially in the 1920s.

Never again would the OLA be a partner in government policy making to the extent it had been when Inspectors Leavitt and Nursey were at the Public Libraries Branch. In fact, the Conservative government suspended publication of OLA's proceedings after 1918 and, in 1924, it decided to eliminate the government's annual grant as part of a cost-cutting exercise.[157] When Edwin Hardy stepped down as secretary of OLA, after a quarter century of helping to organize libraries, its annual budget was set at $635 and its executive remained few in number (Illus. 53). The year 1925/26 saw Hardy's last major commitment: he served as president and produced *The Ontario Library Association; An Historical Sketch 1900-1925* to mark the OLA's twenty-fifth anniversary. Hardy's presidential address observed that the OLA had indeed accomplished many goals between 1900 and 1925, and that the public library had become an essential element in the education of individuals.[158]

However, as Hardy was lavishing praise on OLA, there was a growing interest in forming a Canadian library association. At the Seattle meeting of ALA in July 1925, Canadian librarians had held three meetings ("national round tables, so to speak") presided over by William Carson.[159] Canadians wanted more tangible recognition from their American peers; they no longer were content to be seated with foreign delegates as they were in 1926 at the New York ALA conference, when George Locke was chosen as the incoming president for 1926/27 (Illus. 54). Locke was keen on bringing the Americans to Toronto in June 1927. It was Canada's sixtieth year of nationhood, and Locke's motivation stemmed from the same civic pride which had prompted John Hallam and James Bain to court ALA in 1883. An unprecedented opportunity was at hand to celebrate Canada's heritage and rejuvenate library service.

Friday of the American Library Association week will be a big day. It is Canadian day. In the morning there will be a meeting of Canadian librarians. In the afternoon the Mayor and Corporation of the city are giving a garden party in University College Quadrangle, and in the evening in Convocation Hall, Principal W.L. Grant will speak on Canada, and Mr. Charles Marchand and his quartette – the Bytown Troubadours – will sing the chansons of the voyageur, the habitant and the coureur-de-bois of early days, the lumbermen of the north country. It will be a great send-off for the convention.[160]

The chance to organize a national library fellowship had never looked more promising.

A number of Ontario's librarians presided over meetings at the ALA's 1927 Toronto convention. More than four hundred Canadian delegates, the majority of whom were from Ontario, pondered the merits of a Canadian association. At a preliminary session on library extension work in Canada, chaired by Mary J. L. Black, the delegates learned of the growing need for library service in many parts of Canada.[161] Concrete action was taken at a second gathering, on 24 June, chaired by Fred Landon, OLA president for 1926/27. At this session, one hundred and fifty Canadian delegates decided to establish a Canadian Library Association. However, a further step – independence – was not seriously contemplated. Delegates, cautious to a fault, decided that Canadian sessions would be held in conjunction with ALA's annual convention.[162]

It was made very clear by the speakers that there was no intention of organizing a rival for the American Library Association... The Canadian libraries have received very great assistance from the organization of the A.L.A. and will, it is hoped, continue to retain their present connection by membership in the A.L.A. and participation in the varied work of its committees.[163]

A provisional committee was struck, with Fred Landon as chair, to report on the prospects for such an association. John Ridington, Librarian of the University of British Columbia, was appointed president, but no formal body was ever instituted. Instead, the members solicited money from the Carnegie Corporation to investigate in greater detail the state of library service in the nine provinces. The commission's survey results appeared in 1933.

The June 1927 ALA conference offered an important rostrum for George Locke, now at the zenith of his career. Locke spoke eloquently about the library's educational role, a subject dear to his heart, but his comments were tinged with concern for "excessive standardization," which he foresaw as an impediment to growth and development. He cautioned his audience. The ALA had become "formidable in numbers and dangerous in possibilities of power." It was a sobering remark.

> I am not anxious to be connected with only an efficient insti-
> tution – one logically complete – but I want always to be a
> part of an institution that is effective – where there is not
> only a sustaining power but a stimulating influence which
> urges experiment and rewards individual development, which
> buries failures even with the turf and invites all to celebrate
> the victories of one another. What every institution needs is
> the pioneer spirit. We can't be pioneers in action in the sense
> that our fathers were – times have greatly changed – but we
> can be pioneers in spirit and transfer the impulse of conquest
> from the physical to the social and educational life.[164]

Locke was delivering a belated message to more informed ALA delegates from larger urban centres: Los Angeles, Chicago, Boston, and New York. Many Americans already understood that the standardization inherent in bureaucratic organizations and government threatened individual initiative and personal autonomy. But Locke's address marked an important milestone. It publicly recognized that the individualism and enterprise that had sustained the library movement – its pioneer vigour – had been replaced by a permanent library infrastructure. Municipal public libraries had grown steadily, as *Maclean's Magazine* noted in the same month, to the point where they were part of "the very bone and sinew of a nation's development."[165]

EPILOGUE: OTHER DAYS

My study of the public library movement has focused on the identity of the many people who helped frame its ideology, the assessment of its social significance, and the general course of its progress to 1930. It is to be expected that any history of the movement will reveal some troublesome baggage. The movement's successful thrusts ultimately had some disquieting effects on library development. The public library system that emerged in the 1920s was not completely unified. Free public library service had succeeded in reaching almost two-thirds of the population by the third decade of the century (Map 4: Free and Association Public Libraries by County or Census District in 1931), but its immediate prospects for extension were not promising. Libraries had developed unevenly across Ontario. Many small subscription public libraries continued to exist in rural areas; they were a residue from a previous era and outside the mainstream of library theory and practice. Leadership resided mostly in urban libraries where lay managers and librarians worked at implementing economy and efficiency. Moreover, library governance by special purpose bodies was somewhat removed from the core of Ontario's political and educational polity.

The typical free library in a rural setting was small and encircled by fee-paying non-residents. It relied on municipal tax revenue and it was governed by a "depoliticized" special purpose board that had to reckon with the reality of "hard services" (sewers, roads, lighting, etc.). The rule of economy dominated municipal politics and underscored the fact that local tax bases were consistently perceived to be inadequate when library budgets were presented to council. The legacy of optional, local-based service was encouraged by small conditional provincial grants, which dated from the earliest days of the Mechanics' Institutes. Too frequently there was a dearth of energetic leadership on library boards because the demand for local lay talent often outstripped the supply in many areas of the province. In the 1920s, trained librarians from the Ontario Library School assumed leadership roles and promoted the principles of managerial efficiency and professional expertise. The emphasis on internal management in librarianship at the expense of external policy matters assured a subordinate "political" status for libraries at a time when the growing apparatus of provincial and federal government programs was beginning to eclipse municipal authorities.[1] These were potentially serious impediments to future growth.

Only belatedly were Canadian library leaders reaching out beyond the local municipal jurisdiction for additional assistance. In Ontario, the free library movement had spent its energy positively. According to the 1931 census information and statistics from the library inspector's office, there were only a handful of incorporated towns in excess of 2,500 persons which had not achieved free library status. More than half of these places were already association libraries:

Association Libraries	*No library service*
Blind River, 2,805	Bridgeburg, 3,521
Bowmanville, 4,080	Eastview, 6,686
Burlington, 3,046	East Windsor, 14,251
Cobalt, 3,885	Forest Hill, 5,207
Cobourg, 5,834	Hawkesbury, 5,177
Cochrane, 3,963	Kapuskasing, 3,819
Copper Cliff, 3,173	Petrolia, 2,596
Dunnville, 3,405	Portsmouth, 2,741
Haileybury, 2,813	Riverside, 4,432
Huntsville, 2,817	Sturgeon Falls, 4,234
Long Branch, 3,962	
Napanee, 3,497	
Sandwich, 10,715	

Association library status was not unusual – there were five hundred such smaller communities. But it was unlikely any significant changes in library status would occur even if economic conditions improved. Only county or regional library systems seemed to offer any hope for providing adequate rural library service, given three decades of American practice and the recommendations of the Mitchell and Kenyon reports for the United Kingdom in the 1920s.[2]

Across Ontario and Canada, there was less rhetoric concerning the efficacy of local self-help, the mobilization of public opinion for free library bylaws, and the potency of the "library movement." There was more enquiry and concern for organizational improvements; legislation that would allow larger units of service; better education for librarians; improved administrative ideas and practices; and the introduction of new service programs already in place in the United States and Britain for many years.[3] Now the time had come for Ontario to keep pace. When the Carnegie Commission of Enquiry toured the country in 1930, its commissioners – John Ridington, Mary J.L. Black, and George Locke – spouted modern library thought. In their final report,

Libraries in Canada, they wrote a new prescription for Ontario's main problem: "That remedy is co-operation – the pooling of the resources, in funds, in books and in personnel, of these little libraries into a unified regional library system, soundly financed, ably led, competently staffed, and efficiently administered."[4] Could the Banner Province reorient its thinking and face the complexities of this challenge?

There were difficult internal incongruities to overcome, ones that prevented extension of free library service to rural areas and blocked expansion on a national stage, where a network of interests and personal relationships could interact and offer new directions for growth. The subscription library continued to persist in the countryside despite all efforts to transform it. The 1909 and 1920 legislation officially recognized the survival of these libraries by designating them association libraries, an acceptable legal terminology that remained in use until 1966. From a public administration viewpoint, the universal model for public library service was distressingly dependent upon an urban phenomenon – a central library and its branches funded by one jurisdiction. In a youthful profession that claimed to emphasize service to individuals, library management theory and practice too often revolved around economy and efficiency. These were spartan principles which had the effect of limiting service options and consolidating decision making in a few hands.

Most opportunities to gather information, discuss ideas, and share plans about libraries remained confined within provincial borders. Despite preliminary steps in the mid-1920s towards the formation of a national library association, an interprovincial organization remained an elusive goal. Ontario formed the kernel of library strength in Canada, but at this time it was not strong enough to bring to fruition a national library infrastructure. As a substitute, the ALA provided a benign security and focus for the professional activities of librarians in the province's larger urban centres. Consequently, they failed to establish firmer relationships with kindred voluntary associations and cultural organizations that sprang up across the country in the 1920s. For example, libraries were considered auxiliaries, not partners, in the vital field of public education. The public library's ambition to serve adult educational needs, as defined by the Canadian branch of the Workers' Educational Association and university extension departments, generally was ignored by schools, universities, and the department of education. Even well-placed provincial officials, such as OLA President Frederick Gavin, principal of the Ontario School for Technical Education, did not have much influence in expanding the educational role of libraries.[5]

Closer library connections were initiated with some organizations in art and literature. From 1921 on, libraries cooperated with the Canadian Authors Association (CAA) in organizing Canadian Book Week. It was a joint venture undertaken in the promotion of national literature, a natural alliance for libraries. During the twenties the annual book week became a major promotional event for authors and readers alike. But it is difficult to judge the effect of these episodic, localized efforts, or their relation to the fact that total book circulation in Ontario exceeded twelve million in 1930 and would continue to increase during the first part of the Great Depression. At any rate, in the 1920s the official membership rolls of the CAA and OLA were relatively small.[6] Librarians and trustees directed their energies towards organizing local groups in drama, music, and art. Notable in this regard was the work of TPL's Marjorie Jarvis, who spent much of her career promoting community theatre and plays through TPL's branch system.[7] Yet activities at the cultural grassroots did not generate many accolades. Not surprisingly, libraries have received scant attention in cultural histories of this period.[8]

Gender relationships within libraries also were far from satisfactory. The feminization of librarianship gave women more opportunities to enter the library labour force, but moderate wages, low status, and limited autonomy assured their marginalization in professional and management work: "Library work offers fascinating possibilities to the woman whose first consideration is not remuneration."[9] Of course, orthodox social mores determined that married women should resign their positions, thus inhibiting genuine long-term career opportunities. Talented women, such as Mary Black and Mabel Dunham, contributed to librarianship within a social and political framework bounded by municipal concerns. This framework was essentially restrictive. Locally, the work of library boards was normally conducted within a board/chief librarian structure dominated by male trustees who had few interests or contacts in the library field outside OLA. On a provincial or national scale, opportunities for developing services or participating in organizations were limited to voluntary associations.

The high visibility of females in libraries was therefore somewhat deceptive, for their independence was restricted by the parameters of prevailing social structures and social conventions, male paternalism, and gender-biased employment practices.[10] In fact, the enormous impact of the Carnegie building program and the concomitant increase in library activities burdened the advancement of women, who had pioneered the transformation of libraries from a nineteenth-century master-client relationship to one in which different groups of users determined the types of information to be dispensed. There was a widespread (but mistaken) perception that the local library had come a long way and that the range of its services was virtually complete. All these obstacles and misconceptions made it difficult for Ontario's mostly female library leaders to recast service in a different character, to say what it was and what it should become. They had few opportunities to effect real change for the future.

On balance, after decades of development there were many library accomplishments deserving recognition. Edwin Hardy might reveal a dream about a better future in his 1926 presidential address, but Norman Gurd, another articulate library promoter from the Carnegie era, preferred to accentuate the past achievements. As he harked back to "other days," Gurd was sanguine about the striking transformation that had taken place.

> In contrasting the average town library in Ontario of say, thirty years ago with the same library as it exists to-day, the changes that have taken place may be summarized in the statement that the library now had an atmosphere of freedom and hospitality instead of restriction and red tape ...
>
> Those days happily have passed away. The library of to-day has so enlarged the scope of its service that it has become in a real sense a true community centre, eager to extend its hospitality to every good work in the community. Librarians are so keen to increase the service of the library to the community that it is difficult to suggest any new work for the library.[11]

Gurd's enthusiasm and confidence are understandable; he had personally participated in implementing reforms. He was a lawyer in a small city, a pragmatist who saw the public library's agenda in terms of interaction with local cultural groups and reform on a municipal scale.

There were frequent reminders about public library history in the late twenties and early thirties. A few of the "old time" library board members were still active. Charles A. Haehnel, a Waterloo trustee, was one of them. He had served continuously for three decades and could recall the slow transformation of the local Mechanics' Institute library into a free library.[12] A self-consciousness had evolved to the point where librarians were interested in their collective past and willing to recognize the deeds of builders and the history of their buildings. Contributors to the *Ontario Library Review* wrote about old techniques and furnishings, marked the anniversaries of the founding of libraries in Mechanics' Institutes, and recorded the life and work of trustees upon their retirement or death. On one occasion, the small quarterly explained in detail the workings of an old charging board preserved intact at Carleton Place and a handmade facsimile at Cobalt (likened to a telephone exchange switchboard!). The obscure "relic" was actually an indicator. Aged devices like these were regarded by the editor as vestiges from "bygone days," and the article concluded, "Needless to add, neither has functioned for many years."[13] In the depression era, a critique of past customs and equipment could elicit some comfort among library staff. They had firsthand knowledge of contemporary public library theory and practice and the mechanical improvements that had eliminated the drudgery inherent in obsolete daily routines.

During the thirties the public library movement's memory and methods – the problems it had confronted, the state of mind (or ideology) it represented, and the type of society it purported to create – had become valuable historical points of reference. Despite the economic gloom of the depression years, it was possible to rekindle a spirit akin to the early days. Ottawa's chief librarian, William Sykes, submitted a confident analysis of the current status of Ontario's public libraries to an ALA publication dedicated to public libraries throughout the world.

> It would appear that the public library situation in Ontario today might be called by the familiar name of 'depression.' Some years ago Ontario was well abreast of the current library movement, but it has not kept pace with the times. There are serious obstacles to be overcome and much hard work ahead; but there are hopeful signs of unrest and aspiration among librarians and in the provincial department concerned.[14]

It was a traditional formula for recovery and advancement, one that had served the province well for eighty years but now required sustained institutional support and stimulus.

The public library had drawn upon a vast reservoir of attitudes, beliefs, and values, concentrating its efforts in local communities, as it made its own contribution to an evolving Canadian identity. No single, decisive historical event marked the disappearance of the public library movement in Ontario.[15] As long as the campaign for the formation of more free public libraries and associated services proceeded apace, it had the force and character of a movement. However, it was no longer necessary to espouse the rhetoric of "movement" in the face of multiple nodes of modernized and municipally supported free library service, a strengthened library bureau in the department of education, and the OLA's active promotion of libraries. Indeed, libraries, librarians, and trustees had become entrenched features of municipal life within a national, bureaucratic society. After 1930, the year of the Carnegie survey of Canadian libraries, institutional tasks and self-sufficiency, not social reform, comprised the major goals set by most library leaders, activists, and organizations. Increasing reliance on state aid and assimilation into formal organizations had produced a common structural pattern headed by like-minded people.

The redefinition of library roles and relationships within a receptive societal framework – a consumer society based on mass-produced goods, pluralism, and personal satisfaction – was the *modus vivendi* of public library leaders. No longer did they seek to change people's beliefs or behaviour. Libraries were service points for persons seeking information and recreational works. In the "golden age" of the detective novel, when writers of the stature of Agatha Christie, John Buchan, and S.S. Van Dine were entertaining their readers, the Victorian rationale for library service remained serviceable, but its societal goals seemed more dated with each passing year. Decisions about what knowledge should be disseminated or how it should be used were left to individual learners. On this basis, slogans such as "freedom to read" easily replaced didactic nineteenth-century conventions. The ramifications of Modernism, the passionate revolt against irksome Victorian cultural dictates, were evident in librarianship by 1930.

The public library movement had succeeded in attaining most of its goals in Ontario by the beginning of the fourth decade of the twentieth century. The movement's sense of permanence was grounded on a more precise conception of public libraries and more informed knowledge about their general character, functions, and potential. Receptive public attitudes to libraries indicated the magnitude of the cultural shift which had occurred since the movement took up its work in the days of Egerton Ryerson. Homogeneity had replaced the diversity and embryonic quality of public library service associated with the latter part of the nineteenth century. As urban communities had matured in strength, population, and purpose, the public's attachment to the concept of free public library service also matured. People came to rely on their local library and its promotion of educational uplift, conservation of ideas, and accessibility of culture. However, the universal social objectives set for libraries by Victorian advocates had proved to be more difficult to attain. Free libraries were the norm in urban centres, but in rural areas the outcome was more problematic because equivalent social, economic, and political opportunities did not apply. Different appeals and strategies beyond local initiative had to be developed to plan cultural and structural library changes in Ontario. A new agenda for library action was necessary, one that governments at different levels would have to sponsor.

APPENDIX A

Table 1
Public Libraries in 1850 by County

County	Common School Libraries		Public Libraries	
	Number	Vols.	Number	Vols.
Brant	0	0	1	800
Carleton	2	490	0	0
Dundas	1	45	0	0
Durham	2	88	2	455
Essex	3	0	0	0
Frontenac	0	0	1	1,200
Glengarry	0	0	0	0
Halton	3	177	4	933
Hastings	3	155	2	125
Huron	2	180	2	50
Kent	1	60	1	100
Lambton	1	70	0	0
Lanark	1	20	7	2,707
Leeds	6	440	1	350
Lennox-Addington	1	100	0	0
Lincoln	0	0	2	900
Middlesex	8	555	14	2,574
Norfolk	3	300	1	400
Northumberland	0	0	2	230
Oxford	9	373	4	300
Perth	0	0	2	210
Peterborough	4	503	0	0
Prince Edward	0	0	3	1,075
Renfrew	0	0	2	280
Russell	0	0	1	102
Simcoe	1	250	1	100
Stormont	3	129	0	0
Waterloo	5	111	10	2,130
Welland	2	140	4	770
Wentworth	5	406	1	50
York	4	160	9	1,910
Total	70	4,752	77	17,751

Source: Upper Canada, Superintendent of Education, Annual Report.

Table 2
Books Sent Out from the Depository, 1853-75

Year	Library Books	Teachers' Library	Prize Books	Total
1853	21,922	208	.	21,922
1854	66,711	578	.	66,711
1855	28,659	432	.	28,659
1856	13,669	258	.	13,669
1857	29,833	244	2,557	32,390
1858	7,587	84	8,045	15,632
1859	9,308	172	12,089	21,397
1860	9,072	142	20,194	29,266
1861	6,488	117	26,931	33,419
1862	5,599	112	29,760	35,359
1863	6,274	112	32,890	39,164
1864	3,361	57	33,381	36,742
1865	3,882	58	44,601	48,483
1866	6,856	148	58,871	65,727
1867	5,426	66	64,103	69,529
1868	6,573	52	54,715	61,288
1869	6,428	60	54,657	61,085
1870	5,024	52	60,655	65,679
1871	4,825	37	60,420	65,245
1872	6,015	323	63,721	69,736
1873	5,367	351	71,557	76,924
1874	7,167	471	67,498	74,665
1875	7,744	631	72,810	80,554
Totals	273,790	4,765	839,455	1,113,245

Sent to Mechanics' Institutes and Sunday Schools:	22,885	
Grand total library and prize books despatched:	1,136,130	

Source: Ontario. Superintendent of Education, *Annual Report.*

Table 3
Public Libraries in Urban Centres, 1862

Place	1860-61 Pop.	Common School Libs.	Vols.	Other Public Libs.	Vols.
Amherstburg	2,360	.	.	.	.
Arnprior	670	.	.	.	.
Ashburnham	.	.	.	.	.
Barrie	2,154	3	496	1	260
Bath	.	.	.	.	.
Belleville	6,277	.	.	1	900
Berlin	1,956	1	325	2	1,720
Bowmanville	2,721	1	438	1	800
Bradford	961	.	.	1	120
Brampton	1,627	1	413	1	360
Brantford	6,251	1	42	1	1,150
Brighton	1,182	.	.	2	703
Brockville	4,112	1	154	2	850
Caledonia	1,081	.	.	1	120
Cayuga	.	.	.	1	1,000
Chatham	4,466	2	120	1	1,000
Chippewa	1,095	.	.	1	500
Clifton	1,292	1	285	1	808
Clinton	1,000	.	.	2	400
Cobourg	4,975	3	1,183	3	1,400
Colborne	806	.	.	1	200
Collingwood	1,408	2	862	1	848
Cornwall	1,915	1	403	.	.
Dundas	2,852	1	129	1	2,000
Dunnville	1,268	.	.	1	1,100
Elora	1,043	2	921	1	100
Embro	551	.	.	.	.
Fergus	1,117	2	179	1	750
Fort Erie	706	.	.	1	87
Galt	3,069	1	280	1	953
Goderich	3,227	2	582	1	900
Guelph	5,076	1	94	1	1,560
Hamilton	19,096	1	2,725	4	6,129
Hawkesbury	1,259	.	.	1	329
Hespeler	604	.	.	.	.
Holland Landing	741	.	.	.	.
Ingersoll	2,577	1	696	1	604
Iroquois	618	.	.	.	.

(Table 3 continued)

Place	1860-61 Pop.	Common School Libs.	Vols.	Other Public Libs.	Vols.
Kemptville	1,068	1	246	1	600
Kincardine	981	1	86	.	.
Kingston	13,743	2	2,382	2	2,800
Lanark	.	.	.	.	.
Lindsay	1,907	.	.	1	106
London	11,555	2	1,427	2	2,500
Merrickville	908	.	.	1	300
Milton	905	.	.	1	800
Mitchell	1,216	.	.	1	500
Morrisburgh	855	.	.	.	.
Napanee	1,773	.	.	1	800
New Hamburg	868	.	.	.	.
Newburgh	.	.	.	1	366
Newcastle	1,029	.	.	.	.
Newmarket	.	.	.	2	762
Niagara	2,070	.	.	1	1,000
Oakville	1,450	2	224	2	962
Oshawa	2,009	2	762	1	650
Ottawa	14,669	.	.	1	1,600
Owen Sound	2,216	.	.	1	700
Paris	2,373	1	296	1	1,000
Pembroke	637	.	.	1	50
Perth	2,465	.	.	1	700
Peterborough	3,979	1	335	1	1,000
Picton	2,067	1	43	2	1,000
Port Hope	4,162	1	550	3	600
Portsmouth	892	.	.	.	.
Prescott	2,591	.	.	1	100
Preston	1,538	1	392	1	400
Renfrew	700	.	.	1	500
Sandwich	988	.	.	1	500
Sarnia	2,091	1	93	2	350
Simcoe	1,858	2	819	1	260
Smith's Falls	1,137	1	643	3	1,800
Southhampton	609	.	.	1	200
Stirling	753	.	.	.	.
Straford	2,809	.	.	1	1,000
Strathroy	751	1	72	1	100

(Table 3 continued)

Place	1860-61 Pop.	Common School Libs.	Vols.	Other Public Libs.	Vols.
Streetsville	730	.	.	1	400
St. Catharines	6,284	.	.	2	1,408
St. Mary's	2,778	.	.	1	750
St. Thomas	1,631	.	.	1	900
Thorold	1,616	1	59	1	400
Toronto	44,821	4	6,336	9	41,421
Trenton	1,398	.	.	1	300
Vienna	908	.	.	1	486
Waterloo	1,273	.	.	.	.
Welland	731	.	.	1	400
Wellington	.	.	.	.	.
Whitby	2,697	2	414	1	850
Windsor	2,501	.	.	1	350
Woodstock	3,353	1	82	1	1,500
Yorkville	1,570	.	.	1	650
Totals	214,826	56	25,588	101	101,472

Sources: Upper Canada. Superintendent of Education, *Annual Report; Census of Canadas 1860-61.*

Table 4
Public Libraries in Canada West, 1864

Libraries	*Number*	*Vols.*	*% of Total*
Univ. of Toronto and University College	1	15,500	2.8
" Victoria College, Cobourg	1	1,000	0.2
" Queen's College, Kingston	1	3,000	0.6
" Trinity College, Toronto	1	3,500	0.6
Regiopolis College, Kingston	1	2,500	0.5
Knox's College, Toronto	1	4,000	0.7
St. Joseph's College, Ottawa	1	2,000	0.4
St. Michael's College, Toronto	1	1,500	0.3
Upper Canada College, Toronto	1	500	0.1
Congregational College, Toronto	1	2,260	0.4
Osgoode Hall, Toronto	1	8,000	1.5
Canadian Institute, Toronto	1	2,600	0.5
Educational Department, U.C.	1	2,000	0.4
Board of Arts & Manufactures	1	1,050	0.2
Mechanics' Institute, Toronto	1	5,400	1.0
" Kingston	1	2,300	0.4
Hamilton & Gore Mechanics' Institute	1	2,740	0.5
Public School Libraries	481	193,258	35.5
Sunday School Libraries	1,875	288,664	53.0
Jail and Asylum Libraries	22	3,218	0.6
Totals	2,395	544,990	100

Source: Hind, *Eighty Years' Progress in British North America.*

Table 5
Library Volumes Held, Circulation, and Fiction, 1879-80

Institutes	*Vols.*	*Fiction*	*Total Circ.*	*Fiction Circ.*	*% Vols. Fic.*	*Vols.: Circ.*	*% Circ. Fic.*
Ailsa Craig	804	150	1,770	618	19	1:2.2	35
Alexandria	203	0	.	.	0	1:0.0	.
Alliston	340	139	.	.	41	1:0.0	.
Arkona	387	67	.	.	17	1:0.0	.
Arthur	557	150	2,320	800	27	1:4.2	34
Aylmer	1,052	154	2,371	.	15	1:2.3	0
Ayr	1,852	492	.	.	27	1:0.0	.
Barrie	1,011	346	960	599	34	1:9.5	62
Belleville	1,053	443	8,418	6,302	42	1:8.0	75
Berlin	1,915	345	2,153	659	18	1:1.1	31
Blyth	607	102	845	224	17	1:1.4	27
Bolton	289	0	868	0	0	1:3.0	0
Bowmanville	1,361	191	3,278	.	14	1:2.4	0
Bradford	788	102	1,536	.	13	1:1.9	0
Brantford	3,542	1,043	6,816	3,811	29	1:1.9	56
Brighton	794	148	685	102	19	1:8.6	15
Brussels	572	34	.	.	6	1:0.0	.
Chatham	628	114	739	271	18	1:1.2	37
Clarksburg	221	66	.	.	30	1:0.0	.
Claude	495	83	543	215	17	1:1.1	40
Clinton	470	149	526	222	32	1:1.1	42
Collingwood	2,708	217	3,734	1,172	8	1:1.4	31
Dundas	4,100	626	1,750	947	15	1:4.3	54
Durham	1,201	362	2,316	1,087	30	1:1.9	47
Elora	4,643	787	5,362	1,337	17	1:1.2	25
Ennotville	569	49	200	.	9	1:3.5	0
Exeter	590	350	2,340	.	59	1:4.0	0
Fenelon Falls	569	160	2,402	1,444	28	1:4.2	60
Fergus	2,439	285	3,012	589	12	1:1.2	20
Forest	156	59	55	34	38	1:3.5	62
Galt	2,895	401	6,563	2,679	14	1:2.3	41
Garden Island	1,690	115	2,492	687	7	1:1.5	28
Georgetown	380	43	.	.	11	1:0.0	.
Goderich	542	42	.	.	8	1:0.0	.
Grimsby	1,710	223	1,965	.	13	1:1.1	0
Guelph	2,710	691	.	.	25	1:0.0	.
Hamilton	7,140	2,484	27,277	18,398	35	1:3.8	67
Harriston	1,139	340	2,092	1,318	30	1:1.8	63
Hespeler	1,095	175	3,064	432	16	1:2.8	14

(Table 5 continued)

Institutes	Vols.	Fiction	Total Circ.	Fiction Circ.	% Vols. Fic.	Vols.: Circ.	% Circ. Fic.
Kemptville	705	411	.	.	58	1:0.0	.
Kingston	1,723	466	568	220	27	1:3.3	39
Lindsay	399	171	518	383	43	1:1.3	74
Listowel	541	139	.	.	26	1:0.0	.
London	2,081	479	2,862	1,726	23	1:1.4	60
Lucan	143	51	.	.	36	1:0.0	.
Markham	686	145	1,539	943	21	1:2.2	61
Meaford	750	125	930	200	17	1:1.2	22
Milton	2,413	172	2,859	.	7	1:1.2	0
Mitchell	1,625	264	2,252	996	16	1:1.4	44
Mount Forest	660	84	.	.	13	1:0.0	.
Napanee	429	97	1,870	833	23	1:4.4	45
Newmarket	802	225	898	672	28	1:1.1	75
Niagara	2,644	402	.	.	15	1:0.0	.
Niagara Falls	697	237	1,665	1,085	34	1:2.4	65
Norwood	639	130	.	.	20	1:0.0	.
Oakville	597	22	1,257	.	4	1:2.1	0
Orangeville	593	271	2,597	1,850	46	1:4.4	71
Orillia	205	.	.	.	0	1:0.0	.
Paris	2,930	382	3,006	1,380	13	1:1.0	46
Parkhill	932	240	1,315	.	26	1:1.4	0
Penetanguishene	209	68	50	12	33	1:2.4	24
Peterborough	3,292	447	.	.	14	1:0.0	.
Picton	200	17	.	.	9	1:0.0	.
Point Edward	43	8	.	.	19	1:0.0	.
Port Colborne	610	247	635	468	40	1:1.0	74
Port Elgin	1,442	125	1,144	300	9	1:7.9	26
Port Hope	874	384	2,226	1,518	44	1:2.5	68
Prescott	688	348	508	297	51	1:7.4	58
Preston	2,676	148	2,082	394	6	1:7.8	19
Richmond Hill	1,239	137	507	146	11	1:4.1	29
Ridgetown	192	100	986	553	52	1:5.1	56
Sarnia	1,163	364	1,813	993	31	1:1.6	55
Scarborough	1,200	240	1,204	630	20	1:1.0	52
Seaforth	1,564	389	6,039	.	25	1:3.9	0
Simcoe	1,242	.	1,600	.	0	1:1.3	0
Smith's Falls	2,357	275	1,963	.	12	1:8.3	0
Stouffville	254	36	754	280	14	1:3.0	37
Stratford	2,630	921	3,743	1,281	35	1:1.4	34

(Table 5 continued)

Institutes	Vols.	Fiction	Total Circ.	Fiction Circ.	% Vols. Fic.	Vols.: Circ.	% Circ. Fic.
Strathroy	1,623	435	3,056	1,659	27	1:1.9	54
Streetsville	1,425	376	3,827	3,362	26	1:2.7	88
St. Catharines	3,524	958	5,042	1,481	27	1:1.4	29
St. George	357	146	558	.	41	1:1.6	0
St. Mary's	3,103	580	4,469	2,110	19	1:1.4	47
Thorold	3016	664	6,588	.	22	1:2.2	0
Toronto	10,053	3,456	32,986	26,596	34	1:3.3	81
Uxbridge	2,323	570	10,579	3,867	25	1:4.6	37
Wardsville	1,090	69	1,026	156	6	1:9.4	15
Waterdown	1,304	65	.	.	5	1:0.0	.
Waterloo	1,644	318	2,894	1,256	19	1:1.8	43
Watford	153	51	86	50	33	1:5.6	58
Welland	890	238	695	200	27	1:7.8	29
Whitby	1,387	458	3,394	2,132	33	1:2.4	63
Wingham	743	95	1,123	519	13	1:1.5	46
Woodbridge	319	.	.	.	0	1:0.0	.
Woodstock	2,679	978	19,610	7,764	37	1:7.3	40
Wroxeter	792	76	490	155	10	1:6.2	32
Totals	135,711	30,027	244,265	114,365	22	1:1.8	47

Source: Special Report of the Minister of Education.

Table 6
Free Public Library Bylaws, 1883-95

Date	Place	Population[1]	Rate-payers[2]	Votes For	Votes Against	Majority	Total
1883	Guelph	10,190	2,486	646	137	509	783
1883	Toronto	94,755	27,981	5,405	2,862	2,543	8,267
1884	London	25,792	6,713	1,583	942	641	2,525
1884	Simcoe	3,000	na	328	47	281	375
1884	Berlin	4,473	na	376	167	209	543
1884	St. Thomas	10,811	2,433	na	na	na	-
1884	Brantford	11,783	2,165	1,086	275	811	1,361
1885	Hamilton	41,280	10,640	1,358	1,547	-189	2,905
1888	London[3]	26,960	8,356	838	245	593	1,083
1888	Waterloo	2,664	na	na	na	na	-
1888	St. Catharines	10,080	3,452	na	na	na	-
1889	Hamilton	44,653	11,774	3,697	2,030	1,667	727
1890	Ingersoll	5,200	na	486	232	254	718
1890	Chatham	8,730	1,835	540	500	40	1,040
1893	London	33,427	8,400	3,522	1,279	2,243	4,801
1894	Windsor	11,468	2,748	919	254	665	1,173

1 Population given is provincially assessed
2 Ratepayers excludes tenants and other qualified electors
3 The 1888 London bylaw repealed 1884 bylaw

Sources: Ontario. Bureau of Industries. *Annual Report;* Newspapers, local reports, bylaw results.

Table 7
Grants for Mechanics' Institutes Libraries, 1882-96

Year	Institutes Receiving Grants	Legislative Aid $	Average Grant $	Index 1900= 100	Grant Adjusted to 1885/86=101 $
1882/83	79	21,447	271	120.3	323
1883/84	81	22,058	272	114.4	308
1884/85	97	25,170	259	110.5	283
1885/86	100	22,904	229	101.0	229
1886/87[1]	116	20,079	173	97.3	167
1887/88	123	21,884	178	102.5	181
1888/89	154	27,186	177	105.8	185
1889/90	161	28,466	177	104.7	183
1890/91	177	31,711	179	103.4	183
1891/92	192	35,448	185	104.7	191
1892/93	195	37,178	191	96.5	182
1893/94	263[2]	-	-	99.2	-
1894/95	292	-	-	92.1	-
1895/96	207	35,200	170	88.3	149

1 Grant regulations revised
2 Total number of institutes reporting

Sources: Ontario. Dept. of Education, *Report of the Minister of Education;* Curtis, Taylor & Michell, *Statistical Contributions to Canadian Economic History.*

Table 8

Comparative Statistics of Ontario Cities, 1901

City	1902 Pop.	Mill Rate 1902	Street Lighting $	Water & Fire $	Expenditures for 1901				Total Expenses $
					Board of Health $	Poor & Charities $	Schools $	Library $	
Belleville	9,300	23.3	4,893	18,122	177	1,856	16,589	100	429,369
Brantford	17,143	23.5	8,919	37,212	2,387	7,403	34,219	2,200	403,780
Chatham	8,867	30	4,689	14,289	1,133	2,097	19,382	947	229,924
Guelph	11,347	23	5,850	16,060	823	4,253	25,630	1,714	248,479
Hamilton	54,035	19.9	34,415	121,112	14,323	46,720	113,715	9,057	1,157,131
Kingston	18,463	20.5	7,914	19,854	797	3,500	37,563	na	377,015
London	39,265	24.5	24,621	55,811	4,877	25,943	124,096	9,051	1,416,625
Ottawa	61,151	22.2	28,258	99,769	29,873	3,599	174,593	na	1,793,211
St. Catharines	10,604	22.6	8,030	19,524	1,509	970	28,769	1,649	277,651
St. Thomas	11,810	26.3	7,893	21,995	685	5,818	26,400	650	415,170
Stratford	10,741	26.1	5,621	8,711	883	1,961	24,250	800	220,972
Toronto	211,727	23.5	119,076	403,519	45,150	81,224	626,526	28,882	7,247,340
Windsor	12,642	28.5	8,290	21,758	2,305	2,452	32,698	2,410	403,968
Woodstock	9,357	23.1	7,866	17,398	399	855	16,552	na	228,660

(Table 8 continued)

City Totals	Pop.	Mill Rate $	Street Lighting $	Water & Fire $	Board of Health $	Expenditures Poor & Charities $	1895-1901 Schools $	Library $	Total Expenses $
Totals 1902:	486,452	23.2	na	na	na	na	na	na	na
Totals 1901:	479,460	22.5	276,235	875,134	105,402	188,651	1,300,982	57,469	14,849,295
Totals 1900:	467,960	22.9	255,806	839,166	71,332	199,077	1,430,853	57,025	13,440,598
Totals 1899:	448,876	21.8	239,666	736,012	72,770	183,319	1,130,466	56,576	14,754,108
Totals 1898:	440,889	21.6	251,379	828,061	67,205	175,233	1,258,986	55,775	13,966,046
Totals 1897:	430,940	21.8	245,456	720,294	68,145	175,327	1,068,928	57,666	13,301,342
Totals 1896:	420,934	21.4	254,797	716,095	63,648	157,318	1,141,815	57,047	12,432,208
Totals 1895:	416,215	21.1	282,986	727,622	59,416	147,994	1,134,140	51,631	12,250,357

Source: Ontario. Dept. of Agriculture, *Annual Report of the Bureau of Industries 1902. Part III – Municipal Statistics,* 66-69.

Table 9
Public Library (Not Free) Revenue and Expenses, 1895-1910

Year	Bds.	Member Fees $	Prov. Grant $	Local Revenue $	Total Exp. $	Liabilities $	Average Exp. $
1895	292	19,177	35,200	8,140	85,706	11,850	294
1896	245	na	na	na	72,209	13,603	295
1897	244	na	na	na	71,219	12,560	292
1898	247	na	na	na	69,906	16,021	283
1899	253	na	na	na	59,037	17,845	233
1900	263	na	na	na	79,151	20,492	301
1901	283	17,344	26,930	10,929	83,512	25,677	295
1902	306	17,852	29,959	9,755	85,150	28,458	278
1903	288	15,868	26,580	10,602	70,179	16,339	244
1904	264	14,071	12,646	10,251	51,251	9,180	194
1905	242	12,853	8,354	11,538	47,174	6,641	195
1906	233	13,021	8,406	11,307	47,153	7,799	202
1907	221	12,301	8,069	10,597	42,842	6,271	194
1908	234	11,555	8,649	12,207	41,592	3,617	178
1909	230	10,902	9,387	13,830	40,573	3,299	176
1910	224	9,717	9,471	12,003	37,588	2,713	168

Source: Ontario. Dept. of Education, *Report of the Minister of Education*

Table 10
Provincial Expenditures for Libraries, 1902-14

Year	Public Library Grants $	Travelling Libraries* $	Rural School Library Grants $	Total Library Grants $
1902	50,344	475	no grants	50,819
1903	49,039	662	2,904	49,701
1904	26,591	856	3,656	27,447
1905	20,521	1,170	5,273	21,691
1906	21,382	1,084	4,343	22,466
1907	21,888	5,514	4,870	27,402
1908	29,042	1,839	no report	30,881
1909	33,743	1,843	6,060	35,586
1910	37,764	2,515	5,847	40,279
1911	38,483	2,789	8,060	41,272
1912	37,168	2,810	8,241	39,978
1913	38,644	2,257	7,962	40,901
1914	38,008	1,543	8,294	39,551
Total	442,617	25,357	65,510	467,974

* Includes grants to Canadian Reading Camp Association, 1902-07

Source: Ontario. Provincial Auditor, *Public Accounts.*

Table 11
Libraries Represented at OLA and Library Institutes, 1907-14

District	1907	1908	1909	1910	1911	1912	1913	1914
Brantford	21	17	22	18	29	25	25	23
Chatham		7	16	19	25	25	25	28
Niagara		5	9	17	18	15	19	12
Eastern			23	26	32	24	30	33
Belleville				16	19	18*	16	15
Georgian				10*	16	16	16	10
Guelph				25	22	21*	21	28
Lindsay				20	20	21*	24	27
London				25	21	18*	22	21
Orangeville				20	18	19*	18	17
Stratford				30	26	30*	33	33
York				8	18	13	13	12
Northern					11	7	10	8
Western					5	5	5	6
Toronto							1	1
Institutes Total	21	29	70	234	280	257	276	274
OLA Total	34	37	49	55	62	60	64	69

*Higher number from one of the two institutes held this year.

Sources: Report of the Minister of Education; Proceedings of the Ontario Library Association.

Table 12
Public Library Service in Ontario, 1910/11
1. Population Served

| | Municipalities | | | All Libraries | | | |
Status	Assessed Population	Pop. Served	% of Ont. Population	% of Pop. Served	Pop. Unserved	% of Ont. Population	% of Pop. Unserved
Cities	752,280	752,280	32.8	58.6	-	-	-
Towns	397,364	347,837	15.1	27.1	49,527	2.2	4.9
Villages	121,343	87,379	3.8	6.8	33,964	1.5	3.4
Police Villages	na	27,356	1.2	2.1	na	na	na
Twps 'with' libs	647,990	68,216	3.0	5.3	552,418	24.1	54.5
Twps with none	377,170	-	-	-	377,170	16.4	37.2
Urban total	1,270,987	1,187,496	51.7	92.6	83,491	3.6	8.2
Rural total	1,025,160	95,572	4.2	7.4	929,588	40.5	91.8
Ontario total	2,296,147	1,283,068	55.9	100.0	1,013,079	44.1	100.0

(Table 12 continued)

2. Population Served by Library Type

Status	Free Libraries Pop. Served	Free Libraries % of Ont. Population	% of Pop. Served	Pop. Served	Association Libraries % of Ont. Population	% of Pop. Served
Cities	716,443	31.2	55.8	35,837	1.6	2.8
Towns	260,314	11.3	20.3	87,523	3.8	6.8
Villages	42,946	1.9	3.3	44,433	1.9	3.5
Police Villages	1,000	0.0	0.0	26,356	1.1	2.1
Twps 'with' libs[1]	-	-	-	68,216	3.0	5.3
Urban total	1,019,703	44.4	79.5	167,793	7.3	13.1
Rural total	1,000	0.0	0.1	94,572	4.1	7.4
Ontario total	1,020,703	44.5	79.6	262,365	11.4	20.4

1 Townships served by police village free libraries also had larger association libraries.

Sources: Report of the Minister of Education; Bureau of Industries; Canadian Almanac and Directory.

Table 13
Functional Space in Selected Ontario Libraries

Place	Date Opened	Shape	Size Sq. Ft.	Population	Per Capita Sq. Ft.
Belleville	1908	Rec.	3,840	9,117	.42
Berlin	1904	Rec.	3,600	9,747	.37
Bracebridge	1907	Rec.	1,800	2,479	.73
Brantford	1904	"T"	9,392	16,619	.57
Brockville	1904	Sq.	3,965	8,940	.44
Burlington	1907	Sq.**	1,935	1,119	1.73
Chatham	1903	Sq.	3,600	9,068	.40
Collingwood	1904	Rec.	3,280	5,755	.57
Cornwall	1904	Rec.	1,728	6,704	.26
Elora	1909	Rec.	1,728	1,187	1.46
Ft. William*	1912	Rec.	6,960	16,499	.42
Galt	1905	Irr.	3,196	7,866	.41
Guelph	1905	Rec.	4,200	11,496	.37
*Hamilton**	1890	Rec.	5,529	47,245	.12
Hamilton*	1913	Rec.	22,579	81,969	.28
Harriston	1910	Sq.**	2,500	1,637	1.53
Lindsay	1904	Sq.	2,587	7,003	.37
London	1895	Rec.	5,984	37,976	.16
Napanee	1900	Sq.	900	3,143	.29
Niagara Falls*	1910	Sq.	2,500	9,248	.27
Paris	1904	Rec.	2,280	3,229	.71
Peterborough*	1911	Sq.	5,325	18,360	.29
Picton	1907	Rec.	2,492	3,698	.67
St. Catharines	1905	Rec.	3,649	9,946	.37
St. Mary's	1905	Sq.	2,500	3,384	.74
Sarnia	1903	Rec.	5,200	8,176	.64
Smith's Falls	1904	Sq.	2,907	5,155	.56
Stratford	1903	Rec.	3,286	9,959	.33
*Toronto**	1884	Rec.	8,414	86,415	.09
*Uxbridge**	1887	Rec.	1,512	2,023	.75
Waterloo	1905	Rec.	2,376	3,537	.67
Windsor	1903	Rec.	5,868	12,153	.48

* Census populations for Hamilton are 1891 and 1911; Uxbridge is 1891; Toronto is 1881; Fort William, Niagara Falls and Peterborough are 1911; all other populations are 1901.

** Rear stack room was semi-circular.

Notes: Dimensions are approximate.
The average per capita floor space is .54 sq. ft.
Italics indicate non-Carnegie buildings.

Sources: Report of the Minister of Education; newspapers and articles.

Table 14
Interior Features of Carnegie Libraries

Library	Date Opened	Stack Access	Separate Children's Area	Age Limit	Ladies' Reading Room	Catalogue Type
Berlin	1904	F-closed NF-open	yes	14	no	card
Bracebridge	1907	open	no	12	no	card
Brantford	1904	closed	no	14	yes	-
Brockville	1904	closed	no	14	no	indicator
Chatham	1903	open	no	none	yes	card
Collingwood	1904	aft-open eve-closed	no	12	yes	book
Cornwall	1904	closed	no	12	no	-
Elora	1909	open	no	10	no	-
Fort William	1912	open	yes	none	yes	_
Galt	1905	closed	no	-	no	-
Goderich	1905	closed	no*	12	no*	book
Guelph	1905	open	no	14	yes	card
Hamilton	1913	open	yes	-	yes	card
Harriston	1909	open	yes	10	yes	-
Lindsay	1904	open	yes	none	no	none
Orillia	1912	open	no	none	yes	card
Ottawa	1906	closed	yes	none	yes	card
Paris	1904	open	no	14	no	manuscript
Picton	1907	open	yes	none	yes	card
St. Catharines	1905	closed	yes	none	yes	card
St. Mary's	1905	closed	yes	14	no	book
St. Thomas	1906	F-closed NF-open	no	12	no	book & card
Sarnia	1903	open	yes	none	no	card
Smith's Falls	1904	closed	no	none	yes	-
Stratford	1903	F-closed NF-open	yes	12	no	book
Toronto (main)	1909	closed	no	-	no	card
Waterloo	1905	closed	yes	12	no	-
Windsor	1903	open	no	16	no	-
Woodstock	1909	open	no	none	no	card

* At Goderich the women's and children's areas was combined in one room.
Note: Some age limits were discretionary.

Sources: Report of the Minister of Education; Proceedings of the Ontario Library Association; various articles and reports.

Table 15
Libraries Organized by Patricia Spereman, 1908–16

1908	1909	1910	1911	1912
Brampton	*Brockville*	*Brockville*	Belleville	*Bracebridge*
Brantford	Cobourg	*Collingwood*	*Brampton*	Don
Galt	Gananoque	Drayton	Embro	*Essex*
Goderich	Millbrook	*Dundas*	*Midland*	*Ingersoll*
Gorrie	*Norwood*	Dunnville	*North Bay*	Kincardine
Ingersoll	Oshawa	Elora	*Peterborough*	Leamington
Markdale	*Palmerston*	*Fergus*	Port Arthur	Mt. Brydges
Niagara Falls	Richmond Hill	Kingston	Scarborough	*New Liskeard*
Orangeville	*Smith's Falls*	*Millbrook*	*Windsor*	*Orangeville*
Simcoe	St. Catharines	*Milverton*		Orillia
Streetsville	*Woodstock*	Morrisburg		*Renfrew*
Wallaceburg		North Toronto		Runnymede
Wiarton		*Orillia*		*Simcoe*
Wingham		*Owen Sound*		*Windsor*
		Penetanguishene		
		Pickering		
		Uxbridge		
		Weston		

1913	*1914*	*1915*	*1916*
Amherstburg	Aurora	Acton	*Aylmer*
Blenheim	Beeton	*Ayr*	Beachville
Campbellford	Deseronto	Beamsville	*Exeter*
Fonthill	Georgetown	Burlington	*Hanover*
Grand Valley	Grimsby	Caledon	*Mitchell*
Kingsville	*Harriston*	Cargill	*New Hamburg*
Lindsay	Melbourne	*Dresden*	*Parkhill*
Meaford	*Mount Forest*	*Durham*	Ridgetown
Milton	Newbury	*Galt*	*Wallaceburg*
Mount Albert	Victoria Harbour	Iroquois	*Seaforth*
Port Hope	Wardsville	*Markdale*	Zephyr
St. Mary's	*Whitby*	Mimico	
Welland		Prescott	
		Stirling	
		Tillsonburg	
		Walkerton	

Note: Italics indicates Carnegie funded communities

Source: Report of the Minister of Education.

Table 16
Ontario Public Library Growth under Inspector Carson, 1915–30
A. Free Public Library Boards

Year	No. of Boards	Provincial Grant	Total Expenses	Book Expenditure	Volumes	Circulation	Population Served
1895	54	$7,541	$97,983	$22,201	254,091	1,216,407	.
1905	134	$11,693	$151,504	.	684,539	1,807,122	.
1915	166	$22,129	$521,125	.	1,215,525	4,436,995	.
1916	175	$23,290	$624,887	.	1,262,765	4,626,323	1,356,078
1917	179	$24,006	$557,045	.	1,309,928	5,074,571	1,377,544
1918	183	$24,913	$578,866	$57,182	1,407,666	4,759,049	1,440,091
1919	186	$24,510	$580,052	$100,093	1,470,288	5,628,417	1,479,052
1920	186	$27,686	$738,010	$120,131	1,537,517	6,316,340	1,523,873
1921	193	$28,817	$834,590	$141,821	1,654,424	7,511,391	1,548,511
1922	195	$31,200	$873,686	$149,453	1,731,827	7,791,492	1,582,851
1923	202	$32,083	$980,381	$162,137	1,811,219	7,920,215	1,606,754
1924	208	$33,360	$933,443	$165,221	1,887,434	8,500,973	1,643,475
1925	212	$34,320	$1,037,392	$179,004	1,930,841	9,421,208	1,663,867
1926	214	$35,492	$1,032,795	$191,522	1,991,782	9,498,898	1,702,128
1927	214	$36,546	$1,035,196	$187,111	2,055,858	9,232,887	1,712,163
1928	215	$37,307	$1,104,185	$205,516	2,113,412	9,682,283	1,792,491
1929	219	$38,240	$1,155,026	$225,645	2,082,757	10,261,357	1,847,493
1930	222	$39,079	$1,239,798	$243,145	2,214,245	11,433,208	1,976,678
Change 1920-30:	41.2%		68.0%	102.4%	44.0%	81.0%	29.7%

(Table 16 continued)

B. Association Library Boards

Year	No. of Boards	Provincial Grant	Total Expenses	Book Expenditure	Volumes	Circulation	Population Served
1895	292	$35,200	$85,706	$27,317	404,605	700,958	.
1905	242	$8,354	$47,174	.	473,160	673,958	.
1915	229	$8,223	$32,790	.	427,113	510,287	.
1916	226	$7,944	$34,232	.	447,081	505,607	174,460
1917	229	$8,282	$32,628	.	438,569	515,794	153,315
1918	242	$7,623	$40,561	$12,721	445,090	535,367	161,894
1919	250	$8,292	$39,851	$16,922	436,654	552,288	150,949
1920	264	$9,963	$52,599	$20,637	473,950	635,307	166,368
1921	267	$11,182	$56,272	$22,182	475,292	728,500	170,415
1922	271	$11,511	$52,604	$22,148	476,930	742,019	164,082
1923	273	$12,484	$56,208	$22,288	479,457	707,095	155,520
1924	288	$12,185	$53,911	$21,535	501,289	735,168	166,498
1925	293	$11,782	$57,563	$22,513	502,142	758,166	170,332
1926	296	$12,394	$57,674	$24,601	531,821	800,553	186,083
1927	296	$13,471	$61,672	$25,208	554,810	819,574	187,691
1928	301	$13,455	$62,627	$26,293	584,601	881,080	205,337
1929	287	$13,976	$64,600	$25,029	593,236	890,480	215,663
1930	300	$12,651	$64,828	$36,021	604,323	892,700	211,712
Change 1920-30:	27.0%	23.2%	74.5%	27.5%	40.5%	27.3%	

Source: Ontario. Dept. of Education, *Report of the Minister of Education.*

Table 17
Public Library Finances, 1920–40
A. Free Public Libraries

Year[1]	*Population Served $*	*Provincial Grant*	*Total $*	*Expenditure Per Capita*	*Deflator[2] (100 = 1935-39)*	*Deflated Per Capita Expenditure*
1919/20	1,479,052	27,686	580,052	.39	150.4	.26
1924/25	1,643,475	34,320	933,443	.57	120.4	.47
1927/28	1,712,163	37,307	1,035,196	.60	120.2	.50
1929/30	1,847,493	39,079	1,555,026	.84	120.8	.70
1932/33	1,914,250	26,279	1,253,177	.65	94.3	.69
1934/35	1,992,862	26,545	1,078,892	.56	96.2	.58
1937/38	2,012,041	28,292	1,215,932	.60	102.2	.59
1939/40	2,057,359	29,474	1,283,526	.62	105.6	.59

1 Statistics provided for legislative grant are for latest year, all others for previous year.
2 Cost of living index; deflator for government expenditure not available prior to 1926.

(Table 17 continued)

B. Association Libraries

Year[1]	Population Served[2] $	Provincial Grant	Total $	Expenditure[3] Per Capita	Deflator[4] (100 = 1935-39)	Deflated Per Capita Expenditure
1919/20	150,949	9,963	39,851	.26	150.4	.17
1924/25	166,498	11,782	53,911	.32	120.4	.27
1927/28	187,691	13,455	61,672	.33	120.2	.27
1929/30	215,663	12,651	64,600	.30	120.8	.25
1932/33	213,214	9,945	55,957	.26	94.3	.28
1934/35	-	8,795	48,834	-	96.2	-
1937/38	190,044	9,487	47,952	.25	102.2	.25
1939/40	212,476	11,752	53,573	.25	105.6	.24

1   Statistics provided for legislative grant are for latest year, all other figures for previous year.
2   Only statistics for borrowers available in 1934.
3   Includes county library associations after 1930.
4   Cost of living index; deflator for government expenditure not available prior to 1926.

Sources: Ontario Dept. of Education, *Report of the Ministry of Education; Ontario Library Review;* Dominion Bureau of Statistics, *National Accounts, Income and Expenditure, 1926-1950.*

APPENDIX B

GRAPH 1: TOTAL GRANTS FOR MECHANICS' INSTITUTES
LIBRARIES, 1868 TO 1880

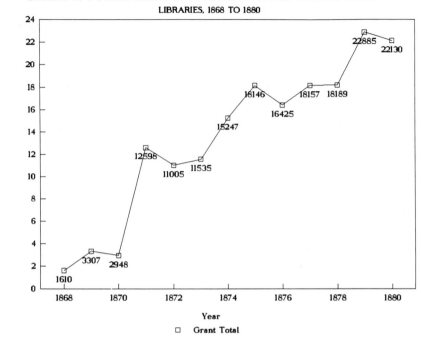

GRAPH 2: TOTAL BOOKS IN MECHANICS' INSTITUTES
LIBRARIES, 1868 TO 1880

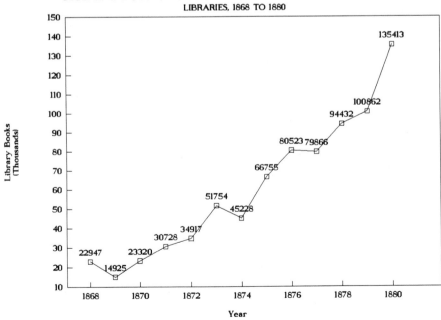

GRAPH 3: LIBRARY CIRCULATION FROM
MECHANICS' INSTITUTES, 1875-1880

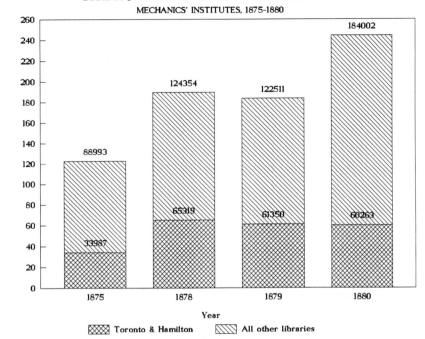

Book Circulation (Thousands)

Year

Toronto & Hamilton   All other libraries

GRAPH 4: FREE LIBRARY BOARDS IN ONTARIO
1882 TO 1918

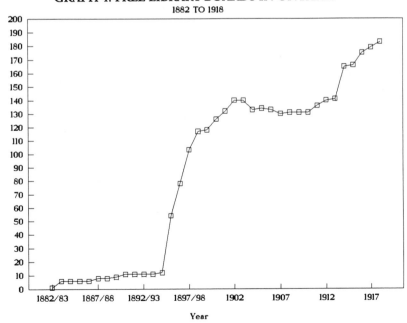

Library Boards

Year

Free Libraries

GRAPH 5: LOCAL PUBLIC LIBRARY REVENUE
1882 to 1914

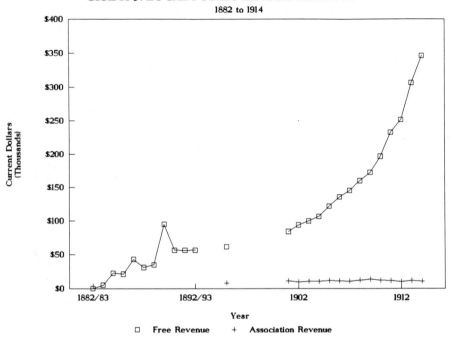

□   Free Revenue   +   Association Revenue

GRAPH 6: FREE LIBRARY VOLUMES AND CIRCULATION
1882 TO 1918

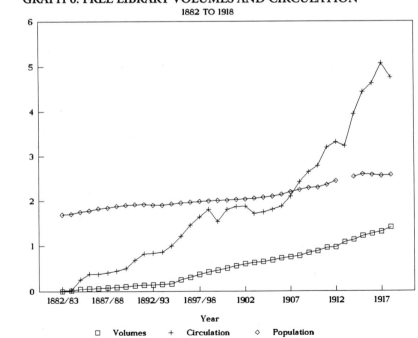

□   Volumes   +   Circulation   ◇   Population

APPENDIX C

MAP 1

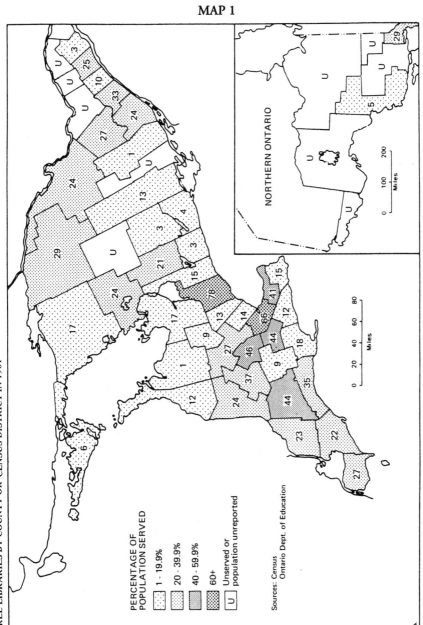

FREE LIBRARIES BY COUNTY OR CENSUS DISTRICT IN 1901

PERCENTAGE OF
POPULATION SERVED

1 - 19.9%

20 - 39.9%

40 - 59.9%

60+

U Unserved or
population unreported

Sources: Census
Ontario Dept. of Education

NORTHERN ONTARIO

MAP 2

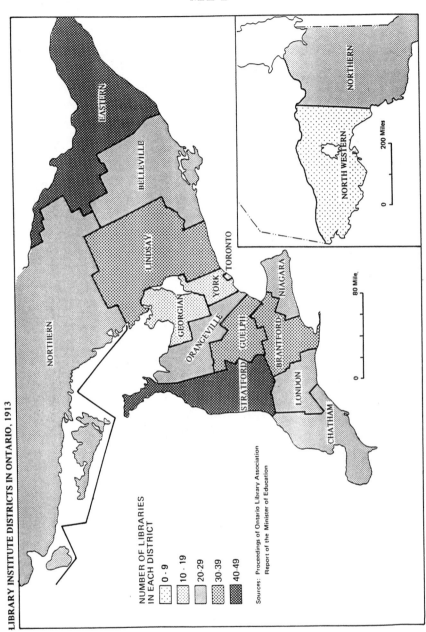

LIBRARY INSTITUTE DISTRICTS IN ONTARIO, 1913

NUMBER OF LIBRARIES
IN EACH DISTRICT

0 - 9
10 - 19
20-29
30-39
40-49

Sources: Proceedings of Ontario Library Association
Report of the Minister of Education

MAP 3

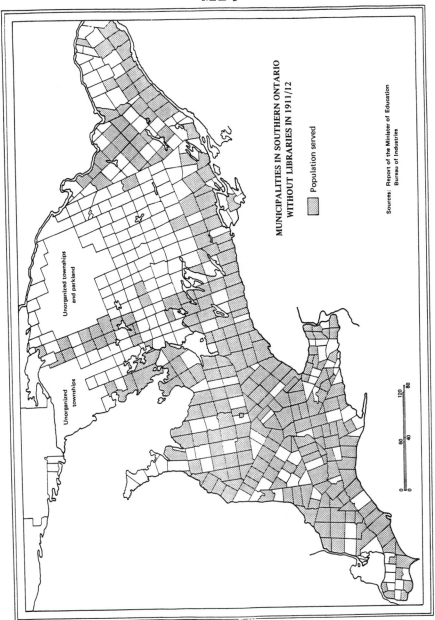

MUNICIPALITIES IN SOUTHERN ONTARIO
WITHOUT LIBRARIES IN 1911/12

Population served

Unorganized townships
and parkland

Unorganized
townships

Sources: Report of the Minister of Education
Bureau of Industries

MAP 4

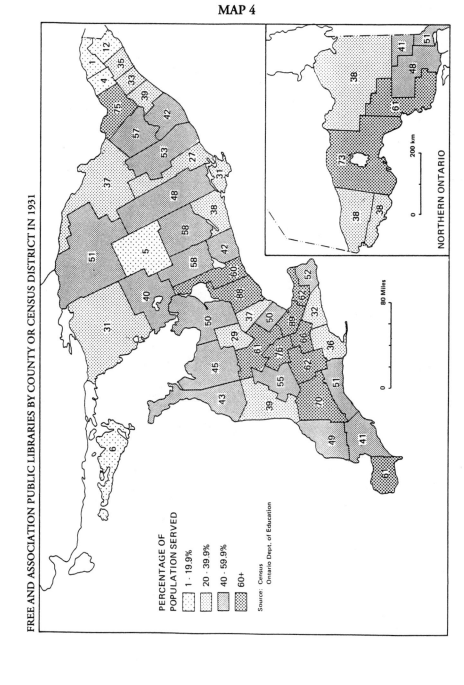

FREE AND ASSOCIATION PUBLIC LIBRARIES BY COUNTY OR CENSUS DISTRICT IN 1931

NORTHERN ONTARIO

PERCENTAGE OF
POPULATION SERVED

1 - 19.9%

20 - 39.9%

40 - 59.9%

60+

Source: Census
Ontario Dept. of Education

NOTES

Abbreviations

AO	Archives of Ontario
ARCA	Ont. Dept. of Agriculture, *Annual Report of the Commissioner of Agriculture* [title varies]
ARUC	E. Ryerson, *Annual Report of Normal, Model, Grammar and Common Schools in Upper Canada* [title varies]
CLC	Carnegie Library Correspondence
CMW	H. Morgan, *Canadian Men and Women of the Time* [two editions, 1898 and 1912]
Cyclopaedia	G.M. Rose, *Cyclopaedia of Canadian Biography*
DALB	*Dictionary of American Library Biography*
DCB	*Dictionary of Canadian Biography*
DHE	J.G. Hodgins, *Documentary History of Education*
JBAMUC	*Journal of the Board of Arts and Manufactures of Upper Canada*
MTRL	Metropolitan Toronto Reference Library
NAC	National Archives of Canada
Ont. Lib. Rev.	*Ontario Library Review*
Proc. of OLA	*Proceedings of the Ontario Library Association Annual Meeting* [title varies]
RME	Ont. Dept. of Education, *Report of the Minister of Education*

Introduction: A Dream for Ontario

1 John Hallam, *Address to the Board of Management of the Toronto Free Library* (Toronto: n.p., 1883).

2 Eugène Rouillard, *Les Bibliothèques Populaires* (Quebec: L.-J. Demers & Frère, 1890), 45-46.

3 James Bain, Jr., "The Library Movement in Ontario," *Public Libraries* 6 (1901): 349. Another condensed version of his speech appears in *Library Journal* 26 (1901): 269-270; and a longer, but incomplete version in the Archives of Ontario [hereafter AO], Ontario Library Association, MU 2239.

4 For Ontario, see Eric C. Bow, "The Public Library Movement in Nineteenth-Century Ontario," *Ontario Library Review* 66 (1982): 1-16.

5 For a basic text, see Paul Wilkinson, *Social Movement* (New York: Praeger Publishers, 1971).

6 Lorne Bruce, "Public Libraries in Ontario, 1882-1920," *Ontario History* 77 (1985): 124-49.

7 Heartsill Young and Terry Belanger, eds., *The ALA Glossary of Library and Information Science* (Chicago: American Library Association, 1983), 181.

8 Young, *ALA Glossary*, 181.

9 William J. Rhees, *Manual of Public Libraries, Institutions, and Societies, in the United States and British Provinces of North America* (Philadelphia: J.B. Lippincott, 1859), 652-65.

10 Great Britain. Parliament, *Report from the Select Committee on Public Libraries* (London: House of Commons, 1849), xii.

11 The best exponent is Sidney Ditzion, *Arsenals of a Democratic Culture; A Social History of the American Public Library Movement in New England and the Middle States from 1850 to 1900* (Chicago: American Library Association, 1947), 51-76.

12 Joseph L. Harrison, "The Public Library Movement in the United States," *New England Magazine* n.s., 10 (1894): 721.

13 Adam Crooks, *Reform Government in Ontario; Eight Years Review* (Toronto: Hunter, Rose & Co., 1879), 33.

14 Edwin A. Hardy, "The Ontario Library Field," *Public Libraries* 9 (1904): 201.

15 See John A. Mayer, "Notes Towards a Working Definition of Social Control in Historical Analysis," in Stanley Cohen and Andrew Scull, eds., *Social Control and the State; Historical and Comparative Essays* (Oxford: Martin Robertson, 1983), 17-38.

16 Ann Robson, "The Intellectual Background of the Public Library Movement in Britain," *Journal of Library History* 11 (1976): 187.

17 For the salient points, see Jean K. Allen, "The History of Libraries in Ontario," in *Canadian Libraries in their Changing Environment*, eds. Loraine Spencer Garry and Carl Garry (Toronto: York University, 1977), 47-65.

18 See Bruce Curtis, "'Littery Merrit', 'Useful Knowledge', and the Organization of Township Libraries in Canada West, 1840-1860," *Ontario History* 78 (1986): 285-311.

19 For an outline of Ontario's progress, see James Bain, Jr., "The Libraries of Canada," *The Library* 7 (1895): 245-48.

20 Thomas D'Arcy McGee, *The Mental Outfit of the New Dominion* (Montreal: n.p., c.1867), 5.

21 For an example, see Rouillard, *Bibliothèques Populaires*, 3-4.

22 Ontario. Education Department, *Educational System of the Province of Ontario; Dominion of Canada* (Toronto: printed for the Dept., 1886), 93.

23 Margaret Beckman, Stephen Langmead, and John Black, *The Best Gift; a Record of the Carnegie Libraries in Ontario* (Toronto: Dundurn Press, 1984).

24 Lawrence J. Burpee, "The Library Outlook in Canada," *Public Libraries* 9 (1904): 195.

25 J.W. Cummings Purves, "A Paper on Library Ideals: Work and Legislation in Canada," *Library Association Record* 14 (1912): 439.

26 E.A. Hardy, *The Pubic Library; its Place in our Educational System* (Toronto: William Briggs, 1912), 55-71.

27 "The New Publication," *Ontario Library Review* 1 (June 1916): 1.

28 National Council of Women of Canada, *Women of Canada; Their Life and Work* (n.p.: n.p., c.1900), 173.

29 George Locke, "Recruiting for Librarianship in Canada," *Ontario Library Review* 7 (1922): 4-7.

30 See Bertha Bassam, *The Faculty of Library Science, University of Toronto and its Predecessors, 1922-1972* (Toronto: Univ. of Toronto Faculty of Library Science, 1978), 8-22.

31 Hugh H. Langton, "Canada and Public Libraries," *Library Journal* 28 (1903): 45.

32   E.A. Hardy, "A Half Century of Retrospect and Prospect," *Ontario Library Review* 11 (1926/27): 44.

33   Coincidentally, library development in the United States and British Isles began to be studied as a social phenomenon. See Arnold Borden, "The Sociological Beginnings of the Library Movement in America," *Library Quarterly* 1 (1931): 278-82; and John Minto, *A History of the Public Library Movement in Great Britain and Ireland* (London: G. Allen & Unwin Ltd., 1932).

Chapter 1: Common School and Mechanics' Institutes Libraries

1   See Chung S. Kim, "The Development of the First Library in Ontario, 1800-1900" (Master's thesis, University of Toronto, c.1985). For Addison's collection, see William J. Cameron, George McKnight, and Michaele-Sue Goldblatt, comps., *Robert Addison's Library; a Short Title Catalogue of Books Brought to Upper Canada in 1792* (Hamilton: McMaster University, 1967).

2   Charles B. Sissons, *Egerton Ryerson, his Life and Letters*, 2 vols. (Toronto: Clarke, Irwin, 1937-47). This remains the standard biography.

3   Canada (Province). Secretary of the Board of Registration and Statistics, *Census of the Canadas; 1851-52* (Quebec: John Lovell, 1853), vol. 1., xvii-xxi.

4   Egerton Ryerson, *Report on a System of Public Elementary Instruction for Upper Canada* (Montreal: Lovell and Gibson, 1847), 188-89.

5   Upper Canada. Dept. of Public Instruction, *Annual Report of the Normal, Model, Grammar, and Common Schools in Upper Canada for the Year 1847* (Montreal: Lovell and Gibson, 1849) [title varies, hereafter *ARUC*].

6   Robert Bell, "Township School Libraries – Means of Establishing Them," *Journal of Education for Upper Canada* 3 (1850): 81.

7   Letter quoted from Bruce Curtis, "'Littery Merrit', 'Useful Knowledge', and the Organization of Township Libraries in Canada West, 1840-1860," *Ontario History* 78 (1986): 287. See also, Frank C. Pitkin, "Dexter D'Everardo," *Welland County Historical Society Papers and Records* 3 (1927): 86-103.

8   Notice in the *Journal of Education* 2 (1849): 150-51; and "British and Continental Libraries," 3 (1850): 161-64.

9   Charles C. Jewett, *Notices of Public Libraries in the United States of America* (Washington: House of Representatives, 1851), 4.

10   See Robert Blackburn, *Evolution of the Heart; a History of the University of Toronto Library up to 1981* (Toronto: Univ. of Toronto Press, 1989), 30-35.

11   Foster Vernon, "The Development of Adult Education in Ontario 1790-1900" (Ed.D. diss., University of Toronto, 1969), 259-61.

12   William J. Rhees, *Manual of Public Libraries*, 653-59. This is an important area for further research.

13   Ryerson to Governor General Elgin, 16 July 1849, reprinted in Canada (Province). Dept. of Public Instruction for Upper Canada, *Special Report of the Separate School Provisions of the School Law of Upper Canada* (Toronto: John Lovell, 1858), 33.

14   Ryerson to Lord Elgin, 16 July 1849, reprinted in *Special Report of the Separate School Provisions*, 34.

15   Bruce Curtis, "'Littery Merrit'," 299-305.

16   John George Hodgins, ed., *Documentary History of Education in Upper Canada from 1791 to 1876* (Toronto: Warwick Bros. & Rutter, 1894-1910), vol. 3, 284 [hereafter Hodgins, *DHE*].

17   The proposed legislation is reprinted in Hodgins, *DHE*, vol. 10, 171.

18   Reprinted in Hodgins, *DHE*, vol. 11, 178.

19   May's early career is detailed in George Maclean Rose, *A Cyclopaedia of Canadian Biography: Being Chiefly Men of the Time* (Toronto: Rose Publishing, 1886), 654-56 [hereafter Rose, *Cyclopaedia*].

20   For this period see J.M.S. Careless, *The Pre-Confederation Premiers: Ontario Government Leaders, 1841-1867* (Toronto: Univ. of Toronto Press, 1980).

21   *ARUC for 1854.*

22   Canada (Province). Dept. of Public Instruction for Upper Canada, *General Catalogue of Books in Every Department of Literature, for Public School Libraries in Upper Canada* (Toronto: Lovell & Gibson, 1858), 242.

23   *General Catalogue of Books*, 243.

24   John G. Hodgins, *The School House; Its Architecture, External and Internal Arrangements* (Toronto: Lovell and Gibson, 1857), 10-55. For Barnard's library contribution, see Robert B. Downs, *Henry Barnard* (Boston: Twayne Publishers, 1977), 95-101.

25   J.M. Bruyère, *Controversy between Dr. Ryerson...and Rev. J.M. Bruyère...on the Appropriation of the Clergy Reserves Funds: Free Schools vs. State Schools; Public Libraries and Common Schools Attacked and Defended* (Toronto: Leader and Patriot, 1857), 17.

26   The depository issue was played out against the backdrop of the larger issue of separate schools. See Franklin A. Walker, *Catholic Education and Politics in Ontario; A Documentary History* (Don Mills, Ont.: Thomas Nelson, 1955-86), vol. 1, 209-12.

27   Egerton Ryerson, *Dr. Ryerson's Letters in Reply to the Attacks of Foreign Ecclesiastics Against the Schools and Municipalities of Upper Canada* (Toronto: Lovell & Gibson, 1857), 35-92.

28   The petition is reprinted in *Special Report of the Separate School Provisions*, 72.

29   This dispute, as well as several others, are recounted by George L. Parker, *The Beginnings of the Book Trade in Canada* (Toronto: Univ. of Toronto Press, 1985), 124-30.

30   *ARUC for 1860.*

31   See Winifred Hughes, *The Maniac in the Cellar: Sensational Novels of the 1860s* (Princeton: Princeton Univ. Press, 1980).

32   Hodgins, *DHE*, vol. 20, 93-95. For Britain, see Colin Manchester, "Lord Campbell's Act: England's First Obscenity Statute," *Journal of Legal History* 9 (1988): 223-41.

33   Canada (Province). Legislative Assembly, *Journals of the Legislative Assembly of the Province of Canada*, 28 April 1862.

34   James Fraser, *Report...on the Common School System of the United States and of the Provinces of Upper and Lower Canada* (London: Eyre and Spottiswoode, 1866), 273-77.

35   "The Free Public Library of Boston – Speeches at the Dedication," *Journal of Education* 11 (1858): 50-52.

36   Henry Y. Hind, ed., *Eighty Years' Progress of British North America; Showing the Wonderful Development of its Natural Resources....* (Toronto: L. Stebbins, 1864), 475.

37   For favourable comments, see Edward Edwards, *Free Town Libraries, their Formation, Management, and History* (New York: John Wiley & Son., 1869), 344-56.

38 Egerton Ryerson, *The School Book Question; Letters in Reply to the Brown-Campbell Crusade against the Educational Department for Upper Canada* (Montreal: John Lovell, 1866). This contains Ryerson's letters of refutation. See also, Linda Wilson Cormon, "James Campbell and the Ontario Education Department 1858-1884," *Papers of the Bibliographical Society of Canada* 14 (1975): 46-52.

39 Walter Eales, *Lecture on the Benefits to be Derived from Mechanics' Institutes* (Toronto: James Stephens, 1851), 1-2.

40 Eales, *Lecture*, 12.

41 For this conclusion, see Foster Vernon, "Adult Education," 309-21. In Britain, social control was also an objective, but it was difficult to achieve. See Steven Shapin and Barry Barnes, "Science, Nature and Control: Interpreting Mechanics' Institutes," *Social Studies of Science* 7 (1977): 31-74.

42 Henry Morgan, ed., *Canadian Parliamentary Guide*, 3d ed., (Quebec: Desbrats & Derbyshire, 1864), 52.

43 National Archives of Canada [hereafter NAC], Carleton Place Library Association and Mechanics' Institute, MG 9, D8-4, annual meetings on 9 March 1850 and 8 March 1851.

44 Douglas A. Stevenson, *A History of the Fonthill Public Library Prepared in Celebration of the One Hundredth Anniversary of its Opening – on 2 February, 1853* (Fonthill: Library Board, 1953), 4-6.

45 Waldon, Freda F. "Early Provision for Libraries in Hamilton," *Wentworth Bygones* 4 (1963): 322-35.

46 Rose, *Cyclopaedia*, 654.

47 "Toronto Mechanics' Institute," *Journal of the Board of Arts and Manufactures for Upper Canada* 1 (1861): 232-33 [hereafter *JBAMUC*].

48 See Vernon, "Adult Education," 407-8, 420-24.

49 Canada (Province). Bureau of Agriculture, *Reports of the Minister of Agriculture, and the Chief Emigrant Agent, for Canada, for the Year 1857* (Toronto: John Lovell, 1858). Title varies, hereafter Canada, Dept. of Agriculture, *Report*.

50 Newspaper hansard in Canada (Province). Parliament, *Canadian Parliamentary Debates – Scrapbook Debates 1846, 1854/1862* (Ottawa: Canadian Library Association, n.d.).

51 Newspaper hansard in Toronto *Globe*, 30 March 1859.

52 See James A. Eadie, "The Napanee Mechanics' Institutes: the Nineteenth Century Ontario Mechanics' Institute Movement in Microcosm," *Ontario History* 68 (1976): 213-15.

53 AO, Niagara Mechanics' Institute Records 1848-1898, MU 2022, vol. 1, Minutebook, 15 Feb. 1860 and 4 Nov. 1862. See also, Janet Carnochan, *History of Niagara (In Part)* (Toronto: William Briggs, 1914), 215.

54 Canada. Dept. of Agriculture, *Report for 1862*, xxx.

55 Canada. Dept. of Agriculture, *Report for 1864*, 6.

56 For the agriculture department between 1857 to 1864, see J.E. Hodgetts, *Pioneer Public Service; an Administrative History of the United Canadas, 1841-1867* (Toronto: Univ. of Toronto Press, 1955), 228-38.

57 For Edwards, see Henry Morgan, ed., *Canadian Men and Women of the Time* (Toronto: William Briggs, 1898), 305 [hereafter Morgan, *CMW* (1898)].

58 "Classified Catalogue of the Free Library of Reference," *JBAMUC* 1 (1861): 234-39.

59 "Correspondence," *JBAMUC* 2 (1862): 370-71; and "Circulating Library," *JBAMUC* 4 (1864): 133-34.

60   "Draft of a Memorial," *JBAMUC* 2 (1862): 105. Also AO, Board of Arts and Manufactures for Upper Canada, MU 279, Minutebook, 14 Jan. 1862.

61   Adam Crooks, "On the Characteristics of the Canadian Community," *Proceedings of the Royal Colonial Institute* 1 (1869): 162-69.

62   For patrons and clients in this era, see Sidney J.R. Noel, *Patrons, Clients, Brokers: Ontario Society and Politics, 1791-1896* (Toronto: Univ. of Toronto Press, 1990), 275-93.

63   Egerton Ryerson, *Rev. Dr. Ryerson's Defence against the Attacks of the Hon. George Brown...Relative to the Ontario System of Public Instruction and its Administration* (Toronto: Copp, Clark & Co., 1872), 94-95.

64   *ARUC for 1872*, Appendix C, 148.

65   *ARUC for 1872*, Appendix C, 156.

66   For example, *Attack on the People's Depository for Ontario* and *The Educational Depository and its Assailants* in AO, Dept. of Education, RG 2, Series N, box 1, envelope 6. See also, Ontario. Education Office, *Case and Correspondence Respecting the Prices of Books for School Libraries and Prizes, 1874* (Toronto: Hunter, Rose & Co., 1874).

67   AO, RG 2, Series N, box 1, envelope 8.

68   For his role in the Depository's demise, see Dianna Cameron, "John George Hodgins and Ontario Education, 1844-1912" (Master's thesis, University of Guelph, 1976), 150-57.

69   "Report of the Association of Mechanics' Institutes," in Ontario. Dept. of Agriculture, *Report of the Commissioner of Agriculture and Arts of the Province of Ontario for the Year 1868* (Toronto: Hunter, Rose & Co., 1869), 157 [hereafter Ontario, Dept. of Agriculture, *ARCA*].

70   William Edwards, "The Best Method of Classification of Books in the Catalogues, and on the Shelves of Mechanics' Institutes Libraries," in Ontario. Dept. of Agriculture, *ARCA for 1872*, 225.

71   Ontario. Dept. of Agriculture, *ARCA for 1875*, 206.

72   Thomas Davison, "Mechanics' Institutes and the Best Means of Improving Them," *Canadian Monthly* (Sept. 1876): 220-23.

73   Ontario. Dept. of Agriculture, *ARCA for 1877*, xi.

74   For Crooks, see George Brown and Marcel Trudel et al., eds., *Dictionary of Canadian Biography* (Toronto: Univ. of Toronto Press, 1966-), vol. 11, 220-23 [hereafter *DCB*].

75   Ontario. Education Dept., *Special Report on the Operations of the Depository Branch of the Education Department, Ontario; from 1850 to 1875, Inclusive* (Toronto: Hunter, Rose & Co., 1877). Ontario. Education Dept., *Papers and Correspondence with Respect to the Depository Branch of the Education Department* (Toronto: Hunter, Rose & Co., 1877); this publication reviews the controversy of 1876-77. Hodgins subsequently issued another review: Ontario. Education Dept., *Special Report upon the Operations of the Depository Branch of the Education Department for the Years 1876 and 1877* (Toronto: Provincial Secretary's Office, 1879).

76   "Memorandum on Village Libraries," printed in *Papers and Correspondence*, 36-37.

77   "Memorandum to Dr. Hodgins...on 'Village Libraries'," in *Papers and Correspondence*, 42.

78   "Memorandum to the Honourable Minister of Education...by Dr. Hodgins, Deputy Minister of Education," in *Papers and Correspondence*, 51.

79   For Scoble, see Morgan, *CMW* (1898), 916.

80   Figures taken from Ontario. Education Dept., *Return to an Order of the Legislative Assembly, Dated 15th March, 1888...Respecting the Question of Aid in Purchasing Libraries Since the Withdrawal of Such Aid* (Toronto: Provincial Secretary's Office, 1888), 7-9.

81   United States. Bureau of Education, *Public Libraries in the United States of America; their History, Condition, and Management* (Washington: Government Printing Office), 1876), xxx, 39-44, and 57.

82   Robert D. Gidney and Winnifred P. J. Millar, *Inventing Secondary Education: the Rise of the High School in Nineteenth-Century Ontario* (Montreal: McGill-Queen's Univ. Press, 1990), 214-30.

83   Adam Crooks, *Educational Statement of the Hon. Adam Crooks, Minister of Education on Moving the Estimates for 1880* (Toronto: C. Blackett Robinson, 1880), 12-13.

84   Ontario. Education Dept., *Report of the Minister of Education of the Province of Ontario for 1880-81* (Toronto: C. Blackett Robinson, 1881), 156-59 [title varies, hereafter *RME*].

85   Ontario. Dept. of Agriculture, *ARCA for 1879*, xvii.

86   AO, Board of Arts and Manufactures, MU 280, Secretary's Letterbook 1867-1880, Edwards to James Young, 5 Dec. 1879.

Chapter 2: British and American Influences

1   Jewett, *Notices of Public Libraries*, 4.

2   Reprinted in Wilkie Collins, *My Miscellanies*, new ed., (London: Chatto and Windus, n.d.), vol. 13, 249-64.

3   Guinevere Griest, *Mudie's Circulating Library and the Victorian Novel* (Bloomington: Indiana Univ. Press, 1970).

4   Joan Magee, "The Wright and McKenny Circulating Library, Amherstburg; a Pioneer Library in Canada West," *Expression* 3, 3 (1981): 11-14.

5   See Gordon Stubbs, *The Role of Egerton Ryerson in the Development of Public Library Service in Ontario* (Ottawa: Canadian Library Association, 1966), 26-28.

6   Mann's library work is outlined by Robert B. Downs, *Horace Mann; Champion of Public Schools* (New York: Twayne Publishers, 1974), 58-68.

7   *Public Libraries in the United States of America*, 39-41. See also, Sidney Ditzion, "The District School Library," *Library Quarterly* 10 (1940): 575-77.

8   Ian Inkster, "The Social Context of an Educational Movement: a Revisionist Approach to the English Mechanics' Institutes, 1820-1850," *Oxford Review of Education* 2 (1976): 277-307; and Edward Royle, "Mechanics' Institutes and the Working Classes, 1840-1860," *Historical Journal* 14 (1971): 305-21.

9   Great Britain. Parliament. House of Commons, *Report from the Select Committee on Public Libraries* (1849; facsimile reprint, Shannon, Ireland: Irish Univ. Press, 1968), 1.

10   For a brief summary of nineteenth-century British legislation prior to 1892, see H.W. Fovargue and J.J. Ogle, *Public Library Legislation* (London: Library Association, 1893), 88-96.

11   Thomas Greenwood, *Edward Edwards; The Chief Pioneer of Municipal Public Libraries* (London: Scott, Greenwood & Co., 1902), 126-41.

12   "Free Libraries and Museums in England," *Journal of Education* 11 (1858): 86-87.

13   "Libraries for the People," *Meliora; A Quarterly Review of Social Science in its Ethical, Economical, Political and Ameliorative Aspects* 2 (1860): 305.

14   John J. Ogle, *The Free Library; Its History and Present Condition* (London: George Allen, 1897), 281-84.

15   Michael H. Harris, ed., *The Age of Jewett: Charles Coffin Jewett and American Librarianship, 1841-1868* (Littleton, Colorado: Libraries Unlimited, 1975), 20-43.

16   Michael Harris, *The Role of the Public Library in American Life; A Speculative Essay* (Urbana, Illinois: University of Illinois Graduate School of Library Science, 1975). Harris emphasizes that motives are identified with social control.

17   Charles F.J. Whebell, "Robert Baldwin and Decentralization, 1841-9," in *Aspects of Nineteenth-Century Ontario; Essays Presented to James J. Talman*, ed. Frederick H. Armstrong (Toronto: Univ. of Toronto, 1974), 48-64.

18   Canada (Province). Legislature, *Debates of the Legislative Assembly of United Canada, 1841-1867* (Montreal: Presses de l'Ecole des hautes études commerciales, 1970-), vol. 11, pt. 1, 606, 20 Sept. 1852. Hodgins notes that no text was available in 1902: see Hodgins, *DHE*, vol. 10, 102.

19   For Boulton, see *DCB*, vol. 10, 80-81.

20   For Morris, see *DCB*, vol. 11, 608-15.

21   Hodgins, *DHE*, vol. 14, 207-210.

22   "Public Free Libraries," *Meliora* 10 (1867): 235-246.

23   William A. Munford, *Edward Edwards 1812-1866: Portrait of a Librarian* (London: Library Association, 1963), 149-206.

24   Edward Edwards, *Free Town Libraries*, 29-30.

25   See Gwladys Spencer, *The Chicago Public Library; Origins and Backgrounds* (Chicago: Univ. of Chicago, 1943), 230-48.

26   See Henry A. Homes, "Library Legislation," *Library Journal* 4 (1879): 300-2; and 5 (1880): 79, 109-11.

27   William F. Poole, "The Organization and Management of Public Libraries," *Public Libraries in the United States*, 477. Poole became ALA president in 1886. See William L. Williamson, *William Frederick Poole and the Modern Library Movement* (New York: Columbia Univ. Press, 1963), 129-37.

28   See Sidney Ditzion, "The Anglo-American Library Scene: a Contribution to the Social History of the Library Movement," *Library Quarterly* 16 (1946): 281-301.

29   Samuel S. Green, *The Public Library Movement in the United States 1853-1893* (Boston: Boston Book Co., 1893), 24. For Green, see Bohdan S. Wynar, George S. Bobinski, Jesse H. Shera, eds., *Dictionary of American Library Biography* (Littleton, Colorado: Libraries Unlimited, 1978), 212-16 [hereafter *DALB*].

30   William A. Munford, *A History of the Library Association 1877-1977* (London: Library Association, 1976), 18-32.

31   "Librarians in Council," Toronto *Globe*, 25 Oct. 1877.

32   John G. Hodgins, *Special Report...on the Ontario Educational Exhibit and the Educational Features of the International Exhibition at Philadelphia, 1876* (Toronto: Hunter, Rose & Co., 1877), 95-96.

33   Hodgins, *Special Report...on the Educational Exhibit*, 34.

34   Tamara Grad, "The Development of Public Libraries in Ontario, 1851-1951" (Master's thesis, Drexel Institute of Technology, School of Library Science, 1951), 25: "The libraries of Ontario from now on entered a new stage of development."

35   For example, "Novels and Mechanics' Institutes," Toronto *Globe*, 18 Feb. 1879.

36   Ontario. Education Dept., *Special Report of the Minister of Education on the Mechanics' Institutes (Ontario)* (Toronto: C. Blackett Robinson, 1881), 66-72, 73-75 [hereafter May, *Special Report*].

37   Ian Inkster, "The Public Lecture as an Instrument for Science Education for Adults – the Case of Great Britain, c.1750-1850," *Paedagogica Historica* 20 (1980): 80-107.

38   Alpheus Todd, "On the Establishment of Free Public Libraries in Canada," *Proceedings and Transactions of the Royal Society of Canada* Series 1, 1, Sec. 2 (1882-83): 14.

39   George Ross, newspaper hansard record, Toronto *World,* 16 March 1888.

40   "A Dufferin Public Library," Toronto *Mail,* 1 Oct. 1878.

41   W.R.G. Mellen, "Wealth and its Uses," *Rose-Belford's Canadian Monthly and National Review* 2 (1879): 349.

42   AO, Dept. of Education, RG 2, D-6, Box 1, file 1878.

43   Anon [An Old Headmaster], "The Arraignment of the Minister of Education," *Canada Educational Monthly* 2 (1880): 336.

44   Toronto *Globe,* 8 March 1882.

45   "Mechanics' Institute," Hamilton *Spectator,* 12 June 1880; and "Mechanics' Institutes," London *Advertiser* 14 June 1880.

46   Otto Klotz, *A Review of the Special Report of the Minister of Education on the Mechanics' Institutes Ontario* (Toronto: Willing & Williamson, 1881), 17-18.

47   May, *Special Report,* 128.

48   "A Public Library," London *Advertiser,* 12 Oct. 1881.

49   William W. Judd, ed., *Minutes of the London Mechanics' Institute (1841-1895); Edited and with Appendices* (London: London Public Libraries, Galleries, Museums, 1976), 38-45.

50   "The Mechanics' Institute," Hamilton *Spectator,* 17 March 1882.

51   One rural stone library was built as early as the 1850s: see Mary Broadfoot, "The Ennotville Library," *Ontario Library Review* 13 (1928/29): 143-45.

52   May, *Special Report,* 161.

53   *Ibid.,* 43 with Table D.

54   *Ibid.,* 97.

55   *Ibid.,* 105.

56   *Ibid.,* 75. See also, Allison Prentice and Susan Houston, *Schooling and Scholars in Nineteenth-century Ontario* (Toronto: Univ. of Toronto Press, 1988), 179-186.

57   May, *Special Report,* 65-66.

58   For this report, see *Canadian Farmer and Grange Record* 4, 32 (12 April 1882): 511.

59   "Mechanics' Institute Libraries," *Canada Educational Monthly* 3 (1881): 189-190.

Chapter 3: The Caliban of the Nineteenth Century

1   "The Free Library Scheme," Guelph *Daily Mercury,* 27 Nov. 1882. For Innes, see Rose, *Cyclopedia,* 373.

2   See William L. Morton, "Victorian Canada," in *The Shield of Achilles; Aspects of Canada in the Victorian Age,* ed. W.L. Morton (Toronto: McClelland & Stewart, 1968), 311-34; and Peter B. Waite, "Sir Oliver Mowat's Canada: Reflections on an Un-Victorian Society," in *Oliver Mowat's Ontario,* ed. Donald Swainson (Toronto: Macmillan, 1972), 12-32.

3   Paul Rutherford, *A Victorian Authority: The Daily Press in Late Nineteenth-Century Canada* (Toronto: University of Toronto Press, 1982), 156-89 gives an analysis of newspaper coverage.

4   For a typical treatise, see Alexander Scott, *Who May Vote? A Compilation of the Statute Law Relating to the Electoral Franchise in Ontario* (Brampton: n.p, 1885), 78-86.

5   John G. Bourinot, *The Intellectual Development of the Canadian People; An Historical Review* (Toronto: Hunter, Rose & Co., 1881), 119-121 and 128.

6   J.G. Bourinot, *Intellectual Development*, 122-23.

7   William Kingsford, *The Early Bibliography of the Province of Ontario, Dominion of Canada, with Other Information* (Toronto: Rowsell & Hutchison, 1892), 128-29.

8   Rosebery's views were reprinted in "A Public Library," Belleville *Daily Intelligencer*, 5 Jan. 1901. By this time Rosebery had withdrawn from politics and was writing historical biographies.

9   "Studies in Sociology," Hamilton *Daily Spectator*, 24 Feb. 1893.

10   "A Dufferin Public Library," Toronto *Mail*, 1 Oct. 1878.

11   "A Free Library," Brantford *Daily Expositor*, 30 Nov. 1883.

12   John Millar, *Books: A Guide to Good Reading* (Toronto: William Briggs, 1897), 64.

13   See Carl Berger, *Science, God, and Nature in Victorian Canada* (Toronto: University of Toronto Press, 1982), 10-27. See also, Bertrum H. MacDonald, "'Public Knowledge': the Dissemination of Scientific Literature in Victorian Canada as Illustrated from the Geological and Agricultural Sciences," (Ph.D. diss., Univ. of Western Ontario, School of Library and Information Science, 1990). MacDonald discusses the availability of international scientific literature in Canada.

14   William H. Withrow, "Public Libraries," *Canada Educational Monthly* 6 (1884): 193.

15   Marie Klotz, "A Public Library," Ottawa *Evening Journal*, 13 April 1895. See also, Anita Rush, "The Establishment of Ottawa's Public Library, 1895-1906" (Ottawa: n.p., 1981), 3.

16   John Taylor, *Toronto's Free Library; Facts for the Citizens* (Toronto: n.p., 1881).

17   See Alexander B. McKillop, *A Disciplined Intelligence: Critical Inquiry and Canadian Thought in the Victorian Era* (Montreal: McGill-Queen's Univ. Press, 1979), 129-32.

18   "The Free Library," *Palladium of Labor*, 25 April 1885.

19   George Iles, "The Library in Education," *The Week* 7 (21 March 1890): 251.

20   George Iles, "The Appraisal of Literature," *The Week* 13 (18 Sept. 1896): 1026.

21   Graeme M. Adam, "About Books," Toronto *Globe*, 10 May 1890.

22   "For a Public Library," Hamilton *Evening Times*, 2 May 1885. Hallam served as the Toronto library's first chairman.

23   "To be or not to be," London *Advertiser*, 9 June 1888. For Essery, see Morgan, *CMW* (1898), 314.

24   The education minister for one showed no alarm at the likelihood of lagging behind. See George Ross, *The Schools of England and Germany* (Toronto?: n.p., 1894); this work summarizes his personal travels and observations.

25   Regulations issued August 1889 reprinted in *RME for 1889*, 225-27.

26   "Proposed Mechanics' Institute," *Palladium of Labor*, 20 Nov. 1886.

27   Newspaper hansard account, Toronto *Globe*, 24 Feb. 1882.

28   Ontario. Education Dept., *Report of the Minister of Education on the Subject of Technical Education* (Toronto: Warwick & Sons, 1889), 167.

29   Ontario. Education Dept., *Supplement to the Report on the Minister of Education, 1892; University Extension* (Toronto: Warwick & Sons, 1892), 12.

30 Anti-Humbug, "Art Instruction in Ontario," *Canadian Architect and Builder* 2 (1889): 79.

31 Editorial observation in Ingersoll *Weekly Chronicle and Canadian Dairyman*, 26 Dec. 1889.

32 William D. Grampp, *The Manchester School of Economics* (Stanford: Stanford Univ. Press, 1960). Grampp stresses that the School's members held divergent views on many social issues.

33 "Principle versus Fraud," Hamilton *Daily Spectator*, 26 Dec. 1888.

34 Alpheus Todd, "Free Public Libraries," *Royal Society of Canada* (1882-83): 16.

35 "The Proposed Free Library," Toronto *Globe*, 18 Dec. 1882.

36 "Wanted a Public Library and Reading Room," Toronto *Globe*, 27 Jan. 1881.

37 For a short account see John Dinwiddy, *Bentham* (Oxford: Oxford Univ. Press, 1989), 90-122.

38 "A Public Meeting in Favor of the Free Library," Hamilton *Evening Times*, 9 May 1885; "The Public Library Question," Hamilton *Daily Spectator*, 7 May 1885.

39 Ottawa *Free Press*, 3 Jan. 1896.

40 "Dedicated to the Citizens," London *Free Press*, 27 November 1895. For Reid, see Rose, *Cyclopedia*, 342-43. J.S. Mill, "Chapters on Socialism" in *Essays on Economics and Society*, ed. John M. Robson (Toronto: Univ. of Toronto Press, 1967), vol. 2, 703-53.

41 "Booming the By-Law," Hamilton *Daily Spectator*, 20 Dec. 1888. For Freed's role, see Gregory S. Kealey, ed., *Canada Investigates Industrialism* (Toronto: Univ. of Toronto Press, 1973), xv-xix.

42 "Citizens of the Municipality of the Town of Chatham," Chatham *Tri-Weekly Planet*, 27 Dec. 1889.

43 Harvey Graff, *The Labyrinths of Literacy: Reflections on Literacy Past and Present* (London: Falmer Press, 1987), 162-86. He finds this argument wanting in Ontario's case.

44 See "Mr. Witton," *Journal and Proceedings of the Hamilton Association* 30 (1919/20-1921/22): 4-14.

45 However, compared to most unions, the London Trades and Labor Council was unusually active. See Eugene Forsey, *Trade Unions in Canada 1812-1902* (Toronto: Univ. of Toronto Press, 1982), 416-17.

46 W. Stanley Jevons, "The Rationale of Free Public Libraries," *Contemporary Review* 39 (1881): 385-402.

47 John Hallam, *Notes by the Way on Free Libraries and Books with a Plea for the Establishment of Rate-Supported Libraries in the Province of Ontario* (Toronto: Globe Printing Co., 1882), 31-32.

48 John A. Cooper, "Canada's Progress in the Victorian Era," *Canadian Magazine of Politics, Science, Art and Literature* 9 (1897/98): 161.

49 Todd, "Free Public Libraries,": 13.

50 "The Free Library; Some Reasons Therefor," Lindsay *Canadian Post*, 2 Dec. 1898.

51 "The Library Opened," Windsor *Evening Record*, 5 Dec. 1894. Curry's speech is reprinted in Gladys Shepley, "60 Years of Service – Windsor Public Library 1894-1954," *Ontario Library Review* 38 (1954): 231-32.

52 Carnegie Library Correspondence, Windsor, reel no. 34, letter of Andrew Braid and R.F. Sutherland to Andrew Carnegie, 25 Jan. 1900.

53 "Rough on Mossbacks," Hamilton *Daily Spectator*, 27 Dec. 1888; editorial on 8 Jan. 1889.

54   Alpheus Todd, "Is Canadian Loyalty a Sentiment or a Principle?" *Canadian Monthly* 7 (Nov. 1881): 523-30.

55   Ramsay Cook, *The Regenerators: Social Criticism in Late Victorian English Canada* (Toronto: Univ. of Toronto Press, 1985). However, the more active liberal Protestant social reformers were not active in the public library movement.

56   W.R.G. Mellen, "Wealth and its Uses," *Canadian Monthly* 2 (March 1879): 349.

57   "The Free Library By-Law; Letter from Dr. Cochrane," Brantford *Daily Expositor*, 5 Jan. 1884. Cochrane continued on the library board for many years and died in 1898. See Rose, *Cyclopedia*, 257-58; Robert N. Grant, *Life of Rev. William Cochrane, D.D.* (Toronto: William Briggs, 1899).

58   See William Westfall, *Two Worlds; The Protestant Culture of Nineteenth-Century Ontario* (Montreal: McGill-Queen's University Press, 1989).

59   T.K. Henderson in *Free Public Libraries for Canada; Working-men's Prize Essays* (Toronto: "The Citizen," 1882), 3 [hereafter *Working-men's Prize Essays*].

60   "Mr. Boville's Census," Hamilton *Daily Spectator*, 29 Dec. 1888.

61   "Free Library," Brampton *Conservator*, 5 Sept. 1895.

62   For an example, see Toronto Public Library, *List of Books, Pamphlets and Magazine Articles on the Subject of Temperance, Total Abstinence, Prohibition, Gothenburg and Other Licensing Systems of the Liquor Traffic, in the Toronto Public Library* (Toronto, n.p., 1902).

63   "Education, Crime and Free Libraries," Ottawa *Evening Journal*, 30 Dec. 1895; and Thomas Greenwood, *Public Libraries: A History of the Movement and a Manual for the Organization and Management of Rate-Supported Libraries*, 4th ed. (London: Cassell & Co., 1894), 30.

64   The editorials are identical: "Vote for the Free Library," Toronto *Globe*, 30 Dec. 1882 and "The Vote for the Free Library on Monday," Guelph *Daily Mercury*, 30 Dec. 1882.

65   "The Free Library," Lindsay *Canadian Post*, 2 Dec. 1898.

66   John Wiseman, "Temples of Democracy: a History of Public Library Development in Ontario, 1880-1920" (Ph.D. diss., Loughborough University of Technology, Library and Information Studies, 1989), especially 306-308. Wiseman emphasizes the democratic role of the public library.

67   *Working-men's Prize Essays*, 4.

68   H. M. Evans in *Working-men's Prize Essays*, 14.

69   "A Free Library," Stratford *Evening Beacon*, 5 Nov. 1895.

70   "The Free Library By-Law," Hamilton *Daily Spectator*, 27 Dec. 1888.

71   "London's Library," London *Advertiser*, 27 Nov. 1895.

72   AO, Ontario Library Association, MU 2239, John Davis Barnett, "The Value of Public Libraries to the Community," 3.

73   For building styles and local support, see Marc de Caraffe, et. al., *Town Halls of Canada; A Collection of Essays on Pre-1930 Town Hall Buildings* (Ottawa: Dept. of Environment, Parks Canada, 1987).

74   For an example at Ottawa, see "Getting a Move On," Ottawa *Evening Journal*, 23 Dec. 1895.

75   See Allan McGillivray, *Uxbridge Library 1859-1987* (Uxbridge: Uxbridge Public Library, 1987), 1-10.

76   "Free Library Question," Uxbridge *Journal*, 20 Jan. 1898.

77   "The Public Library," Napanee *Express*, 1 Nov. 1901. But on this occasion a free library was not created.

78 "Will the Library be Free?" Clinton *News Record,* 7 Dec. 1899 and "Municipal Elections" on 5 Jan. 1900.

79 "The Library Building," Clinton *New Era,* 19 Jan. 1900.

80 Mary E. Manning, *A Village Library Grows,* 2d ed., (Streetsville: Library Board, 1973), 19-20.

81 "Just the Place," Ottawa *Evening Journal,* 4 Jan. 1896.

82 John G. Bourinot, "Notes in My Library," *The Week* 12 (5 April 1895): 445.

Chapter 4: The Days of Advance

1 "The City Council," Toronto *Globe,* 18 Jan. 1881.

2 See "Free Public Library," Toronto *Globe,* 24 Nov. 1881; "Free Library Question," Toronto *Globe,* 13 Dec. 1881; and "Free Public Library," Toronto *Mail,* 13 Dec. 1881.

3 For Hallam, see Rose, *Cyclopaedia,* 82.

4 John Hallam, *The Days of Advance; British Civilization as Shown in Some Institutions. Free Libraries and Water Supply Systems; Interesting Facts Gleaned by Alderman Hallam While Across the Sea* (Toronto: n.p., c.1881).

5 John Hallam, *Notes by the Way on Free Libraries,* preface.

6 See Margaret A. Evans, "The Mowat Era, 1872-1896: Stability and Progress," in *Profiles of a Province; Studies in the History of Ontario* (Toronto: Ontario Historical Society, 1967), 97-106.

7 "The House and Educational Questions," *Canada Educational Monthly* 5 (1882): 48.

8 Ontario. Education Dept., *Catalogue of Works Recommended for Libraries in High Schools, Collegiate Institutes and Other Institutes Receiving Legislative Aid* (Toronto: "Grip" Printing & Publishing, 1884); *Catalogue of General and Educational Books, Specially Recommended for the Libraries in Collegiate Institutes, High Schools and Mechanics' Institutes, by the Education Department, Ontario* (Toronto: Longmans, Green, 1885).

9 For the original bill and its emendations, see AO, Legislative Assembly, RG 49, Series 1-7-14, Bill 104, 28 Feb. 1882.

10 For his comment, see Toronto *Evening Telegram,* 9 March 1882.

11 Editorial in Toronto *Evening Telegram,* 29 Dec. 1882.

12 *Times,* 3 Jan. 1883.

13 "The City Council," Guelph *Daily Mercury,* 21 Nov. 1882.

14 Metropolitan Toronto Reference Library, John Hallam Papers, vol. 2, David W. McCrae to Hallam, 7 March 1884 [hereafter MTRL].

15 For Tytler's early career, see Rose, *Cyclopaedia,* 363-64.

16 For this club see "James Bain, D.C.L.," *Saturday Night* 21 (25 July 1908): 11-12.

17 "Municipal Politics," London *Free Press,* 22 Dec. 1883.

18 For Essery, see Morgan, *CMW* (1898), 314, and his obituary in Toronto *Globe and Mail,* 26 March 1937.

19 For provincial rights, see Margaret Evans, *Sir Oliver Mowat* (Toronto: Univ. of Toronto Press, 1992), 141-81.

20 See Evans, *Sir Oliver Mowat,* 296-326.

21 AO, OLA, MU 2239, Dr. May, "How to Secure the Passing of a Free Public Library By-Law," 2.

22   George W. Ross, *The School System of Ontario (Canada); Its History and Distinctive Features* (New York: D. Appleton, 1896), 159-60.

23   "Singular Objections," Hamilton *Daily Spectator*, 13 May 1885.

24   "Hamilton's Public Library," Toronto *Globe*, 16 Sept. 1890.

25   James Bain, Jr., "Brief Review of the Libraries of Canada," *Library Journal* 12 (1887): 409.

26   "The Public Library," Dundas *Star*, 26 Sept. 1895.

27   "A Public Library," Hamilton *Evening Times*, 6 May 1885.

28   "The Library By-Law," Hamilton *Evening Times*, 16 May 1885.

29   "Booming the By-Law," Hamilton *Daily Spectator*, 20 Dec. 1888.

30   Goldwin Smith, "Current Questions in Education," *Canada Educational Monthly* 4 (1882): 325-26.

31   MTRL, Hallam Papers, vol. 2, W.F. Poole to Hallam, 2 April 1883 and 6 April 1883; and C.A. Cutter to Hallam, 4 April 1883. For Cutter and Poole, see *DALB*, 109-15, 404-12.

32   *"The Free Library,"* Toronto *Mail*, 25 Dec. 1882.

33   "A Free Library For Toronto," Toronto *Mail*, 30 Dec. 1882.

34   "In Favor of the Library," Hamilton *Evening Times*, 7 May 1885. In the Hamilton *Daily Spectator* 7 May account of this meeting, Thomas Brick is identified as the "voice." For Brick, see Gregory S. Kealey and Bryan D. Palmer, *Dreaming of What Might Be; The Knights of Labor in Ontario, 1880-1900* (Cambridge: Cambridge Univ. Press, 1982), 206-7.

35   "The Council Takes Over the Library," Thorold *Post*, 18 Oct. 1895.

36   "The Free Library By-Law," *Norfolk Reformer*, 3 Jan. 1884; and *Simcoe Public Library; An Historical Sketch* (Simcoe: n.p., 1978), 1.

37   AO, RG 2, Series P-2, V, no. 101 (f), St. Catharines Mechanics' Institute report for 1888. For Robertson, see Andrew Fraser, *A History of Ontario; Its Resources and Development* (Toronto: Canada History Co., 1907), vol. 2, 897-900.

38   "Board of Trade," Chatham *Tri-Weekly Planet*, 20 Dec. 1889.

39   AO, RG 2, Series P-2, V, no. 93, letter of John B. Rankin to Dr. May, 2 May 1890.

40   "Hamilton Public Library," Toronto *Globe*, 16 Sept. 1890.

41   "Books Without Buying," Hamilton *Daily Spectator*, 2 May 1885.

42   For contemporary critics' views, see Kenneth Graham, *English Criticism of the Novel 1865-1900* (Oxford: Clarendon Press, 1965).

43   "The Free Library," Hamilton *Daily Spectator*, 28 March 1885.

44   For a broader context, see Robert A. Colby, *Fiction With a Purpose; Major and Minor Nineteenth-Century Novels* (Bloomington: Indiana Univ. Press, 1968).

45   "Books That Are Read; Public Literary Taste Steadily Improving," Toronto *Globe*, 10 Jan. 1884.

46   "Novel Reading," Toronto *Globe*, 26 July 1890.

47   "Public Libraries," Toronto *Evening News*, 17 Dec. 1881.

48   Ester J. Carrier, *Fiction in Public Libraries, 1876-1900* (New York: Scarecrow Press, 1965), 169-78.

49   See Frederick J. Stielow, "Censorship in the Early Professionalization of American Libraries, 1876 to 1929," *Journal of Library History* 18 (1983): 37-54.

50   Ontario. Education Dept., *Catalogue of Books Recommended for Public Libraries by the Education Department, Ontario* (Toronto: Warwick & Rutter, 1895), 96-103.

51   Touchstone, "Novels at the Public Library," Toronto *Saturday Night*, 19 March

1892. In fact, Sullivan was more concerned with facilities in the central library and its branches.

52   For the growth of popular literature, see James D. Hart, *The Popular Book; A History of America's Literary Taste* (New York: Oxford Univ. Press, 1950); Richard D. Altick, *The English Common Reader: A Social History of the Mass Reading Public, 1800-1900* (Chicago: Univ. of Chicago Press, 1957).

53   Lawrence J. Burpee, "Recent Canadian Fiction," *Forum* 27 (1899): 752-60.

54   AO, OLA, MU 2239, Barnett, "Value of Public Libraries," 8. For Barnett, see Henry Morgan, ed., *Canadian Men and Women of the Time* (Toronto: William Briggs, 1912), 62 [hereafter Morgan, *CMW* (1912)]; and "Noted Bibliophile Passes in London," Toronto *Globe*, 22 March 1926.

55   "The People's Forum," London *Advertiser*, 25 May 1892.

56   "The Free Library; Books Which the Workingmen Have on Their Shelves," London *Advertiser*, 26 May 1892; and Eleanor Shaw, *A History of the London Public Library* (London: London Public Library and Art Museum, 1968), 32-33.

57   "The City Library By-Law," Hamilton *Evening Times*, 8 May 1885.

58   Citizen, "Arguments Against the Free Library," Toronto *World*, 30 Dec. 1882.

59   "Trades and Labour Council," Toronto *Globe*, 16 Dec. 1882.

60   AO, RG 49, Series I-7-F-2, 1892, petition no. 835, Toronto Trades and Labour Council, read 11 March 1892.

61   "A Public Library Already," Hamilton *Evening Times*, 8 May 1885.

62   "Public Library," Toronto *Evening Telegram*, 15 Dec. 1882; and "Provincial Library," Toronto *Evening Telegram*, 3 Feb. 1883.

63   Editorial in Ottawa *Free Press*, 5 Feb. 1895.

64   Daniel Wilson, "Free Public Libraries," *Canada Educational Monthly* 6 (1884): 149.

65   See Nancy Z. Tausky and Lynne D. DiStefano, *Victorian Architecture in London and Southwestern Ontario; Symbols of Aspiration* (Toronto: Univ. of Toronto Press, 1986), 211-14.

66   "The Library Board," London *Advertiser*, 11 March 1884.

67   See Eleanor Shaw, *A History of the London Public Library*, 30-31.

68   James Bain, Jr., "Public Libraries in Canada," *Proceedings of the Canadian Institute*, n.s., 1 (1897-98): 95-100; Bain, "Lectures, Museums, Art Galleries, etc., in Connection with Libraries," *Library Journal* 18 (1893): 214-16.

69   AO, OLA, MU 2239, George Ross to E.A. Hardy, 20 July 1899.

70   "John Hallam is Dead," Toronto *Globe*, 22 June 1900.

71   Hallam, *Days of Advance*, 3.

Chapter 5: From One Century to Another

1   AO, Mechanics' Institutes of Ontario Collection, MU 2017, Letterbook of the Association of Mechanics' Institutes 1880-1884, Edwards to May, 12 March 1884.

2   AO, MU 2017, Association Letterbook 1885-1897, Edwards to Ross, 31 Oct. 1885.

3   AO, MU 2017, Edwards to Ross, 2 March 1886.

4   Newspaper hansard record, Toronto *Globe*, 12 March 1886.

5   Regulations reprinted in *RME for 1887*, 182-83.

6   AO, MU 2017, Edwards to Dewey, 27 Aug. 1884 and Edwards' memo to

Warwick & Rutter, 23 April 1888. See also, AO, Association of Mechanics' Institutes, MU 2021, circular letters 1880-1894. This collection contains various flyers publicizing Edwards' scheme. For Dewey, consult *DALB*, 124-34.

7   "The Toronto Public Library," *Canadian Educational Monthly* 7 (1884): 136.

8   MTRL, John Hallam Papers, vol. 2, Leypoldt to Hallam, 1 Feb. 1883. For Leypoldt, see *DALB*, 314-16.

9   "Librarians in Council," Toronto *Globe*, 15 Aug. 1883 and 17 Aug. 1883. MTRL, John Hallam Papers, vol 2., M. Dewey to Hallam, 25 Jan. 1884; and W.F. Poole to Hallam, 4 March 1884.

10   Buffalo conference proceedings in *Library Journal* 8 (Aug. 1883): 280.

11   Bain quoted by Green, *Library Movement*, 162.

12   Richard Bowker, ed., *The Library List* (New York: Library Journal, 1887); for Bowker, see *DALB*, 52-55.

13   G. Mercer Adam, *The Librarian's [Key]; Brief Suggestive List of Books, New and Old* (Toronto?: n.p., c.1882).

14   The resolution of the institute directors and the municipal bylaw are reprinted in Toronto. City Council, *Minutes of the Council of the Corporation of Toronto* (Toronto: Corporation of Toronto, 1884), 202-4, 208.

15   "The Free Library; How the Building will Appear on Thursday," Toronto *Globe*, 3 March 1884.

16   William Archer, *Suggestions as to Public Library Buildings* (Dublin: Browne & Nolan, 1881). He included a postscript disagreeing with William Poole's subject divided concept for libraries.

17   Donald E. Oehlerts, "The Development of American Public Library Architecture from 1850 to 1940," (Ph.D. diss., Indiana University, Graduate Library School, 1975), 41-54. This author describes the slow transition from book halls, which housed readers and featured alcove/perimeter shelves, to the modern separation of readers, staff, and books.

18   "Public Library; Formal Opening by the Lieutenant-Governor," Toronto *Globe*, 7 March 1884.

19   James Bain, "Books in Branch Libraries," in American Library Association, *Papers and Proceedings of the American Library Association 1898* (Chicago: American Library Association, 1898), 100.

20   MTRL, Hallam Papers, vol. 1, Edward Edwards to Hallam, 19 Dec. 1883 re: information for a new edition of *Memoirs of Libraries*.

21   See Toronto Public Library, *Catalogue of Books and Pamphlets Presented to the Toronto Public Library by John Hallam* (Toronto: C.B. Robinson, 1888).

22   Susan McGrath, "The Origins of the Canadiana Collection at the Metropolitan Toronto Central Library: the First Twenty-Five Years," *Papers of the Bibliographic Society of Canada* 13 (1974): 85-100.

23   James Bain, "Canadian Public Documents," *Canadian Magazine of Politics, Science, Art and Literature* 25 (1905): 125-27.

24   Toronto Public Library, *Fifth Annual Report, 1888* (Toronto: Toronto Public Library, 1889), 4.

25   Toronto Public Library, *Report of a Special Committee on the Museums of the United States and Canada* (Toronto: Toronto Public Library, 1892).

26   Council session reported in Toronto *Globe*, 15 March 1892.

27   James Bain, "Lectures, Museums, Art Galleries, etc., in Connection with Libraries," *Library Journal* 18 (1893): 216.

28 Lorna L. Bergey, "Library Facilities of Wilmot Township," *Waterloo Historical Society Annual Report* 50 (1962): 86.

29 "Farmers' Institutes," *Rural Canadian* 9, 2 (Feb. 1886): 33.

30 Newspaper hansard, Toronto *Globe*, 16 March 1888.

31 Ontario. Education Dept., *Return to an Order of the Legislative Assembly, Dated 15th March, 1888 that there Be Laid before this House...Purchasing Libraries since the Withdrawal of Such Aid* (Toronto: Provincial Secretary's Office, 1888).

32 For Lancefield, see Katharine Greenfield, *Hamilton Public Library 1889-1963: a Celebration of Vision and Leadership* (Hamilton: Hamilton Public Library, 1989), 16-34; Gordon Roper, "The Canadian Bibliographer and Library Record and its Editor," *Papers of the Bibliographical Society of Canada* 6 (1967): 27-31; and Morgan, *CMW* (1898), 554.

33 Hamilton Public Library, *Catalogue of Books in the Circulating Department of the Hamilton Public Library* (Hamilton: Griffin & Kidner, 1890). The 1891 supplement was arranged by class.

34 Hamilton Public Library, *Annual Report of the Hamilton Public Library for 1891* (Hamilton: Hamilton Public Library Board, 1892), 7-8.

35 John W. Emery, *The Library, the School and the Child* (Toronto: Macmillan Co, 1917), 48-54.

36 "Hamilton Public Library Building Competition," *Canadian Architect and Builder* 2 (1889): 54-55. For Stewart, see Thomas M. Bailey, ed., *Dictionary of Hamilton Biography* (Hamilton: Dictionary of Hamilton Biography, 1981), vol. 1., 188-89.

37 See Frank J. Burgoyne, *Library Construction, Architecture, Fittings and Furniture* (London: George Allen, 1897), 73-87.

38 "Our Public Library," Hamilton *Daily Spectator*, 17 Sept. 1890.

39 "Board of Trade," Chatham *Tri-Weekly Planet*, 20 Dec. 1889.

40 W.K.P. Kennedy, comp., *North Bay; Past-Present-Prospective* (North Bay?: n.p., 1961), 120-22; and "A.G. Browning," Toronto *Globe and Mail*, 8 July 1941.

41 For its general activities, see Veronica Strong-Boag, *The Parliament of Women: the National Council of Women of Canada, 1893-1929* (Ottawa: National Museum of Canada, 1976).

42 The disappointing 1895/96 bylaw fight is outlined by Anita Rush, "Establishment of Ottawa's Public Library," 2-4. For a discussion of the NCWC's general relationship with libraries, see John Wiseman, "Temples of Democracy," 51-55.

43 John A. Wiseman, "Silent Companions; the Dissemination of Books and Periodicals in Nineteenth-Century Ontario," *Publishing History; the Social, Economic, and Literary History of Book, Newspaper and Magazine Publishing* 12 (1982): 26-34. He emphasizes the positive aspect.

44 See Robert M. Stamp, *The Schools of Ontario, 1876-1976* (Toronto: Ministry of Culture and Recreation, 1982), 45-50.

45 Samuel P. May, *Catalogue of School Appliances, Pupils' Work, etc., Exhibited by the Education Department of Ontario, Canada, at the World's Columbian Exposition, Chicago, 1893* (Toronto: Warwick & Sons, 1893), 8.

46 U.S. Bureau of Education, *Statistics of Public Libraries in the United States and Canada* (Washington: Government Printing Office, 1893), 20.

47 Greenwood, *Public Libraries*, 544. For Greenwood, see R.J. Pritchard, *Thomas Greenwood; Public Library Enthusiast* (Biggleswade, United Kingdom: Clover Publications, 1981).

48 Ontario. Dept. of Agriculture, "Technical Education," in *Annual Report of the*

Bureau of Industries for the Province of Ontario for the Year 1893 (Toronto: Warwick Bros. & Rutter, 1894), part VI, 1-103.

49   AO, Legislative Assembly, RG 49, Series I-7-B-2, 1894, no. 124, *Return to an Order of the House dated the 23rd April instant for A Return...Farmers' Institutes have not been Established.*

50   Newspaper hansard, Toronto *Globe,* 5 April 1895.

51   AO, RG 49, Office of the Legislative Assembly, Series I-7-F-2, 1896, petition no. 354, Dominion Grange Praying Certain Amendments to the Public Libraries Act.

52   For popular fiction tastes, see Mary Vipond, "Best Sellers in English Canada, 1899-1918: An Overview," *Canadian Journal of Fiction* 24 (1979): 96-119.

53   Ontario. Education Dept., *Catalogue of Books,* introduction.

54   Ontario. Education Dept., *Act and Regulations Respecting Public Libraries, Reading Rooms, Evening Classes and Art Schools* (Toronto: Warwick Bros. & Rutter, 1895), 3-4.

55   George Ross, *The School System of Ontario,* 159-60.

56   "London's Library," London *Advertiser,* 27 Nov. 1895; and "Dedicated to the Citizens," London *Free Press,* 27 Nov. 1895.

57   A plan and illustration of the London library appears in the *Canadian Architect and Builder* 7 (1894): 156. For Matthews, see "H.E. Matthews London Native," London *Free Press,* 13 Dec. 1941.

58   American Library Association, *Papers Prepared for the World's Library Congress, Held at the Columbian Exposition* (Washington: Govt. Printing Office, 1896).

59   American Library Association, *Papers and Proceedings of the Twentieth General Meeting 1898* (Chicago: American Library Association, 1898), 36.

60   "Public Librarian Blackwell Passes Away This Morning," London *Free Press,* 19 March 1906.

61   London Public Library. *Class Catalogue; Public Library London, Ont., June 1st, 1897* (London: Thomas Coffey, 1897); it included sections for juvenile literature, magazines and newspapers. Hamilton Public Library, *Catalogue of Books in the Hamilton Public Library, July, 1897* (Hamilton: McPherson & Drope, 1897).

62   For Blackwell's administration, see Elizabeth Spicer, *A History of the London Public Library 1899-1905* (London: London Public Library and Art Museum, 1967).

63   *RME for 1889,* 221.

64   J.W.C. Purves, "A Paper on Library Ideals: Work and Legislation in Canada," *Library Association Record* 14 (Sept. 1912): 446-47.

65   "Toronto Public Library Board v. City of Toronto," in *Ontario Practice Reports* (Toronto, 1899-1900), vol. 19, 329-32.

66   George Iles, "The Appraisal of Literature," *The Week* 13 (18 Sept. 1896): 1025-26.

67   "International Library Conference," *Times,* 17 July 1897.

68   George Iles, "The Trusteeship of Literature," *Library Journal* 26 (1900): 16-22. For Iles, see Morgan, *CMW* (1912), 565-66; and Walter L. Brown, "As it was in the Beginning: George Iles," *Public Libraries* 30 (1925): 367-68.

69   William I. Fletcher, *Public Libraries in America* (Boston: Roberts Brothers, 1894), 113. For Fletcher, see *DALB,* 176-79.

70   Canada's national psyche is ably discussed in Robert G. Moyles and Douglas Owram, *Imperial Dreams and Colonial Realities; British Views of Canada, 1880-1914* (Toronto: Univ. of Toronto Press, 1988); and Carl Berger, *The Sense of Power; Studies in the Ideas of Canadian Imperialism 1867-1914* (Toronto: Univ. of Toronto Press, 1970).

71 John Macfarlane, *Library Administration* (London: George Allen, 1898), 177-79 and 210-12.

72 Greenwood, *Public Libraries*, 22-23.

73 See Jon C. Teaford, *The Unheralded Triumph: City Government in America, 1870-1900* (Baltimore: Johns Hopkins Univ. Press, 1984), 258-62.

74 *RME for 1901*, Part II, 197.

75 For the "new" education, see Neil Sutherland, *Children in English-Canadian Society: Framing the Twentieth-Century Consensus* (Toronto: Univ. of Toronto Press, 1976), 202-24.

76 *RME for 1900*, xliii.

77 John Seath, "Manual Training and High School Courses of Study," in *RME for 1900*, 284.

78 AO, RG 2, Series P-2, V, no. 70, letter of F.W. Hodson to George Ross, 25 June 1897.

79 AO, RG 2, Series P-2, V, no. 60, John Millar to J.R. Cartwright, Deputy Attorney General, 1 June 1900.

80 AO, RG 2, Series P-2, V, no. 69, Circular to Public Libraries dated 15 Nov. 1899.

81 James Bain, "Public Libraries in Canada," *Proceedings of the Canadian Institute* n.s., 1 (1897-98): 99-100.

82 Bain, *Proceedings* n.s., 1 (1897-98): 100.

83 *A Public Reference Library for the Province of Ontario, and Provincial Travelling Libraries* (Toronto: n.p., 21 Jan. 1899) [printed circular].

84 Lawrence J. Burpee, "Modern Public Libraries and Their Methods," *Proceedings and Transactions of the Royal Canadian Society*, 2nd Series, 8 (1902): 43-47 [hereafter Burpee, "Modern Public Libraries," *TRCS*]. For Burpee, see Pelham Edgar, "Lawrence J. Burpee (1873-1946)," *TRCS*, 3rd series, 51 (1947): 115-17.

85 Newspaper hansard, Toronto *Globe*, 19 March 1897.

86 Ontario. Education Dept., *Circular for Librarians on Classification of Books in Public Libraries* (Toronto: n.p., 1900), 1-4.

87 "William Edwards Dead," Toronto *Globe*, 2 May 1904.

88 Burpee, "Modern Public Libraries," *TRCS*: 43.

89 See Marjorie G. Cohen, *Women's Work, Markets, and Economic Development in Nineteenth-Century Ontario* (Toronto: Univ. of Toronto Press, 1988), 146-51.

90 Jean Thomson Scott, "The Conditions of Female Labour in Ontario," in William J. Ashley, ed., *Toronto University Studies in Political Science* series I, 3 (1892): 22.

91 The lengthy TPL careers of Staton and some of her friends are recounted in "Toronto Public Libraries Staff Association," *Ontario Library Review* 28 (1944): 5-6.

92 For the theme of feminization in American libraries, see Dee Garrison, *Apostles of Culture: the Public Librarian and American Society, 1876-1920* (New York: Free Press, 1979), 173-241. Her work is essential, although she does not emphasize the importance of societal structures which (in my view at least) effectively determined the low status of librarianship as it emerged as a service profession.

93 Burpee, "Modern Public Libraries," *TRCS*: 42. Sanders helped pioneer open access, children's services, and the idea of the library as a hospitable centre of culture: see Emily M. Danton, ed., *Pioneering Leaders in Librarianship* (Chicago: American Library Association, 1953), 153-64.

94 See Graham S. Lowe, "Women, Work and the Office: the Feminization of Clerical Occupations in Canada, 1901-1931," *Canadian Journal of Sociology* 5 (1980): 361-81.

95   See the weekly edition of the Sarnia *Observer* between 24 Nov. 1899 and 12 Jan. 1900.

Chapter 6: The Ontario Library Association

1   Hardy's contributions are summarized in John A. Wiseman, "'Champion Has-Been': Edwin Austin Hardy and the Ontario Library Movement," in *Readings in Canadian Library History*, ed. Peter McNally (Ottawa: Canadian Library Association, 1986), 231-43.

2   The minutes of OLA meetings from 1900 to 1925 are conveniently reprinted in Ontario Library Association, *The Ontario Library Association; An Historical Sketch 1900-1925* (Toronto: University of Toronto, 1926), 117-89.

3   Hardy's program for the OLA is reprinted in *The Ontario Library Association*, 26-33.

4   For Robertson's outstanding contributions, see David Williams, "The Collingwood Public Library," *Ontario Library Review* 28 (1944): 69-71.

5   Constitution of the Ontario Library Association as adopted 1901, *The Ontario Library Association*, 25.

6   Editorial section, *Library Journal* 25 (1900): 271.

7   A.A.C., "Public Libraries," *Canadian Magazine of Politics, Science, Art and Literature* 17 (1901): 286.

8   A Librarian in Canada, "A Word About Modern Methods," *Public Libraries* 9 (1904): 222.

9   E.A. Hardy, "The Training of Librarians in the Province of Ontario," *Public Libraries* 11 (1906): 144.

10   See Greenfield, *Hamilton Public Library 1889-1963*, 31-34.

11   AO, RG 2, D-7, box 18, Bill 150, An Act to Amend the Public Libraries Act.

12   For Fitzpatrick, see Morgan, *CMW* (1912), 400. For Brown, see Morgan, *CMW* (1912), 157-58.

13   AO, RG 2, Series P-2, V, no. 64, letter of G.C. Creelman, Superintendent of Farmers' Institutes, to Harcourt, 5 March 1900.

14   AO, RG 2, Series P-2, V, no. 11, Brown to Harcourt, 25 Jan. 1900.

15   AO, RG 2, P-2, V, no. 57, Brown to Harcourt, 31 Jan. 1900.

16   AO, RG 2, P-2, V, no. 66, Brown to Harcourt, 25 March 1900 and John Millar to Brown, 13 July 1900.

17   Walter Brown, "Travelling Library System of Ontario," *O.A.C. Review* 15 (1903): 10-11.

18   AO, RG 2, P-2, V, no. 62, Fitzpartrick to May, 7 Aug. 1900.

19   Alfred Fitzpatrick, *Library Extension in Ontario; Travelling Libraries and Reading Camps* (n.p.: n.p., c.1901), 2-3; and NAC, MG 28, I 24, Frontier College Papers, vol. 132, file 1900-1, circular on travelling libraries, 11 Sept. 1900. The pamphlet on library extension summarizes Fitzpatrick's work in 1900 and includes most of his correspondence.

20   Fitzpatrick, *Library Extension*, 36.

21   AO, RG 2, Series D-7, box 18, Harcourt to Melvil Dewey, 24 Jan. 1901. For Dewey's contribution to travelling libraries and extension work, see Michael M. Lee, "Melvil Dewey (1851-1931): His Educational Contributions and Reforms," (Ph.D. diss., Loyola Univ. of Chicago, 1979), 148-64; and Joanne E. Passet, "Reaching the Rural Reader: Travelling Libraries in America, 1892-1920," *Libraries & Culture* 26 (1991): 100-18.

22 AO, RG 2, Series D-7, box 18, Bain to Harcourt, 24 April 1901.

23 *RME for 1901*, xvii-xx.

24 Richard Harcourt, *Speech of Hon. R. Harcourt at the Opening Meeting of the Ontario Teachers' Association, Normal School Building, April 1st, 1902* (Toronto: n.p., c.1902), 10.

25 Eastman later authored *The Library Building* (Chicago: American Library Association, 1912).

26 *The Ontario Library Association*, 124.

27 AO, RG 2, Series D-7, box 7, Harcourt to H. Langton, 19 Dec. 1902.

28 AO, OLA, MU 2239, Langton to Hardy, 1 Nov. 1902.

29 AO, RG 2, Series P-2, V, no. 57, memorandum for the Minister's Consideration, 2 Feb. 1900.

30 *RME for 1900*, xix.

31 *RME for 1902*, xvi-xx; AO, RG 49, Series 1-7-B-2, 1903, Regulations pertaining to School Libraries, sessional paper no. 63 [adopted 16 July 1902]. Ontario. Education Dept., *Catalogue of Books Recommended for Public School Libraries by the Education Department of Ontario* (Toronto: King's printer, 1902).

32 AO, RG 2, D-7, box 18, Deseronto library board to Samuel Russell, M.P.P. for Hastings East, 1 Oct. 1901.

33 AO, RG 2, D-7, box 18, memorandum of May to Harcourt, 4 April 1900.

34 AO, RG 2, D-7, box 18, memorandum of May to Harcourt, 12 March 1902.

35 AO, RG 2, Series P-2, V, no. 20, memorandum on legislative grants by Dr. May, 15 May 1903.

36 Newspaper hansard, Toronto *Globe*, 1 May 1902.

37 "A Farmers' Institute Library," *Farmer's Advocate and Home Magazine (Eastern Edition)* 36, 536 (15 Oct. 1901): 674. The magazine supplied books to institutes and offered discounts based on subscriptions. See *Farmer's Advocate* 36, 530 (15 July 1901): 480.

38 John Seath, "Some Needed Educational Reforms," in Ontario Educational Association, *Proceedings of the Annual Convention for 1903* (Toronto: William Briggs, 1903), 70.

39 AO, RG 2, D-7, box 18, Harcourt to Seath, 16 March 1903.

40 "Dr. Bain Replies to Dr. Seath," Toronto *Daily News* 17 April 1903.

41 Hugh Langton, *A Provincial Library Commission* (Toronto?: n.p, 1903), 1-2. For Langton, see William S. Wallace, "Hugh Hornby Langton," *Canadian Historical Review* 34 (1953): 388.

42 *RME for 1903*, xxiv-xxvi.

43 *RME for 1903*, 153-54, 156.

44 He died in 1957: Toronto *Globe*, 25 Oct. 1957. Albert Leake wrote two books: *Industrial Education; Its Problems, Methods and Dangers* (New York: Houghton Mifflin, 1913); and *The Vocational Education of Girls and Women* (New York: Macmillan, 1918).

45 *RME for 1904*, 245.

46 Newspaper hansard, Toronto *Globe*, 25 March 1904.

47 AO, OLA, MU 2239, Norman Gurd to E.A. Hardy, 16 Feb. 1904 includes Gurd's objections to W.J. Hanna. For Gurd, see Morgan, *CMW* (1912), 483.

48 E.A. Hardy, "The Ontario Library Field," *Public Libraries* 9 (1904): 201.

49 "Libraries and Librarians," Toronto *Globe*, 5 April 1904. For Macallum, see Morgan, *CMW* (1912), 673.

50 For Gould, see *DALB*, 208-10. Gould was active in the ALA and instrumental in

bringing it to Montreal in 1900. For Bain's interest in the global scientific cata-logue, see James Bain, Jr., "President's Address," *Proceedings of the Canadian Institute*, n.s., 2 (1899-1904): 98-101.

51   W.J. Robertson, "Should the Education Department Issue a Librarian's Certificate?" *Public Libraries* 9 (1904): 209-12. See Morgan, *CMW* (1912), 954-55; and Andrew Fraser, *A History of Ontario; Its Resources and Development* (Toronto: Canada History Co., 1907), vol. 2, 897-900.

52   *The Ontario Library Association*, 131.

53   For Tytler, see Rose, *Cyclopaedia*, 363-64.

54   Hodgins remained until his death. See "Famous Educator Dies at Age of 92," Toronto *Globe*, 23 Dec. 1912.

55   "Men of the Books Confer," Toronto *Globe*, 25 April 1905.

56   See M. Lee, "Melvil Dewey," 164-74.

57   *Journals of the Legislative Assembly of the Province of Ontario* (Toronto: L.K. Cameron, 1904), vol. 38, 170 [15 March 1904].

58   AO, Sir James P. Whitney Papers, MU 3315, T.H.W. Leavitt to J.P. Whitney, 19 Feb. 1905.

59   AO, Whitney Papers, MU 3116, Pyne to Whitney, 21 March 1905. For Leavitt's Conservative ties see Charles W. Humphries, *'Honest Enough to Be Bold': The Life and Times of James Pliny Whitney* (Toronto: Univ. of Toronto Press, 1985), 67-71.

60   "Dr. May Will Retire," Toronto *Globe*, 3 Nov. 1905.

61   Henry J. Cody, "Dr. A.H.U. Colquhoun – An Appreciation," *Ontario Library Review* 20 (1936): 62-63.

62   Arthur H.U. Colquhoun, "Canadian Celebrities; No. XIII – Mr. James Bain, Jr.," *Canadian Magazine of Politics, Science, Art and Literature* 15 (1900): 31-33.

63   "Larger Education Grants and More Normal Schools," Toronto *Globe*, 11 April 1906.

64   AO, OLA, MU 2240, Bain to Hardy, 4 Feb. 1907.

65   Norman Gurd, "How to Deepen Public Interest in the Library," *Public Libraries* 9 (1904): 222-24.

66   Ontario Library Association, *Catalogue of Children's Books Recommended for Public Libraries, Alphabetically Arranged by Authors, Giving Title, Publisher and Price* (Toronto: Warwick Bro's. & Rutter, 1906), 3.

67   *Proceedings of the Ontario Library Association* (1907), 18 [hereafter *Proc. of OLA*].

68   *Proc. of OLA* (1907): 18.

69   An Act Authorizing Certain Payments under the Public Libraries Act, 6 Edw. VII, c. 38.

70   "Carnegie Plan," Toronto *Globe*, 17 April 1906.

71   AO, OLA, MU 2240, Leavitt to Hardy, 14 Dec. 1906.

72   Walter R. Nursey, *The Story of Isaac Brock, Hero, Defender and Saviour of Upper Canada, 1812* (Toronto: William Briggs, 1908). For his extraordinary career, see Morgan, *CMW* (1912), 858.

73   Regulations published in *RME for 1906*, 181-82.

74   T.W.H. Leavitt, "Travelling Libraries in Ontario," *Library Journal* 33 (1908): 231.

75   AO, OLA, MU 2240, Hardy to W.J. Robertson, 31 Jan. 1907.

76   *Proc. of OLA* (1907): 40-42.

77   Reprinted in *RME for 1907*, 198.

78   Newspaper hansard in Toronto *Daily Star*, 7 March 1907.

79   T.W.H. Leavitt, "Some Library Problems," *Proc. of OLA* (1908): 55.

80 Patricia Spereman, "Library Work for Children," *Proc. of OLA* (1908): 36-40.

81 Angus Mowat, "Patricia Spereman," *Ontario Library Review* 30 (1946): 348-49.

82 AO, OLA, MU 2240, Gurd to Hardy, 12 April 1907; and "Not for Small Children Are Public Libraries," Toronto *Evening Telegram*, 3 April 1907.

83 "Plea for Open Library," Toronto *Evening Telegram*, 9 April 1907.

84 Carnegie Library Correspondence, Toronto, reel no. 32, letter of James Bertram to Bain, 8 May 1908.

85 For example, Thomas E. Champion, "A Great Librarian; the Late James Bain, D.C.L.," *Canadian Magazine of Politics, Science, Art and Literature* 31 (1908): 223-26.

86 For the progressive elements of Conservative reform after 1905, see Charles Humphries, *'Honest Enough to Be Bold'*, 123-79.

87 *Proc. of OLA* (1909): 22.

88 T.W.H. Leavitt, "Technical Work in Public Libraries," *Proc. of OLA* (1909): 36-46. Due to illness, this paper was read by Walter Nursey.

89 "Encouragement of Technical Instruction in Ontario Through the Medium of Public Libraries," *Labour Gazette* 9 (1908/09): 973-74.

90 George Locke, "The Public Library as an Educational Institution," in *Addresses Delivered Before the Canadian Club of Toronto 1908-09* (Toronto: Warwick Bros. and Rutter, 1909), 142. For Locke, see *DALB*, 317-19.

91 See "T.W.H. Leavitt Passes Away," Toronto *Mail and Empire* 22 June 1909; and a notice in *RME for 1909*, 331.

92 Alexander D. Hardy, "[Presidential Address]," *Proc. of OLA* (1910): 33.

93 See Ryan Taylor, "Mabel Dunham's Centenary," *Annual Report of the Waterloo Historical Society* 69 (1981): 13-25; Lillian Snider, "Miss Mabel Dunham," *Ontario Library Review* 38 (1954): 221-24; and Constance Banting, "Mabel Dunham," *Ontario Library Review* 12 (1927/28): 66-67.

94 Mabel Dunham, "Methods of Reaching the People," in *Proc. of OLA* (1910): 70.

95 Ontario Library Association, *Report of Special Committee on Technical Education in Public Libraries* (Toronto: William Briggs, 1910), 6.

96 Ontario. Dept. of Education, *Education for Industrial Purposes; a Report by John Seath* (Toronto: L.K. Cameron, 1911), 308-12.

97 Canada. Royal Commission on Industrial Training and Technical Education, *Report of the Commissioners*, part IV (Ottawa: C.H. Parmelee, 1913), 2177.

98 AO, RG 2, Series P-2, no. 42, Charles Gould to A.H.U. Colquhoun, 26 Nov. 1908.

99 "In the Library," *Canadian Magazine of Politics, Science, Art and Literature* 34 (1909): 78.

100 Lewis. E. Hornung and Lawrence J. Burpee, *A Bibliography of Canadian Fiction (English)* (Toronto: William Briggs, 1904).

101 E.A. Hardy, "Training of Librarians," *Public Libraries* 11 (1906): 143-45.

102 William O. Carson, "The Status and Training of the Librarian," *Proc. of OLA* (1912): 111.

103 Mary T. Butters, "[Ontario Summer Library School]," in *RME for 1911*, 556.

104 Mabel Dunham, "The Ontario Library Summer School 1911," *Proc. of OLA* (1912): 66.

105 For Henwood's death notice see *Ontario Library Review* 8 (1923/24): 74.

106 "Library Meeting Is Held," Brantford *Daily Expositor*, 12 July 1907.

107 Edwin D. Henwood, *Notes on Binding* (Toronto: Education Department, 1908).

108   Walter R. Nursey, "The Story of the Library Institutes of Ontario," *RME for 1913*, 733-37.

109   "Visitors Well Entertained," St. Catharines *Daily Standard*, 6 Nov. 1908.

110   George B. Snyder, "How We Started Our Library on 'Modern Lines,'" *RME for 1910*, 513-16.

111   George B. Snyder, *A Study of the Conditions of the Libraries of the Niagara District* (Port Colborne?: n.p., c.1911), 14-15.

112   AO, OLA, MU 2242, Mabel Dunham to E.A. Hardy, 12 Feb. 1913.

113   Otto Klotz, "The Trustee's Duty to the Library," *Proc. of OLA* (1910): 78-81.

114   Robert McAdams, "How Trustees May Help the Library," *RME for 1911*, 569.

115   Andrew Denholm, "Problems of the Small Libraries," *Proc. of OLA* (1910): 42.

116   Nursey's report is contained in *RME for 1912*, 660-81.

117   Lawrence Burpee, "Library Cooperation in Ontario," *Library Journal* 37 (1912): 85.

118   Walter R. Nursey, "Some Library Possibilities," *Proc. of OLA* (1911): 57.

119   William H. Arison, "Library Extension on County Lines," *RME for 1912*, 687. Arison continued with the board in different capacities until 1938. See Niagara Falls Public Library, "History of the Niagara Falls Public Library" (Niagara Falls, n.p., n.d.), unpaged [typescript]; and his obituary in *Ontario Library Review* 22 (1938): 97.

120   A.W. Cameron, "A Provincial Library System," *Proc. of OLA* (1911): 48.

121   AO, OLA, MU 2241, Lawrence Burpee to E.A. Hardy, 16 Feb. 1911.

122   Lawrence J. Burpee, "A Plea for a National Library," *University Magazine* 10 (1911): 152-63.

123   See *Saturday Night* 24 (March 25 1911), 2.

124   NAC, MG 30, D-39, Lawrence Burpee papers, file 1-14, letter of L.J. Burpee to Edmund Walker, 24 Jan. 1918. His disappointing personal crusade is outlined in Francis D. Donnelly, *The National Library of Canada* (Ottawa: Canadian Library Association, 1973), 31-33.

125   Lutie Stearns, "The Library Militant," *Proc. of OLA* (1912): 88-94; and "Library Extension," *Proc. of OLA* (1912): 114-21. For Stearns, see *DALB*, 504-5.

126   The legal committee's report appears in *Proc. of OLA* (1914): 49.

127   E.A. Hardy, "The Library Situation in Ontario: What May Be Done in Organized Effort," *Proc. of OLA* (1914): 121.

128   Andrew Denholm, "Rural and Village Libraries," *Proc. of OLA* (1915): 82.

129   Norman Gurd, "The Public Library in Every Municipality," *RME for 1914*, 732.

130   AO, RG 49, Series I-7-H, Bill no. 127 – 1906, An Act to Amend the Act Respecting Public Free Libraries.

131   AO, OLA, MU 2241, Nursey to Hardy, 17 June 1910.

132   AO, OLA, MU 2241, letter of Burpee to Hardy, 20 June 1910.

133   AO, OLA, MU 2242, notice to boards dated 20 Jan. 1912.

134   AO, OLA, MU 2242, Adeline Kopp to Hardy, 21 May 1912; Hardy to H.B. Coleman, 28 May 1912; and Hardy to Kopp, 31 May 1912.

135   AO, OLA, MU 2242, Nursey to Hardy, 4 June 1912.

136   Ontario. Dept. of Education, *American Library Association, Ottawa, Canada, June 26th to July 2nd, 1912; Advance List of Librarians and Other Representatives in Attendance from Ontario* (Toronto: n.p., 1912).

137   For Ahern, see *DALB*, 5-7. Mary Ahern, "A Day in Toronto," *Papers and Proceedings of the American Library Association 1912*, (Chicago: American Library Association, 1912), 208-9.

138 *ALA Papers and Proceedings 1912*, 66.

139 *Ibid.*, 160.

140 *Ibid.*, 302-7.

141 For example, "Library Convention Sessions Open With Interesting Talks," Ottawa *Evening Citizen* 27 June 1912. The editor could not resist the subhead "Many Ladies Here."

142 William F. Moore, "The Library Situation in Ontario: In Organized Effort What Has Been Done?" *Proc. of OLA* (1914): 59.

143 Moore, "Library Situation," 60.

144 AO, OLA, MU 2242, Hardy to Gibbard, 20 Aug. 1914. See J.S. Wood, "The Saskatchewan Library Association: A Brief History," *Saskatchewan Library Association Bulletin* 8, 2 (1955): 2-13.

145 See Nursey's address, "Library Progress in Ontario," *RME for 1912*, 651-58; and AO, OLA, MU 2242, Hardy to Annie A. Pollard, President of Michigan Library Association, 20 Sept. 1913.

146 Matthew Dudgeon, "The Universality of Library Service," *Proc. of OLA* (1914): 94. For Dudgeon, see *DALB*, 145-46.

147 William H. Keller, "The Character of Books for a Small Library," *Public Libraries* 6 (1901): 347.

148 For this period, see Evelyn Geller, *Forbidden Books in American Public Libraries, 1876-1939; A Study in Cultural Change* (Westport, Conn.: Greenwood Press, 1984), 79-97.

149 William J. Sykes, "Book Selection," *Proc. of OLA* (1914): 102-6.

150 William J. Sykes, *Selected List of Fiction in English; Prepared for Canadian Public Libraries* (Ottawa: James Hope & Sons, 1914); and Geller, *Forbidden Books in American Libraries*, 93-97.

151 E. A. Hardy, "How Ontario Administers Her Libraries," *Library Journal* 41 (1916): 732.

152 *RME for 1914*, 735.

Chapter 7: Carnegie Philanthropy

1 Robert Nixon, Liberal member for Brant, speaking on 15 Nov. 1984. See *Hansard Official Report of Debates; Legislative Assembly of Ontario* (Toronto: Legislative Assembly of Ontario, 1984), fourth session, 32nd parliament.

2 Andrew Carnegie, *The Gospel of Wealth and Other Timely Essays*, ed. by Edward C. Kirkland, (Cambridge, Mass.: Harvard Univ. Press, 1962), 39.

3 Andrew Carnegie, *Triumphant Democracy: or Fifty Years' March of the Republic* (New York: Charles Scribner's Sons, c.1886), 363.

4 "Carnegie Library Formally Opened," Ottawa *Evening Journal*, 30 April 1906.

5 "Mr. Andrew Carnegie's Message to the Association," *Proc. of OLA* (1915): 43.

6 The fundamental study of the Carnegie era in Ontario is Margaret Beckman, John Black, and Stephen Langmead, *The Best Gift; A Record of the Carnegie Libraries in Ontario* (Toronto: Dundurn Press, 1984). See also, George S. Bobinski, *Carnegie Libraries; Their History and Impact on American Public Library Development* (Chicago: American Library Association, 1969).

7 "Carnegie Library Formally Opened," Ottawa *Evening Journal*, 30 April 1906.

8 Carnegie Library Correspondence, Tavistock, reel no. 31, letter of J.G. Fields, municipal clerk, to James Bertram, 2 June 1915 [hereafter CLC].

9 For American opponents, see Bobinski, *Carnegie Libraries*, 87-106.

10   See Susan H. Swetnam, "Pro-Carnegie Library Arguments and Contemporary
      Concerns in the Intermountain West," *Journal of the West* 30 (July 1991): 63-68.
11   Wilfred Campbell, "The Man and His Scottish Home," Ottawa *Evening Journal,*
      28 April 1906.
12   Carnegie's thoughts on a global order can be found in Joseph F. Wall, *Andrew
      Carnegie* (New York: Oxford University Press, 1970), 674-80.
13   Andrew Carnegie, *Triumphant Democracy,* 111.
14   Christopher Howard, *Splendid Isolation* (London: Macmillan, 1967), 14-20.
15   A good review of the furor about Carnegie's 1903 statements regarding Canadian
      sovereignty appears in J. Castell Hopkins, ed., *The Canadian Annual Review of
      Public Affairs 1903* (Toronto: Annual Review Publishing, 1904), 391-93.
16   Responses appear in "Money from Carnegie to Build Four Libraries," Toronto
      World, 28 Jan. 1903.
17   "Opposes the Grant from Andrew Carnegie," Stratford *Evening Herald,* 6 Jan.
      1902.
18   "Rev. A.H. Goring Replies," Stratford *Evening Herald,* 4 Feb. 1902.
19   James Anderson, Sue Bonsteel, and Tom Dolan, *Stratford – Library Services Since
      1846,* 2d ed. (Stratford: Stratford Public Library, 1975), 12-14.
20   A.A.C., "Public Libraries," *Canadian Magazine of Politics, Science, Art and
      Literature* 17 (1901): 286.
21   Margaret Cohoe, "Kingston Mechanics' Institute to Free Public Library," *Historic
      Kingston* 33 (1985): 50. The opening ceremonies attended by Inspector Nursey are
      covered in "At the Library," Kingston *Daily British Whig,* 16 March 1911.
22   See Abigail A. Van Slyck, "Free to All: Carnegie Libraries and the Transformation
      of American Culture, 1886-1917," (Ph.D. diss., University of California, 1989),
      321-33.
23   "A New Library Building Needed," *Saturday Night* 15 (13 Sept. 1902): 7.
24   "Carnegie's Offer to Toronto," Toronto *Globe,* 28 Jan. 1903.
25   "Mr. Carnegie's Offer," Toronto *Globe,* 28 Jan. 1903.
26   For this period of race-thinking see Stuart Anderson, *Race and Rapprochement;
      Anglo-Saxonism and Anglo-American Relations, 1895-1904* (East Brunswick, New
      Jersey: Fairleigh Dickinson Univ. Press, 1981), 17-61.
27   Elisabeth Wallace, "Goldwin Smith on England and America," *American Historical
      Review* 59 (1954): 884-94.
28   "Carnegie and Canada," Toronto *World,* 28 April 1906. Carnegie's speech is
      reported at length in the same issue.
29   Israel T. Naamani, "The 'Anglo-Saxon' Idea and British Public Opinion,"
      Canadian Historical Review 32 (1951): 43-60.
30   "Orangemen Say Accept It," Toronto *World,* 11 Feb. 1903.
31   The bilingual school issue is studied by Franklin A. Walker, *Catholic Education
      and Politics in Ontario; A Documentary History* (Toronto: Thomas Nelson, 1955-
      86), vol. 2, 228-96.
32   Editorial in *Saturday Night,* 16 (Sept. 1911): 2.
33   For the intellectual interchange, see James T. Kloppenberg, *Uncertain Victory;
      Social Democracy and Progressivism in European and American Thought* (New York:
      Oxford Univ. Press, 1986); for national political-business parallels, see Kenneth O.
      Morgan, "The Future at Work: Anglo-American Progressivism 1890-1917," in
      Contrast and Connection: Bicentennial Essays in Anglo-American History, ed. H.C.
      Allen and Roger Thompson (London: G. Bell & Sons, 1976), 245-71.

34   Lawrence Burpee, "Canadian Libraries and Mr. Carnegie," *Public Libraries* 10 (1905): 87.

35   CLC, St. Catharines, reel no. 27, letter of James Bertram to Mayor Marquis, 12 Dec. 1904.

36   "The City Hall That May Be Built," *Sault Star*, 14 Aug. 1902.

37   "Money from Mr. Carnegie," *Sault Star*, 19 Dec. 1901.

38   CLC, Sault Ste. Marie, reel no. 28; and Beckman, *Best Gift*, 35-36.

39   CLC, Toronto, reel no. 32, letters of G. Smith to A. Carnegie, 28 Nov. 1901 and 14 Feb. 1903.

40   Letter of Goldwin Smith to Lord Mount Stephen, 4 March, 1902, in *A Selection from Goldwin Smith's Correspondence*, ed. Arnold Haultain (Toronto: McClelland & Goodchild, 1910), 381.

41   Melvil Dewey, "The Future of the Library Movement in the United States in the Light of Andrew Carnegie's Recent Gift," *Journal of Social Science* 39 (Nov. 1901): 139-47.

42   Lee, "Melvil Dewey (1851-1931): His Educational Contributions and Reforms," 89-107.

43   "Reception of Library King," Ottawa *Evening Journal*, 30 April 1906.

44   For Carnegie's role, see C. Roland Marchand, *The American Peace Movement and Social Reform, 1890-1918* (Princeton: Princeton Univ. Press, 1972), 114-43.

45   See Thomas P. Socknat, *Witness against War; Pacifism in Canada, 1900-1945* (Toronto: Univ. of Toronto Press, 1987), 23-42.

46   Consult Leon Wolfe, *Lockout: The Story of the Homestead Strike of 1892; A Study of Violence, Unionism, and the Carnegie Steel Empire* (London: Longmans, 1965).

47   For unionization between 1867 and 1941, see Ian M. Drummond, et.al., *Progress without Planning; The Economic History of Ontario from Confederation to the Second World War* (Toronto: Univ. of Toronto Press, 1987), 237-44.

48   "Reject Carnegie Offer," Toronto *Globe*, 12 Feb. 1903.

49   "Labor's View of Carnegie's Offer," Ottawa *Evening Journal*, 16 March 1901.

50   "Town Should Not Be Stained by Carnegie Blood Money," and "Went by Default," Welland *Tribune* 21 May 1914.

51   "What Should be Done with Mr. Carnegie's Offer," Ottawa *Evening Journal*, 20 March 1901.

52   "Worked for Carnegie," Guelph *Daily Mercury*, 23 Nov. 1901.

53   "Millionaires' Gifts," *Canadian Magazine of Politics, Science, Art and Literature* 25 (1905): 178.

54   "The Carnegie Offer," Guelph *Daily Mercury*, 31 Oct. 1901.

55   Beckman, *The Best Gift*, 46.

56   CLC, Thorold, reel no. 34, letter of A.M. McCulloch, library board chairman, to James Bertram, 16 March 1915. Bertram refused McCulloch's request for a supplementary $10,000 to build an extension when the insured building was reconstructed.

57   Barbara Forsyth and Barbara Myrvold, *The Most Attractive Resort in Town: Public Library Service in West Toronto Junction, 1888-1989* (Toronto: Toronto Public Library, 1989), 10-14.

58   "Teeswater," Wingham *Advance*, 16 Jan. 1908.

59   CLC, Teeswater, reel no. 31, letter of Dr. George S. Fowler to Robert A. Franks, Carnegie financial agent, 21 March 1913.

60   "Mr. Carnegie's Offer," Owen Sound *Times*, 24 June 1904; "Favor Carnegie

Offer," 18 Nov. 1904; "Town Council," 10 Feb. 1905.

61   "Labor and the Library," Lindsay *Weekly Post,* 20 Feb. 1903; and "The Public Library Bill is Approved," Lindsay *Weekly Post,* 20 March 1903.

62   G.Y. Donaldson, "Palmerston, Ontario, and It's Public Library," *Ontario Library Review* 27 (1943): 243.

63   Editorial in Orillia *Packet,* 20 May 1909.

64   "The Carnegie Library," Orillia *Times,* 3 June 1909.

65   "A Free Library," Orillia *Packet,* 4 March 1909.

66   This also was evident in the United States: see Alvin S. Johnson, *A Report to Carnegie Corporation of New York on the Policy of Donations to Free Public Libraries* (New York: Carnegie Corp., 1919), 37.

67   "The Free Library," Lindsay *Weekly Post,* 27 Feb. 1903.

68   "Men Elected for 1896," St. Mary's *Journal,* 9 Jan. 1896.

69   "Long Petition," St. Mary's *Journal,* 14 April 1904.

70   CLC, St. Mary's, reel no. 27, letter of Maybee and Makins to James Bertram, 30 July 1904.

71   See Goderich *Signal,* 3 April 1902; and the Goderich *Star,* 28 March, 4 April, and 11 April 1902.

72   Robena Kirton, "Gravenhurst Public Library" (Gravenhurst: n.p., 1985), 1-4 [typescript].

73   Beckman, *The Best Gift,* 54-56.

74   CLC, Otterville, reel no. 23, includes Bill 89 (the 1916 legislation for township free libraries) and Otterville correspondence between Bertram and H.C. Downing or M. Durkee between 1915 and 1923.

75   CLC, Port Arthur, reel no. 68, outlines Port Arthur's problems.

76   CLC, Trenton, reel no. 68, letter of Bertram to Lieutenant Colonel A.E. Bywater, 26 Feb. 1919.

77   For the pre-war era, see Drummond, et. al., *Progress without Planning* (Toronto: Univ. of Toronto Press, 1987), 103-33.

78   CLC, Oshawa, reel no. 23, letter of Frederick Fowke to J. Bertram, 3 July 1906, 12 July 1906, etc.

79   For this transformation, see Jacob Spelt, *The Urban Development in South-Central Ontario,* 2nd ed. (Ottawa: Carleton Univ. Press, 1983), 176-86.

80   H.G. Wells, *Social Forces in England and America* (New York: Harper & Brothers, 1914), 203.

81   Charles C. Soule, *Library Rooms and Buildings* (Boston: American Library Association, 1902), 14.

82   Frank Burgoyne, *Library Construction; Architecture, Fittings, and Furniture* (London: George Allen, 1897), 8-9.

83   Burgoyne, *Library Construction,* 14.

84   James D. Brown, *Manual of Library Economy* (London: Scott, Greenwood & Co., 1903), 99.

85   Brown, *Manual of Library Economy,* 93.

86   Soule, *Library Rooms and Buildings,* 22.

87   For design, see Abigail Van Slyck, "Free to All," 279-320.

88   Design is discussed in Beckman, *The Best Gift,* 117-40.

89   William A. Langton, "Library Design," *Canadian Architect and Builder* 15 (1902): 47.

90   Langton, "Library Design," 48.

91 "Would Accept Carnegie Gifts," Toronto *News*, 14 April 1903. See also, Paul G. Boultbee, "The Story of a Small Town Library: Paris Public Library – the Early Years," *Library History Review* 2 (Sept. 1975): 53-56.

92 "Men of the Books Confer," Toronto *Globe*, 25 March 1905.

93 "Carnegie Plan Confer on Books," Toronto *Globe*, 17 April 1906.

94 Editorial in *Sault Star*, 19 June 1902. Halton's initial approach to Bertram began on 9 Sept. 1901 and a promise was awarded on 14 Dec. See CLC, Sault Ste. Marie, reel no. 28.

95 "The City Hall That May Be Built," *Sault Star*, 14 Aug. 1902.

96 For Goderich, see *RME for 1906*, 226-29. For Bertram's frequent criticism of Guelph, consult the CLC, Guelph, reel no. 13. Later he relented and promised $8,000 for an extension in 1914, but the project never materialized.

97 See Barbara Keogh, "Burlington Public Library, 1872-1952: School House to Big White House on Elizabeth Street," *Ontario Library Review* 37 (1953): 75-77. A formula for size based on population, volumes, seats, and circulation first appears in Joseph L. Wheeler and Alfred M. Githens, *The American Public Library Building: Its Planning and Design with Special Reference to Its Administration and Service* (Chicago: American Library Association, 1941), 38-44.

98 For Horwood, see *Who's Who in Canada 1928/29* (Toronto: International Press, 1929), 1390.

99 *RME for 1906*, 284-88.

100 The planning for the Ottawa library is documented by Otto Klotz in Appendix A of the Ottawa Public Library, *First Preliminary Report of the Carnegie Library* (Ottawa: Ottawa Printing Ltd., 1906), 30-33.

101 Lawrence J. Burpee, "Modern Methods in Small Libraries," *Public Libraries* 9 (1904): 218.

102 *RME for 1909*, 416-17.

103 CLC, Ottawa, reel no. 23, letter of W.J. Sykes to A. Carnegie, 10 May 1913; and J. Bertram to W.J. Sykes, 12 May 1913.

104 CLC, Ottawa, reel no. 23, letter of Harold Fisher, Mayor, to J. Bertram, 8 May 1917.

105 "Lots of Branch Libraries Plan Mr. Carnegie Favors," Toronto *World*, 25 April 1906.

106 Toronto Public Library, *Programme of a Competition for the Selection of an Architect for the Public Reference Library Building in the City of Toronto 1905* (Toronto: n.p., 1905).

107 For descriptions, see "Public Reference Library for Toronto," *Canadian Architect and Builder* 19 (1906): 85-86, and *RME for 1906*, 233-42.

108 For Chapman's career, see Howard D. Chapman, *Alfred Chapman: The Man and His Work* (Toronto: Architectural Conservancy of Ontario, 1978). Chapman also designed Carnegie libraries in Dundas and Barrie, and the Dovercourt branch in Toronto.

109 For these forerunners, see Burgoyne, *Library Construction*, 158-62, 144-45, and 177-80.

110 "The New Library Open at Nights," Toronto *Star*, 30 Oct. 1909.

111 Amian L. Champneys, *Public Libraries; A Treatise on Their Design, Construction, and Fittings* (London: B.T. Batsford, 1907), 123-24.

112 Hamilton Public Library Archives, Series I-F-4b-2, "Instructions to Architects for

the Public Library Building to be Erected at Hamilton, Ontario, 1910."

113   Hamilton Public Library Archives, Series I-F-4b-6, "Agreement Between Hamilton Public Library and E.L. Tilton Architect," 24 April 1911. Tilton was contracted "to make sketches that meet the approval of James Bertram" and "to assist in a professional way."

114   Edward L. Tilton, "Scientific Library Planning," *Library Journal* 37 (Sept. 1912): 497-501. For Tilton's influence see Donald Oehlerts, "The Development of American Public Library Architecture," 117-21, 165-68.

115   See Greenfield, *Hamilton Public Library 1889-1963*, 37-42.

116   "Will Trust Them," Hamilton *Times,* 23 May 1913.

117   For a discussion, see Wheeler and Githens, *The American Public Library Building,* 215-22. Bertram's leaflet underwent several revisions.

118   For these branches, see "Toronto Branch Library," *Construction* 10 (1917): 390-91; and Alfred V. Hall, "Toronto Branch Libraries Ground Treatment," *Construction* 10 (1917): 392-94. For Eden Smith, see *Who's Who in Canada 1928/29,* 549.

119   Hester Young, "The Dewey Decimal Classification," *Proc. of OLA* (1908): 24.

120   Amian L. Champneys, *Public Libraries,* 88. For another negative British view, see William Willcock, "Ladies' Reading Rooms," *Library Association Record* 15 (1913): 80-84.

121   Norman Gurd, "Free Access in an Ontario Library," *Public Libraries* 9 (1904): 229-30.

122   *RME for 1910,* 523.

123   CLC, Windsor, reel no. 34, letter of Andrew Braid to James Bertram, 5 March 1910.

124   *RME for 1912,* 622.

125   *RME for 1913,* 740.

126   *RME for 1916,* 108.

127   See Abigail A. Van Slyck, "The Utmost Amount of Effectiv [sic] Accommodation": Andrew Carnegie and the Reform of the American Library," *Journal of the Society of Architectural Historians* 50 (1991): 359-83.

128   For the positive influence of Carnegie, see Bobinski, *Carnegie Libraries,* 183-202; and Beckman, *The Best Gift,* 171-77.

129   Hardy, *The Public Library,* 108.

130   Greenfield, *Hamilton Public Library 1889-1963,* 14-15.

131   "Opening of the New Public Library Building at Renfrew," *Ontario Library Review* 6 (1921/22): 18.

132   Bill Hillier and Julienne Hanson, *The Social Logic of Space* (London: Cambridge Univ. Press, 1984), 143-97. They discuss how various building interiors function in terms of social relations.

Chapter 8: A Province to Be Served

1   For a contemporary record of Ontario's war achievements, see J. Castell Hopkins, *The Province of Ontario in the War; A Record of Government and People* (Toronto: Warwick Bros. & Rutter, 1919).

2   See Gerald A. Hallowell, *Prohibition in Ontario, 1919-1923* (Ottawa: Love Printing, 1972).

3   See Christopher Armstrong, *The Politics of Federalism: Ontario's Relations with the*

Federal Government, 1867-1942 (Toronto: Univ. of Toronto Press, 1981), 114-59.

4   For the development of broadcasting and radio audiences, see Mary Vipond, *Listening In; The First Decade of Canadian Broadcasting, 1922-1932* (Montreal: McGill-Queen's Univ. Press, 1992).

5   For the Conservative collapse, see Peter Oliver, *Public and Private Persons; The Ontario Political Culture, 1914-1934* (Toronto: Clarke, Irwin & Co., 1975), 16-43. For labour's problems, see James Naylor, *The New Democracy; Challenging the Social Order in Industrial Ontario, 1914-1925* (Toronto: Univ. of Toronto Press, 1991).

6   For Mary Black, see "The Librarian and Library of Fort William," *Ontario Library Review* 1 (1916/17): 92-95 [hereafter *Ont. Lib. Rev.*].

7   General meeting discussion, *Proc. of OLA* (1917): 88.

8   For Great Britain, see W.C. Berwick Sayers, "The Immediate Programme of Librarianship," *Library Assistant* 14 (1918): 229-37; for the United States, see Charles C. Williamson, "The Need of a Plan for Library Development," *Library Journal* 44 (1918): 649-55.

9   Mary J.L. Black, "Concerning Some Popular Fallacies," *Proc. of OLA* (1918): 58.

10 The best study of northern libraries before 1920 is John A. Wiseman, "Temples of Democracy," 77-122.

11 Nursey died in 1927: see "W.R. Nursey's Death Ends Stirring, Colorful Career," Toronto *Star*, 14 March 1927.

12 AO, OLA, MU 2245, 1916, E.A. Hardy to David Williams, OLA President, 8 April 1916.

13 For Carson, see *A Standard Dictionary of Canadian Biography; The Canadian Who Was Who*, eds. Charles G.D. Roberts and Arthur L. Tunnell (Toronto: Trans-Canada Press, 1934), vol. 1, 101.

14 For education policies under the farmer government, see Charles M. Johnston, *E.C. Drury: Agrarian Idealist* (Toronto: Univ. of Toronto Press, 1986), 83-98.

15 William Carson, "The Canadian Public Library as a Social Force," *Proc. of OLA* (1915): 37.

16 Wayne A. Wiegand, "British Propaganda in American Public Libraries, 1914-1917," *Journal of Library History* 18 (1983): 237-54. He outlines Parker's clandestine work.

17 John A. Wiseman, "A Genteel Patriotism; Ontario's Public-Library Movement and the First World War," in *Readings in Canadian Library History*, ed. Peter F. McNally (Ottawa: Canadian Library Association, 1986), 181-90.

18 Toronto Public Library, *Thirty-fifth Annual Report, 1918* (Toronto: Toronto Public Library, 1919), 18-19.

19 William O. Carson, "Libraries in War-Time and Some Factors that Require Consideration," *Proc. of OLA* (1917): 62.

20 Charles C. Williamson, *Andrew Carnegie: His Contribution to the Public Library Movement* (Cleveland: n.p., 1920).

21 William G.S. Adams, *A Report on Library Provision and Policy* (Edinburgh: Neill & Company, 1915).

22 Alvin S. Johnson, *A Report to Carnegie Corporation of New York on the Policy of Donations to Free Public Libraries* (New York: n.p., 1919), 45-49.

23 *A Selected List of Books Recommended by the Ontario Library Association*. Title varies between 1902-1916.

24 Edgar M. Zavitz, "From A Rural Library Trustee," *Ont. Lib. Rev.* 1 (1916/17): 6.

25   Transmission of the disease by library books was a worrisome problem. See Hibbert W. Hill, "Library Books Rarely, If Ever, Carry Disease," *Ont. Lib. Rev.* 3 (1918/19): 34.

26   *RME for 1916*, 113.

27   For Barnstead, see Freda F. Waldon, "W.G.B.: A Personal Reminiscence," *Ont. Lib. Rev.* 35 (1951): 203-5.

28   Toronto Public Library, *An Extension of the Dewey Decimal Classification Applied to Canada* (Toronto: n.p., 1912); and Winifred Barnstead, "Expansion of Dewey Decimal System for Canada," in *Proc. of OLA* (1912): 76-79. Also, Winifred G. Barnstead, *Filing Rules for Dictionary Catalogues, Recommended by the Minister of Education for Use in the Public Libraries of Ontario* (Toronto: A.T. Wilgress, 1918).

29   *RME for 1916*, 106.

30   "Statistics of City Libraries," *Ont. Lib. Rev.* 2 (1917/18): 111-14; and "Statistics for 1917 – Free Public Libraries in Places of Less than 10,000," *Ont. Lib. Rev.* 3 (1918/19): 12-15.

31   Letter of W.O. Carson to W.A. Hutton, municipal clerk of Tilbury, 22 Feb. 1917, CLC, reel no. 31. Tilbury was contemplating a commitment of $500 per annum.

32   *RME for 1917*, 99.

33   *RME for 1919*, 76.

34   Rev. Father J.T. Foley, "A Public Library Confers a Benefit on Its Whole Community," *Ont. Lib. Rev.* 1 (1916/17): 12.

35   Ontario. Dept. of Education, *Reference Work and Reference Works* (Toronto: A.T. Wilgress, 1920), 2.

36   "Loan System for Rural, Village and School Libraries," *Ont. Lib. Rev.* 4 (1919/20): 60-63.

37   Sir Robert Falconer, "What a Public Library Can Do for the Development of a Community," *Proc. of OLA* (1918): 60-61 [also printed in *Ont. Lib. Rev.* 2 (1917/18): 105-6].

38   For the intellectual postwar milieu, see James G. Greenlee, *Sir Robert Falconer: A Biography* (Toronto: Univ. of Toronto Press, 1988), 242-73.

39   *RME for 1919*, 81.

40   See Charles Johnston, *E.C. Drury*, 99-181.

41   Frederick F. Schindeler, *Responsible Government in Ontario* (Toronto: Univ. of Toronto Press, 1969), 12-27.

42   George Locke, "Canadian Libraries and the War," *Ont. Lib. Rev.* 3 (1918/19): 5.

43   William J. Sykes, "Why Should a Community Support a Free Library?" *Ont. Lib. Rev.* 1 (1916/17): 5.

44   W.G. Peacock, "The Educative Value of Fiction," *Ont. Lib. Rev.* 3 (1918/19): 61-63.

45   "Librarians and Their Work," Toronto *Mail and Empire*, 23 April 1919.

46   For a synopsis, see "The Public Libraries Act of 1920," *Ont. Lib. Rev.* 5 (1920/21): 9-13.

47   Mary J. L. Black, "New Library Legislation in Ontario," *Canadian Bookman* n.s., 2 (Dec. 1920): 18.

48   William O. Carson, "The Ontario Public Library Rate," *Bulletin of the American Library Association* 15 (July 1921): 126-28.

49   Samuel H. Ranke, "The Ontario Library Law and American Libraries," *Bulletin of the American Library Association* 15 (July 1921): 128-30; see also, "Standards for Public Libraries," *Bulletin* 27 (Nov. 1933): 513-14.

50   "Claimable Public Library Rates Compared," *Ont. Lib. Rev.* 5 (1920/21): 14-17.

51   "Regulations Governing Grants to Public Libraries, 1921-1922," *Ont. Lib. Rev.* 5 (1920/21): 107-8.

52   For the Carnegie work, consult Carl M. White, *A Historical Introduction to Library Education: Problems and Progress to 1951* (Metuchen, New Jersey: Scarecrow Press, 1976), 157-87.

53   Ontario. Dept. of Education, *Ontario Library School* (Toronto: n.p., c.1923-24), 1-19. This publication describes all the school's activities.

54   See Bertha Bassam, *The Faculty of Library Science University of Toronto and its Predecessors 1911-1972,* 23-34.

55   *RME for 1921,* 74.

56   C.E. Freeman, "Travelling Libraries," (B.A. thesis, Ontario Agricultural College, 1925), 11.

57   For example, Ontario. Dept. of Agriculture, *Report of the Women's Institutes of the Province of Ontario 1920 and 1921* (Toronto: Clarkson W. James, 1922), 27-30.

58   See *Report of the Women's Institutes 1923,* 64-66 for early twenties undertakings.

59   *RME for 1918,* 138.

60   Mary J. L. Black, "Twentieth Century Librarianship, *Canadian Bookman* n.s., 1 (Jan. 1919): 58.

61   Mary S. Saxe, "The Library from the Inside, Out!" *Canadian Bookman* n.s., 2 (April 1920): 17.

62   Mary Kingley Ingraham, "Librarianship as a Profession," *Canadian Bookman* n.s., 3 (June 1921): 39-40. For Canadian concerns on censorship, see Henry Alexander, "Obscenity and The Law," *Queen's Quarterly* 60 (1953): 161-69.

63   Evelyn Geller, *Forbidden Books in American Public Libraries, 1876-1939,* 127-46.

64   AO, OLA, MU 2246, 1919, B. Mabel Dunham, "The Public Library of To-Morrow," unpaged typescript.

65   "Editorial Comment: Duties of All Trustees," *Ont. Lib. Rev.* 13 (1928/29): 130.

66   For Taylor's impact on American libraries during this period, see Marion Casey, "Efficiency, Taylorism, and Libraries in Progressive America," *Journal of Library History* 16 (1981): 265-79.

67   David Williams, "Publicity, a Factor in Library Work," *Ont. Lib. Rev.* 2 (1917/18): 83-84.

68   Talk given by B.W.N. Grigg, Waterloo Public Library, on the Kitchener radio station, 1922: see *Ont. Lib. Rev.* 7 (1922/23): 18.

69   [William O. Carson], "Adult Education and the Library," *Ont. Lib. Rev.* 10 (1925/26): 8.

70   American Library Association, *Libraries and Adult Education* (Chicago: American Library Association, 1926), 97.

71   The role of the provincial library service branch is discussed by Stephen F. Cummings, "Angus McGill Mowat and the Development of Ontario Public Libraries, 1920-1960," (Ph.D. diss., University of Western Ontario, School of Library and Information Science, 1986), 133-53.

72   W.A. Craick, "Little Sketches of Busy Men; V. – Dr. George H. Locke," Toronto *Globe,* 12 April 1913.

73   George H. Locke, "Revery of a Bookish Librarian," *Canadian Bookman* n.s., 1 (Jan. 1919): 43.

74   George Locke, "The Library and Adult Education," *Libraries* 35 (1930): 433-37.

75   George Locke, "An Experiment Station in Education," *The Nineteenth Century*

and After; A Monthly Review 97 (Aug. 1925): 199.

76 Margaret Penman, *A Century of Service: Toronto Public Library 1883-1983* (Toronto: Toronto Public Library, 1984), 19-35. For architectural comments, see George H. Locke, "The Toronto Public Libraries," *Journal of the Royal Architectural Institute of Canada* 3 (May-June 1926): 87-103; and Charles R. Sanderson, "Beauty with Utility," *Construction* 23 (1930): 282-88, 293-96.

77 Augustus Bridle, *The Story of the Club* (Toronto: Arts & Letters Club, 1945), 41. Locke was the second president, 1909-10.

78 Charles R. Sanderson, "A Library in a Shopping Centre," *Library Journal* 55 (1930): 257-59.

79 Teresa O'Connor, "The Old Order Changeth," *Ont. Lib. Rev.* 12 (1927/28): 72-73.

80 For example Septimus Pitt, *Libraries of the United States and Canada: Report of Visit by the City Librarian, Glasgow; September-October, 1926* (Glasgow: n.p., n.d.), 13-14 [typescript].

81 Frances Staton, "The Compilation of a Bibliography of the Rebellion of 1837-38," *Canadian Historical Association Annual Report* (1924): 66.

82 Lillian Smith, "The Children's Librarian," *Acta Victoriana* 42, 2 (1917): 65.

83 See Mary Vipond, "The Nationalist Network: English Canada's Intellectuals and Artists in the 1920s," *Canadian Review of Studies in Nationalism* 5 (1980): 32-52.

84 William O. Carson, "Public Libraries of Ontario," *Library Journal* 52 (1927): 451.

85 The Hamilton controversy (and its origin) is studied by Greenfield, *Hamilton Public Library 1889-1963*, 46-54.

86 "Hamilton's Library," Hamilton *Spectator*, 22 Nov. 1920.

87 "Library Inquiry Has Been Refused," Hamilton *Spectator*, 18 Dec. 1920.

88 Hamilton Public Library Archives, Series I-A-3, Ontario. Dept. of Education, Public Libraries Branch, "Report of Special Inspection of the Hamilton Public Library," Dec. 1921 (?), 31 [typescript].

89 Carson also issued a supplementary report on the collection, Hamilton Public Library Archives, Series I-A-3, "Notes on the Book Collections."

90 For Hunter's career, see Jesse E. Middleton and Fred Landon, *The Province of Ontario – a History 1615-1927* (Toronto: Dominion Publishing, 1927), vol. 3, 198-99.

91 Carlton published a number of works, e.g., William Carlton, *English Literature* (Chicago: American Library Association, 1925). For the American Library in Paris and American influence in France, see Mary N. Maack, "Americans in France: Cross-Cultural Exchange and the Diffusion of Innovations," *Journal of Library History* 21 (1986): 315-33.

92 Hamilton Public Library Archives, Series I-A-3, William Carlton, "General Outline of Library Administration," 1921(?) [typescript].

93 See Greenfield, *Hamilton Public Library*, 55-64.

94 "Report of Special Investigation of the Hamilton Public Library," 27.

95 Hamilton Public Library Archives, Series I-A-3, letter of Winifred Barnstead to Freda Walton, 16 Feb. 1963.

96 Lurene McDonald Lyle, "Reference Work in the Depression," *Ont. Lib. Rev.* 18 (1934): 59-61.

97 See Greenfield, *Hamilton Public Library*, 65-79.

98 William Sykes, "Adult Education in Ottawa," *Ont. Lib. Rev.* 9 (1924/25): 35-36.

99 Wilfred Campbell, *The Poetical Works of Wilfred Campbell; Edited with a Memoir by W.J. Sykes* (London: Hodder and Stoughton, 1923).

100 Ottawa Carnegie Library, *The Ottawa Public Library 1921-1931; A Retrospect and Forecast* (Ottawa: n.p., 1932), 7.

101 *Ottawa Public Library*, 5.

102 For an investigation of the Americanization of Canadian culture in the twenties, see A.B. McKillop, *Contours of Canadian Thought* (Toronto: Univ. of Toronto Press, 1987), 111-28.

103 See Arthur R. Ford, "Fred Landon, Journalist, Librarian, Historian," *Ont. Lib. Rev.* 27 (1943): 119-20; Frederick H. Armstrong, "Fred Landon, 1880-1969," *Ontario History* 62 (1970): 1-4; and Elizabeth Spicer, "Our Fourth Librarian – Fred Landon," *Ex Libris News; Newsletter of the Ex Libris Association* 12 (Fall 1992): 22-24.

104 Fred Landon, "A City Library's Work," *Ont. Lib. Rev.* 6 (1921/22): 10-13.

105 Fred Landon, "The Library and Local Material," *Ont. Lib. Rev.* 1 (1916/17): 61-62.

106 Fred Landon, "John Davis Barnett, 1849-1926," *Ont. Lib. Rev.* 10 (1926/27): 75-77.

107 "New Library is Badly Needed," London *Free Press*, 28 Sept. 1920.

108 See "Richard Crouch, New Librarian," London *Free Press*, 8 June 1923; and "Richard Edwin Crouch," *Ont. Lib. Rev.* 46 (1962): 28.

109 "Ask Vote on Debenture Issue of $250,000 for New Library Building," London *Free Press*, 24 Sept. 1926.

110 "Library Building is Needed Here," London *Free Press*, 11 Nov. 1927.

111 London *Advertiser*, 6 Dec. 1927.

112 London Public Library, *Thirty-Third Annual Report* (London: n.p., 1928), unpaged [typescript].

113 "Why London Should Vote for Public Library By-Law," London *Free Press*, 28 Nov. 1930.

114 "London's Library Situation," London *Free Press*, 3 May 1933.

115 "Library By-Law Carried," Kingston *Daily British Whig*, 26 March 1920.

116 Advertisement in Kingston *Daily British Whig*, 24 March 1920, 12.

117 "Kingston's New Public Library Formally Opened on Wednesday," Kingston *Daily British Whig*, 17 Dec. 1925.

118 Mildred A. Clow, "Kingston Public Library," *Ont. Lib. Rev.* 11 (1926/27): 39-40.

119 A.M. Kennedy, "The Librarian in Her Relationship to Books and Readers," *Ont. Lib. Rev.* 15 (1930): 42.

120 "Kingston Librarian Retires," *Ont. Lib. Rev.* 34 (1950): 13.

121 Brooke Abbott, "An Accidental Librarian," *Canadian Magazine* 76 (1931): 18.

122 Ena Kirker, "The Woman Who Put Charm into a Public Library," *Canadian Magazine* 68 (1927): 32.

123 Mary J.L. Black, "The Ideal Librarian," *Ont. Lib. Rev.* 19 (1935): 125.

124 For the early period, see Mary J. L. Black, "Our Public Library," *Thunder Bay Historical Society Papers and Annual Reports* 3 (1911/12): 6-7; and Mary Black, "Early History of the Fort William Public Library," *Thunder Bay Historical Society* 16/17 (1924/26): 28-31.

125 See *The Library Story in Fort William* (Fort William: n.p., 1959), unpaged; "Retirement of Miss M.J.L. Black from the Fort William Pubic Library," *Ont. Lib. Rev.* 21 (1937): 132; and "Mary J.L. Black Dies in Vancouver," *Ont. Lib. Rev.* 23 (1939): 5-7.

126 Mabel Dunham, "Leaves from the Diary of a Librarian," *Acta Victoriana* 33, 4 (1910): 270-76.

127   AO, OLA, MU 2246, 1921, Mabel Dunham, "Library Work As a Profession for Canadian Women," 2 [typescript].

128   Mabel Dunham, "What of the Canadian Historical Novel?" *Ont. Lib. Rev.* 16 (1932): 114.

129   Lillian Snider, "Miss Mabel Dunham," *Ont. Lib. Rev.* 38 (1954): 221-24.

130   John Ridington, Mary J.L. Black and George Locke, *Libraries in Canada; A Study of Library Conditions and Needs* (Toronto: Ryerson Press, 1933), 51.

131   A.E. Borland, "Fred DelaFosse," *Ont. Lib. Rev.* 30 (1946): 27-28.

132   Fred DelaFosse, "The Influence of a Good Book," *Ont. Lib. Rev.* 3 (1918/19): 57-59.

133   Fred DelaFosse, "Library Service," *Ont. Lib. Rev.* 27 (1943): 471.

134   For an example, see Andrew Braid, "Bookish Edinburgh," *Ont. Lib. Rev.* 4 (1919/20): 8-11.

135   Braid died in 1925: see *Ont. Lib. Rev.* 10 (1925/26): 3.

136   Agnes Lancefield, "[Windsor]," *Proc. of OLA* (1928): 12-17 [typescript].

137   See "First Woman Chairman of Barrie Library," *Ont. Lib. Rev.* 22 (1938): 85; and Mrs. J.E. Montagu-Leeds, "Trustee and the Library," *Bulletin of the Canadian Library Association* 7 (Jan. 1951): 148.

138   "The Walkerville Public Library," *Ont. Lib. Rev.* 8 (1923/24): 54.

139   Margaret Fralick, "Anne Hume Retires," *Ont. Lib. Rev.* 41 (1957): 209-10.

140   Anne Hume, "The Librarian in the Community," *Quill and Quire* 14 (Oct. 1948): 18.

141   "Sarnia Librarian Retires," *Ont. Lib. Rev.* 38 (1954): 220.

142   Dorothy Carlisle, "Steps Toward County Library Work in Lambton County," *Ont. Lib. Rev.* 15 (1931): 138-40.

143   Mowat's early career appears in Stephen Cummings, "Angus McGill Mowat and the Development of Ontario Public Libraries," 196-223.

144   Angus Mowat, "Better Reading and How to Attain It from the Viewpoint of the Adult," *Ont. Lib. Rev.* 8 (1923/24): 3-6.

145   See Angus Mowat, "Reference Work in the Smaller Library," *Proc. of OLA* (1928): 2-12 [typescript]; and "Adult Education," *Proc. of OLA* (1929): 12-16 [typescript].

146   See Mary Vipond, "Canadian Nationalism and the Plight of Canadian Magazines in the 1920s," *Canadian Historical Review* 58 (1977): 43-63.

147   For Ferguson's administration, see Peter Oliver, *G. Howard Ferguson: Ontario Tory* (Toronto: Univ. of Toronto Press, 1977), 144-370.

148   AO, RG 3, Premier's Office and Cabinet Office, Ferguson Papers, box 89, general correspondence and letters, libraries and censorship bill, letter of G.H. Ferguson to W. Doreen, editor of Bookseller and Stationer and Office Equipment Journal, 25 Feb. 1926.

149   Inconstant Reader, "Preferences," *Canadian Forum* 9 (Aug. 1929): 386-87.

150   His viewpoints are evident from his unpublished works. See MTRL, George Herbert Locke papers, undated typescripts of speeches.

151   "Two Public Libraries on Rails," *Ont. Lib. Rev.* 11 (1926/27): 8; see also, Karl and Mary Schuessler, *School on Wheels; Reaching and Teaching the Isolated Children of the North* (Erin, Ont.: Boston Mills Press, 1986).

152   "Mr. W.O. Carson," *Ont. Lib. Rev.* 14 (1929/30): 40-41.

153   AO, OLA, MU 2246, 1920, "Annual Report of the O.L.A. Secretary for the Year 1919-20," 15-16. For the defeat of the enlarged program, consult Dennis Thompson, *A History of the American Library Association, 1876-1972* (Chicago: American Library Assn., 1978), 72-83.

154 AO, OLA, MU 2247, 1922, Hugh S. Eayrs, "Canadian Authors Association;" and "Annual Report of the O.L.A. Secretary for the Year 1921-22," 17-23.

155 All these addresses, in typescript, can be found in the *Proc. of the OLA* for the particular years.

156 Lieut.-Col. John Malcolm Mitchell, "[Libraries in Great Britain]," *Proc. of OLA* (1925): 40-49 [typescript]; and Charles F.D. Belden, Achievements and Hopes of the American Library Association," *Proc. of OLA* (1926): 20-28 [typescript].

157 AO, OLA, MU 2247, 1924, letter of George H. Ferguson to E.A. Hardy, 18 Dec. 1924.

158 Edwin A. Hardy, "A Half Century of Retrospect and Prospect; Annual Presidential Address," *Ont. Lib. Rev.* 11 (1926/27): 41-46.

159 Beatrice W. Welling, "Canadian Librarians Meet at the American Librarian [sic] Association," *Ont. Lib. Rev.* 10 (1925/26): 11-12.

160 Toronto Public Library, *Gossip! Of the American Library Association Conference, Held in Toronto, June 10th to June 25th, 1927* (Toronto: n.p., 1927), 3.

161 Mary J. L. Black, "Canadian Library Extension Meeting," *Proceedings and Transactions of the American Library Association, Forty-Ninth Meeting, 1927*, 338-40.

162 "Organization of the Canadian Library Association," *Library Journal* 52 (1927): 705-6.

163 Fred Landon, "The Toronto Conference – II; Canadian Library Association," *Library Journal* 52 (1927): 749.

164 George Locke, "President's Address," *Proceedings and Transactions of the ALA for 1927*, 271.

165 A. Raymond Mullens, "Bringing Books to Brains," *MacLean's Magazine* 40 (1 June 1927): 83.

Epilogue: Other Days

1 See John Taylor, "Urban Autonomy in Canada: It's Evolution and Decline," in *The Canadian City: Essays in Urban and Social History*, rev., eds. Gilbert Stelter and Alan Artibise (Ottawa: Carleton Univ. Press, 1984), 478-500.

2 For a brief synopsis, see Charles R. Sanderson, "The Extension of Library Privileges to the Rural Parts of England and Scotland Through the County Library System," *Proc. of OLA* (1930): 9-10 [typescript]. For the Mitchell and Kenyon reports, see Thomas Kelly, *History of Public Libraries in Great Britain, 1845-1975*, 2nd ed. (London: Library Assn., 1977), 232-54.

3 For a general introduction to regional systems in Canada, see Violet L. Coughlin, *Larger Units of Public Library Service in Canada* (Metuchen, New Jersey: Scarecrow Press, 1968), 55-73.

4 Carnegie Corporation. Commission of Enquiry. *Libraries in Canada; A Study of Library Conditions and Needs* (Toronto: Ryerson Press, 1933), 61-62.

5 Frederick P. Gavin, "Vocational Training for Adults in Ontario," *Ont. Lib. Rev.* 9 (1924/25): 30-32. For Gavin, see "Was Technical School Leader," Toronto *Globe and Mail*, 3 Oct. 1944.

6 For the CAA in the 1920s, see Lyn Harrington, *Syllables of Recorded Time* (Toronto: Simon & Pierre, 1981), 15-113.

7 Marjorie Jarvis, "The Librarian and Community Drama," *Ont. Lib. Rev.* 9 (1923/24): 9-13.

8 For example, see Maria Tippett, *Making Culture: English-Canadian Institutions and*

the Arts Before the Massey Commission (Toronto: Univ. of Toronto Press, 1990).

9   See Meyeme C. Althouse, "The Librarian's Job," *Chatelaine* (Sept. 1931): 40-41.

10   For the broader context, see Veronica Strong-Boag, *The New Day Recalled: Lives of Girls and Women in English Canada, 1919-1945* (Toronto: Copp Clarke Pitman, 1988), 41-80.

11   N. Gurd, "Other Days," *Ont. Lib. Rev.* 16 (1931/32): 114-15.

12   Waterloo Public Library, *The Waterloo Public Library Golden Jubilee 1876-1926* (Waterloo: n.p., c.1926), 10.

13   "Other Days," *Ont. Lib. Rev.* 19 (1935): 153-54.

14   William J. Sykes, "Canada," in *Popular Libraries of the World*, ed. Arthur E. Bostwick (Chicago: American Library Association, 1933), 47.

15   In chronological terms, William J. Murison, *The Public Library; Its Origins, Purpose, and Significance*, 3rd ed. (London: Clive Bingley, 1988), 10-73 delimits the British "movement" by using the convenient date of 1918 after which "modern" developments commenced.

BIBLIOGRAPHY

Primary Sources

A number of principal sources on library history, librarians, and trustees in Ontario can be located at larger public libraries, the National Archives in Ottawa, and the Archives of Ontario in Toronto. There are few scholarly studies in the secondary literature. Following the formation of the Canadian Library Association's Library History Interest Group in 1980, more academic publications have appeared, but much work remains to be done. I have consulted sources at the following major collections and microfilmed some records at the Ontario Archives during the course of my research. These items are designated with an "Mf" and now can be purchased for study purposes.

A. Archives of Ontario
1. The Mechanics' Institutes of Ontario collection, MU 2017-2022: Mf
2. The Board of Arts and Manufactures for Upper Canada, MU 279-80: Mf
3. Dept. of Education records, R.G. 2.
   a. Office of the Minister, correspondence 1880-1905, Series D-7 box 18 (Richard Harcourt): Mf
   b. Educational Depository records 1849-1905, Series N: Mf
   c. Registrar's branch select files 1885-1913, Series P-2 (mostly Dr. May's administrative records): Mf
   d. Central registry files 1911-1968, Series P-3, Deputy Minister-7 (inspectors' records 1911-1937)
   e. Provincial library service records 1874-1924, Series R (reports from various agencies): Mf
   f. Provincial library service branch unprocessed material (mostly library school records)
4. Ministry of Culture and Recreation records, R.G. 47
   a. Provincial Library Service, library financial reports 1911-1972 (annual reports filed for grant purposes)
5. Ontario Library Association records, 1899-1926, MU 2239-2248 (incomplete papers, correspondence, etc.): Mf
6. Niagara-on-the-Lake library records, MS 540 (reels 1-4)
7. Photography collection
8. Scarborough Public Library records, MU 2567: Mf
9. Alton and Caledon Public Library records, MU 2332-33: Mf

B. Ontario Library Association
1. Proceedings of annual meetings, 1901-1930 (printed and typescript records)

C. Metropolitan Toronto Reference Library
1. Toronto Mechanics' Institute papers
   a. Letter books of the librarian-secretaries, 1857-83
   b. Minutes of monthly board meetings, 1840-83
   c. Library catalogues
   d. Annual reports, 1854-83
2. Toronto Public Library papers
   a. Board minutes, 1883-1938
   b. Applications for chief librarian, 1908
   c. Committee minutes, 1887-1911
   d. Catalogues of circulating library
3. John Ross Robertson picture collection
4. John Hallam Papers. Letters concerning the founding and administration of a public library in Toronto from persons interested in the movement for public libraries in England, United States, and Canada
5. George Herbert Locke papers. Speeches, 1910-36 (typescripts)

D. Hamilton Public Library
1. General administrative files
   a. Chief librarians, 1899-1925
   b. Library history (includes Mechanics' Institute)
   c. Library board minutes, annual reports, photographs, and book catalogues
   d. Reports of branch libraries and departments

E. Ottawa Pubic Library
1. General administrative files
   a. Annual reports, 1906-1932
   b. Library board minutes, 1906-1930

F. London Public Library
1. General administrative files
   a. Library board minutes, 1895-1930
   b. Library history, photographs

G. National Archives of Canada
1. Carleton Place Mechanics' Institute records: MG 9, D-8-4
2. Photography collection
3. Frontier College records, annual reports and correspondence: MG 28, I-124, vol. 1 and 132
4. Lawrence J. Burpee papers: MG 30, D-39

H. Carnegie Corporation of New York
1. Carnegie library correspondence as to gifts and grants, 35 reels of 16 mm film.
2. Carnegie library correspondence as to buildings promised but lapsed, 3 reels of 16 mm film.

Contemporary Books, Pamphlets and Articles

Adam, Graeme Mercer. "Free Public Libraries." *Canada Educational Monthly* 4 (1882): 94.

———. *The Librarian's [Key]: Brief Suggestive List of Books, New and Old, in All Classes of Literature, the Arts and Sciences, etc., Compiled for the Use of Librarians, Committees of Management and Custodians of Free Public Libraries.* Toronto?: n.p., c. 1882.

———. *Testimonials in Favor of the Candidature of Mr. G. Mercer Adam for the Position of Librarian of the Free Public Library.* Toronto: n.p., 1883.

———. "The Toronto Public Library." *Canada Educational Monthly* 6 (1884): 135-36.

"Adult Education and the Library." *Ontario Library Review* 10 (1925/26): 8-11.

Ahern, Mary. "What Seems to Me an Important Aspect of the Work of Public Libraries at the Present Time." *Proceedings of the Ontario Library Association Annual Meeting* (1917): 38-42.

Anon [A Librarian in Canada]. "A Word About Modern Methods." *Public Libraries* 9 (1904): 222.

Arison, William H. "Library Extension on County Lines." In Ontario. Dept. of Education, *Report of the Minister of Education for 1912.* Toronto: L.K. Cameron, 1913, 685-88.

———. "The Library Situation: in Administration; Local." *Proceedings of the Ontario Library Association Annual Meeting* (1914): 73-78.

Aylesworth, George A. "Newburgh Public Library." *Ontario Library Review* 14 (1929/30): 135.

Bain, James Jr. "Books in Branch Libraries." *Papers and Proceedings of the General Meeting of the American Library Association* (1898): 100-1. [also in *Library Journal* 23 (1898): C100-C101]

———. "Brief Review of the Libraries of Canada." *Library Journal* 12 (1887): 406-9.

———. "Canadian Public Documents." *Canadian Magazine of Politics, Science, Art and Literature* 25 (1905): 125-27.

———. "The International Scientific Catalogue." *Proceedings of the Canadian Institute* n.s., 2 (1899-1904): 27-29.

———. "Lectures, Museums, Art Galleries, etc., in Connection with Libraries." *Library Journal* 18 (1893): 214-17.

———. "The Libraries of Canada." *The Library* 7 (1895): 241-49.

———. "Library Movement in Ontario." *Library Journal* 26 (May 1901): 269-70.

———. "The President's Address." *Proceedings of the Canadian Institute* n.s., 2 (1899-1904): 96-101.

———. "Public Libraries in Canada." *Proceedings of the Canadian Institute* n.s., 1 (1897-1898): 95-100.

———. "Public Libraries in the Dominion of Canada." *Library Journal* 12 (1887): 217-20.

Bancroft, F.A. "The Relation of the Public Library to Technical Education, from the View Point of Organized Labour." *Proceedings of the Ontario Library Association Annual Meeting* (1911): 96-100.

Barnett, J. Davis. "The Mechanic and the Book." *Ontario Library Review* 1 (1916/17): 16.

———. "A National Library For Canada." *Ontario Library Review* 2 (1917/18): 107-8.

Barnstead, Winifred G. "Expansion of Dewey Decimal System for Canada." *Proceedings of the Ontario Library Association Annual Meeting* (1912): 76-79.

Belden, Charles F.D. "Achievements and Hopes of the American Library Association." *Proceedings of the Ontario Library Association Annual Meeting* (1926): 20-28. [typescript]

Bell, Robert. "Township School Libraries – Means of Establishing Them." *Journal of Education for Upper Canada* 3 (1850): 81.

Black, Mary J.L. "Adult Education." *Proceedings of the Ontario Library Association Annual Meeting* (1928): 61-64. [typescript]

——. "Concerning Some Popular Fallacies." *Proceedings of the Ontario Library Association Annual Meeting* (1918): 52-58. [also in *Public Libraries* 23 (1918): 199-204]

——. "New Library Legislation in Ontario." *Canadian Bookman* n.s., 2 (Dec. 1920): 18-19.

——. "Town Survey: in Theory and in Practice." *Proceedings of the Ontario Library Association Annual Meeting* (1915): 72-80.

——. "Twentieth Century Librarianship." *Canadian Bookman* n.s., 1 (Jan. 1919): 58-59.

——. "Walks and Talks With Wilfred Campbell." *Ontario Library Review* 3 (1918/19): 30-31.

——. "What Seems to Me an Important Aspect of the Work of Public Libraries at the Present Time." *Proceedings of the Ontario Library Association Annual Meeting* (1917): 30-34.

Bleeker, Mrs C.A. "Marmora and the Memorial Building." *Ontario Library Review* 13 (1928/29): 71-73.

Bourinot, John George. "Notes in My Library." *The Week* 12 (5 April 1895): 444-45.

Boyd, A.L. "The Personal Element in the Work of the Librarian." *Proceedings of the Ontario Library Association Annual Meeting* (1918): 28-34.

"Boys' and Girls' Librarians in Special Conference." *Ontario Library Review* 7 (1922/23): 50-52.

Bradley, W.A. "[The Larger Place of the Public Library in Our Educational Life]." *Proceedings of the Ontario Library Association Annual Meeting* (1909): 5-8.

——. "The Public Library and the Local Clubs and Kindred Organizations in Its Own Town or Village." *Proceedings of the Ontario Library Association Annual Meeting* (1908): 55-57.

Briden, William. "Materials for Efficient Library Service." *Proceedings of the Ontario Library Association Annual Meeting* (1918): 42-45.

Bridle, Augustus. "Hansen [a Novel of Canadianization]." *Proceedings of the Ontario Library Association Annual Meeting* (1926): 6-15. [typescript]

Broadfoot, Mary. "The Ennotville Library." *Ontario Library Review* 13 (1928/29): 143-44.

Brown, Walter James. "Travelling Library System of Ontario." *O.A.C. Review* 15, 6 (Mar. 1903): 3, 8-11.

Burpee, Lawrence J. "As Others See Us." *Proceedings of the Ontario Library Association Annual Meeting* (1912): 50-62.

——. "Canadian Libraries and Mr. Carnegie." *Public Libraries* 10 (1905): 87.

——. "How We Purchase Our Books." *Proceedings of the Ontario Library Association Annual Meeting* (1907): 52-53.

——. "Library Cooperation in Ontario." *Library Journal* 37 (1912): 85-86.

——. "The Library Outlook in Canada." *Public Libraries* 9 (1904): 195-97.

——. "Modern Public Libraries and Their Methods." *Proceedings and Transactions of the Royal Canadian Society* 2nd Series, 8 (1902): 3-47.

————. "Modern Methods in Small Libraries." *Public Libraries* 9 (1904): 217-21.

————. "A Plea for a Canadian National Library." *Canadian Historical Review* 1 (1920): 191-94.

————. "A Plea for a National Library." *University Magazine* 10 (1911): 152-63.

————. "What the Canadian Government is Doing for Canadian Libraries." *Library Journal* 33 (1908): 17-18.

Butler, Miss. "Newcastle." *Proceedings of the Ontario Library Association Annual Meeting* (1928): 50-53. [typescript]

Butters, Mary T. "[Summer Library School 1911]." In Ontario. Dept. of Education, *Report of the Minister of Education for 1911.* Toronto: L.K. Cameron, 1912, 553-56.

Byam, C.A. "The Finances of the Public Library." *Proceedings of the Ontario Library Association Annual Meeting* (1914): 62-65.

Cameron, A.W. "The Decimal System in Streetsville Public Library." *Proceedings of the Ontario Library Association Annual Meeting* (1908): 27-28.

————. "How Books are Purchased in the Smaller Libraries." *Proceedings of the Ontario Library Association Annual Meeting* (1907): 46.

————. "A Provincial Library System." *Proceedings of the Ontario Library Association Annual Meeting* (1911): 46-51.

Campbell, William Wilfred. "[Ethical and Intellectual Responsibility to Canada and to the Empire]." *Proceedings of the Ontario Library Association Annual Meeting* (1909): 50-62.

Canadian Institute, Toronto. "A Public Reference Library for the Province of Ontario, and Provincial Travelling Libraries." Toronto: n.p., 21 January 1899. [printed circular]

Carson, William O. "Book Purchasing." *Proceedings of the Ontario Library Association Annual Meeting* (1914): 110-16.

————. "Canadian Chapter." *Ontario Library Review* 11 (1926/27): 28-35.

————. "The Canadian Public Library as a Social Force." *Proceedings of the Ontario Library Association Annual Meeting* (1915): 36-42.

————. "Libraries in War-Time and Some Factors that Require Consideration." *Proceedings of the Ontario Library Association Annual Meeting* (1917): 59-62.

————. "Newark (Modified) Charging System." *Proceedings of the Ontario Library Association Annual Meeting* (1909): 68-69.

————. "The Ontario Public Library Rate." *Bulletin of the American Library Association* 15 (1921): 126-28.

————. "Public Libraries of Ontario." *Library Journal* 52 (1927): 451-56.

————. "Reference Work in the Library." *Proceedings of the Ontario Library Association Annual Meeting* (1909): 22-35.

————. "The Status and Training of the Public Librarian." *Proceedings of the Ontario Library Association Annual Meeting* (1912): 106-14.

Cartwright, Adeline. "Children's Literature from the Canadian Point of View." *Proceedings of the Ontario Library Association Annual Meeting* (1915): 66-72.

Charteris, Charles R. "Library Work." *Proceedings of the Ontario Library Association Annual Meeting* (1913): 63-66.

Chivers, Cedric. "[Book Binding]." *Proceedings of the Ontario Library Association Annual Meeting* (1909): 72-73.

Chown, Alice A. "[League of Nations]." *Proceedings of the Ontario Library Association Annual Meeting* (1928): 53-61. [typescript]

"Claimable Public Library Rates Compared." *Ontario Library Review* 5 (1920/21): 14-17.

Clow, Mildred. "Kingston Public Library." *Ontario Library Review* 11 (1926/27): 39-40.

Cockburn, K.A. "Story of a Town Library." [Weston] *Ontario Library Review* 10 (1925/26): 15-16.

Cody, Henry J. "Real Measure of Progress; Intellectual and Spiritual." *Proceedings of the Ontario Library Association Annual Meeting* (1930): 29-32. [typescript]

———. "The Education of the Adult." *Ontario Library Review* 4 (1919/20): 1.

Colquhoun, Arthur H.U. "[Informal Talk on Public Libraries]." *Proceedings of the Ontario Library Association Annual Meeting* (1907): 26-29.

Cuttle, A.H. "Library Publicity." *Proceedings of the Ontario Library Association Annual Meeting* (1911): 109-11.

Davison, Thomas. "Mechanics' Institutes and the Best Means of Improving Them." *Canadian Monthly* (Sept. 1876): 220-23.

DelaFosse, Fred M. "The Influence of a Good Book." *Ontario Library Review* 3 (1918/19): 57-59.

Denholm, Andrew. "Problems of the Small Libraries." *Proceedings of the Ontario Library Association Annual Meeting* (1910): 42- 45.

———. "Rural and Village Libraries." *Proceedings of the Ontario Library Association Annual Meeting* (1915): 81-83.

De Peyster, Frederic. *The Moral and Intellectual Influence of Libraries upon Social Progress.* New York: New York Historical Society, 1866.

Dorrington, Mrs William. "What People Think and Say About the Public Library and Why?" *Proceedings of the Ontario Library Association Annual Meeting* (1918): 34-36.

Dudgeon, Matthew S. "The Universality of Library Service." *Proceedings of the Ontario Library Association Annual Meeting* (1914): 90-100.

Duncan, Mary. "Sketch of the Don Library." *Ontario Library Review* 2 (1917/18): 50-51.

Dunham, B. Mabel. "Leaves from the Diary of a Librarian." *Acta Victoriana* 33, 4 (1910): 270-76.

———. "Library Work as a Profession for Canadian Women." in Archives of Ontario, Ontario Library Association, MU 2245, 1921. [typescript]

———. "Methods of Reaching the People." *Proceedings of the Ontario Library Association Annual Meeting* (1910): 68-76.

———. "Report on the Ontario Library Summer School, 1911." *Proceedings of the Ontario Library Association Annual Meeting* (1912): 63-66.

———. "What is the Place and Use of Newspapers and Periodicals in Our Public Libraries in Towns." *Proceedings of the Ontario Library Association Annual Meeting* (1917): 68-76.

Dunlop, William J. "Adult Education through Organized Groups." *Proceedings of the Ontario Library Association Annual Meeting* (1925): 6-14. [typescript]

"Editorial Comment: Duties of All Trustees." *Ontario Library Review* 13 (1928/29): 130-33.

"Editorial Notes and Comment: Duties of Library Trustees." *Ontario Library Review* 7 (1922/23): 2-3.

"Editorial Notes and Comment: Wisdom of Library Boards." *Ontario Library Review* 10 (1925/16): 26.

Edwards, C.B. "The Public Library and the Public School." *Proceedings of the Ontario Library Association Annual Meeting* (1913): 107-110.

Edwards, Edward. *Free Town Libraries, Their Formation, Management, and History.* New York: John Wiley & Son, 1869.

"Encouragement of Technical Instruction in Ontario through the Medium of Public Libraries." *Labour Gazette* 9, 9 (1908/09): 973-74.

Falconer, Robert. "What a Public Library Can Do For The Development of a Community." *Ontario Library Review* 2 (1917/ 18): 105-7. [also in *Proceedings of the Ontario Library Association Annual Meeting* (1918): 59-62]

Fitzpatrick, Alfred. "Camp Libraries in Ontario." *Public Libraries* 9 (1904): 201-3.

————. *Library Extension in Ontario: Travelling Libraries and Reading Camps.* N.p.: c. 1901.

————. "Life in the Lumbering Camps." *Canadian Magazine of Politics, Science, Art and Literature* 17 (1901): 49-52.

————. "The Neglected Citizen in the Camps." *Canadian Magazine of Politics, Science, Art and Literature* 25 (1905): 43-48.

Flavelle, Ethel G. "The Use of a Public Library by the General Reader." *Proceedings of the Ontario Library Association Annual Meeting* (1916): 61-66.

Foley, Rev. J.T. "A Public Library Confers a Benefit On Its Whole Community." *Ontario Library Review* 1 (1916/17): 11-12.

Fowler, John Coke. *On Public Libraries. Address Delivered at the Winter Course of Lectures at the Royal Institution of South Wales, 1870.* Swansea: Pearce and Brown, 1871.

"The Free Library." *The Bystander* 3 (April 1883): 105-6.

"Free Public Libraries." *The Bystander* 3 (Jan. 1883): 66-67.

Gavin, Frederick P. "The Public Library and the High School." *Proceedings of the Ontario Library Association Annual Meeting* (1913): 110-13.

————. "Vocational Training For Adults in Ontario." *Ontario Library Review* 9 (1924/25): 30-32.

Gordon, Rev. D.L. "Life Stories of Live Libraries: Agincourt." *Proceedings of the Ontario Library Association Annual Meeting* (1926): 37-40. [typescript]

Gould, Charles H. "The Cutter Expansive Classification." *Proceedings of the Ontario Library Association Annual Meeting* (1908): 17-20.

Grier, E. Wyly. "Canadian Art and Its Relationship to the Library." *Proceedings of the Ontario Library Association Annual Meeting* (1918): 45-51.

Grieve, Weir. "Tobermory Village Library Association." *Ontario Library Review* 14 (1929/30): 52-53.

Gurd, Norman St Clair. "Free Access in an Ontario Library." *Public Libraries* 9 (1904): 229-30.

————. "How to Deepen Public Interest in the Library." *Public Libraries* 9 (1904): 222-24.

————. "Other Days." *Ontario Library Review* 16 (1931/32): 114-16.

————. "Present Problems of Libraries in Canada." *Public Libraries* 12 (1907): 176-80.

Haines, Rev. R. "Some Interesting Library Stories: Powassin [sic]." *Proceedings of the Ontario Library Association Annual Meeting* (1923): 51-52. [typescript]

Hall, Alfred V. "Toronto Branch Libraries Ground Treatment." *Construction* 10 (1917): 392-94.

Hallam, John. *An Address to the Board of Management of the Toronto Free Library.* Toronto: n.p., c. 1883.

————. *The Days of Advance: British Civilization as Shown in Some Institutions, Free Libraries and Water Supply Systems. Interesting Facts Gleaned by Alderman Hallam while across the Sea.* Toronto: n.p., c. 1881.

————. *Notes by the Way on Free Libraries and Books with a Plea for the Establishment of Rate-Supported Libraries in the Province of Ontario.* Toronto: Globe Printing Company, 1882.

Hanna, Mrs W.J. "Books for the Little Ones." *Proceedings of the Ontario Library Association Annual Meeting* (1913): 80-83.

Hardy, Alexander D. "[President's Address]." *Proceedings of the Ontario Library Association Annual Meeting* (1910): 33-35.

Hardy, Edwin Austin. "How Ontario Administers Her Libraries." *Library Journal* 41 (1916): 729-733. [also in *Bulletin of the American Library Association* 10 (1916): 181-185]

———. "The Library Situation in Ontario: What May be Done in Organized Effort." *Proceedings of the Ontario Library Association Annual Meeting* (1914): 118-21.

———. "The Ontario Library Field." *Public Libraries* 9 (1904): 198-201.

———. "An Outline Program of the Work of the Ontario Library Association." *Public libraries* 6 (1901): 414-18.

———. "The Training of Librarians in the Province of Ontario." *Public Libraries* 11 (1906): 143-45.

Henderson, T.K. *Free Public Libraries for Canada: Working-men's Prize Essays.* Toronto: "Citizen," 1882.

Henwood, Edwin D. *Notes on Binding.* Toronto: Education Department, 1908.

Hibbert, James. *Notes on Free Public Libraries and Museums.* Preston: Guardian General Printing, 1881.

Hoag, J.P. "Cooperation of Public Library and Public School." *Public Libraries* 9 (1904): 225-27.

Holmes, Eleanor. "[Town Beautifying]; The Public Library, Picton." *Proceedings of the Ontario Library Association Annual Meeting* (1924): 53-60. [typescript]

———. "What the People Think and Say about the Public Library and Why?" *Proceedings of the Ontario Library Association Annual Meeting* (1918): 36-38.

Howard, Rev. Thomas B. "Life Stories of Live Libraries: Listowel." *Proceedings of the Ontario Library Association Annual Meeting* (1926): 30-34. [typescript]

———. "Shall We Revive the Library Institutes?" *Proceedings of the Ontario Library Association Annual Meeting* (1930): 42-44. [typescript]

Howell, George. "The Library as an Aid to Technical Education." *Proceedings of the Ontario Library Association Annual Meeting* (1911): 92-95.

Hunt, Clara W. "Boys and Girls and the Public Library." *Proceedings of the Ontario Library Association Annual Meeting* (1913): 99-100.

Iles, George. "The Appraisal of Literature." *The Week* 13 (18 Sept. 1896): 1025-26.

———. "The Library in Education." *The Week* 7 (21 March 1890): 251.

"In the Library." *Canadian Magazine of Politics, Science, Art and Literature* 34 (1909): 78-79.

Ingraham, Mary Kinley. "Librarianship as a Profession." *Canadian Bookman* n.s., 3 (June 1921): 38-40.

Jackson, Henrietta. "Children in the Public Library." *Public Libraries* 9 (1904): 228-29.

Jarvis, Marjorie. "The Librarian and Community Drama." *Ontario Library Review* 9 (1923/24): 9-13.

Keller, W.H. "The Character of Books for a Small Library, Uxbridge." *Public Libraries* 6 (1901): 347-49.

Keough, Andrew. "Libraries Both Past and Present." *Proceedings of the Ontario Library Association Annual Meeting* (1930): 13-27. [typescript]

Kerr, H.O. "Some Interesting Library Stories: Walkerville." *Proceedings of the Ontario Library Association Annual Meeting* (1923): 54-61. [typescript]

Kinsinger, Arthur. "What the People Think and Say about the Public Library and Why?" *Proceedings of the Ontario Library Association Annual Meeting* (1918): 38-40.

Klotz, Otto Sr. *A Review of the Special Report of the Minister of Education on the Mechanics' Institutes Ontario.* Toronto: Willing & Williamson, 1881.

Klotz, Otto Jr. "The Trustee's Duty to the Public." *Proceedings of the Ontario Library Association Annual Meeting* (1910): 78- 81. [also in *Bulletin of the American Library Association* 6 (1912): 302-4]

Lancefield, Agnes. "[Windsor Public Library]." *Proceedings of the Ontario Library Association Annual Meeting* (1928): 12-17. [typescript]

Landon, Fred. "A City Library's Work." *Ontario Library Review* 6 (1921/22): 10-13.

———. "J. Davis Barnett's Gift to the Western University." *Ontario Library Review* 3 (1918/19): 16.

———. "Libraries and Extra-Mural Students." *Ontario Library Review* 11 (1926/27): 8-9.

———. "The Library and Local Material." *Ontario Library Review* 1 (1916/17): 61-62.

———. "Public Spirit at Brownsville." *Ontario Library Review* 4 (1919/20): 53-54.

———. "A Special Duty For Every Public Library in War-Time." *Ontario Library Review* 2 (1917/18): 51-52.

———. "The Toronto Conference – II: Canadian Library Association." *Library Journal* 52 (1927): 749-50.

Langley, O.A. "The Library Situation in Finances (Provincial)." *Proceedings of the Ontario Library Association Annual Meeting* (1914): 65-69.

Langton, Hugh Hornby. "Canada and Public Libraries." *Library Journal* 28 (1903): C43-C46.

———. *A Provincial Library Commission.* Toronto: n.p., c. 1903.

———. "What a Permanent Library Commission Can Do to Aid Libraries." *Public Libraries* 9 (1904): 212-16.

Langton, William Alexander. "Library Design." *Canadian Architect and Builder* 15 (1902): 47-48.

Leavitt, Thaddeus W.H. "Some Library Problems." *Proceedings of the Ontario Library Association Annual Meeting* (1908): 51-55.

———. "Travelling Libraries." *Proceedings of the Ontario Library Association Annual Meeting* (1907): 17-21.

———. "Travelling Libraries in Ontario." *Library Journal* 33 (1908): 231-32.

———. "The Working Man and the Library." *Proceedings of the Ontario Library Association Annual Meeting* (1909): 36-46.

Lewis, Richard. "Mechanics' Institutes and the Best Means of Improving Them." *Canadian Monthly* (Sept. 1876): 223-38.

"The Librarian and Library of Fort William." *Ontario Library Review* 1 (1916/17): 92-95.

"Library and the Soldier." *Canadian Bookman* n.s., 1 (January 1919): 60.

"Loan System For Rural Villages and School Libraries." *Ontario Library Review* 4 (1919/20): 60-63.

Locke, George H. "Canadian Libraries and the War." *Canadian Magazine of Politics, Science, Art and Literature* 52 (1918/ 19): 588-591. [also in *Public Libraries* 23 (1918): 357-360 and *Ontario Library Review* 3 (1918/19): 3-6]

———. "How a Public Librarian Hears of Books and Orders Books." *Proceedings of the Ontario Library Association Annual Meeting* (1912): 121-24.

———. "Libraries in Great Britain." *Proceedings of the Ontario Library Association Annual Meeting* (1928): 17-21. [typescript]

———. "The Library and Adult Education." *Libraries* 35 (1930): 433-37.

———. "[Library Work in Canada]." *Library Association Record* 12 (1910): 561-62.

———. "Presidential Address at the A.L.A. Conference, Toronto." *Ontario Library Review* 12 (1927/28): 4-7.

———. "The Privileges and Obligations of our Public Libraries in These Days of Unrest." *Ontario Library Review* 1 (1916/17): 96-99. [also in *Proceedings of the Ontario Library Association Annual Meeting* (1917): 43-45]

———. "The Public Library as an Educational Institution." In *Addresses Delivered before the Canadian Club of Toronto, 1908-09.* Toronto: Warwick Bro's and Rutter, 1909, 138-43.

———. "Recent Legislation Affecting Public Libraries in Ontario." *Proceedings of the Ontario Library Association Annual Meeting* (1914): 69-71.

———. "Recruiting for Librarianship in Canada." *Ontario Library Review* 7 (1922/23): 4-7.

———. "Revery of a Bookish Librarian." *Canadian Bookman* n.s., 1 (Jan. 1919): 42-43.

———. "The Toronto Public Libraries." *Journal of the Royal Architectural Institute of Canada* 3, 3 (1926): 87-103.

McAdams, Robert. "How Trustees May Help the Library." In Ontario. Dept. of Education, *Report of the Minister of Education for 1911.* Toronto: L.K. Cameron, 1912, 567-69.

McClung, Nellie. "What Books Have Meant To Me." *Ontario Library Review* 14 (1929/30): 37-39.

McDonald, Barbara. "Browne Charging System." *Proceedings of the Ontario Library Association Annual Meeting* (1909): 70-71.

McLaren, Justice John James. "[The Mission of the Public Library]." *Proceedings of the Ontario Library Association Annual Meeting* (1908): 41-44.

Manners, Janetta, Duchess of Rutland. *Some of the Advantages of Easily Accessible Reading and Recreation Rooms and Free Libraries.* 2d ed. London: William Blackwood and Sons, 1885.

Mitchell, Lieut-Col. John Malcolm. "[Libraries in Great Britain]." *Proceedings of the Ontario Library Association Annual Meeting* (1925): 40-49. [typescript]

"The Modern Public Library." *Ontario Library Review* 5 (1920/21): 93.

Moir, Elizabeth. "Popular Reference Books and How to Use Them." *Proceedings of the Ontario Library Association Annual Meeting* (1911): 69-81.

Moore, W.F. "The Library Situation in Ontario: in Organized Effort; What Has Been Done." *Proceedings of the Ontario Library Association Annual Meeting* (1914): 59-62.

Mowat, Angus. "Adult Education." *Proceedings of the Ontario Library Association Annual Meeting* (1929): 12-16. [typescript]

———. "Better Reading and How To Attain It." *Ontario Library Review* 8 (1923/24): 3-6.

———. "[Reference Work in the Smaller Library]." *Proceedings of the Ontario Library Association Annual Meeting* (1928): 2-12. [typescript]

Mullins, John D. *Free Libraries and Newsrooms: Their Formation and Management.* 3d ed. London: H. Sotheran and Co., 1879.

Murch, W. H. "Proportionate Expenditure in Library Administration." *Proceedings of the Ontario Library Association Annual Meeting* (1913): 114-16.

"A New Library Building Needed." *Toronto Saturday Night* 15 (13 Sept. 1902): 7.

"The New Public Library at Agincourt." *Ontario Library Review* 10 (1925/26): 33-35.

Nursey, Walter R. "Library Progress in Ontario." In Ontario. Dept. of Education, *Report of the Minister of Education for 1912.* Toronto: L.K. Cameron, 1913, 651-58.

————. "Our Library Situation." *Proceedings of the Ontario Library Association Annual Meeting* (1910): 36-41.

————. "Our Library Situation." *Proceedings of the Ontario Library Association Annual Meeting* (1912): 80-87.

————. "Some Library Possibilities." *Proceedings of the Ontario Library Association Annual Meeting* (1911): 54-59.

————. "The Story of the Library Institutes of Ontario." In Ontario. Dept. of Education, *Report of the Minister of Education for 1913.* Toronto: L.K. Cameron, 1914, 733-37.

————. "[Travelling Libraries]." In Ontario. Dept. of Education, *Report of the Minister of Education for 1910.* Toronto: L.K. Cameron, 1911, 531-35.

————. "The Trustees' Duty to the Public." In Ontario. Dept. of Education, *Report of the Minister of Education for 1912.* Toronto: L.K. Cameron, 1913, 641-646. [also in *Bulletin of the American Library Association* 6 (1912): 304-7]

————. "The Trustee and the Children's Department." *Proceedings of the Ontario Library Association Annual Meeting* (1913): 90-96. [reprinted in *Report of the Minister of Education for 1913,* 747-753]

O'Connor, Teresa. "'The Old Order Changeth'." *Ontario Library Review* 12 (1927/28): 72-73.

O'Meara, Annie T. "Classification of Public Documents, Pamphlets, and Miscellaneous Matter." *Proceedings of the Ontario Library Association Annual Meeting* (1912): 68-70.

Ontario. Dept. of Education. *Catalogue of Books Recommended for Public Libraries by the Education Department, Ontario; November 1895.* Toronto: Warwick Bros. & Rutter, 1895.

————. *Circular for Librarians on Classification of Books in Public Libraries.* Toronto: n.p., 1900.

————. *Ontario Library School.* Toronto: n.p., c. 1924.

————. Public Libraries Branch. *Reference Work and Reference Works.* Toronto: n.p., 1920.

————. *Special Report of the Minister of Education on the Mechanics' Institutes (Ontario).* Toronto: C. Blackett Robinson, 1881.

————. *Special Report on the Operations of the Depository Branch of the Education Department, Ontario; from 1850 to 1875, Inclusive.* Toronto: Hunter, Rose & Co., 1877.

Ontario Library Association. *Catalogue of Children's Books Recommended for Public Libraries, Alphabetically Arranged by Authors, Giving Title, Publisher and Price.* Compiled by Norman S. Gurd, Carrie A. Rowe and Effie A. Schmidt. Toronto: Ontario Library Association, 1906.

————. *Report of Special Committee on Technical Education in Public Libraries.* Toronto: William Briggs, 1910.

"The Opening of the New Public Library Building at Renfrew." *Ontario Library Review* 6 (1921/22): 18-20.

"Organization of the Canadian Library Association." *Library Journal* 52 (1927): 705-6.

"Outline of the Report of the Commission on the Library and Adult Education." *Ontario Library Review* 11 (1926/27): 35-37.

Peacock, W. G. "The Educative Value of Fiction." *Ontario Library Review* 3 (1918/19): 61-63.

Pitt, Septimus Albert. *Libraries of the United States and Canada: Report of [a] Visit by the City Librarian, Glasgow, September-October, 1926.* Glasgow: n.p., c. 1926. [typescript]

Poole, Edna W. "Classification of Some Recent Books." *Proceedings of the Ontario Library Association Annual Meeting* (1912): 66- 67.

Potter, Jessie C. "Library Work with Children." *Proceedings of the Ontario Library Association Annual Meeting* (1911): 100-4.

"Public Libraries." *Canadian Magazine of Politics, Science, Art and Literature* 17 (1901): 285-86.

"The Public Libraries Act of 1920." *Ontario Library Review* 5 (1920/21): 9-13.

Purves, J. W. Cummings. "A Paper on Library Ideals: Work and Legislation in Canada." *Library Association Record* 14 (1912): 439-61.

Ranck, Samuel H. "The Ontario Library Law and American Libraries." *Bulletin of the American Library Association* 15 (1921): 128-30.

————. "The Relation of the Public Library to Technical Education." *Proceedings of the Ontario Library Association Annual Meeting* (1911): 83-91. [also in *Library Journal* 36 (1911): 279-85]

"Reference Work and Reference Works." *Ontario Library Review* 4 (1919/20): 98-131.

Reid, Jennie S. "Charging System." *Proceedings of the Ontario Library Association Annual Meeting* (1909): 71.

————. "Fines and Charges for Overdue, Damaged and Lost Books." *Proceedings of the Ontario Library Association Annual Meeting* (1912): 71-72.

Riddell, William R. "The Use of a Public Library by a Public Man." *Proceedings of the Ontario Library Association Annual Meeting* (1916): 67-72.

Robertson, William John. "Should the Education Department Issue a Librarian's Certificate?" *Public Libraries* 9 (1904): 209-12.

Rorke, Jesse. "The Canadian Novel and the New Revolutionary Movement in Literature." *Ontario Library Review* 8 (1923/24): 56-58.

————. "The Lending Department and Its Possibilities in Adult Education." *Proceedings of the Ontario Library Association Annual Meeting* (1929): 8-12. [typescript]

Rothwell, Ruby M. "The Card Catalogue." *Proceedings of the Ontario Library Association Annual Meeting* (1908): 28-36.

Rouillard, Eugène. *Les Bibliothèques Populaires.* Quebec: L.-J. Demers & Frère, 1890.

Sanderson, Charles R. "Beauty with Utility." *Construction* 23 (1930): 282-88, 293-96.

————. "A Library in a Shopping Centre." *Library Journal* 35 (1930): 257-59.

Saxe, Mary J. L. "Books and Their Classification." *Canadian Bookman* n.s., 1 (July 1919): 56-58.

Saxe, Mary S. "The Canadian Library's Opportunities to Encourage the Reading of Canadian Authors." *Proceedings of the Ontario Library Association Annual Meeting* (1915): 48-52.

————. "Classification of Books." *Proceedings of the Ontario Library Association Annual Meeting* (1911): 59-64.

————. "The Library from the Inside, Out!" *Canadian Bookman* n.s., 2 (April 1920): 16-17.

————. "What Seems to Me an Important Aspect of the Work of Public Libraries at the Present Time." *Proceedings of the Ontario Library Association Annual Meeting* (1917): 35-37.

Schmidt, Effie A. "Rules for Numbering Books." *Proceedings of the Ontario Library Association Annual Meeting* (1908): 47-48.

Scroggie, George E. "Library Publicity." *Proceedings of the Ontario Library Association Annual Meeting* (1911): 111-16.

Seath, John. "Some Needed Educational Reforms." In Ontario Educational Association, *Proceedings of the Forty-Second Annual Convention of the Ontario Educational Association*. Toronto: William Briggs, 1903, 66-79.

Smallfield, W. E. "How We Carried the Public Library By-Law in Renfrew." *Proceedings of the Ontario Library Association Annual Meeting* (1916): 34-36.

Smith, Lillian H. "Boys and Girls and the Public Library." *Proceedings of the Ontario Library Association Annual Meeting* (1913): 68-70.

———. "Buying Books For the Youngest Children." *Ontario Library Review* 8 (1923/24): 29-30.

———. "The Children's Librarian." *Acta Victoriana* 42, 2 (1917): 63-65.

———. "Considerations Which Enter into the Making of a List of Books for Canadian Girls." *Proceedings of the Ontario Library Association Annual Meeting* (1916): 37-39.

———. "Holiday Reading for Boys and Girls." *Canadian Bookman* n.s., 2 (December 1920): 71-73.

———. "A List of Books for Boys and Girls." *Ontario Library Review* 2 (1917/18): 11-33.

Smith, Rev. Edward F. McL. "The Story of the Alliston Library." *Proceedings of the Ontario Library Association Annual Meeting* (1925): 54-58. [typescript]

Snyder, George B. "How We Started our Library on 'Modern Lines'." In Ontario. Dept. of Education, *Report of the Minister of Education for 1910*. Toronto: L.K. Cameron, 1911, 513-15.

———. *A Study of the Conditions of the Libraries of the Niagara District.* Port Colborne?: n.p., c. 1911. [paper read at Niagara District Library Institute Convention at Port Colborne 24 Oct. 1911]

Spereman, James. "Methods in Book Purchasing." *Proceedings of the Ontario Library Association Annual Meeting* (1907): 47-49.

Spereman, Patricia. "Library Work with Children." *Proceedings of the Ontario Library Association Annual Meeting* (1908): 36-40.

Staton, Frances Maria. *Books and Pamphlets Published in Canada up to the Year 1837, Copies of Which are in the Public Reference Library.* Toronto: Toronto Public Library, 1916.

———. *The Canadian North West; a Bibliography of the Sources of Information in the Public Reference Library of the City of Toronto, Canada in Regard to the Hudson's Bay Company, the Fur Trade and the Early History of the Canadian North West.* Toronto: Toronto Public Library, 1931.

———. "The Compilation of a Bibliography of the Rebellion of 1837-38." *Canadian Historical Association Annual Report* (1924): 66-72.

———. *The Rebellion of 1837-38; a Bibliography of the Sources of Information in the Public Reference Library of the City of Toronto, Canada.* Toronto: Toronto Public Library, 1924.

———. "Reference Libraries and Reference Work." *Proceedings of the Ontario Library Association Annual Meeting* (1911): 64-69.

Stead, Robert J. C. "Canadian Literature as a National Asset." *Proceedings of the Ontario Library Association Annual Meeting* (1924): 40-46. [typescript]

Stearns, Lutie E. "Library Extension." *Proceedings of the Ontario Library Association Annual Meeting* (1912): 114-21.

———. "The Library Militant." *Proceedings of the Ontario Library Association Annual Meeting* (1912): 88-94.

"Story of a Rural School." *Canadian Farm* 2 (March 1910): 8.

Sykes, William J. "Adult Education in Ottawa." *Ontario Library Review* 9 (1924/25): 35-36.

———. "Book Selection." *Proceedings of the Ontario Library Association Annual Meeting* (1914): 102-6.

———. *Selected List of Fiction in English.* Ottawa: James Hope & Sons, 1914.

———. "Why Should a Community Support a Public Library?" *Ontario Library Review* 1 (1916/17): 4-5.

Tait, Rev. Murray C. "Some Interesting Library Stories: Wallaceburg." *Proceedings of the Ontario Library Association Annual Meeting* (1923): 46-50. [typescript]

Tanner, Hazel G. "An Experiment in Boys' Clubs." *Ontario Library Review* 4 (1919/20): 91-93.

Taylor, John. *Toronto's Free Library: Facts for the Citizens.* Toronto: n.p., c. 1881.

Thomson, Norah. "The Story Hour as a Means of Popularizing the Public Library." *Ontario Library Review* 1 (1916/17): 36-38.

Todd, Alpheus. "On the Establishment of Free Public Libraries in Canada." *Proceedings and Transactions of the Royal Society of Canada* 1st series, 1, sec. 2 (1882-83): 13-16.

Toronto Public Library. *List of Books, Pamphlets and Magazine Articles on the Subject of Temperance, Total Abstinence, Prohibition, Gothenburg and Other Licensing Systems of the Liquor Traffic, in the Toronto Public Library.* Toronto: n.p., 1902.

———. *On the Opening of the Toronto Free Public Library on the City's Semi-Centennial Day, March 6th, 1884.* Toronto: n.p., 1884.

———. *Programme of a Competition for the Selection of an Architect for the Public Reference Library Building in the City of Toronto.* Toronto: n.p., 1905.

———. *Report of a Special Committee on the Museums of the United States and Canada.* Toronto: n.p., 1892.

"Toronto Branch Library." *Construction* 10 (1917): 390-91. [High Park Branch]

"Travelling Libraries." *The Farmer's Advocate and Home Magazine* 36 (1 Nov. 1901): 699.

"Unwise Library Legislation in Canada." *Public Libraries* 18 (1913): 257-58.

"Walkerville Public Library." *Ontario Library Review* 8 (1923/24): 51-56.

Waller, Rev. Charles C. "The General Public and the Modern Catalogue." *Ontario Library Review* 6 (1921/22): 51-52.

———. "Inter-Library Loan Privileges." *Ontario Library Review* 4 (1919/20): 11-12.

———. "The Possibilities of the Small Library." *Ontario Library Review* 4 (1919/20): 55-58.

Welling, Beatrice W. "Canadian Librarians Meet at the American Librarian [sic] Association." *Ontario Library Review* 10 (1925/26): 11-12.

Williams, David. "The Press as Related to the Public Library." *Proceedings of the Ontario Library Association Annual Meeting* (1916): 31-33.

———. "Publicity, A Factor in Library Work." *Ontario Library Review* 2 (1917/18): 83-84.

Wilson, Daniel. "Free Public Libraries." *Canada Educational Monthly* 6 (1884): 145-50.

Withrow, William Henry. "Free Public Library." *Canada Educational Monthly* 6 (1884): 193-96.

Wodson, H. M. "The Story Hour." *Proceedings of the Ontario Library Association Annual Meeting* (1913): 87-89.

Young, Hester. "Subject Headings [for Card Catalogues]." *Proceedings of the Ontario Library Association Annual Meeting* (1912): 73-75.

———. "The Dewey Decimal Classification." *Proceedings of the Ontario Library Association Annual Meeting* (1908): 20-27.

Zavitz, Edgar M. "From a Rural Library Trustee." *Ontario Library Review* 1 (1916/17): 6-7.

———. "The Need of Books in a Rural District." *Ontario Library Review* 4 (1919/20): 54-55.

Secondary Books, Articles, and Theses

Abbott, Brook. "An Accidental Librarian; Mary Black of Fort William, Ont." *Canadian Magazine* 76 (1931): 18, 29.

Allen, Jean Kerfoot. "The History of Libraries in Ontario." In Lorraine and Carl Garry, eds. *Canadian Libraries in Their Changing Environment.* Toronto: York University Centre for Continuing Education, 1977, 47-77.

Anderson, James, Sue Bonsteel and Tom Dolan. *Stratford - Library Services Since 1846.* Stratford: Stratford Public Library, c. 1975.

Bain, James Jr. "Canadian Libraries." *Canadian Magazine of Politics, Science, Art and Literature* 16 (1900): 28-32. [also in *Library Journal* 25, no. 8 (1900): C7-C10]

———. "The Public Libraries of Canada." In J. Castell Hopkins, ed., *Canada: An Encyclopaedia of the Country.* Toronto: Linscott Publishing, 1898-1900, vol. 5, 207-11.

Banting, Constance. "Mabel Dunham." *Ontario Library Review* 12 (1927/28): 66.

Bassam, Bertha. *The Faculty of Library Science, University of Toronto and its Predecessors, 1922-1972.* Toronto: Univ. of Toronto Faculty of Library Science, 1978.

Beckman, Margaret, John Black and Stephen Langmead. *The Best Gift: a Record of the Carnegie Libraries in Ontario.* Toronto: Dundurn Press, 1984.

Bergey, Lorna L. "History of New Dundee Library." *Waterloo Historical Society Annual Report* 50 (1962): 86-87.

———. "Library Facilities of Wilmot Township 1853- 1889." *Waterloo Historical Society Annual Report* 50 (1962): 85-86.

Black, Mary J. L. "Early History of the Fort William Public Library." *Papers and Annual Reports of the Thunder Bay Historical Society* 16-17 (1924/25-1925/26): 28-31.

———. "Our Public Library." *Papers and Annual Reports of the Thunder Bay Historical Society* 3 (1911/12): 6-7.

Blanchard, Jim. "Anatomy of Failure: Ontario Mechanics' Institutes, 1835-1895." *Canadian Library Journal* 38 (1981): 393-98.

———. "Predecessor to the Public Library: Mechanics' Institutes in Upper Canada and Ontario." *Expression* 3, 3 (1981): 25-28.

Boultbee, Paul G. "The Story of a Small Town Library: Paris Public Library – the Early Years." *Library History Review* 2, 3 (1975): 48-56.

Bow, Eric. "The Public Library Movement in Nineteenth-Century Ontario." *Ontario Library Review* 66 (1982): 1-16.

Bowron, Margaret. "A Short History of the Galt Public Library, 1835-1905." *Waterloo Historical Society Annual Report* 43 (1955): 37-44.

Brown, Walter L. "As it was in the Beginning: George Iles." *Public Libraries* 30 (1925): 367-68.

Bruce, Lorne. "Public Libraries in Ontario, 1882-1920." *Ontario History* 77 (1985): 123-49.

———. "Recreating the Past: Library Service in Elora, 1858-1920." *Collection Update* 8 (1984): 17-34.

Burpee, Lawrence J. "Canadian Libraries of Long Ago." *Bulletin of the American Library Association* 2 (1908): 136-43.

Cameron, Marion D. "Windsor's Public Libraries." *Ontario Library Review* 34 (1950): 9-12.

Cameron, William J., George McKnight and Michaele-Sue Goldblatt. *Robert Addison's Library: A Short-Title Catalogue of the Books Brought to Upper Canada in 1792.* Hamilton: McMaster University, 1967.

Carnochan, Janet. "First Library in Upper Canada." *Ontario Library Review* 2 (1917/18): 2-3.

Champion, Thomas E. "A Great Librarian; the Late James Bain, D.C.L." *Canadian Magazine of Politics, Science, Art and Literature* 31 (1908): 223-26.

Clarke, E. A. L. "100 Years of Library Work in Dundas." *Ontario Library Review* 26 (1942): 148-51.

Cohoe, Margaret. "Kingston Mechanics' Institute to Free Public Library." *Historic Kingston* 33 (1985): 42-55.

Colquhoun, Arthur H. U. "Canadian Celebrities: no. xiii - Mr. James Bain, Jr." *Canadian Magazine of Politics, Science, Art and Literature* 15 (1900): 31-33.

Cook, George L. "Alfred Fitzpatrick and the Foundation of Frontier College (1899-1922)." *Canada; an Historical Magazine* 3 (1976): 15-39.

Corman, Linda Wilson. "James Campbell and the Ontario Education Department, 1858-1884." *Papers of the Bibliographical Society of Canada* 14 (1975): 17-52.

Curtis, Bruce. "'Littery Merrit', 'Useful Knowledge', and the Organization of Township Libraries in Canada West, 1840- 1860." *Ontario History* 78 (1986): 285-311.

Dickson, Mrs F. V. "Diamond Jubilee of Wroxeter Public Library." *Ontario Library Review* 9 (1924/25): 65-66.

Donaldson, G. Y. "Palmerston, Ontario, and It's Public Library." *Ontario Library Review* 27 (1943): 243-45.

Donnelly, Francis Dolores. *The National Library of Canada: a Historical Analysis of the Forces which Contributed to its Establishment and to the Identification of its Role and Responsibilities.* Ottawa: Canadian Library Association, 1973.

Dunham, B. Mabel. *History of the Kitchener Public Library.* Kitchener: n.p., c. 1934. [typescript]

Eadie, James A. "The Napanee Mechanics'Institute: the Nineteenth Century Ontario Mechanics' Institute Movement in Microcosm." *Ontario History* 68 (1976): 209-21.

Emery, John W. *The Library, the School, and the Child.* Toronto: Macmillan, 1917.

Fasick Adele M., Margaret Johnston and Ruth Osler, eds. *Lands of Pleasure: Essays on Lillian H. Smith and the Development of Children's Libraries.* Metuchen, New Jersey: Scarecrow Press, 1990.

Forsyth, Barbara and Barbara Myrvold. *The Most Attractive Resort in Town: Public Library Service in West Toronto Junction, 1888-1989.* Toronto: Toronto Public Library, 1989.

Freeman, C. E. "Travelling Libraries." B.A. thesis, Ontario Agricultural College, 1925.

Gale, Phyllis. "The Development of the Public Library in Canada." M.L.S. thesis, University of Chicago Graduate Library School, 1965.

Gary, Lorraine Spencer, and Carl Garry, eds. *Canadian Libraries in Their Changing Environment.* Toronto: York University Centre for Continuing Education, 1977.

Grad, Tamara E. "The Development of Public Libraries in Ontario, 1851-1951." M.S in L.S. thesis, Drexel Institute of Technology, 1952.

Grant, Robert N. *Life of Rev. William Cochrane, D.D.* Toronto: William Briggs, 1899.

Greenfield, J. Katharine. *Hamilton Public Library 1889-1963: a Celebration of Vision and Leadership.* Hamilton: Hamilton Public Library, 1989.

Grigg, Dorothy and Mabel Dunham. "The Kitchener Public Library." *Waterloo Historical Society Annual Report* 16 (1928): 68-76.

Gundy, H. Pearson. "Libraries in Kingston 1811-1949." *Ontario Library Review* 33 (1949): 7-11.

Hardy, Edwin Austin. "A Half Century of Retrospect and Prospect; Annual Presidential Address." *Ontario Library Review* 11 (1926/27): 41-46.

———. "The Ontario Library Association: Forty Years, 1900-1940." *Ontario Library Review* 25 (1941): 9-13.

———. *The Public Library; Its Place in our Educational System.* Toronto: William Briggs, 1912.

Harrop, Esther Grace. "Some Early Canadian Libraries." M.S. in L.S. thesis, Western Reserve University, School of Library Science, 1950.

Judd, William W., ed. *Minutes of the London Mechanics' Institute (1841-1895); Edited and with Appendices.* London: London Libraries, Galleries, Museums, 1976.

Keane, Patrick. "Library Policies and Early Canadian Adult Education." *Humanities Association Review* 29 (1978): 1-20.

Keil, Doris Parkin. *Chatham's Thirteen Public Libraries from 1839-1903.* Chatham: Chatham Public Library, 1953.

Keogh, Barbara. "Burlington Public Library, 1872-1952: School House to Big White House on Elizabeth Street." *Ontario Library Review* 37 (1953): 75-77.

Kerr, James E. "History of the Galt Public Library." *Waterloo Historical Society Annual Report* 2 (1914): 17-19.

Kim, Chung S. "The Development of the First Library in Ontario, 1800-1900." M.A. thesis, University of Toronto, Faculty of Education, c. 1985.

Kirker, Ena. "The Woman Who Put Charm into a Public Library." *Canadian Magazine* 68 (1927): 32, 41.

Kirkness, Mary Anne and Bruce Miller, comps. *The Elmira Library: A History - a Heritage, 1888-1988.* Elmira, Ont.: Waterloo Regional Library, c. 1990.

Kirkton, Robena. "Gravenhurst Public Library." Gravenhurst: n.p., 1985. [typescript]

Kitchener Public Library. *KPL, Kitchener Public Library: 100 Years of Service; Centennial 1884-1984.* Kitchener: Kitchener Public Library, 1984.

Kyte, E. C. "Ex Libris: for Librarians; George Herbert Locke." *Queen's Quarterly* 44 (1937): 85-89.

Landon, Fred. "George H. Locke as a Librarian; Address Delivered at Dedication of G.H. Locke Memorial Room in Victoria University Library, Nov. 27, 1937." [typescript]

———. "John Davis Barnett." *Ontario Library Review* 10 (1925/26): 75-77.

Library Story in Fort William [50th Anniversary Booklet]. Fort William: Fort William Public Library Historical Committee, 1959.

Lumby, J. R. "Retirement of Miss M.J.L. Black from the Fort William Public Library." *Ontario Library Review* 21 (1937): 132.

Magee, Joan. "The Wright and McKenny Circulating Library, Amherstburg; a Pioneer Library in Canada West." *Expression* 3, 3 (1981): 11-14.

Manning, Mary E. and Rev. T.D. Jones. *A Village Library Grows.* Streetsville, Ont.: Streetsville Library Board, 1973.

McGillivray, Allan. *Uxbridge Library 1859-1987.* Uxbridge: Township of Uxbridge Library Board, 1987.

McGrath, Susan. "The Origins of the Canadiana Collection at the Metropolitan Toronto Central Library: the First Twenty-Five Years." *Papers of the Bibliographical Society of Canada* 13 (1974): 85-100.

"Mr. W.O. Carson." *Ontario Library Review* 14 (1929/30): 40-41.

Ontario Library Association. *The Ontario Library Association: an Historical Sketch 1900-1925*. Toronto: Univ. of Toronto Press, 1926.

The Ottawa Public Library 1921-1931; A Retrospect and Forecast. Ottawa: n.p., 1932.

Parker, George L. "Egerton Ryerson and the Ontario Book Trade in the Mid-Nineteenth Century." *Signum* 2 (Jan. 1975): 21-38.

Penman, Margaret. *A Century of Service: Toronto Public Library, 1883-1983*. Toronto: Toronto Public Library, 1983.

Ramsay, J. D. "The Hespeler Mechanics' Institute and Public Library." *Waterloo Historical Society Annual Report* 15 (1927): 300-2.

Ridington, John, Mary J.L. Black and George H. Locke. *Libraries in Canada; a Study of Library Conditions and Needs*. Toronto: Ryerson Press, 1933.

Roper, Gordon. "The Canadian Bibliographer and Library Record and Its Editor." *Papers of the Bibliographical Society of Canada* 6 (1967): 27-31.

Rush, Anita. "The Establishment of Ottawa's Public Library, 1895- 1906." Ottawa: n.p., 1981. [typescript]

Shaw, Eleanor. *A History of the London Public Library*. London: London Public Library and Art Museum, 1941 (reprinted 1968).

Shepley, Gladys. "60 Years of Service – Windsor Public Library 1894-1954." *Ontario Library Review* 38 (1954): 231-32.

Sifton, Pat. "The Making of a Public Library; Woodstock Ontario." *Expression* 3, 3 (1981): 5-10.

Simcoe Public Library; an Historical Sketch. Simcoe, Ont.: n.p., 1978.

Snider, Lillian. "Miss Mabel Dunham." *Ontario Library Review* 38 (1954): 221-24.

Spicer, Elizabeth. *A History of the London Public Library 1899- 1905*. London: London Public Library and Art Museum, 1967.

Stevenson, Douglas A. *A History of the Fonthill Public Library Prepared in Celebration of the One Hundredth Anniversary of Its Opening - on 2 February 1853*. Thorold: The Fonthill Public Library Board, 1953.

Stubbs, Gordon Thomas. *The Role of Egerton Ryerson in the Development of Public Library Service in Ontario*. Ottawa: Canadian Library Association, 1966.

Sudbury Public Library. *A Half Century of Continuous Service, Sudbury Public Library, 1912-1962*. Sudbury: Public Library, 1962.

Taylor, Ryan. "Mabel Dunham's Centenary." *Waterloo Historical Society Annual Report* 69 (1981): 13-25.

Vernon, Foster. "The Development of Adult Education in Ontario, 1790-1900." Ed.D. diss., University of Toronto, 1969.

Waldon, Freda F. "Early Provisions for Libraries in Hamilton." *Wentworth Bygones* 4 (1963): 22-35.

Walker, Jean. "History of the Stayner Library." Stayner: n.p., 1988. [typescript]

Wallace, Malcolm W. "Dr. George Herbert Locke (1870-1937)." *Ontario Library Review* 21 (1937): 59-60.

Wallace, William Stewart. "Hugh Hornby Langton." *Canadian Historical Review* 34 (1953): 388.

———. "The Ontario Library Association, 1901- 1955; a Brief History." *Bulletin of the Canadian Library Association* 12 (Oct. 1955): 77-78.

Waterloo Public Library. *The Waterloo Public Library Golden Jubilee, 1876-1926*. Waterloo: n.p., c. 1926.

Wilkinson, John. "The Bain and Rhees Lists." *IPLO Quarterly* 9, 3 (1968): 41-45.

Wiseman, John. "'Champion Has-Been': Edwin Austin Hardy and the Ontario Library Movement." In Peter F. McNally, ed. *Readings in Canadian Library History.* Ottawa: Canadian Library Association, 1986, 231-43.

———. "A Genteel Patriotism; Ontario's Public-Library Movement and the First World War." In Peter F. McNally, ed. *Readings in Canadian Library History.* Ottawa: Canadian Library Association, 1986, 181-90.

———. "Phoenix in Flight: Ontario Mechanics' Institutes, 1880-1920." *Canadian Library Journal* 38 (1981): 401-5.

———. "Silent Companions; the Dissemination of Books and Periodicals in Nineteenth-Century Ontario." *Publishing History; the Social, Economic and Literary History of Book, Newspaper and Magazine Publishing* 12 (1982): 17-50.

———. "Temples of Democracy: a History of Public Library Development in Ontario, 1880-1920." Ph.D. diss., Loughborough University of Technology, 1989.

Wragg, Gordon. "Library Service in Ontario and Some Possible Improvements, Especially in Rural Library Service." B.A. thesis, Ontario Agricultural College, 1943.

INDEX